P 37

BOOKS BY THE SAME AUTHOR—

HISTORY OF ITALIAN PAINTING IN THE
  RENAISSANCE

THE COLLECTORS

HOMER MARTIN, POET IN LANDSCAPE

ESTIMATES IN ART, SERIES I AND II

THE PORTRAITS OF DANTE

MODERN PAINTING: 1664–1914

CONCERNING BEAUTY

VENETIAN PAINTERS

WESTERN EUROPEAN PAINTING OF THE
  RENAISSANCE (in preparation)

GIOTTO: DORMITION OF THE VIRGIN

Berlin

A HISTORY OF
ITALIAN
PAINTING

By

FRANK JEWETT MATHER, JR.

PH.D., L.H.D.

Professor of Art and Archaeology in
Princeton University

NEW YORK

HENRY HOLT AND COMPANY

To

B. B.

IN FRIENDSHIP

PREFACE TO REVISED EDITION

In this new edition some slight corrections of the text have been made, and "Notes" and "Hints for Reading" have been brought up-to-date with the friendly aid of my colleague Professor E. T. Dewald.

F. J. M., Jr.

October 1, 1938

PREFACE

This book has grown out of lectures which were delivered at the Cleveland Art Museum in 1919–20. There I had ideal hearers, beginners who wanted to learn and were willing to follow a serious discussion. Since I aim at the same sort of a reader now, I have only slightly retouched and amplified the original manuscript. This is frankly a beginner's book. I have had to omit whatever might confuse the novice, including many painters inherently delightful. Controversial problems for the same reason have been when possible avoided. When, however, I have had to cope with such, I have depended more on my own eyes and judgment than on the written words of others. But the latest literature has also been used, so that even the adept should here and there find something to his purpose.

For opinions on contested points, I have given my authority or personal reason in notes, which, in order not to clutter up the text, are printed at the end. By the same token, hints on reading and private study are tucked away in the last pages where they will not bother readers who do not need or want them. While I hope the book will be welcome in the class-room, I have had as much in mind the intelligent traveller in Europe and the private student. Throughout I have had before me the kind of introduction to Italian painting that would have been helpful to me thirty years ago in those days of bewildered enthusiasm when I was making my *Grand Tour*.

THE AUTHOR

CONTENTS

Chapter I

GIOTTO AND THE NEW FLORENTINE HUMANISM

The Florentine ideal of Mass and Emotion — Its Humanism — The City of Florence about 1300 — The Position and Methods of the Painter — The General demand for Religious Painting — Accelerated by the religious reforms of 1200, and changed in character — Insufficiency of the current Italo-Byzantine Style — Experiments towards a new manner: Duccio and the Sienese, Cimabue, Cavallini and the "Isaac Master" — Giotto — Immediate followers of Giotto, Andrea Orcagna and the return to sculptural methods — Later Panoramists, Andrea Bonaiuti and the Spanish Chapel.

Leonardo da Vinci, from the summit of Florentine art, has written "What should first be judged in seeing if a picture be good is whether the movements are appropriate to the mind of the figure that moves. And again he has expressed somewhat differently the highest merits of painting as "the creation of relief (projection) where there is none." For Florence, at least, these notions are authoritative, and they may well serve as text for most that I shall say about Florentine painting. To give significant emotion convincing mass — this was the problem of the Florentine painter from the moment when Giotto about the year 1300 began to find himself, to that day more than two centuries and a half later when Michelangelo died. No Florentine master of a strenuous sort ever failed to perceive this mission, and no unstrenuous artist was ever fully Florentine. This twofold aim — humanistic, in choice and mastery of emotion; scientific, in search for those indications which most vividly express mass where no mass is — this twofold endeavor Florence shared with the only greater city of art, Athens. Thus Florence is to the art of today what Athens was to that of classical antiquity.

In these two little communal republics were discovered and worked out to perfection all our ideals of humanistic beauty. Florence saw God, His Divine Son, the Blessed Virgin, and the saints quite as Athens had seen the gods of Olympus, the demi-gods, and the heroes, simply as men and women of the noblest physical and moral type. Both agreed in magnifying and idealizing the people one ordinarily sees. For greater beauty, Athens represented them nude or lightly draped; for greater dignity, Florence chose the solemn garb of the Roman forum. Whether pagan or Christian, the guardians of a people's morality were to be above haste, excitement, or any transient emotion. They were to express intensities of feeling, but a feeling more composed, permanent, and disciplined, than that of every day. Judgment and criticism count for as much in both arts as emotional inspiration. The great Florentine artist is a thinker; he is often poet and scientist, sculptor and architect, besides being a painter. Behind his painting lies always a problem of mind, and as sheer personalities the greatest painters of Siena, Venice, and Lombardy often seem mere nobodies when compared even with the minor Florentines. We should know something about a city that produced personality so generously, and before considering Giotto, the first great painter Florence bred, we shall do well to look at Florence as he saw it about the year 1300, being a man in the thirties.

Florence was then as now a little city, its population about 100,000 souls, but it was growing. The old second wall of about two miles' circuit was already condemned in favor of a turreted circuit of over six. Up the Arno the forest-clad ridge of Vallombrosa was much as it is today; down the valley the jagged peaks of the Carrara mountains barred the way to the sea. The surrounding vineyards and olive orchards by reason of encroaching forest were less extensive than they are now, but through every gate and from every tower one could see smiling fields guarded by battlemented villas. In the city, the fortress towers of the old nobility, partizans mostly of the foreign Emperor, rose thickly, but already dismantled at their fighting tops, for the people, meaning strictly the ruling merchant and manufacturing classes, had lately taken the rule from the old nobles. Many of these had fled; some had been banished, as was soon to be that reckless advocate of the emperor, Dante Alighieri, an excellent poet of love foolishly dabbling in politics. Other patricians sulked in their fortress palaces. Some shrewdly got themselves demoted and joined the ruling trade guilds. Of these guilds a big four, five, or six, governed the city, while a minor dozen had political privilege. Only guild members voted for the city officers. The guilds combined the function of a trade union and an employer's association, including all members of the craft from the youngest apprentice to the richest boss-contractor. Such a guild as the notaries, must have been much like a bar association, while the wholesale merchants' guild must have resembled a chamber of commerce. The guild folk had early allied themselves with the Pope, the only permanent representative of the principle of order in Italy. The Pope was also the bulwark of the new free communes against the claims of the Teutonic Emperors. So in Florence piety, liberty, and prosperity were convertible terms.

Within the narrow walls was a bustling, neighborly, squabbling and making-up life. Everybody knew everybody else. The craftsman worked in the little open archways you may still see in the Via San Gallo, in sight and hearing of the passing world. Of weavers' shops alone there were 300. No western city was ever prouder than Florence in those days. Her credit was good from the Urals to the Pentland Hills. Her gold florin was everywhere standard exchange. She had secret ways of finishing the fine cloths that came in ships and caravans from Ghent, Ypres, and Arras; she handled the silks of China and converted the raw pelts of the north into objects of fashion. Her civic pride was actively expressing itself in building. Between 1294 and 1299 she had projected a new cathedral, the great Franciscan church of Santa Croce, a new town hall, and the massive walls we still see. For stately buildings she had earlier had only the Baptistry, in which every baby was promptly christened, and the new church of the Friars Preachers (Dominicans), Santa María Novella. In considering this Florence you must think of a hard-headed, full-blooded, ambitious community, frankly devoted to money-making, but desiring wealth chiefly as a step towards fame. Since the painter could provide fame in this world and advance one's position in the next, his estate was a favored one.

The painter himself was just a fine craftsman. He kept a shop and called it such — a *bottega*. He worked only to order. There were no exhibitions, no museums, no academies, no art schools, no prizes no dealers. The painters modestly joined the guild of the druggists (*speziali*), who were their color makers, quite as the up-to-date newspaper reporter affiliates himself with the typographical union. When a rich man wanted a picture, he simply went to a painter's shop and ordered it, laying down as a matter of course the subject and everything about the treatment that interested him. If the work was of importance, a contract and specifications were drawn up. The kind of colors, pay by the job or by the day, the amount to be painted by the contracting artist himself, the time of completion, with or without penalty — all this was precisely nominated in the bond. Naturally the painter used his shop-assistants and apprentices as much as possible. Often he did little himself except heads and principal figures. But he made the designs and carefully supervised their execution on panel or wall. A Florentine painter's *bottega* then had none of the preciousness of a modern painter's studio. It was rather like a decorator's shop of today, the master being merely the business head and guiding artistic taste. When we speak of a fresco by Giotto, we do not mean that Giotto painted much of it, any more than a La Farge window implies that our great American master of stained-glass design himself cut and set the glass. The painter of Florence had to be a jack-of-all-trades, a color grinder, a cabinet maker, and a wood carver; a gilder; to be capable of copying any design and of inventing fine decorative features himself. He must be equally competent in the delicate methods of tempera painting as in the resolute procedures of fresco.

These two methods set distinct limits to the work and its effects. The colors were ground up day by day in the shop. Each had its little pot. There was no palette. Hence only a few colors were used, and with little mixing. For tempera painting a good wooden panel — preferably of poplar — was grounded with successive coats of finest plaster of Paris in glue and rubbed down to ivory smoothness. The composition was then copied in minutely from a working drawing. The gold background inherited from the workers in mosaic was laid on in pure leaf. The composition was first lightly shaded and modelled either in green or brown earth, and then finished up a bit at a time, in colors tempered with egg or vegetable albumen. The paints were thick and could not be swiftly manipulated; the whole surface set and so hardened that retouching was difficult. How so niggling a method produced so broad and harmonious effects will seem a mystery to the modern artist. It was due to system and sacrifice. Though the work was done piecemeal, everything was thought out in advance. Dark shadows and accidents of lighting which would mar the general blond effect were ignored. The beauty desired was not that of nature, but that of enamels and semi-precious stones. These panels are glorious in azures, cinnabars, crimsons, emerald-greens, and whites partaking of all of these hues

Their delicacy is enhanced by carved frames, at this moment, 1300, simply gabled and moulded; later built up and arched and fretted with the most fantastic gothic features.

If the painter in tempera required chiefly patience and delicacy, the painter in fresco must have resolution and audacity. He must calculate each day's work exactly, and a whole day's work could be spoiled by a single slip of the hand in the tired evening hour. For fresco, the working sketch was roughly copied in outline on a plaster wall. Then any part selected for a day's work was covered with a new coat of fine plaster. The effaced part of the design must be rapidly redrawn on the wet ground. Then the colors were laid on from their little pots, and only the sound mineral colors which resist lime could be employed. The vehicle was simply water. The colors were sucked deep into the wet plaster, and united with it to form a surface as durable as the wall itself. Generally the colors were merely divided into three values, — light, pure colors, and dark. Everything was kept clear, rather flat, and blond, highly simple and beautifully decorative. One of the later painters, Cennino Cennini (active about 1400), tells us that a single head was a day's work for a good *frescante*. The touch had to be sure, for a misstroke meant scraping the wet plaster off, relaying it, and starting all over again. The fresco painter accordingly needed discipline and method. Nothing could be farther from modern inspirational methods. Where everything was systematized and calculated in advance, you will see it was quite safe for a master to entrust his designs to pupils who knew his wishes. Every fresco when dry was more or less retouched in tempera, but the best artists did this sparingly, knowing that the retouches would soon blacken badly or flake off.

So much for the shop methods. Now for him who makes shops possible — the patron. A wealthy Florentine as naturally wanted to invest in a frescoed chapel as a wealthy American does in a fleet of motor cars. Considering the changed value of money, one indulgence was about as costly as the other. But the Florentine never quite regarded paintings as luxuries. They were necessary to him. He loved them. They enhanced his prestige in this world and improved his chances in the next. Then to beautify a church was really to magnify the liberty and prosperity of Florence, which largely derived from the Holy See. Recall that every Florentine was born a Catholic, baptized in the fair Church of St. John with the name of a saint. This saint, he believed, could aid him morally and materially, was in every sense his celestial patron. It paid to do the saint honor, and that could best be done through the painter's art. The poorest man might have a small portrait of his patron, a rich man might endow a chapel and cause all his patron's miracles to be pictured on the wall. Think also that every altar — a dozen or more in every large church — was a shrine[1], containing the bread and wine that by the never-ceasing miracle of the Mass became the Saviour's body and blood; and was also a reliquary or tomb, containing in whole or part the body of some saint. Every altar then, and every chapel inclosing one, cried out for a twofold interpretation of its meaning. Everything about the Eucharist had to be explained (involving pretty nearly all of Biblical history), and the particular relic required similar illumination. Since many of the faithful could not read, and the Catholic Church has ever been merciful as regards sermonizing, these explanations of the altar as miracle shrine of Our Lord and as tomb of a particular saint were best made pictorially, and generally were so made.

Such motives for picture-making Florence of course shared with the entire Christian world. It remains to explain why she wanted more painting and better than any other mediæval city. She wanted more painting chiefly because of her exceptional civic pride and prosperity, she wanted better painting because she had moved ahead of the world towards finer, more passionate, and conscious experiences of life which the older painting was powerless to express. About the year 1200, a century before the time we are considering, there flourished two great religious leaders who gave to Christianity a new dignity and appeal. St. Dominic, with his disciple, St. Thomas Aquinas, endeavored to make Christianity more reasonable, St. Francis of Assisi endeavored to make it more heartfelt and compassionate. They founded two monastic orders with divergent yet harmonious aims. The Dominicans called men to a life of study and self-examination, enlisting the human reason to explain and justify the universe under the Christian scheme; the Franciscans called men to poverty, humility, and chastity, and service to the unfortunate. Between the two — one supplying the light of the reason and the other the light of the heart — they overcame heresies which had menaced both Christianity and civilization and roused the Church out of its dogmatic slumber. It was no longer enough for the Church to threaten. Men yielded to her now only on condition that their heads be convinced or their hearts touched. In Florence, where a rationalizing shrewdness and a real warm-heartedness singularly blended, the double appeal was irresistible. By and large the whole city either schematized with the Dominicans or slummed with the Franciscans. Here was urgent new matter requiring an art that could move and persuade.

Together with this religious revival and the political and commercial progress we have noted, came a literary revival. Before the end of the 13th century such poets as Guido Guinizelli, Guido Cavalcanti, and Dante Alighieri had so reshaped the rude vulgar tongue that it became worthy of its Latin succession. The refinements of chivalric love came to Florence in melodious verse, and what the poets called the "sweet new style," *il dolce stil nuovo*, in diction presaged a similar sweet new style of painting. Alongside of the poets, Brunetto Latini in the *Tesoro* shows glimmerings of scientific interest, and Giovanni Villani lends substance and dignity to the work of the chronicler. Already the sculptors Nicola and Giovanni of neighboring Pisa had grasped the beauties respectively of classic sculpture and the noble intensity of that of the Gothic North. All this immensely increased that sum of fine thinking, feeling, and seeing which underlies all great art.

To express these new emotions the old painting was inadequate. Italy through the so-called Dark Ages produced art abundantly. Wherever power and order asserted themselves amid the welter of war and oppression, stately buildings rose and these were decorated. Thus at Rome, where the popes gradually added temporal to spiritual power, splendid basilicas grew over the tombs of the martyrs. At Ravenna, through the 5th and 6th centuries the seat of the Byzantine and Gothic sovereignties, magnificent churches and baptistries were covered with pictorial mosaics. In Sicily, at Messina, Cefalù and Palermo, the sway of the Norman kings in the late 12th and the 13th centuries expressed itself in churches and civic buildings of the utmost splendor, which were adorned with mosaics by Greek masters. When the fugitives from the valleys of the Po, Adige, and Piave, and Brenta fled from Attila to the Venetian fens, there again was a beginning of great building. Whereever there was a powerful primate as at Milan, Como, Parma, Pisa, or a wide ruling abbot as at Subiaco, Monte Cassino, Capua, you will find art.

But hardly, except perhaps in architecture, Italian art. We have sporadic provincial expressions dominated from afar by the prestige of the Eastern Roman Empire. At Constantinople there was a permanent court, a ceremonious civilization, an artistic blending of the traditions of old Greece and of the mysterious Levant. The merchants of the world sought from Byzantium, jewelry, enamels, embroideries, brocades, carved ivories, and pictured manuscripts. She was to the early Middle Ages what Paris is to ours — the æsthetic fashion

maker of the world, — and her skilled artists went far afield
as so many missionaries of the Byzantine style. We find them
making the mosaics of Ravenna in the 5th and 6th centuries,
of St. Mark's at Venice from the 11th century, of many Roman

FIG. 1.   Byzantine Narrative Style about 1300.   Detail from Mosaic
Book Covers in the Opera del Duomo.

churches from an even earlier date, of Palermo in the 12th,
and of the Baptistry at Florence in the 13th. This Byzantine
manner, as practiced by the travelling Greek artists and by
their innumerable Italian imitators, is the real starting point
and jump-off place for Italian painting. Hence in first studying the Byzantine style we do but imitate the Italian painters
who immediately preceded Giotto.

Byzantine pictures have come down to us on the largest and
on the smallest scale — in the great mosaics and wall paintings, and as well on small panels and in the illustrated books
used in the ritual of the church. Both are important. The
mural decorations are what the early Italian painter had constantly before his eye; the miniatured psalters, Gospels, lec-
tionaries, chorals and prayer books, afforded the patterns
from which he drew with little alteration the standard compositions of the Annunciation to Mary, the Nativity of Christ.

His Adoration by the Shepherds and Kings, His Baptism, the
Raising of Lazarus, the Last Supper, Crucifixion, Descent into
Hell, Resurrection, and Ascension. But Byzantine design is
most imposing in its monumental phase. The most careless

FIG. 2. Mosaic in the Cathedral, Pisa. St. John, left, is by Cimabue,
1302; the Christ is in good Byzantine tradition; the Virgin, right,
is some twenty years later.

traveller still feels awe before those solemn figures of Christ
supreme ruler (*Pankrator*) and his Mother queen of heaven which
are seen throned against a background of azure or gold and attended by solemn figures of apostles and martyrs, Figure 2.
The forms are flat, — silhouettes enriched by interior tracery,
the arrangement in the space formal, symmetrical, highly decorative. The smaller narrative compositions,[2] Figure 1, are
clearly conceived but have small emotional appeal. For this
reason the Italians of the Golden Age spoke of the Byzantine
style as rude. This is an error. Rude in the hands of half-
trained local imitators, the style as formulated in the 9th century

at Constantinople was highly sophisticated and decoratively of great refinement. It was based on an admirable system of color spotting and a fine understanding of silhouette. The contours were cast in easy conventional curves. These were enriched within by hatchings and splintery angles of gold which contrasted effectively with the fluent outlines. Everything was done by precept and copybook. In four centuries before the year 1300, the style showed little change, indeed is still alive in the mountains of Macedonia and, until the Revolution, in Russia. The Byzantine artist seldom looked at a fellow mortal with artistic intent. He looked at some earlier picture or considered his own color preferences. Conventional and anæmic as the narrative style was, it did all that was required of it. Nothing better serves the purpose of an authoritative Church than the awe-inspiring Christs of the Lombard and Sicilian and Roman apses, and so long as the Church felt no duty beyond that of plain statement of her claims, the unfelt narratives from the Scriptures served every religious need.

It was different when under the leading of St. Dominic and St. Francis,[3] the Church eagerly wished to persuade men. Men may well have been frightened or even instructed by a Byzantine picture; nobody was ever persuaded by one. It took a century to work away from the Byzantine style, so deeply was it rooted. In fact, from the year 1226, that of St. Francis's death, to about the end of the century, such artists as Guido of Siena, Coppo di Marcovaldo, Giunta of Pisa, Jacopo Torriti, Giovanni Cosma, Duccio, and Cimabue chiefly restudied the old Byzantine manner. They wished to learn how to build creditably before they began to tear down. Such reverent experiment extending over two generations only proved that the breach with Byzantine formalism was inevitable.

With the deepening and broadening of personal, civic, and religious emotions, the painter found new exactions laid upon him which the bloodless art of Byzantium could not satisfy.

New life called for new forms to express it. We find in sculpture from about the year 1260, that of Niccolò Pisano's first pulpit — wholly classical in its dignity — a kindred endeavor in advance of the art of painting. The renewal took three forms: the more conservative spirits accepted the By-

FIG. 3. Tuscan Master about 1285. — *Mrs. Otto Kahn, N. Y.*

FIG. 4. Cimabue. Madonna in Majesty — *Uffizi.*

zantine formulas but endeavored to refine on them in a realistic sense, to add grace to austerity. Such moderate development of the old style fixed the character of the school of Siena and was magnificently initiated by its greatest artist, Duccio, active about 1300. A very beautiful Madonna of this general tendency is in the collection of Mrs. Otto Kahn at New York, Figure 3. It has been quite variously attributed.[4] It seems to me, however, a pure Tuscan work by Coppo or a painter akin to him. For the greater spirits such a reform was inadequate. Refine the Byzantine formulas to the utmost — there was no gain, rather loss in strength. Accordingly a vehement spirit like Cimabue,[5] acknowledgedly father of the Florentine school, accepts the Byzantine tradition loyally, but seeks to make its rigid mannerisms express the new religious passions. At times he is successful at this unlikely task of putting new wine into old bottles. His great enthroned Madonna at Florence, Figure 4, with solemn angels in attendance and grim patriarchs below her throne, may have been painted as early as 1285. It is faithful to the old monumental tradition — akin to the Christs and Marys of the mosaics — in its impressive richness is one of the most majestic things the century produced. It reveals the docility of its creator but only partially his power. We have hardly his hand but surely an echo of his influence in the tragic crucifix in the museum of Santa Croce. It is the moment of agony, and the powerful body writhes against the nails, while the head sinks in death. It may represent hundreds of similar crosses that stood high in air on the rood beam before the chancel, in sight both of the preacher and his public.

Somewhere about 1290, Cimabue was called to Assisi to decorate the church in which St. Francis was buried. His part was the choir and transepts of the upper church. In the cross vault he painted the four evangelists, on the walls he spread the stories of St. Peter and St. Paul, the legends of the Virgin scenes from the Apocalypse, the gigantic forms of the archangels and a Calvary, Figure 5, that is one of the most moving expressions of Christian art. Chipped and blackened, their lights become dark through chemical change, these wall paintings retain an immense power and veracity. The Byzantine forms gain a paradoxical solidity, like that of bronze. The convulsion of the figure of Christ is given back in the wild gestures of the mourning women and the terrified Jews. It is the moment of the earthquake and the opening of tombs; a cosmic terror and despair pervade the place. The work is hampered and rude but completely expressive. The sensitive

Japanese critic and man of the world, Okakura Kakuzo, used to regard these sooty frescoes in the transepts of the Franciscan basilica as the high point of all European art, which should at least induce the tourist and the student to give a second look at these battered and fading masterpieces. Cimabue seems

Fig. 5.   Cimabue.   Calvary.   Fresco. — *Upper Church, Assisi.*

to have planned and superintended the entire decoration of the Upper Church, with several Roman and Florentine aides to whom the bays in the nave were assigned. These masters probably worked simultaneously from perhaps 1290 to 1298, preparing the Franciscan Basilica for the great influx of pilgrims expected during the Papal Jubilee of 1300. Cimabue died about 1302 while working on the apsidal mosaic at Pisa, where the St. John is by his hand, Figure 2. He had brought life and passion into Italian painting, as his younger contemporary Giovanni Pisano had into Italian sculpture. Cimabue's defect — that of a noble spirit — was the faith that the old pictorial form could contain the new surging emotions.

Colder spirits, as is often the case, more readily found the right way. And the discovery was made at Rome where the sculptured columns, arches, and sarcophaghi, the pagan wall

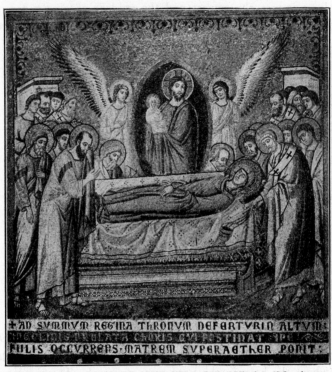

Fig. 6. Pietro Cavallini. Dormition of the Virgin. Mosaic. — *S. M. in Trastevere, Rome.*

paintings and the earliest Christian mosaics combined to continue the lesson of classic humanism. A remarkable family of decorators, the Cosmati; with such contemporaries as Jacopo Torriti and Filippo Rusuti begin very cautiously to free themselves from Byzantine trammels. But it was a painter, Pietro Cavallini,[5] who more fully grasped that glory that had been Rome. In 1291 he designed for the church of Santa Maria in Trastevere a Madonna and four stories of the Christ Child in mosaic. Here we glimpse a new pictorial form, Figure 6. Those Byzantine hooks and hatchings which were quite false to form give way to a reasonable structure in light and dark, the hair no longer wild and ropy, is disposed in sculpturesque

FIG. 7. Pietro Cavallini. Apostles, fresco, from Last Judgment. — *Santa Cecelia in Trastevere.*

locks, the draperies are no longer a cobweb pattern, but cast in broad and classic folds. All these improvements may be noted in more complete form in the frescoed Last Judgment which has recently been uncovered in the church of Santa Cecilia, Figure 7. Here the heads of Christ and the Apostles are well built in carefully graduated light and shade, while the draperies suggest Hellenistic statuary. But the renovation is on the whole cold and academic. Cavallini has not much more to say than the Byzantines, but that little he says with far greater gravity and truthfulness. He was a lucid and industrious but not a fine or strong spirit. His work later at Naples — in the Church of the Donna Regina, about 1310 — shows that when he will express strong emotions he becomes merely hectic. Yet he recovered for Italian painting more than a hint of the choice naturalism of old Rome, and

that is his sufficient glory. There is greater power and knowledge than his in the work of such contemporaries as the unknown painters of the frescoed heads of prophets in Santa
Maria Maggiore at Rome and of the stories of Isaac in the
Upper Church at Assisi.[6] These show a resolute and intelligent
effort to draw in masses of light and shade, and as well an
ambition to recover the gravity of the early Christian mosaics.
It is no wonder that some critics ascribe such dramatic and
superbly constructed frescoes as The Betrayal of Esau to
young Giotto, Figure 8, but the art is too mature for any
young artist. We have rather to do with a great personality
of Roman training who broke the way for Giotto. Cavalcaselle suggests, I think rightly, that the Florentine, Gaddo
Gaddi, may have done some of this work. But we are safe
only in calling this great painter "The Isaac Master."

To recapitulate, there were three ways, all imperfect, open
to a young and progressive painter who like Giotto di Bondone
was forming a style about the year 1300. He might with the
Sienese evade the issue of passion and naturalism, choosing for
gracefulness, he might try over again the great adventure of
his master Cimabue, endeavoring to bring emotion into the old
unfit forms, or he might, like Pietro Cavallini, let emotion
take care of itself and work academically towards better structure, drapery, light, and shade. His choice was absolutely
momentous for modern painting, and I want you to feel that
the issue was quite consciously and vividly before him, for he
had spent much of his youth as a humble assistant in the
basilica at Assisi, where frescoes in the vehement Tuscan manner of Cimabue and in the dignified Roman style of the Isaac
Master were being painted side by side. His decision was to
combine the merits of the two manners — to seek, like his
master, sincerity and depth of emotion, but to embody it in
the new and nobler forms of the Roman school. This decision
virtually fixed the character of Christian art in Italy — it was

to be warm and humanistic, but it was to revive much of that abstract nobility which old Rome had inherited from Greece. Thus Italian painting at the outset took a classic stamp which

Fig. 8.   "The Isaac Master."   Esau before Isaac.   Fresco.
— *Upper Church, Assisi.*

when true to itself it has never lost.   In fundamental ideas of beauty, there is no real difference between Giotto, Masaccio, Leonardo da Vinci, Raphael, Titian, Michelangelo.

Giotto di Bondone,[7] according to the best information we

have on a disputed point, was born in 1266, at the village of Colle, in the lovely valley of the Mugello. His people were prosperous and his way smooth. I see no reason for doubting the charming legend told by Ghiberti that Cimabue found the lad Giotto by the roadside diligently scratching the outlines of a sheep on a slate, and that that was the beginning of their association. In any case, we may surmise that he was early with Cimabue as apprentice and eventually went with the Master to Assisi to grind colors, clean brushes, and paint under direction. To be at that moment in the Franciscan Basilica was to be at the greatest creative center of the world. It seems to me likely that Giotto may have had a considerable part in the actual painting of the Old and New Testament stories in the nave, and I believe we may find his earliest designs in certain frescoes of the upper rows. The Lamenting over Christ's Body, for example, singularly combines the energy of Cimabue with the dignity of Cavallini, and there are significant echoes of the composition in Giotto's later version of the same theme at Padua. Tradition also ascribes to Giotto, maybe correctly, the Resurrection and Pentecost on the entrance wall.[8]

After 1296, according to Vasari's entirely credible account, young Giotto took over the direction of the work for the newly elected Franciscan General, Giovanni di Muro. What share he had in the vivacious and justly loved stories of St. Francis,[9] in the lower range of the nave, is greatly disputed. Of the twenty-eight frescoes involved, it seems clear to me that the first and the last three are by an artist more nearly in the Sienese tradition, that Nos. II to XVIII inclusive are designed by Giotto in the style of the Old Testament stories above and painted by him with a certain amount of assistance, and that the rest are largely inspired by Giotto but executed in his absence and without his final control. What is more important is the variety and vivacity of these narratives. Young

FIG. 10. The Sermon to the Birds. — *Upper Church, Assisi.*

FIG. 9. — St. Francis renounces His Father. — *Upper Church, Assisi.*

FIG. 11. St. Francis before the Soldan. — *Upper Church, Assisi.*

Giotto is free to improvise, as he was not in the standard Bible subjects, and the mood shifts readily. We have charity, with St. Francis giving his cloak to a beggar, in an idyllic landscape; family strife in St. Francis renouncing his father, Figure 9;

Fig. 12. Early Sketch Copy after Giotto's Mosaic of the Navicella. Compare Fig. 31. — *Metropolitan Museum, New York.*

sorcery in the exorcism of the devils from Arezzo; an odd mixture of ogreishness and witchcraft, in St. Francis's Fire Ordeal before the Soldan, Figure 11; a great pious intentness, in the choristers at the Cradle Rite; intense physical appetite, in the Miracle of the Spring; an entrancing blend of reverence and humor, in the Sermon to the Birds, Figure 10; stark tragedy in the Death of the Knight of Celano.

Giotto is still chiefly a sprightly illustrator. He is as yet insensitive to composition. He often perfunctorily splits his groups, giving each a landscape — or architectural back-screen quite in the Byzantine manner. His story-telling is brusque and without rhythm. His sense of form is already strong and growing, but there is little of the ease and style of the Isaac frescoes just above. In vitality the stories of St. Francis mark a great advance, but they lack the gravity and exquisiteness of balance proper to the best mural decoration.

It was at Rome that young Giotto was to broaden and refine his art. He was called thither before the year 1300 to design the great mosaic of Christ walking on the Sea of Galilee beside the tempest-tossed boat of the Apostles. It stood over the inside cloister-portal of old St. Peter's, and has been many times moved in the rebuilding of the church, and with each move restored, so that what we now see in the porch is entirely remade. From certain fragments of the old mosaic, and old sketch-copies, Figure 12, we may judge that the Navicella, as the Italians loved to call it, was an elaborate composition of great dramatic power, the logical consummation of the experiments at Assisi. Our best version of the Navicella is Andrea Bonaiuti's adaptation, Figure 31, for the vault of the Spanish Chapel, 1365.

But Giotto was soon to renounce the facile method of diffuse and genial narrative in favor of a concise and massive style, akin to sculptured relief, and deeply influenced by the antique. The arches and the columns of Imperial Rome are teaching their silent lesson, the simple and noble forms of Cavallini and his nameless rivals show how painting may vie with sculpture in sense of mass and reality. With the problem of the representation of mass on a flat surface, Giotto wrestled eagerly and triumphantly. With a genius that few painters have equalled, he grasped the truth that the figure painter's problem of representing space is chiefly that of emphatically suggesting mass. If you convince the eye of the tangibility of your objects, the mind will supply elbow room and air to breathe. It isn't necessary to simulate a box, as the Sienese painters often did. The painter who can give a convincing sense of mass may handle accessories and perspective with the utmost freedom, according to the inner law of his design. The painter who thinks first of his space is in every way more bound to the smaller probabilities. Much thinking of this sort must have been done by Giotto before he worked out his new style at Padua.

After his return from Rome, Giotto sojourned for a time in Florence, and in 1304 or thereabouts painted the gigantic Madonna formerly in Ognissanti, Figure 13. It is impressive in mass, admirable in the intent expression of the attendant angels, rich in color, but the great figure is unhappily crowded by the canopy. Giotto is still a bit uncertain as to the rendering of space, and makes a good if unpleasing effort to suggest depth despite the limitations of a gold background. With all its nobility and tenderness, this is by no means so good a decoration as the great Madonna by Cimabue, Figure 4, which hangs nearby in the Uffizi.

With the problems of space and mass, Giotto was soon to cope triumphantly. A wealthy citizen of Padua, Enrico Scrovegni, was planning a new chapel to the Virgin Annunciate. Doubtless he wished the repose of his father's soul, for his father had been a notorious usurer. Dante incontinently puts him in hell with other profiteers. Enrico Scrovegni built his chapel near the ruins of a Roman arena and dedicated it March 25, 1305. The Arena Chapel was a brick box, barrel vaulted within — a magnificent space for a fresco painter. Giotto spread upon it the noblest cycle of pictures known to Christian art. Over the chancel arch he painted the Eternal, surrounded by swaying angels, and listening to the counter-pleas of Justice and Mercy concerning doomed mankind, with the Archangel Gabriel serenely awaiting the message that should bring Christ to Mary's womb and salvation to earth. This is the Prologue. Opposite on the entrance wall is the Epilogue — a last judgment, with Christ enthroned as Supreme Judge amid the Apostles, and the just being parted from the wicked. Amid the just you may see Enrico Scrovegni presenting the chapel to three angels.

The side walls are ruled off into three rows of pictures, with ornate border bands and a basement of sculpturesque figures symbolizing the seven virtues and vices. The story reads down from above. Below the azure vault and still a little in the curve are the stories of the Childhood of the Virgin—nothing in the chapel more simple and stately than these.[10] The middle course is devoted to the early deeds of Christ, from his birth to the expulsion of the money lenders from the temple. The lower row depicts His Passion ending with the Miracle of Pentecost. Much later a disciple of Giotto completed the story with the last days of the Virgin, in the Choir. Thus the narrative in its broadest sense is a life of the Virgin Mary, including that of her Divine Son, and both lives are brought into an eternal

Fig. 13. Giotto. Madonna Enthroned. — *Uffizi.*

scheme of things by the prologue, which shows a relenting God, and the Epilogue which shows a now relentless Christ awarding bliss and woe to the race for all eternity.

The first impression of a visitor to the chapel will be a feeling of awe qualified by joy in the loveliest of colors. The whites of the classical draperies dominate. They are shot with rose, or pale blue, or grey green. Certain old enamels have the same quality of making the most splendid crimsons, blues, and greens seem merely foils to foreground masses of white which seem to include by implication all the positive colors. It is this bright and original color scheme balancing crimsons and azures with violets and greens which makes a thing of beauty out of what would otherwise be a stilted checkerboard arrangement.

Next the eye will realize splendid people gravely occupied with solemn acts. There is the strangest blend of passion and

Fig. 13a.   Giotto.   St. Joachim and St. Anna at the Beautiful Gate.
—*Arena, Padua.*

decorum.   See the eager old man who clutches his wife before a massive city gate while she caresses him tenderly, Figure 13a, note the firm gentleness of the bearded priest who handles a screaming baby before the altar, mark the sense of strain and hurry where a mother and child mounted on an ass, Figure 14, are pushed and dragged along by an old man and attendants.   Or again, what sinister power in the scene where three Jewish magistrates press money upon a haggard, bearded,

nervous man. You do not need the bat-like demon prompting
him to know that it is the arch-traitor Judas, Figure 15. Then
there is a strange, serene, processional composition, with the
Virgin moving homeward among her friends to a solemn

Fig. 14. Giotto. The Flight into Egypt. — *Arena, Padua.*

music, Figure 16. It has a rhythm like the frieze of the
Parthenon. Perhaps your eye will fix longest on the scene
where about the pale body of the dead Christ women wail with
outstretched hands, or tend the broken body, while bearded
men, accustomed to the hardness of life, stand in mute sympathy with folded hands, Figure 17. It is what the Gospel
ought to look like. How Giotto shows every feeling, push-
ing its expression just to the verge, and there stopping, so

that idyl and tragedy, devotion and wrath, treachery and
fealty, fear and courage, each keeps its proper and distinguish-
ing aspect, while all are invested in a common dignity and
nobility. You will perhaps never have seen an art at once

so varied and moving, and nevertheless so monumental, and you
may well be curious as to the
method.

You will see readily that
these compositions are conceived
sculpturally. Every one with the
slightest change could be cut in
marble. Indeed the seven Virtues, Figure 18, and seven Vices
impersonated in monochrome on
the dado of the chapel are direct
imitations of sculpture. The

FIG. 15. Giotto. Judas betraying
Christ. — *Arena, Padua.*

figures throughout the life of
Christ and the Virgin are of even size, and usually all on one
plane. The landscapes and architectural features are arranged
simply as frames or backgrounds for the figure groups. The
figures are, whenever the subject permits, clad in drapery of
a classic cast. Expression is conveyed not much by the faces,
which have a uniform Gothic intentness, but by the action of
the entire figure and especially of the hands. The forms are
rather squat and massive, yet have a homely gracefulness.
There is nothing like perspective, and small regard for distance,
yet the figures have convincing bulk and move gravely in
adequate space. All this is due to the most consummate
draughtsmanship. Giotto simplifies his seeing; what he cares
for is the thrust of the shoulder, or the poise of hip, the swing
of the back from the pelvis, the projection of the chest, the
balance of the head on the neck and its attachment to the
shoulders. All these essential facts of mass he represents by

the simplest lines of direction, by broad masses of light and shade, often merely by the tugging lines in drapery that tell of the form beneath. The cave men would have understood Giotto, and so would the post-impressionists of today. Con-

FIG. 16. Giotto.   The Virgin returning from her wedding.—
Arena, Padua.

ciseness, economy, force, mass — these are the technical qualities of the work, as human insight and tenderness are its grace. As the great analytical critic Bernard Berenson has well remarked, this painting makes the strongest possible appeal to our tactile sense, stirring powerfully all our memories of touch, and presenting the painted indications as so many swiftly grasped clues to reality. We have to do with a magnificently conceived shorthand. No artist before or since has made a greater expenditure of mind or achieved a more notable inventiveness than Giotto in the Arena Chapel.

It was dedicated March 25, 1305, Giotto being nearly forty
years old, and it was probably not completely painted on the
day of dedication, since many draperies were borrowed from
St. Mark's, Venice, to cover, presumably, the still unpictured

Fig. 17.   Giotto.   Lamentation over Christ. — *Arena, Padua.*

parts of the walls.   Giotto lived some four years in Padua,
brought his family there, received the exiled poet Dante and
with him joked not too decorously about his own ugliness and
that of his children.   It seems likely enough, though not certain, that he followed the banished Pope to Avignon about
1309, and spent some years in Southern France.   What is
certain is that he was again in Florence by 1312, and that,
having found his own solution of the problem of mass in the

Arena Chapel, he thereafter rested comfortably on his discovery, never was quite as strenuous again, and spent his
later years at a new problem — that of decorative symmetry.

The first experiment towards a sweeter and more complex
style was made in the cross vaults
of the Lower Church of Assisi,
immediately above the tomb of
St. Francis. The subjects were
the three virtues of the Franciscan vow — Poverty, Chastity,
and Obedience — with a St.
Francis in a glory of angels. In
these great triangular compositions, allegory and symbolism
run riot, and we do well to recall
Hazlitt's shrewd remark on
Spenser's "Faery Queene" —
"the allegory will not bite."
Indeed one might forget it for
the radiance of the azures, moss-
greens, rose pinks, and deeper
violets, for the delightful contrast of the freely composed
groups with the intricate geometrical formality of the rich bor-

Fig. 18.   Giotto.   Hope. —
Arena, Padua.

ders. Yet to ignore the allegory completely would be to forget
the master's intention. We may savor it best in the great composition: St. Francis Marries his Lady Poverty, Figure 18a. The
bridal group stands on a central crag, Christ serving as priest,
St. Francis slipping a ring on the gaunt hand of a haggard, yet
strangely fascinating bride clothed in a single ragged garment.
Her bare feet show through a crisply drawn and blossomless rose
tree. Two urchins at the foot of the little cliff stand ready to
stone so unseemly a bride. From the central group to right

and left, earnest groups of angels spread in a descending curve. In the lower angle, left, a young man gives his rich cloak to an old beggar, while an angel points to the bridal: Poverty is accepted. At the lower right corner, another angel attempts

Fig. 18a.   Giotto.   St. Francis' Mystic Marriage with Poverty.
— *Lower Church, Assisi.*

to detain a young man who passes with a gesture of contempt in the company of two portly priests: Poverty is rejected by such. From the apex of the great triangle, the hands of God descend to welcome two angels, one of which offers the cloak given to the beggar, and the other a model of the church which is the splendid covering for the body of the Saint. The fantastic beauty of this and its companion pieces can only be appreciated on the spot. No frescoes of Italy surpass these for loveliness of color and perfection of condition. It is the most beautiful pictured Gothic ceiling in the world, perhaps the most fantastically beautiful of all figured ceilings whatever. Because the figures are a little slight and the expression a bit sentimentalized, and the proportions rather arbitrarily handled to meet the exigencies of the curved spaces, many good critics, including Venturi and Berenson, deny these compositions to Giotto. One of them, the St. Francis in Glory, is clearly of inferior design and quality. For the others, it seems to me that the designs can only be by Giotto, while the execution is mostly by a charming assistant whose work in this ceiling and elsewhere in this church makes us wish we knew his name. No middle-aged painter of established repute was likely to undertake personally the dirty and fatiguing work of painting a ceiling in fresco. If we are right in supposing that Giotto may have designed this ceiling, shortly after his return from Avignon, say, after 1312, he would have been towards fifty years old, and provided with a shop-staff of well-trained assistants. From this time on, indeed, we may assume that he rather directed the work of others than painted himself. Such a view will permit us to accept as school works many fine pictures the design of which a too strict criticism has denied to Giotto. For example, the admirable Coronation of the Virgin, in Santa Croce, Florence, seems to me completely designed by Giotto, and the logical next step after the Franciscan allegories, though there can be little actual painting by the master on the panel, and his personal contribution may have been limited to a small working drawing. Indeed the only one of the later panels which seems to show much of his actual handiwork is the lovely Dormition of the Virgin at Berlin, Frontispiece, which was painted for the Church of Ognissanti.

At about this period I think we may set the several crucifixes in Florentine churches, without inquiring too narrowly whether they are by the master or by scholars. Giotto has developed a singularly noble type. The Christ is no longer contorted in agony as in the crucifixes by Cimabue. He is dead, with his head quietly sunk on the powerful breast, and the body relaxed. The conception is humanistic. One feels chiefly the pity of stretching that glorious thing that is a man's body on a cross. Probably the earliest of these crucifixes is that at Santa Maria Novella, while the finest is at San Felice. About 1320 we may set the dismembered *ancona*, painted for

FIG. 19.   Giotto.   Naming of St. John the Baptist. — *Peruzzi Chapel, Santa Croce.*

Cardinal Gaetano Stefaneschi, which originally stood on the high altar of St. Peter's, Rome. The tarnished fragments which you may still see in the sacristy, are more splendid in color than any other tempera painting whatsoever. Probably only the central panels, Christ and St. Peter enthroned, are from Giotto's hand, the side panels representing the martyrdom of Peter and Paul may well be both designed and executed by the accomplished assistant who carried out the allegories at Assisi.

So far we have seen Giotto a wanderer. Assisi, Rome, Padua, Rimini, delighted to do him honor, but apparently Florence had claimed few works from his hand. We have record of frescoes in the Badia which may have been early works. It was the decoration of Arnolfo's great Franciscan church of Santa Croce that finally recalled Giotto and evoked his most accomplished work. He completed in the transepts of Santa Croce four chapels and as many altar-pieces. The frescoes were white-washed in the 16th century, and the panels broken up and lost. But in the last century the white-wash was scraped off from two of the chapels, and there we may see, so far as defacement and repainting permit, the masterpieces of the early Florentine school. We may reasonably guess the date of this work to be somewhere about 1320, Giotto being nearly sixty.

In the chapel maintained by that noble family, the Peruzzi, Giotto spread on the side walls three stories from the life of St. John the Baptist, and as many more from that of St. John the Evangelist. The figures are superb, magisterial in pose;

FIG. 20. Giotto. Resuscitation of Drusiana by St. John. — *Peruzzi Chapel, Santa Croce.*

the draperies grand and ample after the classical fashion. Upon bulk and relief there is less insistence than at Padua. Giotto has passed the experimental stage as regards form, is less strenuous and more at his ease. Nothing is more stately in the chapel than the presentation of the infant Baptist to his father, who is temporarily stricken with dumbness, Figure 19. Simeon gravely writes the name John; Elizabeth with her adoring group of attendants carefully offers the vivacious child to his father's gaze. The gestures are slow, definite, determined. The group beautifully fills the square space without crowding it. The composition, unlike the widely spaced Paduan designs, is drawn together into a mass.

Upon the Feast of Herod with Salome modestly dancing John Ruskin [11] has expended just eulogies in the petulant yet important little book "Mornings in Florence." What is notable in the scene is its general decorum and the pathetic indecision of the weak King.

But the most accomplished design as such is the miracle of the Resuscitation of Drusiana by St. John the Evangelist, Figure 20. Even the inscenation before a fine Romanesque city is adequately, if very simply, realized. The gesture of the apostle is of majestic power, the contrast of the massive, upright, columnar forms of the elders, with the sharply bent forms of Drusiana, her mourners and bier bearers, is admirably invented, and the drastic portraiture of a cripple at the left adds a tang of reality while in no wise detracting from the dignity of the scene. We have a work in the grand style, massively conceived, warmly felt, wrought into an elaborate and satisfying symmetry. The Ascension of St. John has an even graver and more ample rhythm. The Golden Age of Raphael and Titian will have little to add to this except the minor graces.

In the adjoining chapel of the Bardi family, Giotto, a little later, I believe, painted six stories of St. Francis, and four figures of the great Franciscan saints, St. Louis of France, St. Louis of Toulouse, St. Clare, and St. Elizabeth of Hungary. Over the entrance arch he set an animated picture of St. Francis receiving the stigmata, the wounds of the Saviour. Nearly thirty years earlier he had done this subject for the Church at Assisi, and in an altar-piece which has passed from Pisa to the Louvre. By comparing the rigid, angular figures of the earlier composition and their ill-adjusted accessories, with this easy and beautifully balanced arrangement, you may see how far Giotto had gone in the direction of grace, and you will not fail also to note how much more tragic the earlier and less calculated work is.

For the first time, in the Bardi chapel, Giotto conceives the decoration of the side walls as a whole. From the pointed lunettes above, through the three compositions on each wall, there is an architectural axis, sometimes arbitrarily imposed, about which the figures are symmetrically distributed. Often

FIG. 21. Giotto. St. Francis renounces his Father. Compare FIG. 9. — *Bardi Chapel, Santa Croce.*

the scene is a screen with projecting wings as in the St. Francis before the Sultan of Morocco, or a similar forecourt, as in the Mourning for St. Francis. It will be well to compare the story of St. Francis renouncing his father, Figure 21, with the same subject at Assisi. You will recall that St. Francis, when rebuked by his father for a rash and impulsive act of charity, stripped off his clothes, then threw them at his father's feet, and took refuge under the robe of the Bishop of Assisi. In the earlier version the architectural background splits the composition in two, adding to its intensity perhaps, but displeasing to the eye. Here in the late version a fine building seen in perspective both unifies the two groups and serves as apex for the decorative axis of the entire side wall.

More remarkable still is the contrast between St. Francis Braving the Fire Ordeal before the Soldan, Figure 22, as depicted at Assisi and Florence. We have to do not merely with an immense advance in decorative composition, the accessories at Assisi being trivial and fantastic; not merely with progress towards a gracious symmetry and more massive and impressive form, but also with a complete change of moral point of view. At Assisi the Soldan is an ogre exacting a cruel test. The Moslem priests are a cowardly pack of magicians ignobly slinking away, St. Francis a grim fanatic. At Florence the Soldan is a noble and humane gentleman, amazed at an unreasonable ordeal forced upon his wise men. The Moslem doctors are splendid scholars grudgingly shrinking from an unfair test, St. Francis an alert little enthusiast half gloating over the confusion he has thrown into the enemy camp. With a by no means orthodox feeling, old Giotto, humanistic Giotto, almost seems to take, or at least to see, the pagans' side of it. He who had written a manly poem against the excesses and hypocrisies of the Franciscan ideal of poverty, is now capable of criticizing the more extravagant propagandism of the saint himself.

It is a criticism that admits all tenderness and sympathy, as may be seen in the famous fresco representing the Mourning over the body of St. Francis while his soul is translated to heaven, Figure 23. Again John Ruskin is your best interpreter to this picture, which after all only needs to be seen. It combines all the qualities for which Giotto had striven—warmth, vivacity, ingenuity, unexpectedness in the narrative details; massiveness and dignity of the individual forms; and a decorative symmetry at once monumental, formal, and delightfully varied.

With this noble and deeply felt composition we virtually take leave of Giotto. For though he lived for many years yet, the works of his old age have largely perished. In the chapel at Assisi dedicated to St. Mary Magdalen are fine frescoes in which he surely had a leading part. From 1330 to 1333 he worked at Naples for King Robert of Anjou. Nothing re-

Fig. 22. Giotto. St. Francis before the Soldan. Compare Fig. 11.
— *Bardi Chapel, Santa Croce.*

Fig. 23. Giotto. Death of St. Francis. — *Bardi Chapel, Santa Croce.*

mains from this visit except certain shrewd jests which the painter exchanged with the King. In 1334 Florence recalled him, and made him *capomaestro* of the Cathedral. Giotto designed the flower-like tower which rises lightly beside the temple of Our Lady of the Flower, invented and perhaps cut in marble certain reliefs on the base representing the crafts of men, but did not live to see the loveliest of bell towers finished. The task was completed by his pupil and artistic executor, Taddeo Gaddi. In the last years Giotto conceived vast compositions of a religious and political sort for the public buildings of the Commune. There were allegories of a strong and weak state, in the Bargello, the prison-fortress of the Captain of the People.

FIG. 24. Giotto. Dante, tracing from the ruined fresco in the Bargello.

These great symbolical designs are a kind of missing link between Giotto and the panoramic painters who followed him. We may find an echo of this lost work in the Civic Allegories in the Palazzo Pubblico of Siena. These were doing at the moment of Giotto's death by a Sienese painter, Ambrogio Lorenzetti, who had studied the great Florentine master devoutly. Nothing of Giotto's latest phase is left save a few figures in the battered frescoes in the Bargello which contain the idealized portrait of youthful Dante, Figure 24, and the gracious Dormition of the Virgin at Berlin, Frontispiece.

Just before Giotto died, the tyrant of Milan borrowed him from Florence. Giotto soon returned, to die early in the year 1337, being seventy years old. Almost single-handed he had made Italian painting. He had lent life and warmth to the cold and academic reform of the Roman painters. He had expressed a maximum of feeling, without sacrifice of dignity. He had worked out beautiful and impressive forms of composition wherein symmetry and contrast met harmoniously. He had mastered the expression of mass on a plane surface with a certainty and energy no artist before had even imagined, and that few since have equalled. He had forecast and led the way in every manner of realistic figure painting.

Florence, when true to herself, could only repeat Giotto in one phase or another of his activity. In her casual and sprightly mood, she carries on the method of Giotto's stories of St. Francis at Assisi, in mystical reflection and symbolism she must build on the allegories over St. Francis' tomb and on the lost political frescoes; in her mood of strenuous search for reality she can but repeat the Paduan chapter of Giotto's strivings, in rare moments of vision and fulfilment she will merely begin where the Santa Croce frescoes of Giotto ended.

However Giotto be ranked, and personally I see no greater artist on the rolls of history, his is indisputably the greatest single achievement; for no other artist who accomplished so much began with so little. It was no exaggeration that made Lorenzo Ghiberti regard the advent of Giotto as the coming to life of an art that had been buried for centuries. It is indeed the measured classicism of Giotto's art that constitutes its greatness — its sweet and lucid reasonableness, its rugged yet disciplined strength. Seneca or Marcus Aurelius would have understood it perfectly, as Giotto himself, for his mellow wisdom and wit, would have been a welcome visitor at Horace's Sabine farm. In his broad and flexible insight, his love of mankind, his clear perceptions of aims and ready acceptance of limitations, in his pathos without exaggeration, in his constructive skill without ostentation, in his simplicity without bareness, he is the authentic and indispensable link between the beauty of Greece and Rome and that of the Italian Golden Age. To know him is to know almost everything that is needful about older European painting, not to know him is to lack the very rudiments of an artistic education.

Giotto left many followers,[12] not one of whom at all understood his greatness. Like his friend Dante, he was distantly admired, but really loved only in bits. As perceptive a person as the artist biographer Vasari lavishes praise upon Giotto for his more trivial inventions — the Christ Child struggling out of the arms of the High Priest, for example. So Giotto's followers picked unintelligently from his great accomplishment, choosing what the master himself would least have valued — his simple contours without his significant mass, his variety and vivacity without his warmth and restraint. On their own account they added complication. The sparse economy of Giotto's best work could never have appealed to Florence at large. Something richer and gayer was wanted, more like Florentine life itself as it became after the general loosening up of manners and morals following the plague of 1348. Its chronicler, the author of the "Decameron," fairly represents the new spirit. The best of the younger painters have indeed something of Boccaccio's mentality — his light touch, his charm, his panoramic richness, his fluid and undisciplined grace. Thus arises what I may call the panoramic style of fresco painting — superficial, full of episodes and accessories, still religious in theme, but mundane in spirit, often cleverly conceived, and very superficially felt. These artists had grasped neither the meaning of Giotto's drawing nor the beauty of his decorative formulas, they saw only his variety and energy. Meanwhile a great Sienese painter, Ambrogio Lorenzetti, a profound admirer of Giotto, had worked out a nobly spectacular form of painting in which the stage setting was elaborate and realistic. He painted much in Florence about 1334 and his novelties allured the new men. So we find fresco painting tending in a scenic direction, and panel painting following the same course more conservatively — not merely in Florence and Siena, but throughout Northern Italy as well.

FIG. 25. Giotto's Assistant at Assisi. Flight into Egypt. Compare Figure 14. — *Lower Church, Assisi.*

Many of Giotto's immediate pupils are mere names to us. Maso, whom the sculptor commentator Ghiberti praised for his sweetness, Stefano whom he dubbed the "ape of nature," Puccio Capanna — their work must be at Assisi, but criticism has not succeeded in clearly disengaging it. The nameless master who executed the Franciscan allegories at Assisi and designed the stories of Christ's youthful days, in the adjoining right transept, is the most accomplished and individual follower of Giotto. He works for grace, pathos, sumptuousness, and decorative breadth. He is a Giotto with the angles rubbed down. By comparing Giotto's Flight of the Holy Family to

Egypt, with the later version at Assisi, Figure 25, we may grasp the difference between master and scholar. Giotto is brusque, harsh, noble; the flight through a rocky defile gives a sense of urgency and peril; the composition carries forward like the

Fig. 26. Taddeo Gaddi. St. Joachim Meets St. Anna. Compare Fig. 13a. — *Baroncelli Chapel, Santa Croce.*

ram of a battleship. In the version at Assisi the flight has become an attractive family excursion through a romantic valley; the mood is gentle, charming, unspecific. A moment in an epic has been attenuated into an idyl. This master never fails to express a dreamy sort of poetry, and in such compositions as the Massacre of the Innocents, and the Calvary, he commands a genuine pathos. He is exactly what Giotto might have been, had he skipped the strenuous Paduan

phase, and become a decorator without the preliminary discipline of the draughtsman. There are reasons for thinking that
this work was done by a shop assistant of Giotto's, who for
many years directed the decoration of the Lower Church at
Assisi in Giotto's stead. Some of the work in the Childhood
of Christ, I believe, may be as late as 1330 to 1335.

Taddeo Gaddi is a more definite and less pleasing personality. He was Giotto's godson and his assistant for twenty-
four years, presumably from 1313 to 1337, as well as his
artistic executor. Whether in panel or fresco, he was an admirable craftsman; in tempera, a fine colorist. His panels are
widely scattered, some ten being in the United States; his
frescoes, all that we need to note, are in Santa Croce. In the
Baroncelli Chapel, just after Giotto's death, Taddeo finished
these frescoes of the early life of the Virgin, repeating
themes which Giotto had used both in Padua and elsewhere
in Santa Croce itself. His way of competing with Giotto is to
stir and add and mix things up. Compare the meeting of Anna
and Joachim at the Beautiful Gate in the two masters; Giotto
at Padua is grave, noble, heartfelt; how he discriminates
between the masculine clutch of the old husband and the
tender embrace of the wife — how drastic the conception is,
but also how clear and stately. Poor Taddeo on the other
hand brings the sacred pair together with the bounce of a modern
dance, Figure 26. He brings no brains to bear, and almost no
feelings, just a sprightly and wholly casual inventiveness. Certain delightful little panels with stories of Christ and St. Francis
which he did in Giotto's shop for the doors of the sacristy
wardrobes of Santa Croce remind us of the pity that he ever
ceased to be an interpreter of a greater man's designs. In
the fresco of Job's trials, in the Campo Santo, Pisa, he seems
nearly a great artist. Conceivably he worked on designs of
his late master. At least he had a certain critical sense, for
at an artist's reunion at San Miniato, about 1360, he told

Andrea Orcagna and the rest of the company that painting had constantly declined since Giotto and was declining every day. He transmitted his sound craftsmanship to a son, Agnolo, who decorated the Choir of Santa Croce with the legends of the Cross. He carried down the panoramic style to the end of the 14th century, practicing it with more taste than his father, achieving a grace without much inwardness or force.

FIG. 27. Giottino. Deposition.
— *Uffizi.*

A later contemporary of Giotto's, Buonamico Buffalmacco,[13] seems to have inherited something of Giotto's power, but the identification of his work is very uncertain, and he lives for us chiefly as an egregious wag in the pages of the Italian story writers.

From another contemporary and possibly a scholar of Giotto, Bernardo Daddi, we have many panel pictures and a few frescoes at Santa Croce. He is an admirable craftsman, and a sincere illustrator, within his limitations, applying very competently to panel painting something of the panoramic realism of Ambrogio Lorenzetti. A prolific artist, his exquisitely finished little panels are quite common. In America are good examples in the New York Historical Society, in the Platt Collection, Englewood, and a more monumental piece in the Johnson Collection, Philadelphia. He lived well beyond the middle of the century.

Giottino, who possibly is to be identified with Giotto's pupil Maso, is a more delicate spirit with unusual resources of pathos. His best work is an altar-piece of the Deposition, Figure 27.

painted about 1360 for the Church of San Remigio at Florence
and now in the Uffizi. A preference for isolated figures and for
vertical lines is noteworthy, as is the wistfulness of the
attendant donors. Similar qualities of delicate precision as

FIG. 28. Andrea Orcagna. Christ conferring authority upon St. Peter
and St. Thomas Aquinas. — *Strozzi Chapel, Santa Maria Novella.*

of dispersion are in the frescoes in Santa Croce which represent the Miracles of Pope Sylvester. The note is feminine
and rather Sienese than genuinely Florentine.

Outside of Giotto's *bottega* arose the rare continuers of his
tradition. Such an artist flourished about the middle of the
century in the person of Andrea di Cione, better known by
his nickname of Orcagna. He was more of a sculptor and
architect than a painter, a man of dignity and force, a poet
and thinker. Although not a pupil of Giotto, he studied that
master's work admiringly, and sought to reproduce its massiveness. Its brusqueness he largely rejected. Instead of
sketching the draperies summarily, he drew the folds care-

fully after the model; he liked to treat the panel and wall as a whole, where Giotto had accepted the tradition of subdivision; he gave to his faces a greater sweetness and he occasionally attempted foreshortenings and impetuousities of gesture that Giotto would have avoided. Unluckily Orcagna's most important frescoes have perished. We may grasp his nobility in the altar-piece which he finished and dated in 1357, Figure 28, for the chapel of the Strozzi family at Santa Maria Novella. The formality of the composition is noteworthy, as is the stately sweetness of the Madonna. The subject is Christ delegating his Power and Wisdom respectively to St. Peter and to St. Thomas Aquinas.

In the same chapel the figure of Christ leaning forward over a cloud and making the sublime gesture that decrees the end of the world and the Judgment Day, Figure 29, is probably designed by Orcagna, as are the larger figures below. We have here one of the freest and grandest conceptions of the period. The lovely garden-like heaven and the quaint and ingenious hell on the side walls are by Orcagna's brother, Nardo di Cione. The mood is less grave than Orcagna's, variety counts for more. The heads of the saints are of a most delicate beauty. Nardo has many of the qualities of the panoramic painters without their heedlessness. He represents a compromise between the severity of Giotto and the diffuseness of his own day. He worked indefatigably until 1366, and his younger brother, Jacopo, and his imitator, Mariotto, continued the manner almost into the new century.

Orcagna was perhaps more versatile than critics have supposed. Recently discovered fragments of frescoes in Santa Croce, Figure 30, show a drastic power that no other Florentine possessed. The theme is miserable folk in time of pestilence crying out to Death to end their sorrows. The entire fresco would have shown Death passing them by and poising the scythe for prosperous and happy folk beyond. The whole scene

Fig. 30.   Andrea Orcagna.   They call Death in Vain.   Fragment from ruined fresco of the Triumph of Death. — *Santa Croce.*

Fig. 29.   Andrea Orcagna.   Upper part of Fresco of Last Judgment.
— *Strozzi Chapel, Santa Maria Novella.*

exists in the famous frescoes of the Pisan Campo Santo which, while traditionally ascribed to Orcagna, are unquestionably by Francesco Traini. They will occupy us later. Orcagna's solitary position in Florence reminds us that artistic succession is rarely from master to pupil, but from great soul to great soul across intervening mediocrity.

Giorgio Vasari regarded Gherardo Starnina (active before 1400) as an important link between Giotto and the Renaissance, and if Professor Suida is right in ascribing the frescoes of the legend of St. Nicholas in the Castellani Chapel, Santa Croce, to Starnina, Vasari was quite right. About this mysterious pupil of Antonio Veneziano who worked in Spain, we really know almost nothing. But the St. Nicholas frescoes have a grimness and gravity which points back to Giotto and withal a careful fusion of light and shade which anticipates Masolino and Masaccio. Meanwhile Giotto's own great compositions in still undiminished splendor and impressiveness stood ready to give lessons to the eye and mind that could read them aright. Before such later panoramists as Niccolò di Pietro Gerini, Mariotto di Nardo, and Spinello Aretino were gone, that eye was already busy, in the person of a rugged little boy of San Giovanni in Valdarno. He may have already been called Masaccio for his untidiness. He was to rebuild on Giotto and create the grand style of the Renaissance.

A mere catalogue of those painters who pursued the panoramic method with ability can hardly be expected. One and all they followed the Sienese narrative style. Prominent would be certain incomers from other cities, Giovanni da Milano, Antonio Veneziano, and Spinello Aretino. These are typical decorators of the last quarter of the 14th century.

We do better to fix our attention upon the most remarkable example of the Florentine panoramic style, the decoration of the Spanish Chapel, the chapter house attached to the Dominican Church of Santa Maria Novella.[14]   The work was begun by Andrea Bonaiuti in the year 1365, as we know from a recently discovered document. As decoration it is delightful, if rather superficially so. The artist treats his

FIG. 31. Andrea Bonaiuti, The Navicella, fresco, closely imitated from Giotto's Mosaic at St. Peter's, Rome. — *Spanish Chapel.*

spaces as wholes, declining to cut them up into oblongs after the earlier fashion. He covers his great surfaces with ease and taste, has a knack at illustration, and a fine sense of color. The great Calvary over the triumphal arch imposes from its very vastness; the triangles of the cross vault, including a spirited

transcript of Giotto's Navicella, Figure 31, are composed with
clarity and skill; the famous composition of the Dominican theo-
logian, St. Thomas Aquinas, enthroned above the Liberal
Arts and Sciences, and their representatives in history, combines an almost Byzantine formality and grandeur with
prettiness and ingenuity in details. But the method is better
shown in the decoration opposite, which represents the dual
earthly powers, the Pope and the Emperor, enthroned equally,
and supported by the representatives of the spiritual orders
and secular estates, Figure 32.   The group which symbolizes the
right government of society, according to mediæval ideas, is set
before a church which quite faithfully shows what the Cathedral of Florence was then intended to be.   High up in the
arch is the goal of all earthly endeavor — Heaven with Christ
enthroned amid the angels; an altar with a lamb before Him,
symbolizing His sacrifice; His Mother kneeling as intercessor
for mankind. The Gate of Heaven with St. Peter in attendance, is naïvely set above the church on a sort of aerial raft.
Below is a novel realistic touch, the villa-studded sky line of
hills which encloses Florence. The real guide to St. Peter's
presence is always a Dominican monk, usually St. Dominic
himself is intended — the founder and militant evangelist of
the order, as St. Thomas Aquinas was its systematic theolo-
gian. In the lower range of the picture, St. Dominic confutes
the heretics, who tear their wicked books in despair. Above
he vainly beseeches careless gentlefolk at dalliance in an orange
grove; still higher, he leads the truly penitent to Heaven's gate.
At the foot the Domini Canes (a bad pun for Dominicans)
are vigilant. The moral of the fresco is, happy the world
which trusts its worldly and religious business to the Emperor
and the Pope, and its personal religious problems to the Dominicans. It is a kind of glorified poster for the order.

In its sprightliness, variety, complication and facile charm,
it is a fine example of the panoramic style. It lacks every

quality of seriousness whether as a composition or in the drawing of the figures.   But its fairy-tale profuseness and ease have made it ever since it was painted, one of the most popular decorations in Italy.   Its success shows the kind of taste with

Fig. 32.   Andrea Bonaiuti.   Dominican Allegory of Church and State. Fresco. — *Spanish Chapel*.

which the few disciplined artists of the fourteenth century had to contend.   Such obstacles have ever been the fate of the artist who cares enough for his art to practice it austerely.

Work of the facile and superficial character of the Spanish Chapel Florence produced in abundance for two generations after Giotto's death.   His faithful but dull disciple, Taddeo Gaddi, as we have seen, gloomily foresaw the downfall of the art of painting.   But as in a great personality the recreations and even dissipations seldom permanently eclipse the greater purpose, so Florence was big enough to indulge for a time her weaker side. Had Taddeo Gaddi been more intelligent, or even more hopeful, he would have seen that new masters must arise, and that there would soon be pictures in Florence at which Giotto come back to earth would gaze with that humility with which he had once viewed the marble gods of Rome, with that understanding sympathy which he had borne to all his fellow mortals.

ILLUSTRATIONS FOR CHAPTER I

ON THE DIGNITY AND WEALTH OF OLD FLORENCE

Giovanni Villani, *Historie*, XII, 4, regrets the passing of decorum with the advent of the French and the Duke of Athens in 1342, but wealth increased.

"Formerly the clothing and costumes [of the Florentines] was the most beautiful, noble and distinguished of any nation, in the manner of the togaed Romans." Evidently the look of things favored the art of a Giotto.

In book XI, ch. 91-93, Villani gives remarkable and quite modern statistics which I paraphrase and quote, in part from the Giunta edition, Venice, 1559. The time is about 1340.

"We found by diligence that in these times there were in Florence 25,000 men fit to bear arms, from 15 to 70 years old, among whom there were 1506 nobles . . . There were then in Florence 65 fully equipped knights, though before the middle class which now rules was organized, there were more than 250 knights . . . There was estimated to be 90,000 . . . men, women and children in the city. There is supposed to be generally in the city 1,500 foreigners, travellers, and soldiers not counting in the population the clergy, monks, and nuns . . . In the outlying districts are supposed to be 80,000 people. We have found from the rector who baptizes the children (since for every male who was baptized in San Giovanni — in order to have the count — was dropped a black bean, and for every female a white) that for every year in these times there were from 5,800 to 6,000, the males generally exceeding by 300 to 500 a year.

"We find that the boys and girls at [primary] school were from 8,000 to 10,000. The boys who study the abacus (calculation) and arabic numbers, in six schools, from 1,000 to 1,200. And those who are learning [Latin] grammar and logic, in four great schools, from 550 to 600.

"The churches, which were then in Florence and in the suburbs, counting the abbeys, and monastic churches, we find to be 110, of which 57, parish churches . . . 5 abbeys and two priories with 80 monks, 24 convents of nuns, with more than 500 women, 10 friaries with more than 700 friars, 30 hospitals with more than 1000 beds to lodge the poor and infirm, and from 250 to 300 chaplain priests.

"The shops of the cloth makers (*arte della lana*) were 200 and more, and they made from 70,000 to 80,000 bolts, at a value of more than 1,200,000 gold florins, although fully a third part staid in the city for the workers, without gain for the cloth handlers, and the workers are more than 30,000 persons. . .

"The warehouses of the art of the *Calimala*, for the French and transalpine cloth, were 20, which brought in per year more than 10,000 bolts of a value of 300,000 gold florins, all of which was sold in Florence. . .

Banks of money changers 80 . . . Shops of bootmakers . . . 300. The college of judges, from 80 to 100. And notaries from 600 up, doctors of physic and surgery 60, and druggists' shops 100. . . .

"The greater part of the well-to-do, rich, and noble citizens with their families, staid in the country for four months, and some, more, a year." . . .

"Other dignities and magnificences of our city of Florence I should not fail to bring to memory, for information of such as shall come after us. It was, within, well built with many beautiful palaces and houses, and in these times they were continually demolishing, thus bettering the building by making it more comfortable and rich, bringing in from outside the examples for every sort of betterment and beauty. Churches, cathedrals, friaries of every rule, monasteries, magnificent and rich. Furthermore, there was no citizen who did not have a country place, great or small, which was not richly built, indeed far greater buildings than in the city; and every citizen sinned by inordinate spending, whence they were thought crazy. But it was so magnificent a thing to see, that a foreigner, not used to coming in, believed, because of the rich structures for three miles about, that it was all one city after the manner of Rome, not to mention the rich palaces, towers, court yards, terraced gardens, still further from the city, which in any other country would have been called the rural districts. In short one would have thought that within six miles of the city were more rich and noble inhabitants, than, taking them together, two Florences could have produced. And let this suffice for telling of the facts of Florence."

GIOTTO'S VIEW OF FRANCISCAN POVERTY

Giotto's humanistic detachment from the Franciscan doctrine of
voluntary poverty is well illustrated in his poem which is quoted in part
from Dante Gabriel Rosetti's translation. The original is in G.
Milanesi's edition of Vasari, *Le Vite*, Vol. I, Florence 1878, pp. 426-8.

> "Many there are, praisers of Poverty;
>   The which as man's best state is register'd
>   When by free choice preferr'd,
>   With strict observance, having nothing here.
>   For this they find certain authority
>   Wrought of an over-nice interpreting.
>   Now as concerns such thing,
>   A hard extreme to me it doth appear,
>   Which to commend I fear,
>   For seldom are extremes without some vice,
>   Let every edifice,
>   Of work or word, secure foundation find;
>   Against the potent wind,
>   And all things perilous, so well prepared —
>   That it needs no correction afterward."

A CONTRACT WITH ORCAGNA FOR THE ALTAR-PIECE OF 1357

Tommaso di Rossello Strozzi left a rough note of the terms of the
contract for the altar-piece of his chapel. Doubtless the actual contract
was much fuller. The minute is published by Filippo Baldinucci, *Opere*,
Milano 1811, Vol IV. p. 397.

"Herewith is to be written [on my part] and Andrea called Orcagna
that I Tommaso di Rossello aforesaid have given to paint for the altar-
piece which is made for the altar of [the chapel] in Santa Maria Novella,
of a breadth of five braccia, 1 sol. [over 10 feet] there or thereabouts.
The aforesaid Andrea is to paint in fine and splendid colors; and gold,
silver and everything else are truly to be used in the entire panel and
pinnacles, that is [gold] leaf.   Only in the side columns may silver
be used. . .   And [with] as many figures as [directed] by me
Tommaso it shall be completed.   And the said panel to be entirely
painted by his own hand.

"[1] 354 in twenty months . . . .

"Should it come about that the aforesaid Andrea should not give it to us completed and painted."

"He should pay me for every additional week that he works at the painting as it shall seem right to the judgment of the here named arbitrators." . . .

"Should it come to more than the aforesaid price, we will take the judgment of Carlo, Paolo and Fra Jacopo."

Such is approximately the sense of this very difficult and quite grammarless annotation of Tommaso Strozzi. The arbitrators must have had occasion to act, for the panel is dated 1357, two years after the promised time.

FIG. 33. Ambrogio Lorenzetti. Madonna of San Francesco.

CHAPTER II

SIENA AND THE CONTINUING OF THE MEDIÆVAL STYLE

On the Romantic instability of Siena — Fidelity to Byzantine Ideals —
Guido, Coppo, the Master of the Altar-front of St. Peter — Duccio and
his great Majesty of the Madonna — His two-fold tendency: to
elaborated staged narrative; to sparse and exquisite decoration — Simone
Martini and the Idealistic chivalric style — The Brothers Lorenzetti
and the popular panoramic style — Second half of the Fourteenth
Century — The Fifteenth Century: Sassetta and Giovanni de Paolo —
Matteo, Benvenuto and Neroccio — The Renaissance and the downfall
of the School, Francesco di Giorgio, Sodoma.

As you enter Siena by the wide Camollia gate you will read
in Latin "Siena opens her Heart still wider to thee": — *Cor
magis tibi Sena pandit.* Thus Siena avows herself the city of
the heart. Where Florence studied and calculated, she mused
and dreamed; where Florence was solid, she was volatile.
For unrewarding idealisms she had a kind of genius. Long
after the other Italian communes had seen it was worst possible business to support the emperor, Siena was faithful to
that lost cause. Every few years she changed her form of
government, and seldom for the better. Merrymaking and
pageantry were universal in old Italy, but Siena alone had a
Spendthrift Club (*Brigata Spendereccia*) devoted to continual
pleasure, and a poet, Folgore da San Gemignano, to celebrate
its gaieties. Siena was ardent in inconstant fashion. Early
in the 14th century was found a nude marble Venus so beautiful
that it was set up in the great square and thronged with ad-

mirers. Then the war with Florence went badly, and at a few words from a pious fanatic, the citizenry smashed up the image and secretly buried the bits on Florentine soil to bring bad luck to the foe. Naturally no bad luck ensued to Florence, but Siena had enjoyed two delightful emotional crises. You will see why Siena never could produce a realistic art, any more than Ireland has produced one. Her eye was not on the object but on her own state of mind. Thus Florence will produce historians, scientists, and politicians, while Siena will produce saints and miracles.

Amid this romantic inconstancy, the continuing thread was the cult of the Blessed Virgin. No other city thought so delicately of her, and no other art has represented her so ideally. Had she not saved the city? In 1259 the Florentine Guelfs and their allies marched with overwhelming force to the very gates of Siena. Ruin was imminent and despair abroad, when by a common impulse the populace marched penitently to the Cathedral and before the rude picture of the Queen of Heaven solemnly committed the city into her hands. In ecstacy of renewed faith the inferior army of Siena fell upon the invaders at Montaperti and utterly routed them. In gratitude Siena remained the city of the Virgin. When in 1311 the painter Duccio replaced the rude effigy of the Madonna of Victory with one of the finest Madonnas known to art, Fig. 37, the whole city suspended business and escorted the picture from the studio to the Cathedral with hymns and litanies in honor of their divine patroness.

Nowhere else has painting paid such homage to the Virgin Mary. In other cities it was enough to represent her enthroned with a handful of angels or saints in attendance. The Sienese painters multiplied the celestial escort until it became a heavenly court over which the Mother of God presides in sweet majesty. Siena also grasped at the then not quite orthodox subject of the Assumption of the Virgin into Heaven. You see her slender form rising amid a glory of angels more than a hundred years before the theme was common elsewhere.

These brief hints will tell of the temper of Siena. You will not expect such a city to be like Florence, interested in facts and charmed by the human spectacle. She will be rather engrossed with the beauty of old legends and in rare forward-looking moments concerned with her own devout imaginings. She will not wish the saints to be like the people one knows, but like denizens of some divine, far-off fairyland. Her painting will not be humanistic but of an unworldly idealism.

FIG. 34. Guido of Siena. Madonna.—*Accademia, Florence.*

Such being the temper of Siena, her artists, unlike those of Florence, had no quarrel with the Byzantine style. Its splendid irreality only needed to be made flexible and gracious. Siena has really no new ideas to express, merely feelings more tender and exquisite. Her pictorial reforms are reverent and gradual, backward-looking, mediæval. Her art from 1300 to 1500, as lovely within its narrow limits as the closed garden of the Virgin, has the great interest of teaching us what capacities for growth lay in the mediæval tradition itself — what painting in Italy would have been had Siena exercised her temporary might after Montaperti and razed Florence five years before Giotto was born.

A little earlier than the year 1225, when Florence called in strangers to adorn the Baptistery with mosaics in the Greek style, Guido of Siena signed and dated 1221 the most famous of his madonnas. Unhappily the enthroned Virgin of the Palazzo Pubblico was repainted some fifty years later, a fact which has led many critics unnecessarily to doubt the date.[1] But from half a dozen other pictures by Guido

FIG. 35. Sienese about 1275. Altar-front of St. Peter. — *Siena.*

we may learn that he was a diligent and rather heavy-handed imitator of the current Greek formulas, Figure 34. At the battle of Montaperti the Sienese captured an excellent Florentine painter, Coppo di Marcovaldo, and in 1261 he painted the admirable madonna which is still in the church of the Servi. It shows a sensitive use of the Byzantine conventions. There is pensiveness and almost shyness in the face and posture of the Virgin, and loving intentness in that of the Child. Their relation is to each other and not as in earlier madonnas to the devout public. These intimate qualities have been ascribed, I think wrongly, to restoration. But they appear even more emphatically in the entirely unrestored Madonna, Figure 3, in the collection of Mr. Otto Kahn, which I think may be a Coppo[2], and is in any case of similar date and feeling.

The same process of sweetening the old style while accepting it, is shown in the famous altar-piece of St. Peter in the Academy at Siena, Figure 35. The gaunt figure of the Saint is completely traditional, the little stories of the Annunciation and Nativity at the side show a new vivacity and a new grace. Siena met the innovating painter more than half way, for the indignant citizens soon marred with their knives the crucifiers of the head of the Christian Church. The date of the panel will not be far from 1275, and already the painter of genius who was to create the sweet, new style was learning his trade.

FIG. 36. Duccio. Ruccellai Madonna.—*Santa Maria Novella, Florence.*

Of Duccio di Buoninsegna, the father of the Sienese school, and everything considered its greatest master, we have numerous records,[3] and by no means all to his credit. He must have had the artistic temperament in a degree then unusual. The court records show half a dozen fines against him, and he was not scrupulous about paying his debts. One forgets these foibles before those Madonnas which are a consummate expression of taste and those narratives which are a triumph of tact and ingenuity. Duccio's mind does not grasp the harsher and more heroic emotions, but within the realm of the tender and pathetic he is supreme. His elegance appears in his first important work, the famous Rucellai Madonna, Figure 36, in Santa Maria Novella at Florence, which tradition erroneously ascribes to Cimabue. It is presumably

the great panel which Duccio contracted to paint in 1285.[4]
He was probably young and unconsidered, for he took all
the risks, agreeing that the picture might be rejected at the
will of the patrons. The Society of Saint Mary the Virgin

Fig. 37.   Duccio.   Madonna in Majesty. — *Opera del Duomo, Siena.*

would have been foolish indeed to reject the most gracious
Madonna the world had then seen. Characteristic of Duccio
are the swaying curves of the contours and especially of the
draperies, the thin, delicately folded robes of the Child and
the attendant angels and the sensitively drawn bare feet.
Working in Florence and doubtless impressed by Cimabue,
Duccio has retained in this early work a certain austerity
which gives way in his later work to a more feminine sweetness. For that very reason the Rucellai Madonna is perhaps
the greatest Madonna of the century, since without loss of
the stately Byzantine qualities, she gains the new attributes
of grace. It was no wonder that when the name of Duccio
had faded out of the Florentine memory, Florence ascribed
this noble Madonna to the venerated founder of her native
school, Cimabue. Recent criticism has righted the unconscious wrong thus done to Siena.

To mature his style Duccio needed only to intensify the qualities of sweetness and grace which are evident already in the Rucellai Madonna. The stages of his growth are represented in minor works at Siena and in British and Roman collections. But his fame, for the layman, is associated with the magnificent altar-piece which he executed for the Cathedral of Siena, and only the special student need look beyond it. On the 9th of October, 1309, Duccio contracted with the trustees of the Cathedral to do a great altar-piece wholly with his own hands, at the rate of sixteen soldi a day and expenses. He promised to take no other work during the painting. It was finished in June of 1311 and carried in solemn procession from the bottega outside the Porta a Stalloreggi to the Cathedral. A chronicler describes the cortege "parading about the Campo, as is usual, all the bells pealing a glory in devotion for so noble a picture as this is . . . And all that day they kept praying with many alms which were given to poor folk, praying to God and His Mother, who is our advocate, that she defend us in her infinite mercy from every adversity and every ill, and save us from the hands of traitors and foes of Siena." Most characteristic of the febrile patriotism of Siena is this constant dread of the traitor.

About a year before this ceremony the trustees enlarged the scheme for the picture, making an additional contract for thirty-eight stories to be paid at the rate of two florins and a half each. These were put on the back of the altar-piece, covering very fully the life of Christ and that of the Virgin. Thus the front of the altar-piece represents the decorative and monumental ideals of Sienese painting while the back exemplifies its feeling for narrative. Everything that Sienese painting was to be is already in germ in this marvellous work.

In depicting the Virgin "in Majesty," Figure 37, Duccio has magnified the theme. Earlier pictures show only a handful of angels in attendance. Here we have a cloud of celestial witnesses, the four patrons of Siena kneeling in the foreground, at the sides charming alternation of grim, bearded evangelists, orientally soft girl martyrs, and youthful archangels. Seven years earlier Cimabue had conceived a similar great Majesty for the Church of Santa Chiara at Pisa.[5] Doubtless Duccio had seen it, and, though it is lost to us, we may assume, that the Sienese artist outdid his prototype both in sweetness and splendor.

In many ways Duccio's Majesty is highly traditional. It shows the Byzantine horror of voids, is a little crowded. But this defect would be less apparent if it were raised on its historiated base (*predella*) with its original pinnacles above. Everything derives from Byzantine exemplars, reverently improved in a realistic direction. Duccio has dared to paint the Christ as a laddie; and not as a little old man; he has shown the soft forms of His body through light draperies; he has kept the austerity of the Byzantine apostles but has attenuated their harshness; he has worked the insipid female masks of the older art into forms of a positive and dreamy grace. One feels the tender mood of the work in the Latin jingle at the foot of the throne, typical of dozens of similar dedications in Siena:

> Mater Sancta Dei
> Sis caussa Senis requei
> Sis Duccio vita
> Te quia pinxit ita

which I may rudely paraphrase:

> Holy Mother of God: grant Siena rest,
> Grant life to Duccio, — he did his best.

All the sensibility of the City of the Virgin is in these prattling rhymes with which they loved to hallow and offer great pictures.

If the front of this panel shows only moderate innovations,

the case is not so for the back. The two score stories from the Bible or early Christian legend, in the distribution of the figures follow faithfully the standard Italo-Byzantine compositions. Where Duccio steps in is in bettering the forms,

FIG. 38. Duccio. Entry into Jerusalem; Christ Washing the Apostles' Feet; Last Supper. From the back of the great Madonna. — *Opera del Duomo, Siena.*

giving grace to the draperies, and animation to the gestures — above all in providing contemporary architectural accessories, and coping with the problem of space. He also carries to their ultimate refinement certain decorative formulas which the Byzantine painters had glimpsed but not fully realized. Thus two quite opposed tendencies pass into Sienese painting from Duccio; — a rather small preoccupation with accessories and the problem of space, and a pure æstheticism concerned with finesses of decorative arrangement — in short, the prose and the poetry of Sienese painting.

Sienese narrative painting tends to be scrupulous about details and inscenation, quite as a good story-teller naturally provides incidents that make for plausibility. We may see how Duccio's mind works in the familiar theme of Christ entering Jerusalem, Figure 38. Duccio sets the spectator in a garden with an open gate, thus throwing the scene back a little. Above the procession and the rejoicing throng rises a city wall, and still higher against the sky bristle Gothic towers and spires. Thus the theme gains picturesqueness and variety. One forgets that there is hardly space for the welcoming throng before the gate, and that the donkey's four feet are on a level although he is going up hill. These little maladjustments show that while Duccio took infinite pains in inventing the setting, he borrowed the figure groups bodily from earlier Byzantine compositions in which the setting was simpler. In this piecing-together process he turns some pretty sharp corners, but he never sacrifices clarity and expressiveness.

In the scene where the maid servant catches the Galilean burr in Peter's voice, Figure 39, and asks if he be not a follower of Jesus, we find Duccio's method quite at its best. Nothing could be better than the sudden turn of the girl with one foot on the steps. Fine, too, is the concentration of the crowd on the exciting problem of gossip. Well-observed, their actions as they warm their feet and hands at the fire. Vivid, too, the impulsive gesture of Peter as he denies the charge. The place, a court yard with a staircase leading right into the picture above, which represents the court room where Jesus is being questioned, is most elaborately planned. One looks back through a portal into farther spaces. All this was so new and interesting that I presume the Sienese have never noticed to this day that the seated group would never fit in the space assigned to it and that the positions of the figures are ambiguous. The picture does admirably its work of telling a story spiritedly, and that is enough.

Duccio's Calvary, Figure 41, is remarkable for breadth, spectacular effectiveness, and a measured pathos. As usual

FIG. 40. Duccio. The Marys at the Tomb. — *Opera del Duomo*.

FIG. 39. Duccio. Peter denies Christ.— *Opera del Duomo, Siena*.

he multiplies actors and incidents while keeping the orderliness of the arrangement. The slightness of all the forms, their little weight and uncertain balance are apparent. And there is, on the same principle of taste, a similar attenuation of emotion. Where Giotto at Padua gave stark tragedy, Duccio offers a gentle flutter of restrained grief.

Such is the average of these narratives, clear, picturesque, circumstantial, infused with a generalized and never very intense emotion. There are some, mostly composed with few figures, which reveal a great fastidiousness of arrangement. In such a composition as the Marys at the Tomb, Figure 40, Duccio reveals himself as pure æsthete, as consummate master of linear composition. The motive is essentially insignificant, merely that the Marys shrunk at the sight of the angel at the tomb, but out of that motive of withdrawal is wrought through the little panel a lovely rhythm to which everything contributes — the rise of the cliffs and their crinkly edges, the contrasting angles of the tomb and its impossibly tilted lid, the reciprocal curve of the angel. We grasp in the picture a general truth which reaches far beyond Duccio and Siena,

FIG. 41. Duccio. Calvary. — *Opera del Duomo.*

that a too conscious struggle for style precludes any complete expression of emotional significance. For this picture is as trivial as a narrative as it is exquisite as a decoration.

Duccio, who disappears from our sight about the year 1318,

fixed once for all the character of the Sienese school. In narrative it was to adopt the placid and tender tone of legend, most unlike the urgent and dramatic mood of Giotto. The Sienese artist was too reverent to raise the question how did

Fig. 42. Simone Martini. Madonna in Majesty. Fresco. — *Palazzo Pubblico, Siena.*

this happen, and how did the persons feel; he asked rather "How do we feel about it as believers?" The beauty of the work, then, is not that of outer reality but of revery and meditation. It never has the tang and variety of good Florentine narrative painting, but within its lovingly modulated monotony, Sienese narrative painting is supremely charming.

Duccio also started in Siena a somewhat worried and petty concern with accessories, architecture, complications of perspective. He inaugurated a tradition of material splendor in gilding, tooling, delicate graduation of color which remained the glory of Sienese painting for nearly two centuries. So far as we know he painted only in tempera on panel, and the Sienese generally were to triumph in this feminine form of work rather than in the masculine methods of fresco. Finally Duccio took over from Byzantine art and perfected certain finesses of highly simplified and abstract composition, a pure æstheticism distinctly Sienese and wholly alien to the warm humanism of Florence. You will find this austerely lovely style at its best in Simone Martini, and surviving as late as Sassetta and the middle of the fifteenth century.

After Duccio, Sienese painting divides itself into two tendencies, one aristocratic, chivalric and æsthetic, deriving from his decorative manner; the other popular, narrative and realistic, deriving from his minutely staged scenes on the back of the great altar-piece. Of the aristocratic style Simone Martini is the greatest exemplar, of the popular style, the brothers Lorenzetti.

Simone Martini was born in 1283 or thereabouts. We first meet him as an artist in the great frescoed Majesty of the Virgin, Figure 42, completed in 1315 for the Palazzo Pubblico, Siena. The arrangement is like that of Duccio's Majesty, finished only five years earlier, and the facial types are generally those of Duccio. But the great fresco gains clarity and impressiveness from the added space, from the picturesque motive of a canopy, from the isolation and elevation of the Madonna above her escort, and from the rich Gothic forms of the throne, which are a novelty in painting. While most of the faces show the orientalism of Duccio, the Madonna has the level-browed, intent character of Gothic art, and the Child is realistic. Gothic again is the graceful border with its fine medallions, and the bright colors of the whole. It is the most splendid enthroned Virgin in the world, and she is conceived chivalrically as a sort of tournament queen with her paladins upholding a canopy, and angel pages on their knees offering roses and lilies.

To the Sienese this was a political picture, as a rhymed inscription in Italian shows. The saintly patrons of Siena address the Virgin:

"Angelic flowers, roses and lilies
With which the heavenly meadow is adorned,
Delight me less than do good counsels.
But sometimes I see such as verily
Despise me and my city betray,
And gain praise the more for evil words,
With such as merit condemnation."

The Virgin answers the saints patrons somewhat evasively:

"Fix my delights in your minds,
So that I shall, as ye wish,
Fulfil your honorable requests.
But if the powerful molest the weak,
Oppressing whether with shame or harm —
Let not your prayers be made for these
Nor for whomsoever betrays my city.".

In Simone's work this great Majesty is an exception. He preferred generally to work on a more restricted scale, to burn the lamp of æsthetic sacrifice. I can merely allude to the great idealized portrait of St. Louis of Toulouse, in S. Lorenzo, Naples. It was painted for King Robert of Anjou, whose kneeling figure appears in the picture, sometime after 1317. The thing is resplendent in gold and azure, adorned by curiously twisted Gothic borders; in sentiment it is impassive as a Buddhist painting.

FIG. 43. Simone Martini. St. Martin Knighted. — *Lower Church, Assisi.*

About the year 1325,[6] we may surmise, Simone was called to Assisi to fresco the Chapel of St. Martin in the Lower Church. He set upon the walls so many fairy tales, tender and sprightly in sentiment, provided with the few essential

FIG. 44. Simone Martini and Lippo Memmi. The Annunciation. — *Uffizi*.

accessories that a rapid story-teller would need. What more charming than the boy Martin praying while they bind on him the equipment of a knight, Figure 43, and musicians sound a fanfare! What more gallant than the lad setting out on crusade against the Teutons who lurk in a cleft of the background! This gracious childlike quality, quite akin to the tender phase of Duccio, is exceptional in Simone, who habitually is the strenuous decorator.

His sparse and austere methods appear clearly in the commemorative fresco of Guidoriccio, hired general of Siena, and conqueror of Sassoforte. It is in the Palazzo Pubblico and duly dated 1328. Nothing is realistic but the horse and rider. They are isolated, hold alone a field made up of pure symbols for camps, and fortresses and craggy hill-tops, yet the martial effect is unmistakable and the composition most quaintly impressive.

The quintessence of Simone's later art is in the famous Annunciation of the Uffizi, Figure 44. In order to justify the most nervously exquisite of linear arrangements he has chosen the least significant moment of the event. His Virgin is merely a sullen princess resenting an intrusion; the Gabriel, an etherialized courtier pleading a cause with apologies. But the contrast of the advancing and shrinking motives gave Simone precisely what he wanted. He builds up areas richly colored or brocaded, bounded by sharp curves, relieved by flutters and spirals of flying drapery, and accentuated by such details as the olive twigs and the lily which have the crisp incisiveness of finest metal work. As a triumph of pure decoration Gothic painting has nothing better to show than this lovely panel which was finished in 1333 for the chapel of Sant' Ansano at Siena. It has little quality of heart in it, and no reverence save that of consummate workmanship.

Great honors awaited Simone. He was called to the exiled papal court at Avignon in 1339, met Petrarch, painted Petrarch's Laura and is lauded in one of the poet's sonnets. Of Simone's work at Avignon we have only a few small panels scattered between Antwerp, Paris, Liverpool, and Berlin. The compositions, most of which belonged to a composite altar-piece depicting Christ's passion, waver between his old simple style and a crowded and animated mood reminiscent of Duccio, and influenced by the Lorenzetti. Simone is unable to resist the universal tendency towards diffuse narrative, and in so far as he yields to it, he is less than himself. Christ Bearing His Cross, in the Louvre, exemplifies the extravagance and morbidness of this latest manner, Figure 45. His strength lies in sacrifice and abstraction, his real affinities are the contemporary Buddhist painters of China and Japan, though of course he knew nothing of them. He died in 1344,

leaving behind him a tradition of fastidious artistry which was potent in Siena for over a century.

As late as 1450, Lorenzo Ghiberti informs us in his "Commentaries,"[7] the Sienese regarded Simone Martini as their greatest painter. He differed from them, preferring, himself, Ambrogio Lorenzetti. This was an eminently Florentine choice, Ambrogio's warmth, concreteness, and elaboration were on the whole Florentine. He worked for several years at Florence, must have known Giotto, certainly studied him with discerning admiration. With his elder

FIG. 45. Simone Martini. Christ bearing His Cross. — *Louvre.*

brother, Pietro, Ambrogio Lorenzetti gave to Duccio's tradition of detailed narrative painting its perfected form. They were great fresco painters, and most characteristic as such. In panel painting they are less original, but they bring into this highly conventional art a great ardor and curiosity. They represent the popular average of Siena as Simone Martini represented its aristocratic minority.

We first meet Pietro Lorenzetti as an artist in the altarback at the Pieve, Arezzo,[8] Figure 46, which was finished in 1320. It is an *ancona*, or compartmented piece and the most splendid that has come down in Romanesque form. The figures are of two sorts. The Madonna is of intent Gothic type, and the fine motive of holding off the Christchild at elbow length in order to see him better is borrowed from Giovanni Pisano, who in turn took it from French Gothic sculpture.

Fig. 46. Pietro Lorenzetti. Madonna with Saints, 1320. — *Pieve, Arezzo.*

So are the forms above in the Annunciation new and graceful, while the little boxed room with its plastic column is also novel. The Assumption of the Madonna in the highest pinnacle is probably the earliest occurrence of this famous Sienese theme in painting. But all the figures of saints in the three orders of the side panels are taken almost without change from Duccio's great altar-piece. It would be interesting to trace Pietro's emancipation through a dozen panels. No one better combined dignity with grace, and feeling, and splendor.

His work in fresco is fragmentary and confused with that of his younger brother. We are certain of nothing except a fragment of a deeply felt Calvary in the Church of St. Francesco, at Siena. Many critics ascribe to him the agitated and wildly

Fig. 47. Pietro Lorenzetti, or Follower. St. Francis receiving the Stigmata. Fresco. — *Lower Church, Assisi.*

picturesque frescoes of the Passion in the left transept of the Lower Church at Assisi.[9] But this, I think, is a mistake. Pietro is never in his certain works so lively and indecorous and casual. We have to do with an artist influenced by Duccio working about 1330, Pietro himself may appear as the Stigmatization, Figure 47, and one or two of the other simpler compositions. The other frescoes are chiefly interesting as showing the dangers of the panoramic method of Siena. Take the Last Supper, Figure 48. The theme is simply lost in the fantastic richness of the accessories. It is hard to find Christ or Judas, for the eye seeks the radiating rafters or the scullery where cats lurk and eager scullions wipe the dishes.

In the Birth of the Virgin, dated 1342, Figure 49, Pietro spoils a carefully studied and well-felt picture by elaboration

Fig. 48.   School of Pietro Lorenzetti.   The Last Supper.   Fresco. — *Lower Church, Assisi.*

of the setting.   The frame is conceived as the plastic front of a Gothic room within and behind which, spaces are multiplied confusingly.   Here the pedantic preoccupation with the problem of space offends the eye and destroys the unity of what in a simpler setting would be a monumental composition. It illustrates the dangers of that smaller realism which from Duccio down afflicted the more progressive painters of Siena. Such a picture enables us to appreciate the tact and thoughtfulness with which Ambrogio Lorenzetti approached his narrative themes.

Ambrogio Lorenzetti was born about the beginning of the century.   In 1331 and later he painted remarkable frescoes

for the Church of St. Francis. These if complete would afford
the most interesting comparisons with Giotto at Florence, but
the two that remain are among the best narrative paintings

Fig. 49.   Pietro Lorenzetti.   Birth of the Virgin. — *Opera del Duomo,
Siena.*

of the time. What will first strike the observer in the story
of St. Louis of Toulouse renouncing his throne as he takes the
Franciscan vow, Figure 50, is the variety and orderliness
of the emotions. The devotion of the saint is well offset by
the intense, melancholy curiosity of his brother Robert, who
becomes king through the sacrifice. The audience is divided
into admiring Franciscans and idly marveling courtiers, the

whole well dominated by the kindly and reverend figure of
the Pope.   Remarkable is the methodical division of the
spaces.   A slender column establishes the picture plane and
sets the figures back.   A sort of desk in a hollow square de-

Fig. 50.   Ambrogio Lorenzetti.   Prince Louis of Toulouse receives the
Franciscan Vow. — *San Francesco, Siena.*

fines and isolates the monastic group, while the courtiers
have their appropriate location in a third plane of alcoves.
Florence has next to nothing of this sort at this period, and
it may be noted that this careful division of spaces is not matter of display and curiosity as in Duccio, but is logical and
effective as regards the persons of the narrative.

Of similar significance, but more dramatic and picturesque,
is the martyrdom of the Franciscan missionaries before the
Sultan of Morocco. The elaborated spaces make for clarity,
the entirely professional and impersonal cruelty of the Moorish
tyrant and his bodyguard is splendidly caught and effectively

contrasted with the courageous submission of the martyrs. Lorenzo Ghiberti praises the energy and character of this work, and the observer of today feels as deeply its romantic appeal. All the figures are set on receding platforms, the

FIG. 51. Ambrogio Lorenzetti. Madonna in Majesty. — *Massa Marittima.*

problem of space is solved along lines of intelligent literalism.[10]

It would be a pleasure to dwell on the Madonnas of Ambrogio. The tragic Madonna of S. Francesco, Figure 33, the Madonna with St. Dorothy and St. Lucy, in the Siena Academy, the Virgin in Mr. Dan Fellowes Platt's collection are among the best. No other early Italian so combined nobility with motherly warmth. His splendor and sweet dignity may best be felt in the Majesty of the Virgin, Figure 51, in the little town of Massa Marittima. The central motive, Mary and the Child embracing, is almost Ambrogio's invention. He rings the changes on it in lovely modulations, while always retaining monumentality. This picture is as stately as Duccio's Majesty, and as resplendent as Simone Martini's, while having qualities of ardor and fancifulness all its own. The fairy-like Virtues on the steps of the Madonna's throne especially show the rich vein of pure fantasy which accompanied Ambrogio's robustness. The picture may be dated about 1336 or later.

Previous to its painting Ambrogio had passed some years at Florence, where he must have studied and known Giotto, and where he himself influenced powerfully the beginnings of the new panoramic style. Whatever frescoes he himself did there have perished, and the only memorials of his visit are certain delightful little panels telling with vivacity and utmost circumstantiality the legends of St. Nicholas. At Florence he must have analyzed Giotto's great political frescoes, now lost, which depicted in symbols good and bad government. These were surely the inspiration for the political symbols and illustrations which Ambrogio, in the year 1337 and later, painted in the great hall of the Palazzo Pubblico at Siena.

The most famous is the Allegory of the State. The Commune sits enthroned, above in the air are the theological virtues — Faith, Hope and Charity; seated at the side are the four secular virtues — Prudence, Temperance, Justice, and Fortitude — and with them two additional personifications useful to a state — Magnanimity and Peace. The graceful relaxed figure of Peace, Figure 52, with her filmy drapery is famous. Below the platform on which the Commune sits with attendant virtues, are the grim, disciplined forms of men-at-arms and a throng of magistrates and citizenry. At the left are symbolized Concord and Justice as the supporters of a well-ruled state. Here the symbolism is childishly obvious. Concord holds her smoothing plane. From her hand go strings which bind in fellowship a group of citizens below and lead above to the figure of Justice. Still higher is Wisdom. Justice deals punishment with one hand and grants aid with the other; the Middle Ages never admitted that Justice was merely punitive. The figures of Justice and Concord are superb,— Ambrogio's Madonna type on a heroic scale.

As a pictorial representation of the finest mediæval ideas of statecraft, this fresco is of incomparable interest. As a decoration it is hardly successful. The theme has hampered the artist, the handling of the figures in several scales with the largest above, produces confusion and topheaviness. Beautiful in the parts, it is disappointing in the whole.

Far better merely as decoration is the companion fresco which represents the Effects of Good Government, Figure 53. We have a peaceful city, the entrancing spectacle of Siena as she was about the year 1339. Girls are dancing a carol in the foreground with the quaintest dignity, mounted merchants are passing, and if the picture were better preserved, we should see the mechanics — or "artists" as they still call themselves in Italy — working cheerily in their shops. In its richness without confusion, this is the very triumph of the panoramic realism which Ambrogio made popular throughout Italy.

There are many more frescoes in this series, mostly by imitators of Ambrogio. The Sienese region is full of works by him or by his faithful followers. His panel pictures are in many galleries of Europe and America. They all confirm the record of Ghiberti that Ambrogio had the habits of a nobleman — a great sympathy, a fine scrupulousness, a real magnanimity. Certain contemporaries seem greater, Giotto surely, Simone Martini perhaps, but no Italian painter until Raphael himself reveals so complete and harmonious a development. We find no trace of the brothers Lorenzetti after 1348. Presumably they perished in the great plague of that year.

For a century after the plague year, 1348, the painters of Siena imitated either the narrative realism of Ambrogio or the decorative sparseness of Simone Martini. It is customary to align them as of one camp or the other. We may indeed

Fig. 52. Ambrogio Lorenzetti. Peace, from the Fresco of Good Government. — *Palazzo Pubblico, Siena.*

Fig. 54. Luca Tommé. The Assumption of the Virgin. — *Jarves Coll., New Haven, Conn.*

Fig. 53. Ambrogio Lorenzetti. Results of Good Government — The Peaceful City. Fresco. — *Palazzo Pubblico, Siena.*

say that such painters as Lippo Memmi, Andrea Vanni, and Naddo Ceccarelli faithfully echo Simone, while such a master as the influential Bartolo di Fredi, who is traceable as late as 1388, seems completely Lorenzettian. But most of the painters follow freely both tendencies, employing Simone's formulas in altar-pieces with few figures, and Ambrogio's in narrative. Such eclecticism produced abundantly works of charm, for delicate sentiment and ornate workmanship, but rather few works of originality. Perhaps because of willingly accepted limitations, the average is higher than that of Florence. Throughout Italy it was a more popular style than the Florentine. It dominated the coast region from Naples to Valencia, penetrated into Umbria and the Adriatic marshes, and even got a temporary foothold in Florence itself. It fitted in better with mediæval ideals than the art of Giotto and Orcagna, which implied classical antiquity and anticipated the humanism of the Renaissance. On the whole Sienese art runs down after the Lorenzetti died, losing the robustness which Ambrogio had learned of Giotto, but its decline is gentle and interrupted by beneficent reactions towards its established glories. We may pass rapidly, and chiefly considering types, the fifty-odd years between the Lorenzetti and the new century.

Luca Tommé is credited with an exquisite little Assumption, Figure 54, in the Jarves Collection at Yale University. The picture, though it may be as late as 1370, repeats loyally the formulas which Pietro Lorenzetti invented nearly fifty years earlier. Perhaps Bartolo di Fredi, a rather superficial and overfecund artist, best represents the average condition as the fourteenth century closed. In such a panel as the Adoration of the Magi, in the Siena Academy, Figure 55, we see the familiar theme for the first time expanded in a Lorenzettian sense. It becomes a pageant, probably under the influence of contemporary mystery plays. It is best conceived in the little scenes in the background; the facial types and the simplified

setting on the whole recall Simone Martini. In other narrative pictures Bartolo vies with Ambrogio Lorenzetti in complication of planes and architecture. On the whole he is a
rather faint echo, but his note while thin is also true.

The declining century produced only one robust painter in
Siena, the mysterious Barna whose damaged frescoes of the

Fig. 56. Barna. The Transfiguration. — *Collegiata, S. Gemignano.*

Fig. 55. Bartolo di Fredi. Adoration of the Magi. — *Siena.*

Passion we see in the Collegiate Church of San Gemignano.
The forms are those of Simone Martini, the compositions even
more sparse than his, denuded of all accessories, and powerfully impressive for this reason. The mood is brusque and
tragic, with nothing of Sienese sweetness. Barna seems a kind
of provincial Giotto misplaced and unrealized in the Sienese
country. In the fresco of the Transfiguration, Figure 56,
he rises to sublimity. Fra Angelico will merely repeat him
in San Marco sixty years later. Vasari tells us that Barna
died from a fall from his painting scaffold in 1381, and that
he was then young. If so, his originality was tremendous, for
he cleared away ruthlessly all the delightful but trivial stage
furniture so diligently collected by Duccio and the Lorenzetti.
Modern criticism ascribes to him several panels, and I venture

to add to the list the simple and stately Marriage of St. Catherine in the Boston Museum of Art. Certainly it is one of the most serious creations of the period. The type of the Christ and the concise and characterful arrangement seem to mark

FIG. 57. The Three Living and Three Dead, detail from The Triumph of Death by Francesco Traini. — *Campo Santo, Pisa.*

it as a fine Barna. The base is interesting, representing the composing of a blood feud, and Miracles of St. Michael and St. Margaret. While the simple pattern continues the tradition of Simone, Barna avoids Simone's linear grace-notes. The finical element of the predecessor yields to a kind of realism. Barna is really the critic of the Sienese school. He silently insists that one may be decorative without too much artifice, and dramatic without overtaxing the stage carpenter, A very solitary and elevated spirit, to whom full justice has not yet been done.

Most remarkable among the works inspired by the Lorenzetti is the coarsely effective Triumph of Death, Figure 57. by Francesco Traini in the Campo Santo, at Pisa. It represents the hazards of the mortal life in view of certain death and judgment. At the left a royal hunting party is

stopped short by the sight and stench of three festering bodies
in coffins. The Hermit, Saint Macarius, points the obvious
lesson that kings and lords and fair ladies will turn to dust.
In the centre, miserable folk beckon and cry to Death to
descend and put them out of their distress. The harridan
death ignores the prayer and flies over a pile of corpses towards
a gay garden party. Death loves to cut down the young and
gay and happy, leaving the old and crippled to prolonged
sorrow. In the upper left hand corner you have monks going
about their quiet pursuits. The whole adjoining fresco is
given up to the lives of such desert saints. At the upper right
are angels and fiends struggling for little nude forms that
represent human souls. This motive is a sort of overflow
from a picture of the Last Judgment. The grim moral of the
three pictures is that the worldly life is one of mortal peril,
which may best be avoided by renouncing the world and joining a monastic order. The work was completed about 1375,
is in the rougher following of the Lorenzetti, and has been
famous ever since it was painted on the cloister wall. Entirely Sienese in its conception, in its ruggedness it transcends
the usual softness of the school. It is the last significant
work of the 14th century.

Siena passed into the fifteenth century without greatly
changing her art. In the work of such traditional figures as
Taddeo Bartoli one may observe a certain coarsening of the
tradition. Mere splendor tends to replace the old delicacy,
narrative painting becomes ever more complicated and confused. The latter tendency is manifested in frescoes which
Domenico di Bartolo painted, between 1440 and 1443 for the
Hospital of the Scala, Figure 58. Their crowded picturesqueness grows legitimately out of the Lorenzettian tradition,
as does the elaboration of architectural accessories. But the
work also implies a certain knowledge of the current Florentine discoveries in linear perspective and in architecture. A

small ingenuity runs pretty wild in these decorations, valuable as they are in picturing the times.

About the time these frescoes were designed, a renovation of Sienese painting was being made along divergent lines by

FIG. 58. Domenico di Bartolo. Clothing the Naked, from fresco series, the Seven Acts of Mercy. — *Scala Hospital, Siena.*

Stefano di Giovanni, nicknamed Sassetta,[11] and by the eager eccentric, Giovanni di Paolo. In both cases we have a reactionary reform. Sassetta restudies devoutly Simone Martini and the Lorenzetti, infusing his own tender mysticism both into decoration and narrative. In a manner he combines the two great currents of Siena's past. We may best approach him through the triptych of the Birth of the Virgin in the Collegiate church at Asciano, Figure 59. It is his earliest work painted not much later than 1428 when, being thirty five years old, he joined the Painters' Guild. The picture is conceived in the strictest Lorenzettian fashion, the frame being treated as the front or extension of the painted architecture. Aside from this carefully constructed setting, with its successive spaces, the casual and familiar distribution of the figures suggests strongly Pietro Lorenzetti. But the rich accessories in Sassetta's hands are delicately selected, the humble gestures have an artless grace, the secondary figures such as the brocaded handmaid entering from the rear are

FIG. 59. Sassetta. The Birth of the Virgin. — *Asciano.*

FIG. 60. Sassetta. Marriage of St. Francis to Poverty. — *Chantilly, France.*

fascinating in their own right. An air of alert gentleness runs through the picture. It is shared by persons of all ages. Such episodes as the chatting of two old men before a respectfully listening urchin add nothing to the story but strongly reinforce the faery charm of the whole. Winsomeness has supplanted the monumental quality of the older school. Above in the side gables are the scenes of the passing of the Virgin's soul and her funeral procession, both conceived in the manner of the Lorenzetti. But the familiar forms are singularly animated by a new spirit of tenderness. By a paradox these little stories are really more like Duccio than any intervening work.

Sassetta painted seven years on his masterpiece, the now scattered *ancona* for the Franciscan Church at Borgo San

Sepolcro. The central panel was a St. Francis in ecstacy, now in Bernard Berenson's collection. On the back were eight of the legends of the "Fioretti." The panel was finished in 1444. Especially delightful is the panel at Chantilly which

FIG. 61. Sassetta. Temptation of St. Antony. — *Jarves Coll., New Haven, Conn.*

represents St. Francis's mystical betrothal with Poverty, Figure 60. This scene is before Monte Amiata, spaced off from the group by checkerboard fields. The maidens, Chastity and Obedience, sway lily-like beside their more resolute sister, Poverty, upon whose timidly offered hand the little saint firmly fixes a ring. Above, the celestial trio rises over the mountain line, Poverty turning a regretful face to her humble bridegroom. The simple pattern with its swaying lines derives from Simone Martini, but there is none of his petulant superiority in it, none of his nervousness. The realm is not the airless heights of a pure æstheticism but a very human dreamland. Again Duccio at his best is the closest analogy. Bernard Berenson in his admirable little book *A Painter of the Franciscan Legend* well describes the technical perfection of such work as this. It is conceived in "outlines which have in themselves an energy and vitality, that, whether they are representative or calligraphic, give off values of movement, and values of movement have the power to suggest the unembodied, life unclogged by matter, something in brief that comes close to the utmost limits of what visual art can do to evoke spirit."

Apart from these sublimated reveries of Sassetta which express themselves in utmost delicacy of line, hue, and touch, he had a refreshing, drastic, almost a humorous side, which may be exemplified in a Temptation of St. Antony, Figure 61, in the Jarves Collection at New Haven. Beside his coral-red hut in a desert bounded by a wood that seems the world's end, the Saint starts away from a demure and very plain little girl. He is perplexed, divining rather than seeing the tiny bats' wings which mark her as a demon. The horizon is so curved that one almost feels the old earth swinging unconcernedly beneath this dilemma. A picture full of grotesque and authentic imagination, most true to the hobgoblin tradition of the expiring Middle Ages.

Sassetta died in 1450, and his two long-lived pupils, Sano di Pietro (1406–1481) and Giovanni di Paolo, (1403–1482) kept something of his influence alive for still thirty years.

Sano needs few words. He took nothing from his master but certain formal patterns, fine gilding and blithe colors. He repeats himself tediously, there are over fifty of his panels in the Siena Academy alone, yet is so genuine and unpretending that one forgets his lack of delicacy and insight. A little Coronation of the Virgin, at New Haven, may sufficiently represent his decorative phase. It is a nosegay of fair colors on burnished gold. In narrative painting he is Lorenzettian without the *finesse* of his master. At least he helped prolong a lovely tradition beyond its natural term, and that

Fig. 62. Giovanni di Paolo. Young St. John Baptist goes to the Desert. — *Formerly Charles Butler Coll., London.*

is his chief merit. "A famous painter and a man wholly dedicated to God" — (*Pictor famosus et homo totus deditus Deo*) — we read in his death notice. Siena knew how to appreciate a traditionalist.

Giovanni di Paolo, on the contrary, suffered not from deficient originality but from its excess. He selects restlessly from the older pictures. You will find pure Duccian figures in his paintings of the fifties. He studies the sparse decorative perfections of Simone Martini and exaggerates their nervousness. He drives expression into caricature, seeks strength in distortion, was the post-impressionist of his day. His extravagance is unpleasing in his larger pieces, but is piquant enough in his numerous small panels. One of a pair in English private possession shows the Youthful St. John jauntily setting off for the desert, with a quite cubistic treatment, Figure 62, of

Fig. 63. Matteo di Giovanni. Saint Barbara with Saints. — *S. Domenico.*

the lines of the fields. The motive is still more ingeniously employed in one of a remarkable set of pictures belonging to Mr. Martin Ryerson of Chicago. Giovanni's predilection for distortion and grimace is shown in The Baptism of Christ, a pendant to the story of the youthful John, both being parts of one predella.

Giovanni died in 1482 at the advanced age of seventy-nine, having faithfully preserved the old Gothic tradition while making it a vehicle of his own resolute eccentricity.

The slight concession which Siena made to the Renaissance was inaugurated by Lorenzo Vecchietta, active from about

1440 to 1480. He was primarily a sculptor and his silver altar-back was deemed worthy, in 1506, to displace the great Majesty of Duccio from the high altar of the Cathedral.

FIG. 64. Matteo di Giovanni. Massacre of the Innocents. — *S. Agostino.*

Vecchietta chiefly shows the effect of his studies as architect and sculptor in a severe regard for anatomy, and in the Renaissance character of his architectural settings. He painted for the Cathedral of Pienza a majestic Assumption, his masterpiece. There are numerous frescoes by him at Siena; he is perhaps most agreeable in little stories elaborately set amid rich architecture, but he lacks the sprightliness of the true narrative tradition. "He was a melancholy and solitary per-

son," writes Vasari, "and always sunk in thought." He did
something to give to the Sienese painting of the end of the
century a new and complicating thoughtfulness.

Fig. 65. Benvenuto of Siena. Assumption of the Virgin. — *Metropolitan
Museum, New York.*

Far the most versatile painter at Siena in the second half
of the fifteenth century was Matteo di Giovanni.[12] He was not
a native, but born about 1430 at Borgo San Sepolcro in upper

Umbria. There he worked for a time with that stern realist Piero della Francesca. Thus Matteo brought to Siena better training than his fellows had, but he soon fell contentedly into the ways of the place. His madonnas and female saints

Fig. 66. Girolamo di Benvenuto. Love bound by Maidens. Birth Salver. — *Jarves Coll., New Haven, Conn.*

have a new touch. They are more girlish and fragile than their predecessors, more exquisite, more fashionable. The type is represented in dozens of panels of which Enthroned Saint Barbara, at Saint Domenico, dated 1477, Figure 63, is a fine example.

In such work Matteo continues the tradition of Sassetta along somewhat superficial lines of prettiness. He is far more original in the several versions of the Massacre of the Innocents, in which seeking a maximum of intensity he achieves only a very interesting sort of caricature. The picture at S. Agostino, Figure 64, dated 1482, is perhaps the best of the group. We are in the realm of the grisly fairy tale, at an ogre's sports. The crowding, tumult, ornate architecture are simply Matteo's attempts to refurbish the old Lorenzettian tradition. His real quality best appears in the outlines prepared for the figure decoration of the pavement of the Cathedral. In general his is an engaging but entirely undisciplined talent, oscillating after the fashion of the moment, alike in Florence and Siena, between mere prettiness and sheer restlessness. He died in 1495, Michelangelo's star being already in the ascendent over neighboring Florence.

A kind of petrification of the traditional charm of Siena is in the work of Benvenuto di Giovanni, scholar of Sassetta. He cultivates a resplendent impassivity, is severe without much background of knowledge. His stiffness is gracious enough, like that of an aristocrat who maintains amid difficulties the dignity of an older school. His sense of formal pattern and skill in modeling in a very blond key may be enjoyed in his versions of the favorite theme of the Assumption. One of the best of these, dated at the end of the century in the year 1498, is in the Metropolitan Museum, Figure 65. Benvenuto was born in 1436 and died about 1518. He might, had he chosen, have studied the whole realistic development from Fra Angelico to Leonardo da Vinci, but his painting keeps a chill virginal quality quite apart from life, its problems and allurements.

His son Girolamo continued the manner with less monumentality until his death in 1524. To his early activity belongs the delightful salver, Love Bound by Maidens, Figure 66, in the Jarves Collection at New Haven. It is merely the tray on which the gifts were presented to a young mother during the visits of congratulation. It was painted for some member of the famous Piccolomini family, presumably about the year 1500. The stern maidens who are plucking and binding the stripling Love, doubtless are personifications of Chastity, Temperance and the like. In the middle distance a knight rides off free to adventure since Love is safely bound. It is an odd theme for a gift to a young bride and mother, but the Italians never required consistency in their compliments. The daintiness of the treatment is typical for Renaissance painting at Siena, which never assumes a robust or realistic or humanistic accent.

There is a refinement which is the harbinger of death. It appears in Siena in the person of Neroccio di Landi. He sublimates the style of his great predecessors, Simone and Sassetta, adding freely the more delicate ornamentation of the Renaissance. There is a peculiar pallor in his coloring and tension in his modelling. It is an art of nerves and ecstasies, wholly etherial. An admirable Annunciation in the Jarves Collection at New Haven shows the rich setting, the odd blend of precision with a languor that marks Neroccio as true grandson of Simone Martini. There are many little panels of Madonnas with saints of amber translucency. They have the startling vividness and irreality of an hallucination. And there is a portrait of a girl in the Widener Collection, Figure 67, which is of a superlatively delicate prettiness. Neroccio was born in 1447 and died in 1500. With him passed the special fragrance of Sienese art.

Until 1475, Neroccio was in partnership with one whose ambition went far to destroy what Neroccio and Siena stood for. Francesco di Giorgio was born in 1439. With an ambition and resolution wholly un-Sienese, he mastered the arts of painting, sculpture, architecture and engineering. He met Leonardo da Vinci at Pavia, worked for the tyrants of Milan, competed for the façade of the Cathedral of St. Mary of the Flower at Florence. As architect and engineer it appears that he became a cosmopolitan, in painting it was hardly so. He is most delightful in his early phase which is represented by a bride chest in the Wheelwright collection, Boston. It represents Prince Paris insolently appraising the charms of the rival goddesses, and at the right riding Troywards in disregard of the despair of forsaken Œnone. The classical theme is tinged with mediævalism, naturalized as Sienese. Later pictures, such as The Nativity, Figure 68, in the Sienese gallery, show Francesco uneasy, twisting his figures for grace and display of knowledge, working over the old landscape formulas in a semi-realistic sense, adding classical architecture, generally trying to break the bounds of the old idealism. The result is restlessness or at

FIG. 67. Neroccio di Landi. Portrait of a Girl. — *Widener Coll., Elkins Park, Pa.*

best an ambiguous charm. Siena is beginning to regret her isolation, to make vain efforts to overtake the tide of humanistic realism, to envy Florence, and even Perugia and Cortona. From the point of view of the Renaissance she was two generations behind, and no longer indifferent to the fact.

Not merely Francesco di Giorgio tries to do in a decade the work of a century, but such younger contemporaries as Fungai and Pacchiarotti look to Florence or Umbria. Siena was given no time to reconstruct, and her old beautiful art could not readily assume new forms. Siena never assimilated the Renaissance. It invaded her, killed her native art and substituted one without local flavor. Before Francesco di Giorgio died, in 1502, he had seen Luca Signorelli called to Siena and the clever decorator Pintorricchio. Siena no longer trusted her own artists.   Francesco probably took little note of the advent in 1501, of a young Piedmontese painter, Antonio Bazzi,[13] nicknamed Sodoma, yet with Sodoma remained what little future there was in Sienese painting.

Fig. 69.   Sodoma.   Vision of St. Catherine of Siena. Fresco.— S. Domenico, Siena.

Sodoma brought to Siena the knowledge of Leonardo da Vinci, the new draughtsmanship in light and shade. He assimilated the sensibility of Siena but coarsened it. No painter of the time was more overtly sentimental. His famous St. Sebastian at Florence tells all that need be known about him, — his considerable skill, his exaggerated pathos, his clever use of poise and balance, his sober modern tonalities. His sentimental power is at its height in the fresco at S. Domenico, Siena, which represents S. Catherine swooning at the vision of her lover, the Christ, Figure 69.   Sodoma worked indefatigably in and about Siena till 1549.   The few local painters of a progressive sort, Domenico Beccafumi, Girolamo del Pacchia, either directly imitate Sodoma or draw from similar alien sources. The only man of genius Siena produced in these years, Baldassare Peruzzi (1481-1536), soon went to Rome where in architecture he held his own with all comers, whereas in painting he became a modest imitator of Raphael.

In the ten years after 1500 the old art perished. Siena from being the last radiant exemplar of the glory of the mediæval spirit sunk to the estate of a fourth class station of the

Renaissance. Her idealism could not bear the test of reality.
Her domain had been that of legend and fairy tale and dream,
she had ruled it exquisitely for two centuries until sheer taste
had absorbed her little strength. She had left unforgettable

FIG. 68.   Francesco di Giorgio.   Nativity.—*S. Domenico, Siena.*

records of her most precious feelings, but little record of her
outer activities. Think how portraits abound in Florentine
and Venetian art after 1450! There are practically none at
Siena. So it would be futile to go to Siena for a greater understanding of the active life. But if you would requicken the
sense of legend, live over again the tenderness mankind has
ever felt for the beautiful past, hear some faint blowing
of the horns of elfland — if you want this experience, then go
to The gracious City of the Virgin and you shall find fulfilled
the generous motto over her main portal — Siena will open
her heart wide to thee.

ILLUSTRATIONS FOR CHAPTER II

A SONNET TO THE SPENDTHRIFT CLUB

by

FOLGORE DA SAN GEMIGNANO

translated by

DANTE GABRIEL ROSSETTI

"I give you horses for your games in May,
    And all of them well trained unto the course —
    Each docile, swift, erect, a goodly horse:
With armor on their chests and bells at play
Between their brows, and pennons fair and gay;
    Fine nets and housings meet for warriors,
    Emblazoned with the shields ye claim for yours,
Gules, argent, or, all dizzy at noon day;

And spears shall split and fruit go flying up
In merry counterchange for wreaths that drop
    From balconies and casements far above;
And tender damsels with young men and youths
Shall kiss together on the cheeks and mouths
    And every day be glad with joyful love."

HOW VENUS FARED IN SIENA

Ghiberti, in his commentaries (ed. Frey, Berlin 1886, p. 57 ff.) tells how a marble Venus, bearing the name of Lysippus was dug up at Siena.

"I saw it only as drawn by a very great painter of the city of Siena, who was called Ambrogio Lorenzetti. This drawing was kept with greatest care by a very old Carthusian. This brother was a goldsmith, and his father, and was a designer and delighted greatly in the art of sculpture; and he began to tell me how that statue was discovered as they were making an excavation where now are the houses of the Mala-volti; how all those instructed and versed in the art of sculpture, with the goldsmiths and painters ran to see this so marvellous and artistic statue. Every one praised it greatly, and also the great painters who then were in Siena — to every one it seemed absolutely perfect. And with all honors they set it upon their fountain, as a most splendid thing. All gathered to place it with greatest rejoicing and honor and they fixed it magnificently upon that fountain, which statue reigned there but passingly."

"For as the city had many adversities in the war with the Florentines, and the flower of the citizenry were assembled in council, a citizen rose and spoke about the statue in this tenor: 'Gentlemen and citizens, having considered that since we have found this statue it has always gone wrong with us, and considering that idolatry is forbidden by our faith, we must believe of all the adversities which we have that God sends them for our errors. And behold in truth that since we have honored this statue we have always gone from bad to worse. I am certain that so long as we keep it in our territory it will always go wrong with us. As a councillor I would advise that it be taken down and shattered and split up and be sent to be buried on the soil of the Florentines.'

"Unanimously they confirmed the words of their citizen and put them in execution, and the statue was buried upon our soil."

A PROCESSION ON THE COMPLETION OF DUCCIO'S MAJESTY

"On the day that it was carried to the Duomo the shops were shut; and the Bishop bade a goodly and devout company of priests and friars should go in solemn procession, accompanied by the Nine Magistrates and all the officers of the Commune and all the people; all the most worthy followed close upon the picture, according to their degree, with lights burning in their hands; and then behind them came the women and children with great devotion. And they accompanied the said picture as far as the Duomo, making procession round the Campo as is the use, all the bells sounding joyously for devotion of so noble a picture as is this. And all that day they offered up prayers, with great alms to the poor, praying God and His Mother who is our advocate, that he may defend us in His infinite mercy from all adversity and all evil, and that He may keep us from the hands of traitors and enemies of Siena."

Translated in Edmund G. Gardiner's *The Story of Siena*, p. 178, from the Anonymous contemporary chronicler published by A. Lisini in *Notizie di Duccio*.

A Contract for an Altar-piece
by pietro lorenzetti

"Master Pietro, son of the late Lorenzetto, who was of Siena, solemnly and willingly promises and agrees with the venerable Father Guido, by God's grace Bishop of Arezzo, who stipulates in the name and stead of the people of St. Mary of Arezzo — to paint a panel of the Blessed Virgin Mary, . . . in the centre of which panel shall be a likeness of the Virgin Mary with her Son and with four side figures according to the wish of the aforesaid Lord Bishop, working in the backgrounds of these figures with finest gold leaf, 100 leaves to a florin, . . . and the other ornaments of silver and of best and choicest colors; and using in these five figures best ultramarine blue; and in the other adjoining and surrounding spaces (panels) of this picture to be painted likenesses of prophets and saints, according to the wish of this Lord Bishop, with good and choice colors."

"It must be six braccia long and five braccia high in the middle, apart from two columns each a half braccia wide, and in each should be six figures worked with the aforesaid gold, and the work shall be approved by this Lord Bishop. . . .

"And he [Pietro Lorenzetti] must begin this work according to the wish of this Lord Bishop, immediately after the wooden panel shall have been made, and must continue in this work until the completion of this picture, not undertaking any other work &c. And therefore the said Lord Bishop Guido promises to have given and assigned to him the panel made of wood; and to pay him for his wages for the picture and for colors, gold and silver one hundred and sixty Pisan lire; that is the third part at the beginning of the work, the third part at the middle of the work, and the remaining third part when the work is finished and complete &c."

"Done in the church of the Holy Angels in Arcalto outside of and next to the cemetery."

Translated and slightly abridged from
Borghesi and Banchi, *Nuovi Documenti per la Storia dell' Arte Senese,* (Doc. 6, p. 10) Siena, 1898.

This contract well illustrates the elaborateness and strictness of such agreements. It may be compared with the picture itself (Fig. 46). Apparently the artist persuaded the Bishop to give up the plan of twelve prophets and saints on two side pilasters, and made instead a greater number (15) of figures in the upper arcade and pinnacles.

MASACCIO AND THE NEW REALISM

FIG. 70. Andrea del Castagno. David, Slayer of Goliath. Parade Shield.
— *Widener Coll., Elkins Park, Pa.*

CHAPTER III

MASACCIO AND THE NEW REALISM

Ghiberti, Brunellesco, and Donatello about 1400 begin to study Nature and the Antique — The new secular spirit — Discontent with the old pictorial style expressed in reaction by Lorenzo Monaco — in cautious reform by Fra Angelico — and Masolino — in revolutionary reform by Masaccio — The Cassone painters as illustrators of contemporary manners — Masaccio and the new structure in light and shade — The Problem of the Brancacci Frescoes — Masaccio's enduring influence — The early Florentine Realists — Paolo Uccello and Perspective — Andrea del Castagno and Anatomy — Domenico Veneziano and Oil Painting — Alesso Baldovinetti.

In the two earlier chapters we have considered what Giorgio Vasari calls the vigorous childhood of Italian painting. We are now to observe its splendid youth. The story appropriately begins with three young men and the year 1401 and with a baby, later nicknamed Masaccio, who was born that same year. The three young Florentines represent the new time-spirit. The lucky one, Lorenzo Ghiberti, has just won a competition for the new bronze doors of the Baptistery, and has in that one commission more than twenty years of happy work ahead. Ghiberti is sensitive and thoughtful beyond the wont of the older craftsmen artists. He writes of an antique statue: "It has sweetness of modelling which cannot be caught either in a strong or a dim light, only the hand and touch can find it." Ghiberti is a critic and analyst as well as a creator. In his "Commentaries," a product of his old age, he writes: "Thus I have always sought for first principles, as to how nature works in herself, and how I may approach her, how the eye knows the varieties of things, how our visual power works, how visual images come about, and in what manner the theory of sculpture and painting should be framed." This is the mood of the Renaissance in its most serious aspect.

This student mood was fully shared by two young friends of Ghiberti. Donatello, the sculptor, and Brunellesco, later the designer of the dome of the Cathedral at Florence, had lost in the competition for the Baptistery doors. They accepted defeat magnanimously, joined forces and went to Rome, where their persistent way of poking among the ruins got them the name of the treasure seekers. Such indeed they were, but the treasure they sought was not gold, but the secrets of the ancient sculptors and architects. So Donatello refined and perfected the rugged realism he had from nature. As early as 1416 he was to carve the alert and noble St. George for Or San Michele. Brunellesco's life dream was that lightest and loveliest of domes which is still the architectural crown of Florence, and almost incidentally he threw off designs that filled Florence with elegant colonnades and churches which renewed the dignity and joyousness of the best Roman building. A resolute spirit, Brunellesco once tramped the sixty miles from Florence to Cortona to see a newly excavated statue. Not incidentally, then, but by hardest study, Brunellesco worked out a correct practice of linear perspective. This needed resource for the painter was now available when any one had the sense to ask for it, and all the time young Masaccio was growing up in San Giovanni up the Arno.

Such is the immediate background for the forward move in painting which begins in 1422, or thereabouts, and runs through fifty years of eager experimentation. As in the first revival the sculptors and architects had shown the way to the painters, so it was again. But there is also a remoter social and commercial background for the Early Renaissance which we must consider briefly. The great plague of 1348 cuts Florentine history sharply in two. It marked an acceleration of gayety and worldliness, of sports and pageantry

The chronicler Matteo Villani [1] noted with amazement that the plague had caused not repentance but dissipation. He was shocked to see the old toga-like costume of the Florentines give place to the bobtailed jerkins and parti-colored hose borrowed from wicked France. Heritages were many and heirs few. You saw the gowns of gentle and noble ladies on backs of hussies or worse — the new wives. People ran to " the sin of gluttony, to feasts and taverns, delicate viands and games." As for the poor folk, they no longer wished to work at their trades, they expected the costliest food, they married "*ad libitum*." So began that loosening up of the old bourgeois morals which culminated in the carnivals of the end of the fifteenth century and in the libertine muse of Lorenzo the Magnificent. All this meant an inspiring spectacle for the artist to record, and plenty of lavish patronage, but also it meant a disintegrating tendency for art. Painting is great in Florence in the measure that it escapes the mere expansiveness of the times and seeks discipline. As if to assert the permanency of the spirit of discipline, the very year that set Matteo Villani in despair, 1348, gave him also a chapter on the founding of the Studio, a school of higher learning which eventually became the University of Florence. And the course of art for most of the fifteenth century was to be a constant interplay and rivalry between the Florence of the tavern and race-course and the Florence of the Studio, with a final victory for the latter.

Oddly enough, the new luxury and gayety and the new scholarship conspired to make the old painting inadequate. The panoramic style of the fourteenth century was too simple and unornate for the Frenchified Florentines; for the new generation of strenuous artists, it was too slight and unskilful. All the finer spirits at the beginning of the fifteenth century are malcontents. Their unrest expressed itself, according to temperament, in progress or reaction. The dominating artist of the moment was a reactionary, Don Lorenzo Monaco,[2] Camaldolese monk. Turning from the superficiality of the current Florentine style, he sought his corrective at Siena, his birthplace, in the decorative exquisiteness of Simone Martini and the narrative warmth and breadth of the Lorenzetti; and he imports these qualities into Florence in an art as aristocratic and retrospective as that of our own Pre-Raphaelites. In his hands Gothic painting takes a new and unwarranted lease of life. He is a brilliant colorist, a fastidious designer, an austere spirit. Even his great Sienese exemplars have hardly surpassed his masterpiece, the Coronation of the Virgin, in the Uffizi. It is dated 1413. In the richness of the Gothic frame, the profusion of small incidental figures, the festooning curves of the swaying saints and angels, and formal symmetry of arrangement, it well represents the most florid type of Gothic painting as developed at Siena. It is hard to realize that this lovely mediæval work was painted at the moment when Brunellesco and his friends were already turning sharply to nature and to the vision of Hellas. But Lorenzo was a cloistered man, and appropriately a votary of past perfections. His devout mood is best expressed in the gracious Annunciation, Figure 71, which has happily never left its original altar in the Church of the Trinità. Here Lorenzo follows the Lorenzettian canons of space. A girlish delicacy in the obedient Virgin is a new note, to be echoed more sweetly by Lorenzo's best follower, Fra Angelico. Lorenzo died in 1425. Masaccio had already created the new style of painting, but for a couple of decades faithful disciples of Don Lorenzo carried on his style.

A lover of Plutarchian parallels and contrasts would swiftly pass from Don Lorenzo Monaco to Masaccio. But one may better understand the new movement by taking first men who gradually and normally accepted the new knowledge. Such are Fra Angelico and Masolino, who began as Gothic painters

FIG. 71. Lorenzo Monaco, Annunciation. — *Trinità*.

FIG. 72. Fra Angelico. Annunciation and Adoration of the Magi. — *Museum of S. Marco.*

FIG. 73. Fra Angelico. Coronation. of the Virgin. — *Louvre.*

and ended as Renaissance masters. They show us better the average drift of the times than does so revolutionary a figure as Masaccio.

Fra Angelico[3] was born in 1387 and at twenty entered the religious state as a Dominican at Fiesole. How soon Fra Giovanni, not yet nicknamed Angelico, became a painter we hardly know. But four little pictures designed to inclose in their frames relics of the saints may represent his beginnings. Three are at San Marco, Florence, one in Mrs. John L. Gardner's collection at Boston. The Little Annunciation with an Adoration of the Magi, Figure 72, may represent the work. It is refined, tender, of jewel-like freshness of color, graceful in linear arrangement, at first sight wholly Sienese in inspiration, and directly dependent on Lorenzo Monaco. A kind of veracity under the richness of the expression marks the work as after all straightforward and Florentine. The date may be about 1425, Fra Angelico, being in his middle thirties, and in his art about a century behind the times. In his early Gothic manner he conceived some of his masterpieces, such as the Coronation of the Virgin, with its glimpse of a celestial cloud land; and the whimsically beautiful Last Judgment. Both are at the Museum of San Marco. One can believe the report of Vasari that each day Fra Angelico prayed before touching brush to such masterpieces. Such pictures have the hush and charm of a celestial dreamland, a meditative beauty quite un-Florentine.

All the time Fra Angelico was placidly and intelligently studying the new realistic movement launched by Donatello and Masaccio. He adopts what suits him, rejecting heavy shadows which would dull his Gothic coloring, but adding freely realistic details in anatomy, drapery, and architecture. The Coronation of the Virgin in the Louvre, Figure 73, though it may be only a few months later than that of the Uffizi, no longer takes place in a cloudland before lucent gold, but in a quite practicable architecture imitating the niche which Michelozzo designed in 1423 for Donatello's St. Louis of Toulouse. The forms too are more substantial, more mun-

FIG. 74. Fra Angelico. Madonna dei Linaiuoli. Originally an outdoor tabernacle. — *Museum of S. Marco.*

dane. Soon the architectural accessories become of Renaissance type, and as Mr. Langton Douglas has shown, every new invention of Michelozzo for a space of ten years is promptly reflected in the painting of Fra Angelico. His greatest Madonna, that of the Linen Guild, Figure 74, painted in 1433, is almost plastic, recalling the severe sweetness of Orcagna. The picture is really cumbered by the rich hangings, which with the slender swaying angels in the bevel of the frame are already an anachronism. In the Descent from the Cross, Figure 75, we find Fra Angelico skilfully adopting the new discoveries in anatomy and landscape. The treatment is broad and panoramic in the tradition of the Lorenzetti but all the details are carefully studied from nature and not furnished by formula. A deeply-felt scene thus gains verisimilitude,

FIG. 75.   Fra Angelico.   Deposition. — S. Marco.

comes out of the realm of legend and becomes an actuality. The panel was finished in 1440, and, now that Masaccio was gone, there was no living painter who could have put into it with equal knowledge so much feeling.

The building of the great Dominican Convent of San Marco between 1437 and 1444 opened to Fra Angelico his great opportunity. It was the gift of Cosimo de' Medici, now unofficial ruler of Florence, who had his good reasons for wishing to assure the occasional repose of his busy soul in this world and its permanent repose in the next. He often sought seclusion in the convent and doubtless saw in progress the fifty or more frescoes that Fra Angelico made to adorn it. Fra Angelico was painting for deeply religious men, for scholars who had the Scriptures at their finger tips, and for this reason perhaps he rejects all smaller realisms, reducing his compositions to the mere figures. Thus the San Marco frescoes are more concise even than those of Giotto, and they reach at their best

Fig. 76. Fra Angelico. Dominicans receive Christ as Pilgrim. Guest house door.—*S. Marco.*

a simple sublimity as yet unattained in Italian art. Highly formal and decorative, they are free from consciously aesthetic taint. Sometimes I think Perugino learned much at San Marco and that we may thus regard Fra Angelico as indirectly a leading influence on Raphael. The sparse, effective method may be illustrated in the fresco set over the door of the guest quarters, the *Forestiera*. It represents a pilgrim Christ being received by Dominican brothers. Figure 76. In the stranger we entertain The Lord Himself is the simple lesson. The figures are set against a conventional blue background but are constructed with the authority of the new learning.

In the Chapter House nearby Fra Angelico painted, about

1440, a great Crucifixion, Figure 77. The three laden crosses stand out sharply against a murky sky. The setting is a mere platform, on which the familiar forms of Mary and the beloved Apostles are almost lost in a throng of witnesses of every age. We have the Latin Fathers, and their succes-

FIG. 77.   Fra Angelico.   Mystical Crucifixion.   Chapter House. — *S. Marco.*

sors — St. Dominic and St. Francis among others. The arrangement is highly formal, the mood that of meditation; the sharper tragedy of the theme is not insisted on. The characterization of the saints is precise and fine, the drawing of their forms admirable. Had the composition been set against a Gothic, blue background, the mood would have seemed merely sentimental. What gives it, with all its abstractness, an almost sensational tang of reality is the arching sky, slaty above and an ominous orange behind the figures. The expedient brings an element of definite place and time of day for this rendezvous of saints at a mystically renewed Calvary.

In the cells of the convent, Fra Angelico and his helpers painted no less than forty-three frescoes. These were intended for the private devotions of the brother occupying the cell, and the subjects were probably chosen not by Fra Angelico himself, but by his cloister mates. The best are conceived like the frescoes of the lower story. The background is just a veiled sky, there are no accessories, the figures loom in an indefinite space. Majestic is the Transfiguration, Figure 78, very lovely the Coronation of the Virgin. The angelic painter draws the maximum effect from the simplest patterns and briefest means. There is the measured and simple dignity of the early Christian mosaics with a warmer and more personal feeling. Fra Angelico, when he wishes, can be elaborately realistic. He is so in the garden scene where the Risen Christ gently rebuffs the Magdalen, in the crowded Adoration

FIG. 78. Fra Angelico. Transfiguration, fresco in a cell at S. Marco.

of the Magi, which tradition assigns to Cosimo de' Medici's cell, and in the Annunciation, Figure 79, in the corridor with its graceful Renaissance *loggia*. In this more circumstantial vein, Fra Angelico is delightful, but I think below his best. In all the frescoes at S. Marco, however, Fra Angelico appears as a wholly Florentine figure with an art based at once on the study of nature and on an understanding admiration for the masterpieces of Giotto and Orcagna.

Something of his mediaevalism, of his Sienese manner, persists in the numerous little predella panels, such as those telling delightfully the story of the doctor saints, Cosmo and Damian, and the series with the life of Christ which adorned the doors of the plate lockers of the Church of S. Marco. With their fully developed pictorialism, their careful regard for the minor realisms of setting, these little pictures are the

prelude to his last phase at Rome. They are also the last
Florentine pictures that observe those traditional iconographi-
cal forms which had persisted for four centuries.

Fra Angelico ever refused to make money or accept promo-

FIG. 79.   Fra Angelico.   Annunciation.   Fresco. — *S. Marco.*

tion, but became despite himself a celebrity. In 1445 he was
ordered to Rome by Pope Eugenius IV. The frescoes which
Fra Angelico then made in the Vatican are lost. There was
an escape to Orvieto, where Fra Angelico painted half the vault
of the Chapel of S. Brixio, which Signorelli was later to complete. Fra Angelico was peremptorily recalled to Rome in
1447 by the new Pope, Nicholas V, who was planning a new
chapel in the Vatican. We see it today still radiant with the
legends of St. Stephen and St. Lawrence that Fra Angelico
thoughtfully composed more than four hundred years ago.
Modern critics have generally agreed in finding Fra Angelico's
masterpieces in this chapel. If they mean his fullest display

of knowledge, the opinion is incontestible.   Nowhere else has
Fra Angelico invented such complications of architecture,
interiors, street perspectives;   nowhere has he drawn better
figures in greater variety.   Such frescoes as the lunette with

FIG. 80.   Fra Angelico.   St. Stephen Preaching, the Saint before the
Council.   Fresco. — *Chapel of Nicholas V., Vatican.*

St. Stephen defending himself before the Jewish doctors and
preaching to the people, Figure 80, or that depicting St.
Lawrence giving alms to cripples and poor folk before a basilica, are learned and rich.   But does not their very richness obscure both the decorative and emotional appeal?
Personally I tend to lose the figures in the complexity of the
setting.   Any of Fra Angelico's little predellas tells its story
more feelingly and clearly, and no less ably.   Under the
pressure of competition at Rome, Fra Angelico for the
first time is ostentatious.   To please the Pope he revives in
more specious form the trivialities of the old panoramic style.
Had he grasped Masaccio's invention of aerial perspective and
construction in light and dark, Fra Angelico might have

carried off his elaborate settings successfully. As it is, they confuse the eye by too many linear elements, and only mildly delight the mind. Even the sensitive mood of legend, which is noteworthy in these frescoes, is better represented in the smaller panels. In fairness of Gothic fresco coloring, however, they are unsurpassed.

FIG. 81. Masolino. Annunciation.
—*Henry Goldman, Esq. New York.*

From the point of view of tendency, these frescoes are profoundly instructive. They show the irresistible drift towards the formation of a new panoramic style, a drift that even Fra Angelico, cloistered saint and exquisite self-critic, was unable to escape. In spite of his record and better knowledge, he becomes an inaugurator of that picturesque, undisciplined, and decentralized manner of narrative which was to be represented by Ghirlandaio, Botticelli, and their contemporaries.

In his later years Fra Angelico declined the archbishopric of Florence and died at Rome in 1455. The tombstone which shows the emaciation of his perishable form is in the Roman Church of the Minerva; his imperishable monument is his frescoed convent home of S. Marco at Florence.

Of the transitional artists Fra Angelico is by far the most important, but his contemporary Masolino of Panicale must be considered, partly because tradition makes him the master of Masaccio, partly because of the problems which cluster about his work. The picture which is here drawn of him represents my own investigations, and differs at several points from the views of Berenson and Toesca. If we judge Masolino

only by the work that is unquestionably his, he is not an impressive figure.   He inherits the grace of the late Gothic
style, and he adds rather partially and inconsequentially the
new discoveries in anatomy and linear perspective.   Chance
took him away from the centre of things, Florence.   He
worked mostly in Lombardy, distant Hungary, provincial
Tuscany, and Rome.   He has industry and charm, but nowhere shows much intelligence.   On the whole he is a poorer
story-teller than his Gothic predecessors, and only their fair
equal in panel painting.   Had Vasari not ascribed to him, I
believe erroneously, the early miracles of St. Peter in the
Church of The Carmine, at Florence, the general historian of
art would need to pay little attention to Masolino.   But he
has been entangled in one of the most important of artistic
problems, that of Masaccio, so we cannot ignore him.

Masolino [4] was born in 1384, and, according to Vasari, was
trained by the mysterious Starnina.   We have no very early
works to show his progress, and it is merely a good guess that
the radiant Annunciation, Figure 81, in the possession of
Mr. Henry Goldman, New York, may be considerably earlier
than 1420.   It shows the gentleness and animation which are
constant in Masolino.   It combines the Sienese calligraphic
manner with those smaller realisms of inscenation which ultimately derive from Duccio.   It has coloristic audacities of
its own in the spotting of brightest vermillion.   It gives small
hint of the Renaissance.   At a later date than 1420, by which
time ordinary perspective began to be understood, I doubt if
Masolino would have indulged in that preposterous and unnecessary central pillar which starts above in middle distance
and ends below in the picture plane.   A Madonna at Bremen,
dated 1423, shows him still as Gothic as Lorenzo Monaco,
who indeed seems to have influenced him dominatingly.

In this same year, it is likely that he painted the frescoes
in the Collegiate Church at Castiglione d'Olona, a lovely

village at the foot of the Alps. Masolino had to deal with refractory spaces, the narrow triangular sectors of the apse.
This has caused elongation of the figures and piling up of
fantastic architecture merely to fill the spaces. The mood
is gentle and graceful, the treatment quite Gothic. These
six stories of the Virgin must have satisfied Masolino's humanist patron, Cardinal Branda Castiglione; for several
years later he re-employed the painter to decorate the adjoining Baptistery. Masolino at forty, in the Collegiate
Church, was still completely Gothic. If we may believe Vasari, at that age he suddenly mastered the new style. Only
on such a theory can he have painted the Adam and Eve and
the St. Peter reviving Tabitha, in the Brancacci Chapel, which
are in the new chiaroscuro technic. Since Masolino, years
after the time when he was working in that chapel, is still
incompletely modern as regards light and shade, it is easier
to suppose that what he actually painted in the Brancacci
Chapel, about 1424, was merely the vault and the three lunettes, which have since been destroyed. Thus all the frescoes
now visible in this famous chapel would be by Masaccio or
his continuer, Filippino Lippi. Such was the view of the
excellent critic Cavalcaselle more than fifty years ago. However that be, Masolino by 1427 was at Buda (now Budapest),
where he worked for that extraordinary Florentine exile and
soldier of fortune, Pippo Spano. After that trip, we hear no
more of Masolino at Florence—rather oddly, since the Brancacci
Chapel, which he had begun, still had three unpictured spaces
after Masaccio's death in 1428. Apparently the Brancacci
family did not consider Masolino competent to complete the
work he had begun. If so, they were wise.

We next find Masolino, after an interval of more than ten
years, decorating the Baptistery at Castiglione d'Olona for
his old patron, Cardinal Branda. The date is 1435. By this
time Masolino had learned a good deal, but had hardly as-

similated his new attainments. Whether as decoration or as
story-telling, the stories of St. John the Baptist are at once
confused and pretentious, with little to recommend them save
the loveliness of their Gothic color, the prettiness of the heads,

FIG. 82.   Masolino.   Baptism of Christ, detail of fresco. —*Baptistery,
Castiglione d'Olona.*

and certain vivacious and well-observed gestures. In the
great fresco of the Baptism of Christ, Figure 82, the incidental nudes are so carefully anatomized that they distract
from the general effect, while the deep river valley unhappily
draws the eye away from the figures in the foreground. A
similarly pictorially inept use of foreshortened Renaissance
colonnades appears in the opposite fresco depicting the Feast
of Herod and the delivery of the head of St. John to Herodias.
If it were not for the physical discomfort of travelling to the
end of those interminable colonnades and returning to note
what is happening nearby in them, these stories themselves

would seem vivacious and well-conceived, the female heads attractive, the color gay and pleasing. The method of com-position is still Lorenzettian and the modern architectural features inorganic.

Fig. 83. Masolino. St. Catherine disputing with the Pagan Doctors. Fresco. — S. *Clemente, Rome.*

A few years later Masolino was swept to Rome by the great wave of rebuilding and redecorating which accompanied Pope Martin V's return from Avignon. There in the Chapel of the Sacrament, in the venerable Basilica of S. Clemente, which had formerly been Cardinal Branda's titular Church, Masolino achieved his maturest work. Completely repainted, we may still see the legends of St. Catherine, and a finely theatrical Calvary by Masolino, and as well legends of St. Ambrose by a follower of Masaccio. Here Masolino's gift as a story-teller is at its best. He has learned to subordinate his accessories, and the childlike character of his themes enlists his talent in its most engaging aspect. Such a fresco as St. Catherine urging the mysteries of the faith before the Roman doctors, Figure 83, is well-felt and skilfully composed, and withal most flimsily drawn. It is incredible that a man who could do the Tabitha in the Brancacci Chapel at forty should have relapsed to this level at fifty-five. The evidence of the armor [5] worn by the horsemen in the Calvary proves that that fresco, and presumably the entire decoration of the chapel, cannot be earlier than 1440, while of course it cannot be later than Masolino's own death in 1447.

To this later period belongs, I believe, the diptych at Naples

which represents two themes rare in early Florentine painting,
the Assumption of the Virgin, and the Miracle of the Snow,
Figure 84. The latter scene
shows Pope Liberius tracing
the foundations of the Basilica
of Santa Maria Maggiore which
were indicated by a miraculous
snow-fall in midsummer. It is
delightful as story-telling, and
some of the minor figures are
entrancing, as is the landscape.
Since Michelangelo and Giorgio
Vasari once admired this picture together at Rome, we
should not grudge it our admiration. Nor should we fail
to note the curious defects in
construction. The heads of the
attendant figures are set on the
shoulders like a ball on a post.
You could blow any of these
heads off without overtaxing
your lungs. The picture shows
the utmost of which Masolino

Fig. 84. Masolino. Pope Liberius
tracing the snow-marked plan of
Santa Maria Maggiore.— *Naples*.

was capable. It reveals him as lightly touched by the new
learning and faithful to the old panoramic ideals of narrative
which had come down from Taddeo Gaddi and the Lorenzetti.

Logically we should next consider Masaccio, but first we
may well give an eye to a minor sort of narrative painting
which worked in the direction of contemporary realism. This
was domestic painting as distinguished from ecclesiastical or
civic.[6] In a prosperous Florentine home the chest was the
most important article of furniture. In the fifteenth century
its front was pictured with races, pageants, feasts, battles, or

the new themes from classical mythology. Every patrician bride normally received two such painted cassoni to contain her trousseau. For example,[7] Giovanna di Filippo Aldobrandini when she married Tommaso di Berto Fini, in 1418, received two bride chests depicting the races on St. John's day. A complete chest in the Bargello, Florence, shows the riders carrying to the Baptistery the *palii*, or lengths of brocade which were the prizes. The front panel of the companion chest is in the Holden Collection, at Cleveland, and commemorates with extraordinary vivacity and fidelity the race itself, Figure 85. The winner is just preparing to touch the *palio* which hangs from the ceremonial car at the finish. Jesters, policemen, eager women, and impatient urchins who pelt the losers make up a remarkable picture of contemporary customs. Besides the pictured chests, a well appointed room had at the height of a sitter's shoulder similar but larger panels which were called *Spalliere*. And still higher there was, on a still larger scale, what were called cornice panels. These too were contemporary or mythological in subject matter. Where many a room thus had three courses of pictures from the floor to the ceiling there was abundant opportunity for the narrative painter and remarkable stimulus to invention. The richness and complexity of this household decoration doubtless influenced all narrative painting, making for the sprightliness which dominates the end of the century.

Besides these chest and wall panels, pictured salvers were prepared to celebrate the birth of a patrician child. Such wooden salvers were used to convey the congratulatory gifts which were offered with appalling promptness to every young mother. These *Deschi da parto*, or birth plates, as the Italians called them, bore pictures alluding either to love and beauty or to childbirth. One of the earlier mythological salvers is in the Bargello and represents the Judgment of Paris. As yet the artist is not sufficiently audacious to display the god-

FIG. 85. School of Uccello. A Horse Race. Detail from a *Cassone* Front. — *Cleveland, O.*

FIG. 86. Masaccio. Birth of St. John Baptist. — *Desco da Parto. Berlin.*

desses in classical nudity. The most famous of all birth-plates may serve as our introduction to the greatest artist of the first half of the century, Masaccio. It is in the Berlin Museum, the subject is the Birth of St. John the Baptist, Figure 86, and the date should be about 1422. In the excellent proportions of the Renaissance portico, in the gravity and mass of the figures, it shows the beginnings of a new and more truthful style, based not on previous artistic formulas but on direct and masterful observation of nature. Mr. Berenson justly calls it "a little giant of a picture."

Masaccio [8] was born December 21, 1401, at San Giovanni up the Arno. His real name was Tommaso di Ser Giovanni di Tommaso Guidi. And the slightly slurring character of his nickname was apparently given for absent-mindedness, untidiness, and a certain clumsiness of person. Tradition as late as Vasari declared that Masaccio lived in a world of intense speculation concerning his art. Contemporary tax-returns show that he died deeply in debt and that he never really knew how much he owed. Tradition again insists that he never troubled to collect payments due him unless his need of money were extreme.

All the same he was one of the most original minds of all ages, and on the formal side, one of the most revolutionary. He came to Florence early, probably learned his elements under Masolino, but really drew more from the sculptor naturalists of Donatello's sort. In particular he frequented the surly architect Brunellesco and from him learned the new art of perspective. January 7, 1422, being twenty-one years old, Masaccio was matriculated in the Druggists' Guild as a licensed painter. By this time he surely had made his great discovery and taken his great decision. Reviewing the painting of his contemporaries and predecessors, he judged that it was all based on unnatural conventions. We can imagine him in the Spanish Chapel viewing the carefully charted and contoured and colored groups, and saying impatiently "things don't look like that." And in truth the older painting at its best was a select inventory or formal description of what the artist saw, and not a representation. One can imagine Masaccio exclaiming, as Francisco Goya was to do more than three centuries later, "Lines, always lines, I don't see them in nature." And, as a matter of fact, there are no lines in nature, just the meeting of areas variously colored and lighted, contrasts of tone which the eye instantaneously interprets as form.

Young Masaccio, then, makes the radical innovation that the brush should work according to nature's laws, distributing color and light and dark so as to give the swiftest and truest representation of mass and distance. Besides functional light and shade, Masaccio introduced into painting the idea of aerial perspective. He saw that distant objects diminished not merely in size but also in definition. He felt the air as a palpable veil between the object and the eye, and he painted not simply the object but, as well, its veil. By a swift impulse of sheer genius this moody lad fixed ideals of naturalistic painting which were to remain until yesterday and the Impressionists. In fundamental principles Velasquez marks no great advance on Masaccio.

It is only in fresco painting that Masaccio fully reveals his powers. So passing with mere mention such panels as The Healing of a Demoniac, in the John G. Johnson Collection, Philadelphia, the widely scattered parts of the altar-piece for the Carmelites at Pisa, dated 1426, and the grim Madonna with St. Ann in the Uffizi, the student will best turn directly to the Carmelite Church at Florence and enter that sanctuary of art, the Chapel of the Brancacci. The Church itself was dedicated April 19, 1422. Shortly after that date, young Masaccio did in fresco the dedicatory procession with many portraits. Its realism produced a profound

impression. Nevertheless it was heedlessly destroyed after a
century or so. By 1424, according to all probability, Masaccio
was associated with Masolino in the decoration of the Brancacci Chapel. It was dedicated to St. Peter, and the prescribed
subjects were drawn from the "Acts of the Apostles" and "The
Golden Legend." The vaults which contained the four evangelists and the three lunettes, which depicted The Calling of
Peter and Andrew, the Tempest-tossed Ship of the Apostles
on Galilee, and Peter denying his Lord, were by Masolino.
Unhappily these upper frescoes have been destroyed. The
Chapel now has only two rows of frescoes in twelve pictures.
Of these three and a part of a fourth, all in the lower row, are
certainly by Filippino Lippi, who about 1484 completed the
chapel, probably with the aid of Masaccio's designs. Three
in the upper row, are ascribed by many critics to Masolino.
According to this view, which is largely based on the opinion
of Vasari, Masaccio would be responsible for only five pictures
and most of a sixth. Other critics, whose views I share, believe that Masaccio painted eight of the pictures and most of
a ninth. The difference of opinion, then, concerns three
pictures which many think unworthy of Masaccio's genius.
The problem cannot be fully debated here. The grounds of
my opinion, which was that of the great Italian critic Cavalcaselle, will appear as we review the frescoes themselves.

In general color effect these frescoes are strangely unlike
their Gothic predecessors. They have nothing of the flower-
bed gayety of the Spanish Chapel, of Lorenzo Monaco, or of
Masolino elsewhere. The effect is of a very rich smokiness, a
kind of monochrome from which only subdued colors emerge.
Yellow-browns and silvery grays predominate. There are no
hard contours. The relief is salient, but one form blends in-
sensibly into another. The edges of the figures are established
not by lines but by contrast of values, the contour is often
completely lost. The strong assertion of light and dark in a

few structural planes builds out the forms from an investing
shadow. Indeed the whole chapel recalls not the Gothic fresco
painters, but such far later artists as Velasquez, Rembrandt,
or even Whistler. The method of the painter, whoever he
was, is completely modern, and uniform throughout the
chapel. He sacrifices minute definition to generalizations for
mass; and color, to emphatic construction in light and shade.
To obtain relief in the figures and distance in the backgrounds
is the main concern. It is in intention a luminist art and a
modelling art. The procedure is nearly uniform throughout
the Brancacci Chapel, though it grows abler from fresco to
fresco. It is a method that Masolino never commanded, not
at Castiglione d'Olona ten years later, nor still ten years later
at San Clemente, Rome. Hence I can only believe that the
admitted inequalities in the Brancacci Chapel merely represent the swift development of Masaccio's genius, and certain
interruptions in the work itself.

The first fresco, in the nave alongside, the entrance of the
chapel, depicts our first parents at the moment of the Temptation in the Garden of Eden, Figure 87. It is stilted and awk-
ward, yet withal dignified. The theme, which indeed has seldom been a happy one for any artist, has not greatly interested
the painter. He has made it an occasion for studying the
nude. We have what the modern student calls an academy.
As such, it is able. The construction is highly simplified and
is wholly in masses of light and dark, the contour
is freely effaced. The mystery of background foliage is well
suggested, the placing of the head of the serpent between the
tree and the figures is a perfect example of the new art of
aerial perspective. No painter but Masaccio had even the
notion of such an effect at this moment. Technically the
handling of this detail is just the same as that of the vastly
more beautiful angel in the Expulsion from Eden, Figure
91. Finally, the impassive mask of the Eve is identical with

that of the Virgin, in Masaccio's panel in the Uffizi. We presumably have to do with an experimental phase of Masaccio about the year 1423–5. About that time Masolino probably was called to Buda to work for the extraordinary

FIG. 87. Masaccio. The Temptation. — *Brancacci Chapel.*   FIG. 91. Masaccio. The Expulsion. — *Brancacci Chapel.*

Florentine soldier of fortune, Filippo Scolari, better known by his nickname of Pippo Spano. If Vasari is right, Masaccio had been required to prove his ability to continue the work by painting a St. Paul near the bellcord of the Church, in competition with a St. Jerome by Masolino. Both are lost.

However that be, Masaccio probably succeeded to the work in 1425, his twenty-fourth year, and the next fresco after the Adam and Eve may well have been the adjoining subjects of

FIG. 88. Masaccio. St. Peter raising Tabitha and healing the Cripple.—
Brancacci Chapel.

Peter raising Tabitha from the Dead and healing a Cripple, Figure 88. As a whole the composition is somewhat marred by inadvertences and afterthoughts. It shows the influence of Masolino in the trite and conventional gestures of the mourners about the bier, and in certain strained facial expressions, notably that of the turbaned bystander. Such survivals are precisely what one would expect in a young painter just emancipated from his master. The entirely Masolino-like pair of strollers in the centre seem to be due to an afterthought. The first intention is registered in the unnaturally straight back of St. Peter's companion, in the centre. The fresco was apparently to have been cut into two compartments by a pilaster at that point.[9] When the plan was abandoned in favor of putting two episodes in one space, the two unrelated figures had to be added to fill space and provide a transition. One is a little ashamed of pointing out small defects in what in all essentials is a noble and impassioned work. Technically there is nothing better in the Chapel than the establishing of the city background. It has scale, admirable atmospheric placing, dignity and pictorial significance. How anybody who knows Masolino's niggling and haphazard treatment of such architectural features at Castiglione d'Olona can imagine that he had earlier created this grandiose setting remains a mystery to me. Even more remarkable are the gravity and grandeur of the Peter and the Tabitha. Here we are reminded of Giotto. Masaccio must often have pored over the Stories of St. John in Santa Croce, and while he by no means adopted Giotto's shorthand indications for mass, he did adopt Giotto's sense for classic dignity, beautifully calculated order, and moderation. As we continue through these remarkable frescoes we shall see continually that the quite ruthless innovator that was Masaccio was also a reverent traditionalist. The particular form of his art was settled between nature and himself, as Leonardo da Vinci later justly observed; the spirit of his art derived mostly from Giotto. It was highly important for the whole ongoing of art in Italy that so revolutionary a spirit was tempered by the finest respect for the great classic tradition. And in this great fresco of St. Peter's miracles one may see how a quite homely and drastic realism can be invested with abstract power and dignity. How different it all is from the small and often charming vivacity which Masolino displays at Castiglione d'Olona and at Rome.

Like the Temptation, the Tabitha is more linear and colorful than the other frescoes of the Chapel. The painter has not quite mastered the radically new method of construction in light and shade. Thus there is a technical break between the Tabitha and the frescoes on the back wall, which are in a more developed manner. We may assume an interruption in the work. Indeed we need not assume it, for records prove that for most of the year 1426 Masaccio was occupied with the great altar-piece for the Carmelites at Pisa. On October 15, 1426, Masaccio solemnly engaged not to do any other work until the altar-piece should be finished. We may believe then that the work in the Brancacci Chapel was taken up anew towards 1427.

The four frescoes on the back wall, which are divided into two groups by the window, are the first of the new work. Of these the most remarkable is St. Peter Baptizing, Figure 89. The drawing is magnificent. Light and dark, without aid of the line, create so many bosses and pits which not merely establish form but suggest the gravest emotions. A few well chosen and well placed figures give the sense of a multitude. Mountains tower in gigantic scale, one feels the run of the little river from its distant source amid high ravines. The simplest modulations of light and dark, so many sweeps of a broad brush, establish the constructional planes of the figures and the mountains. All the early Italian writers mark with wondering admiration the expressiveness of the shivering man waiting his turn at the left. It is the smallest merit of the picture. Masaccio in this great composition commands a homely and impressive majesty, and therein shows himself true successor of Giotto, but he also reveals a power of synthesis entirely modern and hardly excelled since his day. One has only to turn to Masolino's Baptism at Castiglione d'Olona, Figure 82, with its niggling insistence on details, to appreciate the gulf between the master and the pupil.

Across the window from Masaccio's Baptism is St. Peter Preaching. The same towering, mountain background is used. The somewhat linear treatment of the faces has led Mr. Berenson, with other critics, to ascribe this fresco to Masolino. It seems to me merely less strenuously seen, because the subject offers little inspiration. Masaccio has lent the theme real dignity, and, in the eager face of the nun at the front of the audience achieves an unusual sweetness. Technically there are good but not compelling reasons for supposing this fresco may have been done among the first, about 1425.

The lower scenes at the back of the Chapel are, at your right, St. Peter healing the Sick, by the mere fall of his shadow and, at the left, St. Peter giving Alms. In both cases we have Florentine street scenes with a classic air lent by the solemn figures of the apostles. We feel the figures as far or near, and the air that veils them. There is great intentness in the poor folk, and a rugged impersonality in St. Peter and St. James. They are not indulging personal compassion so much as fulfilling a divine mission. Again the combination of a drastic realism with a stylistic majesty is what makes these frescoes unique. They contain vivid portraits, among these the traditional portrait of Masolino, a gentle, heavy, middle-aged face, bearded, and crowned with a sort of tuque — just the man to have conceived the charming but loosely organized compositions at Castiglione d'Olona.

What Masaccio looked like we may see in the upper fresco on the right wall. He is the alert and determined figure impersonating St. Thomas, at the left of the group. The story of the Tribute Money, Figure 90, is one of the grandest creations of European art. If, as Leonardo da Vinci asserts, the highest task of painting is to show by the pose and gestures of the body the emotions of the soul, this is one of the greatest paintings. It is remarkable for the dignity lent to an apparently unpromising theme. The story is simply that Christ is required to pay the *denarius* when there is no money in the company. By a miracle Peter finds the coin in the mouth of a fish and pays it to the tax-gatherer. How the creative imagination has magnified this slender theme! Masaccio has formed a group of potent and formidable individuals, these simple men are fit to shake a world. He has shown them in a moment in which discouragement and determination blend. A technicality threatens to check the salvation of the world. He has discriminated between the assured au-

thority of the Christ and the wrathful energy of St. Peter.
He has invested the majestic forms with massive draperies

Fig. 90.   Masaccio.   The Tribute Money. — *Brancacci Chapel.*

Fig. 89.   Masaccio.   St. Peter
Baptizing. — *Brancacci Chapel.*

Fig. 92.   Masaccio.   The Trinity,
Fresco. — *Santa Maria Novella.*

grandly disposed in simple folds.   He has given even the tax-
gatherer the grace of a Roman athlete.   Finally he has set
the austere company before a noble river plain upon which

press the slopes of lofty mountains, while the undulating crest of a remoter range almost bars off the sky. All objects, human and inanimate, bear firmly on the ground and are wrapped in an enveloping atmosphere. In the quality and arrangement of the figures, it all derives from Giotto; in the vastness of the scale, the introduction of mystery and distance, it is wholly Masaccio's own. Vasari rightly praised the harmony and discretion with which these powerful assertions of form are made, and sees here the beginnings of the modern style of painting.

The organizing power of Masaccio is at its height in the Tribute Money. His emotional intensity is fully involved only in the Expulsion from Eden, Figure 91, the adjoining fresco in the nave of the church. Before the sword of a serenely inexorable angel, Adam and Eve stalk forth into the unknown. Their bodies cringe as they move, with shame and grief. An ominous light reduces their bodies to so many pits of shadow and bosses of light. Drawing of such accurate economy will only rarely reappear in the world, in Leonardo da Vinci, in Rembrandt, in Honoré Daumier. The desperate emotion is well contained within the oblong, in a monumental balance. Remorse in the two first sinners has its shades. The man's head is pressed into his hands in an attempt at restraint, while Eve's is thrown back in anguished ululation. The high emotional pressure is new, and symptomatic, and significantly it is contained within monumental bounds. The Italian Renaissance in its striving for expressiveness will rarely fail to keep expression noble. The ingrained classicism of the Florentine point of view is never more favorably represented than in a subject like this which seeks a maximum emotion on terms of order and lucidity.

What remains of Masaccio is in a sense anticlimax. Very stately is the fresco in this chapel, of the Resurrection of the Prince of Tyre and St. Peter enthroned. The beauty is that of fine arrangement and characterization. The graceful nude boy and about ten distinguished figures behind him were added to the composition, presumably from Masaccio's designs, full fifty years later. They are the work of Filippino Lippi, who also added some portraits at the left of this fresco. He also filled the three unpainted panels, in an excellent imitation of Masaccio's style. Evidently Masaccio was called rather abruptly to his last sojourn at Rome. For the fresco of the Raising of the Boy could have been finished in a fortnight.

I have omitted a fine fresco of a Pietà in the Collegiate Church at Empoli, though I believe it to be a splendid example of Masaccio's early style, and I can only mention for its magnificent architectural setting in Brunellesco's new style the fresco of the Trinity in Santa Maria Novella, Figure 92. It is of his latest manner and of extraordinary gravity and mass.

In 1428, being only twenty-six years old, Masaccio drops out of sight at Rome. Some report that he was poisoned, others that he was slain in a street brawl. We really know nothing about it. What we do know is that in the recorded history of art no painter had achieved so greatly in so short a time. Within six short years Masaccio created that method of painting which stood uncontested till the advent of luminism only forty years ago. And he not merely illustrated the method of construction in light and dark, painting in atmospheric values rather than in lines and charted areas, but he also expressed in the new technic both the noblest traditional emotions as also poignant new emotions quite his own. In one superb aggressive he had moved three generations into the future. For a hundred years the most intelligent and ambitious artists in Florence as a matter of course studied and copied in the Brancacci Chapel to form their style. Botticelli, Ghirlandaio, Leonardo da Vinci, Michelangelo, Raphael, Andrea del Sarto thus paid homage to the untidy youth from Castel San Giovanni, and even the iconoclasts of today, for whom Leonardo da Vinci and his peers are scarcely artists at all, envy the gravity and force of Masaccio. He is the real father of modern painting, which is most true to itself when it tempers an ardent curiosity as regards natural appearances with a respect for the great traditions of moderation and taste.

Masaccio's successors, very wisely, did not closely imitate him.   They saw he was an unsafe and unapproachable model. By a swift impulse of genius, and apparently without analytical study of anatomy and topography, he had mastered the broad effects that register form.   Details he neglected. He gives the action of hands and feet, not their articulations, the scale of landscape and not its component parts. For men of lesser genius, these shortcuts were dangerous. While using Masaccio as inspiration, they had to verify his discoveries through analytical studies before those innovations could become generally available.   The process of verification and minute research occupied about fifty years and may be said to be complete with the maturity of Leonardo da Vinci, say about the date of The Last Supper, 1498.

The successors of Masaccio may be divided into two groups as they quietly adopted and popularized the immediately available part of his discoveries, or strenuously carried his work forward.   To the moderate progressive group belong Fra Filippo Lippi and Benozzo Gozzoli, and still later Ghirlandaio; the experimentalists are birds of quite a different feather.

These Florentine realists may be divided into two generations.   The first asserts itself before the middle of the fifteenth century, and is trained chiefly under the influence of such sculptors as Donatello, Brunellesco and Ghiberti.   These painters work at the problem of light and shade, anatomy, and perspective, accepting in their art the guidance of sculpture. The second generation of realists come to their own after the middle of the century, are mostly trained as silver-

FIG. 93.   Paolo Uccello.   Battle of Cavalry. — *Louvre.*

smiths, and work at the new technic of oil painting, at landscape and at the figure in action. Both groups relatively neglected the important matter of composition. Most of the realists sacriᶜced pictorial efᶠect the better to master detail, but they also accumulated that vast body of knowledge upon which rests the glory of the High Renaissance, and nobody can understand the progress of Florentine painting without following sympathetically their great effort.

Of the first generation, the quaintest figure is Paolo Uccello. Born in 1397, he soon gave himself fanatically to the study of the new science of perspective, especially to feats of foreshortening. His pictures are so many experiments and have a petrified inertness. Yet at his best he commands dignity and a considerable decorative power. About the year 1435 he painted for the Medici palace several battle scenes, three of which are respectively in the Louvre, Figure 93, National Gallery and Uffizi. The last, representing the Florentine victory of San Romano, shows the style. The forms are squared, in a fashion anticipating modern Cubism, in order to simplify the problem of placing and foreshortening. Corpses and lances are deliberately pointed at the spectator to offer so many problems in perspective. The landscape is minute and topographical. The decorative coloring is bold and original with interesting dissonances of oranges, russets, and greens. It is quite splendid after the unreal fashion of a tapestry.

Paolo's masterpiece is the equestrian portrait of Sir John Hawkwood, Figure 94, the English soldier of fortune and occasional captain of the Florentine army, which is in the Cathedral. It is painted in gray-green touched with color, and simulates a tomb. The date is 1437. Since Roman times no equestrian monument of equal dignity had been created, and one is inclined to suspect that Uccello profited by preliminary studies of Donatello, his close friend, which later developed into the superb Gattamelata statue at Padua. Ucello has a lighter vein illustrated by furniture panels at Oxford, (a Hunt), at Paris, and Vienna, (St. George and the Dragon), but his most ambitious work is the decoration of the lunettes in the great cloister of Santa Maria Novella. The stories are drawn from the Old Testament, were started by Paolo, about the year 1446, and continued by several assistants. The medium was gray-green, *terra verde*, and the place accordingly is called the Green Cloister. Uccello's manner may be best sensed in the fresco of the Deluge, in which the endeavor to set problems in perspective clashes unhappily with the desire to present a scene of terror. The figures are felt one at a time, there is little relation between them, and the picture has small merit apart from its probity in the rendering of details and a sort of abstract earnestness.

Uccello lived on till 1475, an indulged eccentric, ignored by the public and ridiculed by his greater friends. His zeal for perspective was unabated with age, and many a night

FIG. 94. Paolo Uccello. Tomb Portrait of Sir John Hawkwood. —*Cathedral*.

FIG. 96. Andrea del Castagno. Portrait of a young man. — *J. P. Morgan Coll., N. Y.*

FIG. 95. Andrea del Castagno. Pippo Spano. — *Sant' Apollonia*.

FIG. 97. Andrea del Castagno. Tomb portrait of Niccolò da Tolentino. — *Cathedral*.

his much-tried wife lost sleep as he murmured in the small hours — "O! thou dear perspective!"

Far the most powerful of these early realists is Andrea del Castagno.[10] His aggressive and truculent forms savor of Donatello without Donatello's fineness. He searches the secrets of anatomy, locates and describes the muscles and sinews, depicts a world ruled by force of arm. Although he builds in heavy shadows, after Masaccio's fashion, he retains an outline that vibrates with nervous strength. His truthful sternness still wins approbation. He was born about 1390. We meet him first in full maturity, perhaps about the year 1435, as decorator of the Villa of the Pandolfini. To strengthen the ambition of that proud race, he painted in their great hall nine figures of heroes and heroines noted in war or in the arts. Recently transferred to the Convent of Sant' Apollonia, which already had a Last Supper and a Calvary by Andrea, you may see the austere forms of Dante, Petrarch, and Boccaccio, of Esther, Queen Thomyris and the Cumean Sibyl, of the warrior Farinata degli Uberti, Niccolò Accaiuoli, and Filippo Scolari. This potent and melancholy figure of Pippo Spano, Figure 95, whom we already know as the patron of Masolino, at Buda, is the most striking representation that painting has given us of those masterful Italian soldiers of fortune who managed war and government for the less advanced nations. Pippo Spano had gone to Buda as a clerk and had quickly become a generalissimo, Obergespann of Temesvár. For King Sigismund of Hungary he stemmed the Turkish onslaught, did much to save Central Europe for Christianity. As he stands thoughtfully confident, holding the scimitar, the weapon of his foes, he is the beau ideal of that Italy soon to be immortalized by Machiavelli, in which virtue meant successful force, and both were on sale. A man's portrait, Figure 96, in the collection of Mr. J. P. Morgan, New York, has an even more

sinister intensity. Equally remarkable for its heroic aggres-
siveness is the young David adorning a tournament shield
in the Widener Collection, Figure 70.

In the fresco of the Crucifixion, now in S. Apollonia, Andrea
reveals great knowledge linked to tragic expressiveness. No
tenderness veils the appalling theme. An athlete suffers
stoically while his mother and cousin shudder with grief.
Of its ruthless kind it is a great masterpiece and quite unforgettable.

In 1456 Andrea painted for the Cathedral the equestrian
portrait of the partisan leader, Niccolò da Tolentino, Figure
97. It is a companion piece to Uccello's Hawkwood, and
like it simulates statuary, in monochrome. It is more martial
and restless, in the toss of the horse's head and the snap of
the rider's cloak. It suggests not ceremonious dignity, but
noise and impending action. It may very powerfully have
influenced Verrocchio twenty years later when he modelled
for Venice the Colleoni statue.

The truculence of Andrea's manner led to a false and
scandalous tradition, promulgated by Vasari, that he slew
his rival Domenico Veneziano out of jealousy. As a matter
of prosaic record, Domenico Veneziano survived his alleged
assassin's death, in 1457, by all of four years.

Domenico came down from Venice somewhere about 1438
and brought with him a new technical method. He finished
the pictures, which he began in tempera, with veilings or
glazes in an oil or varnish medium. He avoided the old frank
Gothic coloring in favor of pale tonalities which oddly forecast our modern open-air school. The new method permitted
of bolder brushwork and successive over paintings. For the
moment it wrought havoc with the old conventional beauty,
but it offered the painter new resources and refinements,
and eventually made possible the triumphs of Leonardo and
Titian.

On the whole, Domenico is merely the shadow of a great name, for we have only a handful of works by him, and those perhaps unrepresentative. The altar-piece of St. Lucy, in

FIG. 98. Domenico Veneziano. Madonna with St. Lucy. — *Uffizi.*

the Uffizi, Figure 98, is novel only in its acid and original dissonance of deep rose and pale green. The rugged St. John the Baptist shows an attempt to obtain force of modelling without exaggerating the shadows. This tendency persists in such disciples of Domenico as Baldovinetti and Piero della Francesca, and rules in Florence until Leonardo's definitive application of Masaccio's methods. In the profile portraiture of the period Domenico was a master, as shown in an admirable female portrait in Mrs. John L. Gardner's collection, Figure 99. Many similar heads, which we can hardly ascribe to particular masters, seem to derive from Domenico. One of the most beautiful is in the Poldi Pezzoli Museum at Milan. All of Domenico's pupils and imitators excel in a minute and topographical style of landscape of which he was probably the inventor. It may be studied in Piero della Francesca, in the Pollaiuoli, in Baldovinetti, and there is even a trace of it in the spacious Alpine background of the Mona Lisa.

Domenico died in 1461. By that time Florentine realism was emerging from its first phase, and was beginning to investigate with its new resources the facts of motion. It was the moment, too, when certain realists sought to regain the

FIG. 99. Domenico Veneziano. Portrait of a Girl.— *Coll. Mrs. John L. Gardner, Boston.*

FIG. 100. A. Baldovinetti. Madonna. — *Louvre.*

grace which had largely been sacrificed in the struggle for sheer knowledge.

Alesso Baldovinetti[11] well represents this moment in a lovely Madonna in the Louvre, Figure 100, which shows in perfection the new topographical landscape and that juvenile graciousness which was to be the staple of the coming generation of artists. Baldovinetti was born in 1425, and this loveliest of all his pictures may represent him about the year 1460. He had been an assistant of Fra Angelico, but in a long career, he died in 1499, he fell behind the times. He taught Domenico Ghirlandaio his elements, and profoundly influenced Andrea Verrocchio and Antonio Pollaiuolo. Thus he keeps a sure if modest place in the progress of Florentine art.

In this chapter we have been dealing in a rough way with the Florence of Cosimo de' Medici. Under his astute and delicate rule from behind the political scenes, Florence developed in wealth, splendor, and worldliness. The old piety was waning or assuming merely æsthetic forms. Greek studies were beginning to pave the way for an enlightened and sceptical humanism and, withal, a revival of the pagan sense of beauty. And when the new beauty came, it was greatfully mindful of those who had made it possible. Leonardo da Vinci lauds Masaccio. He expresses the immense debt that art owes to the first conscious realists. They did good and harm, but to Florence at least they opened the only way of progress. For whatever art may be elsewhere, in Florence it was fruitful only as it was intellectualized. Good theory, good practice — such was the creed imposed by the early realists and later formulated by their great scion, Leonardo. I do not offer it as a universal formula, but in these days when pure spontaneity — that is no theory — and false theory divide the field, the old Florentine credo is at least worthy of consideration by all who produce art and by all who love it. Baldovinetti was untouched by these new stirrings which are associated with the rule of Lorenzo de' Medici, but he dimly forecasts the grace that was soon to come. This new spirit and its exponents must be the theme of our next chapter.

ILLUSTRATIONS FOR CHAPTER III

Vasari on Masaccio

Vasari's general estimate of Masaccio's importance is still sound.

"With regard to the good manner of painting, we are indebted above all to Masaccio, seeing that he, as one desirous of acquiring fame, perceived that painting is nothing but the counterfeiting of all the things of nature, vividly and simply, with drawing and with colours, even as she produced them for us . . . This truth, I say, being recognized by Masaccio, brought it about that by means of continuous study he learned so much that he can be numbered among the first who cleared away, in a great measure, the hardness, the imperfections, and the difficulties of the art, and that he gave a beginning to beautiful attitudes, movements, liveliness, and vivacity, and to a certain relief truly characteristic and natural; which no painter up to his time had done . . . And he painted his works with good unity and softness, harmonizing the flesh-colours of the heads and of the nudes with the colours of the draperies, which he delighted to make with few folds and simple, as they are in life and nature . . .

"For this reason that chapel has been frequented continually up to our own day [1554] by innumerable draughtsmen and masters; and there still are therein some heads so life-like and so beautiful, that it may truly be said that no master of that age approached so nearly as this man did to the moderns. His labours, therefore, deserve infinite praise, and above all because he gave form in his art to the beautiful manner of the times."

Vasari then names twenty-five artists who studied Masaccio's frescoes. From De Vere's translation of the *Lives*, Vol. II, p. 189, 90.

Leonardo da Vinci on Masaccio

Leonardo da Vinci uses Masaccio as the example of a painter who goes to nature rather than to other men's painting.

That Painting declines and deteriorates from age to age, when painters have no standard but painting already done.

"Hence the painter will produce pictures of small merit if he takes for his standard the pictures of others. But if he will study from natural objects he will bear good fruit; as was seen in the painters after the Romans who always imitated each other, and so their art declined from age to age. After these came Giotto the Florentine who — not content with imitating the works of Cimabue; his master — being born in the mountains and in a solitude inhabited only by goats and such beasts, and being guided by nature to his art, began by drawing on the rocks the movements of the goats of which he was keeper. And thus he began to draw all the animals which were to be found in the country, and in such wise that after much study he excelled not only all the masters of his time but all those of many bygone ages."

"Afterwards this art declined again, because everyone imitated the pictures that were already done; thus it went on from century to century until Tomaso, of Florence, nicknamed Masaccio, showed by his perfect works how those who take for their standard any one but nature — the mistress of all masters — weary themselves in vain."

J. P. Richter "Literary Works of L. da V.," Vol. I. p. 660.

But Leonardo approves also imitation of antiquity (Richter, Vol. II, ¶1445). "The imitation of antique things is better than that of modern things." He would probably have sanctioned Masaccio's devout study of Giotto. The warning is against slavish imitation of immediate predecessors.

VASARI ON PAOLO UCCELLO

The admirable and self sacrificing ardor of these first realists is best exemplified in the case of Paolo Uccello.

"For the sake of these investigations [in perspective] he kept himself in seclusion and almost a hermit, having little intercourse with anyone, and staying weeks and months in his house without shaving himself. And although those were difficult and beautiful problems, if he had spent that time in the study of figures, he would have brought them to absolute perfection; for even so he made them with passing good draughtsmanship. But, consuming his time in these researches, he remained throughout his whole life more poor than famous; wherefore the sculptor Donatello, who was very much his friend, said to him very often — when Paolo showed him Mazzocchi (facetted head-fillets) with pointed ornaments, and squares drawn in perspective from diverse aspects; spheres with seventy-two diamond-shaped facets, with wood-shavings wound round sticks on each facet; and other fantastic devices on which he spent and wasted his time — 'Ah, Paolo, this perspective of thine makes thee abandon the substance for the shadow; those are things that are only useful to men who work at the inlaying of wood, seeing that they fill their borders with chips and shavings, with spirals both round and square, and with other similar things.'"

Vasari, in Schele de Vere's translation; Vol. II. p. 132, 3.

AN APPRAISAL OF BALDOVINETTI'S FRESCOES

Here I may illustrate a common practice of the times in an appraisal of Baldovinetti's frescoes in the choir of the Trinità by fellow artists including Benozzo Gozzoli, Cosimo Rosselli and Pietro Perugino.

"In the name of God — on the 19 of January 1496 (n. s. '97)

We Benozzo di Lese, painter; and Piero di Cristofano da Castel della Pieve, painter; and Cosimo di Lorenzo Rosselli, painter, chosen by Alesso di Baldovinetto Baldovinetti, painter, to see and judge and set a price on — empowered by a contract which said Alesso has with M. Bongianni de'Gianfigliazzi and his heirs — a chapel pictured in Santa Trinità of Florence — that is the choir of the said church, having seen, all together and agreeing, having examined all the costs of lime, azure, gold and all other colours, scaffolds and everything else, including his work, we judge from all this that the aforesaid Alesso should have one thousand broad gold florins.

"And for clearness and truth of the said judgment I Cosimo di Lorenzo aforesaid have made this writing with my own hand this aforesaid day, and so I judge; and here at the foot they will sign with their own hands that they are agreed with what is above written, and so judge.

Benozzo di Lese &c.

I Piero Perugino &c.

Translated from Herbert Horne's edition of Alesso's *Ricordi* in *Burlington Magazine*, Vol. II. (1903) p. 383.

FRA FILIPPO LIPPI AND THE NEW NARRATIVE STYLE

FIG. 101. Ghirlandaio. Giovanna degli Albizzi. — *J. P. Morgan Coll.,*
New York.

CHAPTER IV

FRA FILIPPO LIPPI AND THE NEW NARRATIVE STYLE

After Masaccio two tendencies, — towards prettiness and vivacious narrative;
    towards strenuous research — Fra Filippo Lippi celebrant of Gay Flor-
    ence — Benozzo Gozzoli and Pageantry — Antonio Pollaiuolo and human
    dynamics — Piero della Francesca and impersonal observation of ap-
    pearances — Dissolving tendencies in the new panoramic style — illus-
    trated by the early frescoes in the Sistine Chapel — Perugino's return to
    simple symmetries — The *Cassone* painters once more — Domenico
    Ghirlandaio and spectacular narrative — His portraits— The charm
    of the slighter narrative style.

In the last chapter we have dealt chiefly with innovators
and reformers. Whether in art or life, these are not always
the most agreeable companions. The charming person is
generally a traditionalist, or a tactful profiteer by other men's
discoveries. So the popular favor has ever gone not to the
strenuous artists of Masaccio's type or Castagno's, but to
devotees of the charm of common folk and things, like Fra
Filippo Lippi; to masters of pageantry and incident, like
Benozzo Gozzoli; or to chroniclers of the festal richness
of Florence in her short prime, like Domenico Ghirlandaio.
These artists, while by no means giants, are highly representative of their times. They one and all aimed to please, and
amply succeeded. Their importance in the history of art is
rather slight; in the history of taste, on the contrary, they
are very important. And it is from that point of view that
we shall do well to consider them. These three masters cover
the last two-thirds of the fifteenth century. They exemplify

the taste of the new-rich merchants who flourished under the benevolent tyranny of the Medici.

Alongside of these gracious and adaptable spirits, struggled the continuers of the realistic reform — Antonio Pollaiuolo, who first systematically studied the anatomy and dynamics of the human form; Andrea Verrocchio, who imbued accuracy and power with grace ; Sandro Botticelli, who explored solitary roads of sentiment and wrought out of the ruggedness of the realists strange forms of recondite beauty. At all times we find the endeavor for artistic adaptation running alongside the passion for sheer discovery, and producing its own triumphs. It is this complicated, dual process which makes the richness and continuity of the Early Renaissance. If we compare the seventy-two years between the beginnings of Masaccio, say 1422, and the death of Ghirlandaio, in 1494, with the century and a half preceding, we shall note an extraordinary acceleration both of production and progress. There are no gaps and rests; each generation makes its discoveries and cashes them in. Architecture, sculpture, classical scholarship develop with a whirling rapidity which by no means precludes taste and reflection. In an almost reckless expansion of emotion, experience, and creative activity, Florence keeps her head though she risks losing her soul. And the true harbinger of this intoxicating new life is one who often lost his head and whose soul remains enigmatic, the wayward and fascinating painter-monk, Fra Filippo Lippi.[1]

He was the first Italian painter to care greatly for the look of everyday people. Born about the year 1400, he was early orphaned and thrust willy-nilly into the Carmelite Order. As a young man he must have seen Masaccio painting those titanic designs in the Brancacci Chapel. From Masaccio Fra Filippo learned his trade, rather by observation than by direct instruction. But he cared for far different things.

He really follows the tender narrative vein of Lorenzo Monaco.
To the grandeur of miracle-working apostles, he preferred the

FIG. 102. Fra Filippo Lippi. Madonna in Adoration. — *Berlin.*

gentle quaintness of the old man who kept the shops and
practiced the trades of Florence; to the matronly dignity
of Masaccio's women, he preferred the shy and alluring sweetness of the Florentine girls about him; to the majestic sweeps
of mountain and valley in Masaccio, the intimate appeal of
the cypress groves, the little ledges and trickling springs.
In technique, too, he avoided the bold short-cuts of his master.

He hung on to the line, loved details, described everything with solicitude. It is an art of amiability and curiosity, gener-

Fig. 103. Fra Filippo Lippi.
Madonna and Child. — *Uffizi*.

ally disregardful of that grand style towards which in her greater moments Florence ever aspired. The advent of Fra Filippo in the Florence of Giotto and Orcagna and Masaccio, was like that of an irresistibly attractive youth in a solemn company. He loosened everything up. Unconsciously he demoralized the assembly; for two generations the art of Florence was to be boyish and girlish. That is its charm and its limitation, and the difference between the Early Renaissance and the Golden Age will be largely that the latter will prefer to depict with the gravity of maturity a world that has grown up.

One of the earliest and most exquisite panels by Fra Filippo was painted shortly after 1435 for the private chapel of Cosimo de' Medici's new palace, and is now at Berlin. The theme, young Mary kneeling before her Divine Infant, Figure 102, is a favorite with the Florentine artists of this century. Perhaps no one has conceived it more delightfully than Fra Filippo. The picture gets its peculiar sweetness from the gentle, girlish figure of the Maiden Mother, its quality of romance from the ledgy background watered by springs and spangled with modest flowers, its tang of reality from the chubby and stolid Christchild and the boyish St. John the Baptist. You could almost see such a thing today along the shaded upper Mensola when a young Florentine mother has taken the children for a Sunday picnic. For the old Gothic conventions and the

bare majesty of Masaccio's painting, Fra Filippo has substituted the everyday joys of a feeling eye, and the charm of
closely-observed little things.

In most of his pictures this familiar quality is marked.

FIG. 104. Fra Filippo Lippi. Coronation of the Virgin. — *Uffizi*.

His saints are not types, but people of the Florentine middle
class. An early Madonna in the Uffizi, Figure 103, shows the
Virgin as a slight girl with her ash-blond locks elaborately
dressed and braided for a holiday. She is almost overborne
by her sturdy Son, an exacting brute, one may imagine,
while the attendant angel is a grinning street Arab caught
in the intervals of mischief. Such pictures with their winsomeness and actuality worked powerfully to break down both
the old Gothic decorum and the new sublimity of Masaccio.

To grasp the novelty of Fra Filippo's most famous panel
picture, The Coronation of the Virgin, painted for the nuns
of Sant' Ambrogio in 1441, Figure 104, and now in the Uffizi,
one has only to recall the devoutly formal and simple version
of the subject which Fra Angelico painted about the same

time for the convent of San Marco. The composition of Fra
Filippo, on the contrary, is radiantly informal. We breathe
the air of the commencement at a very nice girls' school,
with adoring friends and proud relatives moving at the edges
of the ceremony. Indeed God the Father has merely the air
of a benevolent trustee or visiting minor celebrity awarding
a prize to the best girl. It is all like the crowning of a *Rosière*
in a French village. Robert Browning in one of the most
admirable poems in "Men and Women" makes Fra Filippo
promise

> "I shall paint
> God in the midst, Madonna and her Babe.
> Ringed by a bowery, flowery angel-brood,
> Lilies and vestments and white faces, sweet
> As puff on puff of grated orris-root
> When ladies crowd to church at Midsummer."

Our picture is evidence enough that the time has come to
Florentine art when youth shall be served.

Monastic vows, and in fact duties of any sort, bore lightly
on Fra Filippo. He tasted the forbidden sweets of life reck-
lessly, and worked only when the rare mood urged. He was
in and out of the good graces of the Medici. Called to Prato
to fresco the choir of the Collegiata, in 1455, he was nine
years achieving what a steady workman would have done
in two. But in the meantime Fra Filippo had run away with
the nun, Lucrezia Buti, shuffled off his monastic vows (through
the indulgence of the humanist Pope, Pius II), married and
settled down as the father of a family. His random joyous
course was nearly run, and his last frescoes at Prato show a
kind of discipline that is foreign to his earlier work. In 1464
he completed the Feast of Herod and the Funeral of St.
Stephen, frescoes which forecast the sort of narrative painting
that was to mark the close of the century.

About the brutality of the Feast of Herod, Figure 105, Fra

Filippo has cast a dreamy glamour, as indeed Giotto had before him. The youthful guests are absorbed in Salome's dancing. Following the sculptors of the day, Fra Filippo has made her slight and graceful, as she trips a careless measure.

FIG. 105. Fra Filippo Lippi. Feast of Herod. Salome's Dance. Fresco. — *Collegiata. Prato.*

The air is simply that of a gentle society. The grim motive of the delivery of the head of John the Baptist to Herodias is gently emphasized by the charming act of two little handmaids who clutch each other for fright. The sprightliness of the invention, the generalized idyllic charm of the feeling, the rich variety of accessories, the youthful timbre of the whole — make this not merely one of the best but also one of the most characteristic narrative mural paintings of the Early Renaissance. It strikes the note which will be echoed by Fra Filippo's apprentice, Sandro Botticelli; which will be exaggerated by Fra Filippo's son, Filippino, and distantly imitated by many another Florentine successor.

If the Feast of Herod best exemplifies the element of homely poetry and inventive grace in Fra Filippo, the Burial of St. Stephen, Figure 106, just opposite in the choir proves that he was not oblivious to the high and decorous prose of his master Masaccio. In formality and power of construction few painters then living could have equalled it, and those few could not have rivalled its spacious architectural setting and its suggestion of atmosphere. At first sight it seems nearly equal to the Tribute Money or at least to the Tabitha. On more careful survey it is less noble, more insistently pathetic, and in every way more loosely knit. In particular the portraits at the sides have little but a mechanical relation to the theme. Masaccio himself had admitted a similar gallery of mere bystanders in The Miracle of the Prince, but had he lived to complete the fresco, he would doubtless have brought the portrait figures into some relation of interest in the miracle. Fra Filippo virtually waives that problem and merely flanks his real subject with bordering groups of persons of contemporary importance. As a matter of fact, the Florentine donor was no longer humble-minded and content to appear among the saints in miniature and unobtrusive guise. He now insisted in being painted to the life with his family, friends, and dependents, — a complacent, incongruous apparition amid the humility or heroism of the saints. Fra Filippo made the sensible adjustment that the donors should serve as a sort of human frame for the religious picture in the centre. This solution became tiresomely standard and lasted for fifty years or so, until the High Renaissance had authority enough to impose considerations of taste and self-effacement even upon wealthy donors.

In 1465 Fra Filippo was called to Spoleto, and there having started a lovely apse decoration, A Coronation, for the cathedral, he died and was buried. Quite unconsciously he had temporarily shattered that intellectual formalism which is the very essence of Florentine art, and had inaugurated that moral and artistic holiday which is made visible in the painting of Botticelli and Ghirlandaio and audible in the songs of Lorenzo de' Medici.

This holiday mood is strong in Benozzo Gozzoli, and he spread it through Umbria and the Sienese country. Born in 1420, for a time an assistant of Fra Angelico, Benozzo's task was to depict with more vivacity than insight the splen-

FIG. 106. Fra Filippo Lippi. Funeral of St. Stephen. Fresco. — *Collegiata, Prato.*

dors and humors of life. This he does, whether his theme be the legend of St. Francis, as at Montefalco in 1462, the Caval-cade of the Magi, Florence, 1469, the Life of St. Augustine, San Gimignano, 1465, or the doings of the Old Testament Patriarchs and Matriarchs, at Pisa, 1468-1484. He is always sunny, profuse, witty in an obvious way; and not without his tinge of the poetry of youth. He loves gardens, court-yards, forests, and equally well palaces, colonnades, crowds and incidents. He is indefatigably panoramic, and his fres-coes, if hardly good pictures, are at least good pickings, for their abundant and often refreshing detail.

Very splendid is that pageant of the Wise Men from the East, Figure 107, which he painted about 1469 [2] for the private chapel of Cosimo de' Medici's palace. The gorgeous pro-cession winds about the walls, moving over the mountain roads and through the forests which you may still see up

the Arno valley towards Vallombrosa. Their goal was the
little panel over the altar where Filippo Lippi painted the
Madonna reverently kneeling before her Son, Figure 102.
This little picture was flanked by choirs, in fresco, of singing
angels. For the older of the Three Kings Benozzo chose the
Patriarch of Constantinople and the unfortunate Emperor,
John Palaeologus, who thirty years earlier had come to Florence
on the vain mission of uniting the Eastern and Western branches
of the Christian Church. The youngest of the kings is, somewhat
idealized, Lorenzo the Magnificent. What we really have is a
pictorial version of those religious pageants or representations
which were common at the times. Many times Florence had
seen her patricians in such a cavalcade. Benozzo's fresco in
its undiminished loveliness of color and gold — the Medici apparently either ordered few masses or burned few candles
in their family chapel — is a most precious relic of bygone
splendors. Indeed they passed before Benozzo himself, for
he lived on till 1498, four years after Lorenzo the Magnificent's death, and the year of Savonarola's martyrdom; the
year, too, when Leonardo da Vinci's Last Supper was being
finished. Few artists have had such emphatic intimations
that their world and they themselves were obsolete. It is
in every way to be hoped in Benozzo's case that he was at
once too cheerful and too unintelligent to grasp the situation.
This may be fairly supposed of a man who was content for
fifty years of a swiftly moving world with what could be learned
from Fra Angelico.

Of course some painters declined to keep holiday and fever-
ishly pursued the lines of realistic investigation laid down by
Castagno and his contemporaries. The most notable of these
is Antonio Pollaiuolo.[3] He was trained in sculpture under
Ghiberti, and worked most variously, at sculpture, painting,
engraving, glass designing, and even embroiderers' patterns.
Everywhere he pursued with an almost ferocious intensity

the secrets of anatomy and especially of the human body in violent action. He conceived the body as a powerful machine and rejoiced to display its mechanisms — knotted muscles,

FIG. 107. Benozzo Gozzoli. Detail from Procession of Magi. — *Riccardi Palace.*

FIG. 108. Antonio Pollaiuolo. Martyrdom of St. Sebastian. — *London.*

straining sinews. He chose his subjects with this sort of display in mind: Hercules and his feats, the archers setting their bows and crossbows for the slaying of St. Sebastian, nude men in deadly combat with dirks and axes, nude men wildly dancing. Nearly all these works suffer from their avowed experimentalism, but all are alive with a tingling not to say brutal energy. Antonio Pollaiuolo is the ancestor of all the strong painters who for over four centuries have delighted to appal the mild and sheeplike throng with wolfish antics. He is the first artist who is a specialist, pursuing his own ends in disregard of the surrounding public. As a matter of fact, Antonio's muscular paganism fitted in fairly well with the notions of a Florence that worshipped power. The Medici ordered the twelve feats of Hercules for their palace, about the year 1460. The great pictures are lost, but little copies by Antonio himself give an idea of their truculent force. In the Uffizi are Hercules crushing the breath out of the earth-born demigod Antæus, and Hercules slaying the Hydra. The tension, ardor, and ferocity of these tiny pictures are extraordinary. They seem to enhance our own physical life. At New Haven is the panel of Hercules shooting the Centaur Nessus, who races across a ford with Deinaira on his back. The background is an exact picture of the Arno valley looking from the west towards Florence. The representation of the run of the river is extraordinary. Pollaiuolo had adopted Domenico Veneziano's miniature conception of landscape, but has introduced swing and motion.

Equally remarkable is the Arno landscape in the Martyrdom of St. Sebastian, Figure 108, which was painted in 1475. It has the defects of an experimental and academic performance, is a show piece. The executioners are even repeated, to show both front and rear aspects. All the same, its power is impressive and beyond the range of any artist then living, with the possible exception of Piero della Francesca. In painting Pollaiuolo's accomplishment is so even, and in draped figures so ugly, that we may well pass the series of Virtues which with his brother Piero he did in 1469 for the Mercantile Court, and consider his great engraving known as the Ten Nudes, Figure 109, the odd decorative disposition of which is imitated by Botticelli in the Allegory of Spring; and the fresco of Dancing Men, in which Pollaiuolo successfully vies with the convivial and Bacchic themes of the Greek vase painters. The group is odd and effective as pattern, and inspired by a joyous energy.

Painting only claimed a fraction of Antonio's effort; often he merely made the sketch and left the execution to his rather tame brother, Piero. At the end of his life he was called down to Rome to make the bronze tomb for Sixtus IV. There he died in the year 1498, being sixty-three years old. While his own achievement was somewhat cramped and limited, he had made the most valuable contributions to the art, or rather to the science of painting. He had inspired a titan

FIG. 109. Antonio Pollaiuolo. Fighting Men — "The Ten Nudes."
Engraving.

like Signorelli and a poet like Botticelli, and in certain aspects Leonardo da Vinci and Michelangelo only continued and perfected his work. As late as Benvenuto Cellini's day his sketches were passed about the studios for the instruction of young painters in anatomy.

A kindred strenuous spirit, Piero della Francesca,[4] affords an interesting contrast to Pollaiuolo. Though an Umbrian, he belongs spiritually to Florence. For Piero the world was a frozen thing. He investigated with utmost zeal the mathematical basis of perspective, producing on that topic a laborious and quite unreadable book. He studied anatomy and construction in light and dark, and all the atmospheric problems therewith associated. To attain atmospheric envelopement, he sacrificed color. His pictures exist in silvery grays, suggesting the blondness and tonal unity of modern open-air painting. The drama of life never engrossed him.

His world is passionless and almost motionless, coldly impressive. Although he practiced all refinements of modelling, he never made those relaxations of contour which suggest movement. His figures are finely constructed and beautifully placed but emotionally unrelated. They merely exist rather splendidly, as do some of Manet's figures. Indeed the warning of George Moore as regards Manet applies equally to Piero. It is futile to seek from him anything but fine painting.

Fig. 110. Piero della Francesca. The Resurrection. — *Borgo S. Sepolcro.*

Of his origins we know next to nothing. He was born about 1410 in the Umbrian town of Borgo San Sepolcro. For several years after 1439 we find him at Florence as a paid assistant of Domenico Veneziano, whose pale tonalities and topographically minute landscape reappear throughout Piero's work. His austere power is best represented in the bleak Resurrection, Figure 110, which he painted in 1460 for his native city. The stalwart Conqueror of Death has an apparitional impressiveness. He comes with power from beyond the grave. He dominates the world as represented by the sleeping athletes of the guard. A most potent effect is obtained without sacrifice to sentiment. There is a similar detachment in the Baptism of Christ, in the National Gallery, London. Its pearly loveliness of color is in odd contrast to its evasions of anything like warmth or tenderness. It is less an event than a magnificently posed scene. The landscape is a liberating and informal feature, a skilful adaptation of the method of Domenico Veneziano and Pollaiuolo. It is as crisp and calculated as a Japanese print, yet it gives its effect of space and breadth.

Fig. 111. Piero della Francesca. Battle of Constantine, detail from fresco. — *S. Francesco, Arezzo.*

Piero's great opportunity came about 1465 when he painted in the choir of San Francesco at Arezzo ten stories from the Legend of the Holy Cross. For stark impressiveness it is hard to match them in Italy in this century. Only Masaccio and Leonardo da Vinci will at all bear the comparison. On analysis, the power rests mostly on the seriousness with which Piero takes his technical problem. There is little real grief or pathos in the Last Days of Adam, it is merely impersonally solemn. Even of the admirable fresco which represents Constantine in the uneasy dream in which he saw the vision of the cross, there is no warmth, no unexpected or emotional quality. So it is throughout the series; in the Queen of Sheba visiting Solomon, even in the splendid battlepiece, the Victory over Maxentius, Figure 111, the obvious sentiment of the theme is ignored, the figures have a kind of splendid unrelated existence that requires no apology or explanation. It is an effect that recalls the best archaic Greek sculpture.

Taken all in all, Piero is a formidable and enigmatic figure, an exception in a eager and emotional age. His truth to his vision is what counts. One feels it in the portrait of the humanist sovereign and captain of Urbino, Federigo da Montefeltro. It was painted about 1472 and is in the Uffizi, Figure 112. How sternly honest it is, and what a presentation of a powerful and beneficent personality. Even the little decorative picture on the back of the panel, a Triumph of Fame, has an effect beyond its scale and obvious intention. It suggests wide dominions and heavy responsibilities manfully met.

Piero della Francesca lived out his life mostly in Umbria and far from the artistic centre of things. There is a self-sufficing quality in this voluntary isolation. He lived on to great old age, dying in 1492, and unless his declining years were perturbed by the faintly rising star of Leonardo da Vinci, he might boast himself, in the words of his and Leonardo's friend, Fra Luca Pacioli, "the monarch of his times in the science of painting."

We must leave for the Umbrian chapter such sturdy continuers of Piero della Francesca's experimentalism as Melozzo da Forlì and Luca Signorelli. What is more important to note in leaving him is that such triumphs as his in fresco painting were highly exceptional in the second half of the fifteenth century. The successes of the period are in the minor art of panel painting. The fantasies of Botticelli, the best portraits of Ghirlandaio, the early panels of Perugino and Signorelli and Leonardo da Vinci — these are the outstanding things. In mural painting Florence actually retrograded, not merely as compared with the days of Masaccio, Fra Filippo and Fra Angelico, but even as compared with the earlier days of Andrea Bonaiuti, Agnolo Gaddi and Spinello Aretino. The fact has been obscured by the superficial gain in small realism, in sprightliness, and mere prettiness, but in all the serious qualities of monumental design the decadence is unmistakable. The favorite decorators simply executed on a large scale the sort of compositions that would have been charming on the front of a bridechest. In the general enthusiasm for the parts of pictures the sense of pictures as a whole seemed in danger of being lost.

Fig. 112.   Piero della Francesca. Guidobaldo da Montefeltro, despot of Urbino. — *Uffizi.*

The undiscriminating enthusiasm for the primitive painting of the Early Renaissance which has ruled for two generations has so clouded critical opinion on this point, that I must be at some pains to make my case good.

Perhaps I can do no better than to review some of the frescoes which Pope Sixtus IV ordered about 1481 for the new chapel of the Vatican Palace.[5] He summoned to the Sistine Chapel the best available artists from both Tuscany and Umbria. By the measure of their success we may estimate the mural painting of the time.

Originally the decorative scheme, later amplified by Michelangelo, required sixteen scriptural stories, in which the deeds of Moses were parallelled by those of Christ. The two first and two last subjects, on the end walls, have been destroyed,

but we still see the twelve on the side walls. In general they
all show the old Gothic coloring, are mostly vivacious in a
confused and over-rich way, and lack unity of pattern and
dramatic coherence.

FIG. 113.   Assistant of Perugino.   Baptism.   Fresco. — *Sistine Chapel.*

One of the most admired is the Baptism of Christ, Figure
113, by Pintorricchio, (or, as Venturi suggests, Andrea of
Assisi) who here works as Perugino's assistant.   The story
is told in the centre and reinforced by a spacious landscape
which is confusingly full of attractive features.   The theme
is mechanically stretched to fill the space by adding at both
flanks groups which have slight or no connection with the subject.   These groups are interestingly diversified with fine
portraits of the Pope's relatives, the Roveres, and by the
alert forms of children.   The effect is fairly restful and idyllic,
but the pattern is mechanical, and the emotional effect of the
real theme is frittered away in the accessories.   The method
of enlarging a stock composition by adding portrait groups
is standard for the Sistine Chapel and for the period.   Masaccio

had tried it more effectively in the Miracle of the Boy, and Filippo Lippi had made it seem almost organic in The Funeral of St. Stephen. Pintorricchio, if it be he, is more superfi-

FIG. 114. Botticelli. Moses in the Land of Midian. Fresco. — *Sistine Chapel, Rome.*

cially alluring for his richness and variety, but really stands on a far lower plane of design than his predecessors.

If this mechanical symmetry is the standard method, there are significant exceptions in the Sistine Chapel. The more sensitive spirits, Botticelli and Luca Signorelli, reject so trite a solution. Botticelli's Moses in Midian, Figure 114, offers a delicate evasion, by promoting a minor motive to be the central theme. All the incidents that are dramatically important — the slaying of the Egyptian taskmaster, and the adoration of the Burning Bush from which Jehovah spoke — are done with the most energetic feeling, but are relegated to the background and edges of the composition. The picture is really the fine grove in which Moses gallantly helps the nymph-like daughters of Jethro to draw water. A fantastic idyl is foisted off on us as a substitute for one of the decisive moments in the Providential order. Botticelli is so winning in his evasion, that it seems almost unfeeling to note that no Gothic painter would have done anything so

FIG. 115. Signorelli, Design only. Last Days of Moses. Fresco. —
Sistine Chapel, Rome.

shifty. His success is not merely at the expense of the expression of his real theme, but also at the expense of the order and dignity proper to mural design. Having ordered a canto of an epic, the Pope received a delicious madrigal. His contentment is characteristic of the æsthetic casualness of the times.

Signorelli, in the Last Days of Moses, Figure 115, makes a similar but less egregious evasion. His centre of interest is the nude youth in the foreground, but he does give a certain prominence to the scenes where Moses invests Joshua with authority, and where both view the Promised Land from Mount Horeb. Though without much emotional accent, the crowds are agreeably disposed and diversified by graceful forms of women and children. Only the design is by Signorelli, the execution being by an assistant, Don Bartolommeo della Gatta. The picture is more delightful for such passages as the Apollo-like nude youth and the mother with her children in the right foreground than it is as a whole, though it is full of idyllic charm, and inadequate only when one considers the gravity of its theme.

In his Calling of Peter and Andrew, Figure 116, to be fishers

FIG. 116. Ghirlandaio. Christ calling Peter and Andrew. Fresco. — *Sistine Chapel, Rome.*

of men, Domenico Ghirlandaio makes a skilful and impressive use of that approved mechanical symmetry which has already been noticed in Pintorricchio's Baptism. Everything is well centralized, the river view is a welcome outlet, the stereotyped bystanders on the flanks at least are telling portraits and, while not bound into the central motive, have withal a gravity that sufficiently accords with it. The arrangement is lucid, and the surplus accessories fairly well subordinated. A rather perfunctory quality in the central scene of homage and dedication reveals Ghirlandaio's scanty imagination. His impressiveness has a certain dullness about it.

Few words need be spent on the picturesque and irresponsible confusion which reigns in Cosimo Rosselli's Destruction of Pharaoh's Army in the Red Sea, Figure 117. Cosimo was one of the older painters in the chapel, forty-two years old.

FIG. 117.   Cosimo Rosselli.   Destruction of Pharaoh's Army.   Fresco. — *Sistine Chapel.*

Yet a juvenile sensationalism and uncalculated restlessness prevail, and his attempts at vivacity and grace are as unhappy as his striving for effects of terror. It may well be that his eccentric young pupil, Piero di Cosimo, gave this fresco its febrile energy and its theatrical landscape. Certain it is that the three other frescoes by Cosimo are unmitigatedly dull. Oddly it was he alone who won the praise of Pope Sixtus, mostly for his profuse introduction of gold ornament.

We have seen in the Sistine Chapel a mechanical and rather perfunctory symmetry, various clever evasions of an idyllic sort, and a picturesque disorder side by side. The most ambitious decorative scheme of the time seems to result in a kind of artistic bankruptcy. But fortunately the Sistine Chapel contains its own self-criticism and remedy, in the extraordinary fresco by Pietro Perugino, Christ delivering the Keys to Peter, Figure 118. Perugino is an Umbrian from Città della Pieve, thirty-five years old, and with a certain amount of Florentine training. He has, like Masaccio sixty

FIG. 118. Perugino. Christ giving the Keys to Peter. Fresco. — *Sistine Chapel, Rome.*

years before, looked at the art of his times and found it wanting. He has had the lucidity to see that the malady is surplusage and disorder. Hence, he argues, the remedy is simplicity and order. To this he adds a sense of vastness. In this picture the temple platform, a vastness made by man, is set within the vastness of a river valley made by nature. The foreground group is arranged in a formal half military order which is cunningly made easy and flexible by differences of posture and gesture. Every tilted head and pointed foot has its reason. Without undue insistence, all the apostles are interested in the rite which ordains their chief. Here is no casual pleasure ground in which you may delightfully look about, here is a definite vision of a momentous act which you must see swiftly, completely, and precisely as the artist intends you shall see. It is the only well-considered design among these frescoes. It points the simplest and surest way by which the exuberance of the Early Renaissance might be disciplined into a noble order, and within twenty years the lesson was to be reread for all Italy by young Raphael of Urbino. Meanwhile the somewhat irresponsible exuberance of the new narrative painting has after all its winning aspect, is a sign of an energy and enthusiasm that need not so much to be tamed as to be intellectualized.

In discussing the last twenty years of the fifteenth century in Florence I am embarrassed by the richness of the field. Beside such typical figures as Botticelli and Ghirlandaio, we have to do with such sensitive and morbid spirits as Filippino Lippo and Piero di Cosimo; with Andrea Verrocchio and a group of imitators of his fastidious manner, notable among them young Leonardo da Vinci; with a host of secondary painters, particularly of furniture panels, and small altar-pieces, while if we consider rather artistic training than accident of birth, we must reckon with the Florentine achievement the rugged triumphs of Luca Signorelli. But since the more distinctive and progressive of these artists are really precursors of the Golden Age, or symptomatic of the unrest that was its prelude, they may best be treated later. That will leave us only the painters who are fully representative of the festal moment of Lorenzo the Magnificent's greatness — the furniture painters and Ghirlandaio.

Those excesses of vivacity, those extravagances of invention, those juvenile graces which were a weakness in mural painting, were admirably in place in the decoration of chests and wainscots. The greater artists gladly accepted this little work, and some painters painted exclusively trousseau chests (*cassoni*) for young brides — an enviable occupation, for surely these fair young creatures had to be personally consulted. The subjects glorify love, magnify valor, celebrate the festal life of the day, its pageants, feasts, and dances. Of professional *cassone* painters Francesco Pesellino[6] (1422-1457) is the most famous. He is bewitching in variety and sensitiveness of invention, in refinement of story telling, and in glamour of color. Two admirable *cassone* fronts by

Fig. 119. Francesco Pesellino. Cassone Front. Triumphs of Love, Chastity, and Death. — *Mrs. John L. Gardner, Boston.*

him are owned by Mrs. John L. Gardner, Figure 119. They represent the six triumphs described by Petrarch in so many *Canzoni*. Love, Chastity, Death, Time, Fame, and Eternity are figured forth much as these themes were embodied in contemporary pageants, about the year 1450. The subjects were favorites for *cassoni* less because of their grave moral import than because Petrarch was Love's accredited Poet Laureate.

We have in the New York Historical Society the superb salver, Figure 119a, which was prepared against the birth of Lorenzo de' Medici. Appropriately it shows knights acclaiming fame. The date is 1448, the painter of the school of Domenico Veneziano.

We often see the Queen of Sheba reverently approaching Solomon. It is the admonition that a young bride should seek wisdom. Battles and Roman triumphs are tediously common. They set a mark of valor for the bridegroom. Wedding Feasts are almost tautological on a bride-chest, but they afford charming pictures of the Florence that amused itself.

Mythology often dignifies these painted stories, the refer-

ence being generally to that beauty which is institutional
in brides. Thus we have in a *spalliera* panel in the Fogg
Museum the Judgment of Paris, with the competing goddesses more modestly clothed than Ovid's record justifies.

Fig. 119a.   Follower of Domenico Veneziano, perhaps Baldovinetti.
Triumph of Fame.   Birth Salver for Lorenzo de' Medici. — *N. Y.
Historical Society*.

The work is possibly an exceptionally amiable product of
Cosimo Rosselli, and the date may be about 1475. The Rape of
Helen, which was of course due to her fatal beauty, is a common
if unedifying subject for bride-chests. So is Actaeon torn by
the hounds of the Divine Huntress for his temerity in surprising Diana at her bath. A delightful panel in the possession of Mr. Martin Ryerson at Chicago recounts in many

episodes the adventures of Ulysses from his escape from Polyphemus to his home-coming at Ithaca. The dalliances of the much-experienced wanderer are by no means concealed, but at least the scene opens with prominent display of the episode most creditable to him as a married man, the baffling of the Sirens, and closes with the exemplary figure of constant Penelope weaving her interminable web.

FIG. 120. Bartolommeo di Giovanni under Botticelli's direction. Nastagio degli Onesti's Feast. Spalliera panel. — *Spiridon Coll., Paris.*

In furniture painting we are generally in the realm of comedy. But we touch pathos in Boccaccio's story of patient Griselda, at Bergamo, Modena, and elsewhere; while we approach tragedy in the many versions of chaste Susanna assailed and traduced by the elders, and attain to notable melodrama in Boccaccio's grim vision of the spirit lover eternally harrying the miserable ghost of his merciless lady through the pine-wood of Ravenna. The best of these panels is in the Spiridon Collection, Paris. The ghostly scene of the chase takes place before the picnic party, Figure 120, artfully arranged by Nastagio degli Onesti to prove to his unfeeling lady that there is a penalty in the next world for being too cruel to a lover in this. The lesson Boccaccio tells us was effective, and they lived happily together ever afterwards. The panel was designed by Botticelli and painted by his assistant, Bartolommeo di Giovanni, for the wedding of a Bini groom and a Pucci bride in the year 1487.

With it we take leave of Florentine furniture painting, an art too unpretentious to be considered at length in a general survey, yet too charming in itself and too representative of the heyday of Florentine wealth and gayety to be wholly neglected.

Sandro Botticelli and Domenico Ghirlandaio mark in very different fashions the culmination and the close of the Early Renaissance in Florence. Botticelli is the poet of its nostalgia. He expresses not its joyous average, but the erotic and mystical subtilities of Lorenzo de' Medici's Platonic Academy, and later the Apocalyptic hopes and despairs that gathered around Savonarola. He utters a discontent and ideality which in part are completely contained in his work and in part were only fulfilled in the rapidly approaching Golden Age. He is aristocratic and individual, hence we shall consider him in connection with his fellow *intellectuel*, Leonardo da Vinci. Domenico Ghirlandaio,[7] on the contrary, is the most completely contented creature, imaginable. He never even dreamt of anything desirable beyond his Florence. He loved the local spectacle too dearly to represent it literally. He generally prettified it, more rarely he glorified it. Its mundane ideals were his. Towards its people, its young men and maidens and grave merchants and magistrates he brought, without Fra Filippo Lippi's sensitiveness, an equal curiosity and admiration. And Florence fairly deserved the adoration of such a man as was he. Wisely and generously ruled by Lorenzo de' Medici, who exemplified not merely the practical virtues of the city but also her more engaging vices, author of wise policy and of wittily dissolute songs; combining the self-respecting appearances of liberty with the advantages of benevolent despotism, abounding in new wealth, lavish in pleasure and spectacle, unrestrained by a religion which was becoming merely a social decency and a form of fire-insurance against a not impossible hell — Florence had reached a pitch of complacency and worldly well-being the like of which the world has perhaps never seen before or since. The menacing sword of the spirit was already swaying over it in the eloquence of a young Dominican monk at Ferrara. But Florence trod the primrose path unconscious of the doom at hand for her. And Ghirlandaio was present to immortalize everything that was pleasant in her short prime.

FIG. 121. Domenico Ghirlandaio. St. Jerome. Fresco.—*Ognissanti.*

He was born in 1449, his father appropriately being a garland-maker for gay Florence. He was trained under Alesso Baldovinetti, but prudently declined to compromise his own bright coloring with the new technic of oil painting. He studied with profit the ornate narratives of Benozzo Gozzoli. One of his earliest frescoes, painted about 1470 in Ognissanti, already reveals the grounds of his later popularity. The vivid portraits of the Vespucci family so crowd about a Madonna of Pity as to make her seem quite secondary.

Somewhat later he painted the legend of Santa Fina at San Gimignano. Here Gozzoli's simpler vein is imitated, and the effect has a rusticity befitting the theme. Soon the *bottega* at Florence flourished mightily. There were two younger brothers to help, and all commissions were executed with businesslike dispatch. About 1480 we find him once more painting for the Church of Ognissanti. His St. Jerome there, Figure 121, is a beautifully groomed old prelate in a wonderfully kept study. The Saint is caught in an

FIG. 122. Ghirlandaio. The Last Supper. Fresco. — *Refectory, Ognissanti.*

interval of work, searching perhaps for the right Latin word to render the Hebrew text before him. He is grave and not too stern. The colors are vivid without much regard for harmony. Very little of the fire of the missionary who declined to subject the mysteries of God to the rules of the grammarian Donatus is suggested. One has only to look at Botticelli's St. Augustine, opposite in the church, agonized by the burden of thought, to realize that Ghirlandaio has cared nothing for the psychology of his theme, but has given us any comfortable old Florentine scholar placidly occupied in his *scriptorium.*

A similar lack of emotional content mars the otherwise delightful Last Supper, Figure 122, which was painted that same year for the refectory of Ognissanti. Pathos, not to say tragedy, is carefully kept out of the most solemn of scenes. The eye is likely to go first to the tree-tops and flying birds seen above the screen, then it becomes vaguely aware of a gentle company quietly feasting. Except for a faint trace of classicism in the costumes, it could be any governing board of any religious confraternity of the day, decorously enjoying its annual dinner. The qualities and defects of Ghirlandaio are fully apparent in this fresco — his lucidity and sweetness, his emotional nullity.

The next year, 1481, Ghirlandaio painted in the Sistine Chapel at Rome Christ Calling Peter and Andrew. We have already considered this his nearest approach to monumental design. Shortly before the Roman trip he married, and when his wife Costanza died, after a decent interval, he repeated the adventure. The two wedlocks were blessed by nine children of whom one, Ridolfo, was to become in turn a notable painter. Such fecundity was worthy of the man who once sighed for a commission to fresco the seven-mile circuit of the walls of Florence. On his return from Rome Ghirlandaio decorated the great hall of the Palace of the Priors, and from now on merely a list of his commissions and patrons would be a blue book of the old aristocracy and new wealth of Florence.

Thus in 1485 he contracted with Francesco Sassetti to do a chapel in the Trinità with Stories of St. Francis. Sassetti was confidential treasurer for Lorenzo the Magnificent, about the most important financial position in the world at the moment; a selfmade and ambitious man. He had tried in vain to get a finer chapel in a bigger church, but the patrician vested interests prevented. Still the chapel to the right of the Choir of the Trinità was no mean place, this Vallombrosan foundation being one of the oldest in Florence. Ghirlandaio took special pains with the frescoes, studying with intelligence Giotto's famous versions of the stories at Santa Croce. He is most nearly monumental where he follows Giotto, as in the Death of St. Francis, but he also shows surprising felicities of his own. The scene where Pope Honorius III constitutes St. Francis and his fellows a monastic order, is remarkable for not only fine incidental portraiture, but for a nobility of space-composition faintly anticipating Raphael. One scarcely realizes the subject as such. All the

Fig. 123. Domenico Ghirlandaio. Miracle of the Spini Boy. Fresco.—
Trinità.

dramatic features with which Giotto emphasized the eager-ness of the saint, the humility of his companions, the profes-sional dignity of the Pope and the half-veiled hostility of the papal court are absent. One's eyes go over the group to the familiar grandiose prospect of the Piazza della Signoria at Florence, and one feels that never till now has he rightly ap-prehended its amplitude and splendor. Then there are sharp pleasant surprises. At the left is the ugly and fascinating figure of Lorenzo de' Medici and behind him the gross apparition of Francesco Sassetti himself. And in front there are people coming up from a lower level, only their heads and shoulders emerging. The swarthy man who leads is Angelo Poliziano, greatest of humanistic poets, tutor of Lorenzo's sons. And the boys are these gifted children destined to be popes, and granddukes. The combination of great spacious-ness and centrality with casual unexpected graces is so piquant and original, that I suppose Ghirlandaio may have hit upon it almost accidentally, owing to the inevitable relations of his Gothic lunette to the architectural forms in the fresco. In any case Ghirlandaio never again did anything as impressive.

It is his greatest hymn of praise to the Florence that he so dearly loved.

In the same chapel is a remarkable picture representing the Piazza of the Trinità with St. Francis resuscitating a boy of the Spini family. Figure 123. It has extraordinary bits of invention, but lacks the organization of the fresco just discussed. The altar-piece for the chapel, an Adoration of the Shepherds, now in the Uffizi, represents the graciousness of Ghirlandaio in

FIG. 124. Domenico Ghirlandaio. Adoration of the Magi. — *Innocenti.*

familiar narrative his willing acceptance of the panoramic richness of the age, and his exceptional power of portraiture in these rustics painted from himself and from members of the Sassetti family. The ruggedness of the characterization suggests Flemish painting. Ghirlandaio may well have been influenced by the great Nativity with Portraits which Hugo van der Goes sent down from Ghent, in 1476, to the Hospital Church of Santa Maria Nuova.

Ghirlandaio's altar-pieces are many. They are brilliant without real harmony of color; pretty, without much insight, in the types of the Virgin and youthful saints. The most elaborate of these panels, An Adoration of the Magi, Figure 124, was finished in 1488 for the Foundling Hospital dedicated to the Massacred Innocents of Bethlehem. It still stands on its original altar in the chapel of the Innocenti, and is a radiant thing. The crowded group of adorers in the foreground is well knit together. Ghirlandaio had taken a shrewd look at Botticelli's Epiphany (now at Petrograd), or at Leonardo da Vinci's unfinished masterpiece. By a touching and appropriate invention, Ghirlandaio has set two of the martyred Innocents kneeling in white robes and crowned with a saint's nimbus among the Wise Men. There are, as usual, many portraits, including Ghirlandaio's own, by the pillar at the right. The deep river valley, suggested by northern paintings or engravings, relieves the somewhat congested character of the figure arrangement. The girlish Madonna would do no discredit to the front cover of a nation-wide periodical today. So gracious and ingenious is this picture that one regrets to note that it is rather cleverly staged than deeply felt, its manifold prettiness and picturesqueness, of a quite obvious character.

As Ghirlandaio had moved from success to success, so he was destined to end in his day of highest glory. In 1485 he signed a contract with Giovanni Tornabuoni, of the old nobility, to decorate the choir of the most aristocratic church in Florence, Santa Maria Novella. The subjects, the Life of the Virgin and St. John the Baptist, were already on the wall in the guise of water-soaked and ruined frescoes by Andrea Orcagna. Ghirlandaio provided pastoral scenes with wide landscapes, city prospects with charming girls plentiful in foreground, rich patrician interiors with graceful women and their attendants making visits of ceremony, rare religious events with heavy magistrates and dignitaries standing inattentively by — everything in short that a prosperous and well-bred Florentine of the moment was accustomed to think desirable in beauty, gentleness, or worldly estate. Characteristic are the Salutation of Mary and Elizabeth, a picture in which the solemnity of the scene, so magnificently asserted by Giotto at Padua, slips away into mere spectacle and civility; the Birth of Saint John, Figure 125, with a young girl of the Tornabuoni family making her visit with her maids, and all manner of graceful and rich accessories; or again, the Presentation in The Temple, with a whole tribe of Torna-buonis and Ghirlandaios in negligent attendance on the sacred rite. These may stand for the whole. For their casual and

FIG. 125. Domenico Ghirlandaio. Birth of St. John. — *Santa Maria Novella.*

mundane richness John Ruskin has poured upon these fres-coes his double-distilled vials of wrath. What he says as to their superficiality and emptiness of religious feeling is true enough, yet his denunciatory rhetoric serves but as a trip-hammer to demolish an eggshell which has after all its iri-descent frail beauty. Gentler methods are better with so gently mundane a creature as Ghirlandaio. The Lord's people, as he saw them about him, were good enough for him and for his art. Criticism should rather insist that, being worldly, he was not worldly enough to be strong and lucid, but too readily had recourse to promiscuous richness and per-functory ideals of prettiness. Still, it does not befit the age or race whose characteristic art product is the smiling or pensive girl on the cover of the popular magazine to throw the first stone at Domenico Ghirlandaio.

FIG. 126. Domenico Ghirlandaio. Old Man and Boy. — *Paris.*

Whatever the verdict as to his nominally religious painting, in portraiture Ghirlandaio is one of the greatest figures of his time. Portraits of the finest qualities abound in his frescoes, and he has left a few incomparable things on panel. Few Renaissance portraits have the authority of the amazing old man, Figure 126, in the Louvre, who fondles an adoring boy. In this picture, deformity becomes a grace, and the spiritual and material interpretation are of equal incisiveness and beauty. As fine in another vein is the profile of Giovanna degli Albizzi in the J. P. Morgan Collection, Figure 101. It is dated in 1488. It is the supreme portrait of a Florentine beauty of a passing and lovely moment. An instant of time, when the old simplicity had enriched itself with new learning; when with the new humanism the tournament and court of love persisted; when courtly manners had become an ideal without freezing into an official code — all this is for a sensitive and informed observer in this placid well-poised head of an ill-starred Florentine bride. She died in 1488, a little before the overthrow of the Florence she typifies. Her accomplished young husband, Lorenzo Tornabuoni, equally adequate in the tilt yard, the study, or the council hall, lived on for nine years and shared the death agony of the society of which he was a chief ornament. When his head fell under Savonarola's orders, a splendid chapter of early Florentine humanism closed. Thus these young people died with their Florence, leaving no descendants, but a memory eternally fragrant.

The year of Giovanna's death, 1488, Ghirlandaio, being thirty-nine years old, took a new wife, and continued diligently at the frescoes of Santa Maria Novella. Not being overburdened with imagination, he probably never guessed he was occupied with a memorial of a society already doomed. Doubtless he followed the fashionable throng to San Marco where for a year Fra Girolamo Savonarola had been preaching against the current vanities. Ghirlandaio presumably approved the oratory, with a comfortable sense that while unworldliness might very properly be preached, no sensible city could ever be induced to practice it. Perhaps he never woke up to the appalling fact that Savonarola literally meant business both evangelically and politically.

So Ghirlandaio's Florence moved swiftly to its doom, and the while he saved much of its look and grace on the walls of his choir. For a year a touchy and ugly little boy who carried the disproportionately great name of Michelangelo Buonarotti scrambled discontentedly about the scaffolding of the choir, lending a hand here and there, and learning the old art of fresco painting. Ghirlandaio of course never knew that in the restless apprentice he was training a titan. He probably thought him a nuisance. By the end of 1493 the frescoes of the Virgin and St. John the patron of Florence were nearly finished, and the altar-piece, an Assumption, was already planned. At forty-four Ghirlandaio had at once reached his climax and painted himself down an anachronism. Of course he didn't know it; such self-knowledge is mercifully spared us. The luck of Ghirlandaio was extraordinarily constant. Nowhere is it more signally shown than in the date of his death. Some inkling that things were going ill under Piero de' Medici's fitful rule must have come to him, but he died in January 1494, a good ten months before the Medici were expelled, their palaces sacked, and Savonarola in charge of a Florence terrified into sobriety.

To those painters from Fra Filippo to Ghirlandaio who caught the look and unpretentious poetry of Medicean Florence we owe an especial gratitude. They are not in the direct line of progress and they none of them reached the heights of art. But for centuries they have never failed to give delightful information, while infallibly touching average human sympathies. We do ill to idolize them, for they were after all rather small men, but we do well also to honor them according to their accomplishment. They did their particular task of enlivening decoration with illustrative episodes, with tact, refinement and knowledge; with all the sympathy of the modestly observant eye. Most of their work had to be undone before the Grand Style was possible, but it all evinces the vitality and variety without which as preliminary training the Grand Style itself could hardly have attained. its elaborate and strictly ordered composure. We do well to take Vasari's general view of these artists of the human spectacle — not considering them so much as weak links in a mighty chain, but as complete in themselves, as a youth may be complete even though the young man dies in the glory of his unfolding. Why expect prematurely the sedate splendors of middle age? Take then this art for what it offers — an unsystematic fairy land which is yet half real, and keep your higher standards in reserve for artists who better deserve them. For austere standards are held by a truly civilized person for purposes of discriminate praise and not as a ready means of promiscuous blame.

ILLUSTRATIONS FOR CHAPTER IV

PAGEANTRY IN OLD FLORENCE

The art of Gozzoli and the *cassone* painters, and, in part, that of Filippo Lippi and Ghirlandaio implies the background of public pageantry at Florence. There is a precious piece of old doggerel which describes the festivities, in May 1459, for the reception of Pope Pius II and Gian Galeazzo Sforza, Duke of Milan. The palaces and churches were completely hung with rich stuffs, the sumptuary laws were suspended in favor of the fair sex; besides many processions and feasts, there was bear baiting in the Piazza della Signoria, an all night open air ball in the Mercato Nuovo, and a tournament in the Piazza di Santa Croce. I paraphrase the verses which describes the pageant of a Triumph of Love which was conducted by ten year old Lorenzo de' Medici. The subject is common in *cassoni* and *deschi da parto*. The boy Lorenzo mounted on a marvellously caparisoned horse headed the pageant, and while all the people whispered their admiration —

"As prudent and wise lad he conducted the Triumph of the God of Love . . . In all triumph he made Cupid come, who so gently smites the gentle heart. Upon a car I saw him, and so I tell, most marvellously adorned and wrought, how it was made I dare not say. On four wheels it was finely adorned with a raised stand and fixed on every corner thereof as a column the form and fashion of an angel. And I who saw it thought of a castle. Upon the four columns was a great ball and above it another ornamented piece. This was gilded everywhere . . . so that it sparkled like the sun. I cannot tell of such beauties, but I can tell about the top part which was most delightful. Above all . . . I saw stand a youth, with two great wings of many colors on his shoulders and all the rest nude, holding that bow with which he wounds all hearts, and playfully puts venom therein, so that while burning within, nothing shows without. This Triumph so marvellous and so invested with colors, its adornment very glorious — with so many pearls, carbuncles and sapphires — I couldn't reckon how many florins that Triumph was worth I say."

The whole poem is a real treasure of such lore and should be translated. It is found in the new edition of Muratori, *Rerum Italicarum Scriptores*, Tom. XXVII. The quotation is from page 31, lines 1330-1363.

The Procession of the Magi

On St. John's Day, 1354, Matteo Palmieri tells us in his *Annals*, there were many religious representations of which the most interesting to us, as a probable inspirer of Gozzoli's frescoes, is that of the Three Kings from the East. There was —

"A magnificent and triumphant temple for the habitation [stage setting] of the Magi, in which was inclosed an octagonal temple adorned with the seven Virtues, and on the east side the Virgin with the New Born Christ. [Probably figures in a tableau vivant]

"The three Magi with a cavalcade of more than 200 horse adorned with many splendors came to make offerings to the New Born Christ."

New ed. of Muratori, Tom. XXII, p. 173.

Probably all the artists mentioned in this chapter saw these two splendid pageants and many more. Such sights count for much in the alert and profusely ornamented painting of the fifteenth century.

Pageants in 1466

Piero de' Medici "in order to give men something to think about which should take their thoughts from the state, and a year having passed since Cosimo had died, seized the occasion to enliven the city and ordered two elaborate celebrations, following the others that are customary in that city. One which represented, when the three Kings, the Magi, came from the East behind the star which showed the birth of Christ; the which was of such pomp and so magnificent, that in arranging and holding it the entire city was occupied for several months."

Machiavelli, *Istorie fiorentine*, Lib. VII, cap. xii.

"The other [festival, Machiavelli continues] was a tournament (for so they used to call a spectacle, which represented a cavalry skirmish) where the first youths of the city exercised themselves against the most famous knights of Italy; and among the young men of Florence the most in repute was Lorenzo, first-born son of Piero, who not by favor, but by his own valor carried off the first honours."

Lorenzo was then a likely lad of seventeen.

A Side-light on Ghirlandaio's Patrons

A Trick for getting a Family Chapel in 1488

The choir of Santa Maria Novella was under the patronage of the Ricci family, but they were poor and had been unable to repair the water-stained frescoes of Orcagna, which had been painted a century and a quarter earlier. So Giovanni Tornabuoni got permission to redecorate the chapel on condition of setting the Ricci arms "in the most conspicuous and honourable place in that chapel." And so the contract was drawn. Domenico Ghirlandaio actually set the Tornabuoni arms in huge scale on the side pilasters, whereas he painted the Ricci arms half a foot high on the door of the ciborium in the centre of the base of his altar-piece. The rest in Vasari's words (de Vere's translation, Vol. III, p. 224):

"And a fine jest it was at the opening of the chapel, for these Ricci looked for their arms with much ado, and finally, not being able to find them, went off to the Tribunal of Eight, contract in hand. Whereupon the Tornabuoni showed that these arms had been placed in the most conspicuous and honourable part of the work; and although the others exclaimed that they were invisible, they were told that they were in the wrong, and that they must be content, since the Tornabuoni had caused them to be placed in so honourable a position as the neighborhood of the most Holy Sacrament. And so it was decided by that tribunal that they should be left untouched, as they may be seen to-day. Now, if this should appear to anyone to be outside the scope of the Life that I have to write, let him not be vexed, for it all flowed naturally from the tip of my pen. And it should serve, if for nothing else, at least to show how easily poverty falls a prey to riches, and how riches, if accompanied by discretion, achieve without censure anything that a man desires."

DAWN OF THE GOLDEN AGE: BOTTICELLI AND LEONARDO DA VINCI

FIG. 127. Leonardo da Vinci. Cartoon of Madonna and St. Ann. — *Burlington House, London.*

CHAPTER V

DAWN OF THE GOLDEN AGE: BOTTICELLI AND LEONARDO DA VINCI

Leonardo da Vinci as assimilator of the Realistic reforms — Botticelli as reactionary — His beginnings under Fra Filippo and Pollaiuolo — Height of his realistic achievement in Adoration of the Magi — Assertion of his fantastic vein in the Primavera — The Dante drawings and the distraught style of the later works, its aesthetic value — Minor Eccentrics: Filippino Lippi — Piero di Cosimo — Leonardo da Vinci, his gradual advance towards Chiaroscuro method, his ideals — His work with Verrocchio — The Adoration of the Kings, its disciplined richness — Cartoon of St. Ann — First Madonna of the Rocks — Leonardo at Milan. The Last Supper — At Florence again. The Battle Cartoon. Mona Lisa — Second Sojourn at Milan. The St. Ann, his influence — At Rome, in France and the end — Leonardo's successors at Florence; Fra Bartolommeo — Andrea del Sarto — Agnolo Bronzino — Pontormo — Decline of Florentine independence and of the School.

The task before an ambitious young Florentine artist about 1475 was one of assimilation. Pretty much all the knowledge essential for the new painting existed, but in scattered shape. Masaccio had modernized Giotto's monumental patterns, and had found for himself the new structural values of light and shade. Domenico Veneziano had introduced the handier method of oil painting, and, with Piero della Francesca, had attempted novel refinements in paler tonalities. He and Paolo Uccello had worked out the mysteries of linear perspective. Andrea del Castagno had achieved a systematic and learned anatomy. Antonio Pollaiuolo had added to this an extraordinary knowledge of the human body in violent action. Andrea Verrocchio had demonstrated that these realistic strivings were compatible with grace. It had occurred to no one to combine all these discoveries until Leonardo da Vinci reached his early maturity. The synthesis worked out by him between 1480 and 1498, the dates of his unfinished Adoration of the Kings and Last Supper respectively, is the foundation on which Raphael built. Leonardo da Vinci is the pioneer of the Golden Age.

It will help us to realize the greatness of his accomplishment to study first the career of a contemporary and friend, the exquisite artist, Sandro Botticelli. Botticelli, like Leonardo, came under the spell of Verrocchio's fastidiousness, and went some distance in the direction of the new monumental beauty. Then abruptly he turned aside along solitary lines quite unprecedented, but akin to the mystic past of Siena. His great refusal of progress, his broken and eccentric career, give point to the humanistic centrality and social authority of Leonardo's painting. The two men represent opposite escapes from the superficial brilliance of the art dominated by Ghirlandaio. Leonardo moved out towards the future, and has lived on as a fine inspiration of academic painting ever since. Botticelli withdrew into himself, and has survived flickeringly in the occasional admiration of kindred spirits. Both express, if in very different fashion, the profound discontent that preluded a new era of art. It will help us to perceive how great Botticelli is in his solitary poetry, to consider two younger contemporaries, Filippino Lippi, his pupil, and Piero di Cosimo, an intelligent imitator of Leonardo, both of whom, sharing Botticelli's discontent, also sought escape in self-assertiveness of an eccentric sort. As the modern age begins to dawn, the modern temperamental artist appears. The *bottega* begins to be a studio. Thus Sandro Botticelli[1] has a double importance for us — as an exquisite artist, and even more as the first individualist who strained sorely at the bounds imposed by the collective taste, required a select public, and painted to please himself.

There is nothing of this romantic isolation in his origins. He was born a tanner's son, in 1444, and brought up in the smiling country towards Careggi. At thirteen he was still at school, hence was better educated than the average painter. Soon he was put with a goldsmith, very likely his brother Antonio, whose nickname — Il Botticello, the cask, paradoxically attached itself to the creator of the Primavera. Before his fifteenth year, 1459, young Botticelli was apprenticed to Fra Filippo Lippi, the most sensitive eye of the time. Young Botticelli presumably painted on the later frescoes at Prato, and I believe may have been permitted to design certain of the figures in The Feast of Herod. Two early pictures of the Adoration of the Kings, both in the National Gallery, London, show us how whole-heartedly Botticelli adopted his master's discursive style, how sedulously he sought variety and richness of gesture and facial expression. But these crowded compositions lack Fra Filippo's direct geniality. They are already imagined before they are observed. Fra Filippo went to Spoleto some time before 1468 and soon died there. So Botticelli was perhaps on his own resources from his twenty-fourth year, though he was not inscribed in the Company of St. Luke till 1472. What is certain is that he was fortifying himself by imitation of far more strenuous artists than his master. The delicate incisiveness of Verrocchio appears as an occasional inspiration, the rugged power of Antonio Pollaiuolo dominates his pictorial expression for many years.

A group of early pictures shows strikingly the interplay of realistic influences with the assertion of his own originality. The delicately expressive Madonna, Figure 128, in Mrs. John L. Gardner's collection, is based on Filippo Lippi's Madonna in the Uffizi, Figure 103. The general arrangement is the same. But what a change in feeling! All the overt picturesque relations which Fra Filippo loved — the girlish Virgin praying to her child, the chubby baby clutching at its mother, the impish angel grinning out of the picture — all that is

FIG. 128. Botticelli. Chigi Madonna.—*Mrs. John L. Gardner, Boston.*

FIG. 130.   Botticelli.   Judith. — *Uffizi.*

eliminated. The Virgin wistfully reaches for the ear of wheat signifying her Son's body that must be broken. A well grown, reverent angel, enigmatically smiling, offers the grapes and wheat, symbols of the sacrament. The relation is between the Madonna and this mysterious acolyte. Their consciousness of a prophetic rite gains emphasis and pathos from the only unconscious thing in the picture, the graceful babyish action of the Divine Child. The forms of mother and Child are those of Filippo Lippi, but with elimination of superfluous ornament and commonplace action. The reserved, half-concealed smile of the angel and his strange beauty derive from Andrea Verrocchio. You may trace it from his youthful David to his disciple's Mona Lisa. The date of the picture is merely a good guess, but since it is free from the influence of Pollaiuolo, it may be before 1469.

In that year the brothers Pollaiuolo undertook the painting

of seven figures of the Virtues to decorate the wainscot behind
the magistrates' bench in the Mercanzia, the mercantile court.

Evidently they were pressed for
time, for they assigned one
panel representing Fortitude,
Figure 129, to Botticelli. John
Ruskin has celebrated in eloquent phrase this frail embodiment of the courage of the
mind. "Worn, somewhat, and
not a little weary; instead of
standing ready for all comers,
she is sitting — apparently in
revery; her fingers playing restlessly and idly — nay, I think,
even nervously about the hilt
of her sword.   For her battle is
not to begin today, nor did it
begin yesterday.   Many a morn
and even have passed since it
began, and now — is this to be
the ending of it?   And if this —
by what manner of end?"

FIG. 129.   Botticelli.   Fortitude.
— *Uffizi*.

The passage beautifully illustrates the odd blend of purest
insight and casual chatter in Ruskin's criticism.   Forget that
the sword is a mace — Ruskin is never right in such trifles.
Fortitude sits merely because her sister Virtues do so in the
imposed decorative scheme.   The nervous action of the hands is
chiefly an elegance.   Yet the whole characterization expresses
with singular felicity the alert and thoughtful charm of this
Fortitude amid the stolid effigies of Antonio and Piero Pollaiuolo.   Ruskin, as often, is most wrong where it least matters.
We have more prosaic business with the Fortitude — to note
the pouting snub-nosed type, and the elaborate ornaments,

which are Fra Filippo's, the solidly drawn but ill-shapen foot, which is Pollaiuolo's, and the sensitiveness, which is Botticelli's own.

A still more complete assimilation of Pollaiuolo's energetic mode is revealed in the admirable little Judith, Figure 130, which must have been painted towards 1475. The faces are still Fra Filippo's, and he could have invented the eager dog-like obsequiousness of the maid. But the springy action and the fine, lean ankles and feet, the bony, expressive wrists and hands, the minutely featured landscape, are completely in Pollaiuolo's vein. Botticelli's specific invention is the sublimation of the theme — Judith's sense of walking in a dream after the unspeakable ordeal of the night. And the flutter of the robes in the clean morning wind has a stylistic grace that amounts to Sandro's signature.

As he came into his thirty-fifth year, 1478, Botticelli painted two pictures so different that without conclusive evidence we should hardly believe them the work of a single mind and hand. The Adoration of the Kings, Figure 131, with the sturdy Medici portraits, sums up all Botticelli's realistic achievement, shows him the greatest and most typical Florentine master of the moment, and proves that his way was easy to such triumphs of popularity as Ghirlandaio was soon to enjoy uncontested. The other picture, The Allegory of Spring, evinces a strange and to many repellant originality, indulges dreams not of this earth, appeals to experiences inaccessible save to the æsthetically elect. It was an earnest of neglect and unpopularity, the opening of a solitary road that no artist would travel save under inner imperious impulsion.

The Adoration of the Kings is composed after the fashion of Fra Filippo and rendered with all the improvements of Pollaiuolo. The group of the Mother, Child and Joseph is set high and well back, the minutely drawn ruin, with its grace of wall-flowers, and the peacock on the ruined edge of the masonry are again pure Fra Filippo, as are the juvenile charm of Our Lady and the alertness of the Bambino. In Fra Filippo's best style, too, are the flanking groups of portraits which swing back towards the central motive, leaving the centre free.

FIG. 131.   Botticelli.   Adoration of the Magi. — *Uffizi.*

Here are great personnages set forth with dignity and force. Masaccio also has counted for much in these portraits, and Antonio Pollaiuolo for more. The Mage kneeling by the Child is Piero de' Medici, the one in front with his back turned is Cosimo. The beautiful young king addressing him is probably Giuliano, lately slain by the Pazzi conspirators. Lorenzo is unmistakable at the left with his proud military pose, his hands resting on a great sword. At the right, robed in yellow, is the fine manly figure of Botticelli himself. There are many other portraits of the most authoritative accent, but we have no means of identifying them.

Artistically this magnificent little picture suffers from two centres of interest. It is an ambiguity, however, that would have troubled no contemporary Florentine. He was willing

FIG. 132.   Botticelli.   Primavera — Allegory of Spring. — *Uffizi.*

to take the sacred group for granted and to gaze delightedly at the figures of his rulers and benefactors. In technical expression the picture is established through light, shade, and color, its linear quality counting for rather little in the effect. It is a logical and attractive combination of all the realistic experiments of fifty years past, no single feature being over-emphasized. It is prose of a most convincing and eloquent cadence.

Before turning to a picture which is all poetry, the Primavera, we may profitably consider Botticelli's portrait, the robust body, the moody sensual face. He was a celibate. One need not espouse the vagaries of a Freud to know that such men, when gifted with imagination, dream strange dreams. The Primavera, Figure 132, was painted for the Medici Villa of Castello, where later Botticelli placed his Birth of Venus and Signorelli his Pan as God of Music. All these pictures represent that sudden homesickness for the idyllic scenes of classical antiquity which fell upon the Italian world about this time. The *cassone* painters, working for work-a-day people, had represented the mythologies as so many jolly stories. For the deeply cultured circle of the Medici, these retrospections were fraught with sadness. The life where the gods moved among alluring nymphs and amusing fauns seemed infinitely far off and infinitely desirable. Through Horace and Virgil and Theocritus one could glimpse it tantalizingly. Modern poets, like Angelo Poliziano, could recover it faintly in Greek and Latin, or more rarely in Italian verse. But the Italian loves to see, and here was the difficulty. The brown soil had not yet yielded up the great store of old marbles. The actual look of the by-gone Golden Age, which within half a century was to become matter of archaeological certainty, was now matter of hesitant intuition. One could brood over the old poets, arrange masques in which lightly robed Tuscan girls played the nymph or goddess — whatever expedient was used to live oneself back, the visual ingredients of the dream were inevitably local and Tuscan. Such pictures as the Primavera represent this transient and appealing mood. They tremble with unfulfilled aspirations, breathe exquisite nostalgias, perpetuate as no other records do the very soul of the humanists that surrounded Lorenzo the Magnificent.

For the fundamental decorative arrangement of the picture, white forms swaying before a vertical paling, Botticelli skilfully borrowed the motive of Pollaiuolo's engraving, the Ten Nudes. Figure 109. From Pollaiuolo, too, come the nervous contours, the wiry ankles, and slender feet, and the curiously sprung knees. The old poets Lucretius and Horace give just the hint for the persons of the idyl. Lucretius tells of the coming of Spring blown in by the West wind, of Flora strewing flowers before, Figure 133, with Venus and her son as witnesses.   And Horace tells how the three graces with ungirt robes dance before Mercury.   But Botticelli has contrib-

Fig. 133.   Botticelli.   Primavera.   Detail.   Venus, Flora, Spring, Zephyr. — *Uffizi.*

uted what gives the work its penetrating, sad charm.   His is the gloomy screen of orange trees and olives, the carpet of spring flowers, the billowing lines that sweep across the panel.   It is conceived in two great rhythms of motion.   The wave that

is suave in playful Spring becomes crisp and sharp in the robe
of Flora, and is nearly arrested in the heavy drapery of Venus,
it passes with her raised hand to the shimmering veil of the dancing Graces, and dies in the firmly set form of Mercury, whose
uplifted arm carries the movement into the steady background,
which stabilizes it all. Even to mention the particular finesses
and beauties of this fantastically lovely scene would require
an essay. I have made a fuller if very imperfect analysis in
my book, "Estimates in Art." Now it is best to note merely
that the only joyous forms are Zephyrus, Spring and Cupid,
the rest are sad or enigmatically grave, as is Flora. Though
they celebrate the renewal of life through love in springtime,
those whose immortality has witnessed many springs carry in
their faces and bearing the old knowledge that life and love
are constantly reborn under death sentence, and that what
is renewed spring after spring has but

"The frail duration of a flower."

Again and again the poets have told this to unregarding man.
Nobody has made it visible save Botticelli.

I suppose only a score of people at the time knew how fine
the Primavera was, and a few hundred in the world to-day may
know it. The thing was hidden from the public, and Botticelli was painting himself into the most obscure sort of glory.
In his remaining thirty-two years, there are a few reversions
to his realistic vein, but his most characteristic works merely
carry on the recondite charm, the acute and personal rhythms
of the Primavera.

In 1480 was painted the Faust-like figure of St. Augustine.
Figure 134. One feels in the gnarled features and hand clutching the breast the burden of lifelong meditation on the terrible
mysteries of free will and God's eternal decrees. It is the effigy
of one who has agonized in thought, and is still seeking by
that Calvary of the mind a tense and hazardous peace.

The next year Botticelli went to Rome to take charge of the decoration of the Sistine Chapel. We have already considered his best fresco there, Moses in Midian. Figure 114.

Of the two others—the Temptation of Christ, and the Destruction of Korah—we need only add that they are immensely rich in details, effective as narratives, and as decorative arrangements surpassed on the Sistine walls only by Signorelli and Perugino.

There are rare moments of something like serenity in Botticelli's troubled career. One was when he painted the Pallas and the Centaur, and another when he designed the loveliest of his round panels, the Madonna with

FIG. 134.   Botticelli.   St. Augustine. Fresco. — *Ognissanti.*

Six Angels, in the Uffizi, Figure 135. Unlike the more famous and popular Magnificat, it is in immaculate preservation. The composition is subtler and less obvious, the worn and burdened look of the Madonna oppressed by her tragic fate, more specific and appealing. The late Herbert P. Horne, Botticelli's best biographer, sets the picture about 1487. About the same time were done those nuptial frescoes for Lorenzo Tornabuoni and his

FIG. 135.   Botticelli.   Madonna with six Angels. — *Uffizi.*

bride, Giovanna degli Albizzi. Torn from the villa walls at Careggi, they are now among the treasures of the Louvre.

Lorenzo is represented as received by the seven liberal arts, Giovanna as presented to Venus by the Graces. We have seen in the last chapter how these young people shared and illustrated the doom impending over Medicean Florence.

FIG. 136. Botticelli. Birth of Venus. — *Uffizi*.

Botticelli captures, if not their look, at least a fine symbol for their as yet unchallenged beauty and discretion.

A little earlier perhaps he added to the Primavera at Castello the Birth of Venus, Figure 136. It is conceived in the same bold rhythms, which this time converge on the slight, smooth form of Venus and are steadied by the horizon and the trees. Compared with the Primavera, the whole thing is less rich, varied and naturalistic. Everything is more schematic and conventional; gold is freely used without realistic pretext. The wistful mood is still that of the Primavera. Venus comes to earth with no joyous expectation. She glimpses unfulfilled desires, the eternally deferred goal of earthly love. She obeys a destiny with resignation and a pensive humility — almost asks pardon for the confusion she is fated to produce among mortals. These involutions and refinements have nothing

to do with the whole-souled sensuousness of classical antiquity, they have everything to do with that scrupulous balancing of divine and earthly love which was the standing problem
of the Neo-Platonists surrounding Lorenzo the Magnificent.

FIG. 137.   Botticelli.   Dante and Beatrice in Paradise. — *Print Room,
Berlin.*

During the '80s Botticelli was much occupied with the
illustration of a great manuscript of the "Divine Comedy."
Figure 137.   These outlines in silverpoint retouched with the
pen find their equals only in the best Far Eastern art.   The
line whips and dances and swirls across the parchment, halt-
ing and turning to define a detail, then speeding anew on its task
of suggesting motion.   Figures that float, groups that march or
dance as one, trailing smoke of incense — these volatile fea-

tures are rendered with the most energetic delicacy. And the most incredible episodes of Dante's poem gain credence with the eye through the deftest use of the pure line. It hardens to suggest bone and sinew, tightens to express joints that bear weight and preserve balance, loosens and gallops to give the flutter of drapery over twinkling limbs. And all this is done with a thin pen line that hardly changes thickness or blackness — done with a touch as light as a feather and yet as firm as the swing of a draughtsman's compass. The study of such drawings is a liberal education in the æsthetics of pure line.

These drawings freely distort the actual forms for the sake of greater expressiveness. Such distortion is the characteristic mark of Botticelli's latest style. One may note it in the furniture panels which tell the story of St. Zenobius and the tragic lot of the Roman heroines, Lucretia and Virginia; in the Annunciation of the Uffizi and the Last Communion of St. Jerome, in the Metropolitan Museum. The new manner is characterized by habitually vehement expression. Intensity becomes morbid, effective withal. We have to do with tortured but very fine nerves. What personal history is involved we can merely surmise. We know, however, that Botticelli followed eagerly the theocratic revolution of Savonarola and suffered deep chagrin when the attempt to make Florence a city of God collapsed amid sordid political jealousies. His art becomes that of a *Piagnone*, a Savonarolist, a contemner of the careless world. His method changes. The figures are unmodelled and flat, they hurtle wildly and glisten metallically before airless landscapes. Most of the hard-won Florentine realisms drop out, and the linear rhythms recall the Gothic poignancy of Simone Martini.

Perhaps the finest picture of this sort is the Calumny of Apelles, Figure 138, painted about 1490, and now in the Uffizi. It recreates after an anecdote of Lucian, made current by

Leonbattista Alberti, a lost masterpiece by Apelles, which was painted to convince Alexander the Great of the evil of calumny. An innocent prisoner is haled before an ignorant judge. Calumny bearing a torch drags him by the hair.

FIG. 138. Botticelli.   The Calumny of Apelles. — *Uffizi.*

Treachery and Deceit act as her tiring maids. The sordid figure of Envy is her guide to a judge into whose asses' ears Ignorance and Suspicion whisper their counsels. Naked Truth pleads in vain for the victim as Remorse turns to her with sullen helplessness. By a pictorial irony, the sinister whirling group is set in a stately court adorned with statues of magnanimous heroes of old, and one glimpses through the rich arches a cloudless sky and an untroubled sea. Very rich in imaginative content, ornate in its use of color and gold, sharp and definite in its rhythms, discreet in its expressive distortions, this is perhaps the masterpiece of Botticelli's late style.

But one regards with surely almost pleasure and with more

lively sympathy the little Nativity in the National Gallery, Figure 139, a celestial idyl in sentiment, and of greatest beauty of muted coloring. Above the shed where the Virgin Mother worships her Divine Child, a dancing ring of angels hovers. They hold olive branches from which depend martyrs' crowns. Wreathed shepherds, figures from some Theocritan idyl, kneel outside the shed. Below, angels eagerly embrace three youthful crowned figures, while impish baffled fiends lurk in crevices of the rocks. The three figures may well typify Savonarola and his two fellow-martyrs. A Greek inscription gives the date of 1500 and hints at the fall of Savonarola and the shame of the French invasion. There is a tenderness about the picture that recalls the Primavera, but it is more elusive and unearthly, more implicit in every bit of the workmanship itself than dependent on explicit symbolism.

What Botticelli could achieve in stark tragedy at this time is shown in the Pietà of the Munich gallery, a masterpiece which many critics have quite unaccountably ascribed to an inferior imitator. It is of tremendous effect. The compressing rocks seem to confine a grief too great to be liberated in space. A shudder concentrates itself upon the fair, youthful body of the dead Christ. One assists at a cosmic mourning, the intolerable tension of which is mercifully relieved in the swooning form of the Mother of Sorrows. The colors are sombre, the whole effect fairly sculptural, though mass is attained more by linear accents than by systematic light and shade. Balance and pose obey not a law of physics but one of feeling.

The picture may be one of Botticelli's latest. He lived on till 1510, a lonely and indulged eccentric. He witnessed the youthful triumphs of Raphael and Michelangelo at Florence, and saw the superb maturity of his friend Leonardo da Vinci. He saw the artistic world move away from himself towards ideals of gravity and decorum and disciplined monumentality.

FIG. 139. Botticelli. Mystical Nativity. — *London.*

He could have followed that high road himself. Instead he had sought a romantic self-expression leading to an *impasse*. At least he had made the *impasse* singularly thrilling. Being a wag as well as a poet, he had his compensations for neglect and doubtless he never regretted his impolitic choice. Among artists of febrile and romantic fibre he is one of the greatest. To know him thoroughly is an incomparable exercise in exquisite feeling.

Taken in its social aspect, Botticelli's later style is a protest against the current, superficial, narrative and decorative modes. Against prevailing successful commonplace, he opposes a highly refined idiosyncracy. While the more stolid artists of the end of the century were content to rework Ghirlandaio's glittering vein, the more sensitive spirits sought distinction in eccentricity. Eccentricity appears whenever an old style has gone stale and a new one is imminent. It is the natural expression of souls too independent to conform and too weak to reconstruct. The grotesque was in the air. Luigi Pulci in the "Morgante Maggiore" burlesques the ideal romances of chivalry, and mixes the old clear categories of good and evil. Lorenzo de' Medici at once mimics and caricatures the simplicity of the peasant pastorals. Cynicism runs riot in the short-story writers and in the new comedy. There is a confusion of standards, a new complexity of appreciation, that at once bewilders and allures delicate spirits. Thus they really express such a moment of hesitation better than stronger or more ordinary artists. So a Post-Impressionist of today may have a high symptomatic importance even though his art be null, and a Filippino Lippi and Piero di Cosimo really tell us more about the time-spirit than a Leonardo da Vinci.

Filippino[2] was born in 1457, at Prato, and presumably received his first instruction from his father, Fra Filippo. At fifteen we find him an orphan and studying with Botticelli, whom he probably assisted at Rome in 1482. At twenty-seven, in 1484, he had the extraordinary honor of completing Masaccio's frescoes in the Brancacci Chapel. Doubtless he had his great predecessor's sketches to aid him. With a somewhat lighter accent, he imitated as he might Masaccio's simple and

Fig. 140.   Filippino Lippi.   St. Peter before Nero.   Detail of Fresco.
— *Brancacci Chapel.*

massive construction in light and shade. Filippino's Peter before the Proconsul, Figure 140, and Crucifixion of St. Peter are of a gravity and weight to have passed for Masaccio's with good critics. But the fine portraits are distinctive for the later date, as are the portraits and the graceful kneeling boy painted opposite in the fresco left unfinished by Masaccio.

As a work of pious assimilation, Filippino's frescoes are amazing; all his more original work is so much falling-off from his beginnings. His characteristic sensitive prettiness may be best observed in the altar-piece in the Badia representing St.

Bernard's Vision of the Virgin.   Figure 141.   As he writes her praises, she approaches his desk escorted by eager angels.   The scenic picturesqueness of the landscape, the accentuated prettiness of the faces are characteristic. Superficially like Botticelli, Filippino is less selective and always more sentimental.   He is rudely shaken out of a mode in which he is attractive by the advent of the new giants of painting, Leonardo and Signorelli.   In his last work, painted about 1502 for the Strozzi

FIG. 141. Filippino Lippi. St. Bernard's Vision. — *Badia*.

Chapel of Santa Maria Novella, he spends himself in superfluous and ineffective inventions, — trophies, archæological ornaments.   To lend impressiveness and tragedy to the martyrdom of St. Philip and St. James, or to the miracle of Drusiana, Figure 142, he has recourse to hideous contortions of mouth and brows, to creaking joints and bursting muscles, to clamor and sensationalism of all sorts.   It is the bankruptcy of the gentle spirit who only twenty years earlier had shown himself almost a great artist in the Carmine, and only ten years earlier had proved himself an accomplished decorator, at the Minerva, Rome.   And the pity of this plunge into competitive and hopeless exhibitionism is that Filippino was a man of taste and character, a collector of classical antiques, an obliging and generous spirit.   He died in 1504 at the moment when Leonardo da Vinci was planning a real and successful sensation for Florence, in The Fight for the Standard.

If Filippino became an eccentric through pressure of circumstances, Piero di Cosimo[3] was one by nature.   Born in 1462, he soon came under the dullest of masters, Cosimo Rosselli.   To Cosimo's four hopeless frescoes in the Sistine

FIG. 143.   Piero di Cosimo.   Primitive Man.   Spalliera panel. — *Metropolitan Museum, N. Y.*

FIG. 142.   Filippino Lippi.   Raising of Drusiana by St. John. — *S. M. Novella, Florence.*

Chapel he added certain vivacious features, and there he learned to know some of the ablest artists of his day. Always a bachelor and recluse, he pursued serious studies in imitation of such stern realists as Antonio Pollaiuolo and Luca Signorelli. He lived sordidly in his *bottega*, literally from hand to mouth, on the eggs which he boiled in his glue pot, in weekly batches. Alone he planned strange my-thologies, bestially pungent, and there he thought out odd terrible pageants which shocked and enthralled his Florence. And as he made these bizarre inventions, he mocked them and himself. His admirations were shifting — now Signorelli, again the Flemish realists and Leonardo: incompatible attractions.

Fig. 144. Piero di Cosimo. Cleo-patra. — *Chantilly.*

You may sense his quality in two wall panels, now in the Metropolitan Museum,[4] made for some palace. Piero had read over the legend of primitive man as told by Ovid, and quickly his mind bred phantoms. First he conceived a state where dominion trembled between man and the brute crea-tion. Savage men with the unfair advantage of fire are exterminating the beasts, among whom fight those half-men, the centaurs, Figure 143. In the companion panel the mood changes abruptly from strife and tumult to the quaintly pastoral strains of a stone-age minuet. We assist at a troglodyte water-party. Lovely woman dominates the new scene. The now domesticated centaur proudly bears her. In courtly fashion skin-clad warriors hand her into a rude pleasure raft which may perhaps waft the picnickers to the joys of a cannibal feast. These inventions have immense fantastic power, and their real originality by no means precludes the suspicion that the artist is smiling at his own ingenuity and at our complaisance.

Take again his Cleopatra, Figure 144, at Chantilly. The

FIG. 145.   Piero di Cosimo.   Death of Procris. — *London.*

snub-nosed Florentine beauty airs her abundant charms in a romantic landscape, while the asp does his by no means disagreeable duty. What a travesty of the dignity of Plutarch, and how fetching it is as distinguished burlesque!

Cautiously and perhaps grudgingly, in the early years of the new century, Piero follows the improvements of Leonardo. This influence is palpable in the Rescue of Andromeda, in the Uffizi. The chained princess carelessly displays her appetizing attractions, while the leering and hungry dragon lurches on the beach and surveys his prey. High up in the sky is hope, in the brisk, knightly figure of Perseus. A musical party lolls deliciously on the strand, equally prepared to enjoy a heroic rescue or a monster at feeding time. We are in the superbly irresponsible world of the fairy tale, and the thrilling *raconteur* has his clever tongue in his cheek.

Exceptionally, as in that wistful poesy, The Death of Procris, Figure 145, at London, Piero is serious enough. The girlish body lies very quiet amid meadow flowers. A puzzled faun and a more comprehending hound are very touching mourners amid the unregarding beasts and birds of a tranquil lake-side afternoon. Such refinements of sentiment are often the compensation for an unstable spirit. The vein is rare in Piero, who, aside from his mythological ironies and quite conventional religious pieces, is also a vivacious portraitist as the galleries of New Haven, Conn., the Hague, and London attest.

Piero lived on till 1521, surviving both Leonardo and Raphael. The greatest artistic effort of modern times had spent itself before his eyes, and he had mostly been content to be witty. He represents at least a fine scorn of his flimsy training, and remains a consummate type of the artist who lives, like a bear in winter, on his own fat.

After a long detour, we are once more on the high road. Perugino, with his simple and gracious symmetries, had shown the painting of the end of the century what ailed it. But his cure was too obvious to be acceptable until a youngster of Raphael's entirely modest intelligence should come along. The reform, as often in other than artistic affairs, had to be made from within, and was conducted by one who had much sympathy with the random richness of the Early Renaissance style, Leonardo da Vinci.[5]

Leonardo's discoveries, pursued with the most patient and gradual care, shocked no one and were quickly taken up. He was nearly thirty before he reached consciousness of his mission, and having attained his artistic end, he dropped painting, with a kind of scorn, for mathematical and scientific investigation. In his admirable "Tractate on Painting" he has left the fullest and most eloquent records of his ideals. The first is that the painter must know clearly what he is about. "Without good theory no good practice is possible." Next the artist should be in a filial relation to nature, admiring and imitating her directly, and not through the eyes of other artists. As to the main object of painting, Leonardo wavers between two definitions. Repeatedly he insists that

that painting is greatest which through the postures of the body shows the emotions of the soul. As often, he uses a more technical definition — the chief business of painting is to create a sense of relief or projection where there is none. This relief is effected by delicate and accurate distribution of light and shade. Light and dark are conceived in a double fashion, as factors in relief and as offering intrinsic beauties in their gradations. We have a refinement on the method of Masaccio, which is merely structural and dramatic and without much intrinsic charm. But the new beauty of chiaroscuro soon turns out to be incompatible with the old beauty of frank color. Pictures become dusky and mysterious, tending to black and white values. Ever since Leonardo, academic painting has had the sore limitation of regarding shadow as negation of color. It is the defect of his teaching and practice.

On broader matters, however, Leonardo is profoundly right. Seeing is a mental process and should be selective. Represent all the muscles emphatically, and your nude will look like a sack full of nuts. Accuracy is necessary, but is of no value without accompanying dignity and grace. Choose the most gracious aspects of reality, the pervasive moderate light of evening rather than the sharp glare of the overhead sun. Observe deaf-mutes so that you may learn the possibilities of expression through gestures. Seek equilibrium and an active and vital balance whether in the pose of the single figure or in the relations of the figures to each other. Get the action right, and afterwards add the details. These are some of the precepts which Leonardo scribbled off about the year 1500 when he was nearing fifty and his work as a painter was almost over. He is really describing the principles under which, while accepting the richness and variety of the early Renaissance style, he had once for all put it in order.

Of course this was a very gradual process. To the end Leonardo retained something of a primitive quality, and he was by no means precocious. He was born in 1452, the lovechild of a peasant girl of Vinci and a young Florentine notary, Piero da Vinci. His earliest recollections must have been of the hills and distant mountain prospects of his native hamlet of Vinci, between Florence and Pisa. But he was soon taken into his father's home at Florence, and given an education which hardly exceeded the proverbial "Three R's". Just when he was put with the painter and sculptor, Andrea Verrocchio, is uncertain, but it can hardly have been later than Leonardo's thirteenth year, 1465. As a painter, Verrocchio exists for us chiefly in the work of his pupils. As a sculptor, however, he is a definite enough figure. His aim was plainly to infuse the new realism with an aristocratic elegance. What a young patrician is his David composing himself for the ordeal with a restrained well-bred smile! There is a splendid dandyism in his valor. Or consider the Madonna in terra-cotta, with her ornate head-dress, rich brooch, and carefully arranged robe, her almost too sweet self-possession. She is a clue to the fastidiousness of Verrocchio. Again consider the proud hard face and the marvelously firm and delicate hands of the unknown lady Verrocchio cut in marble. These things are dominant for the early development of Leonardo, as the alert, powerful and aggressive Colleoni monument is for his later heroic creations. Something of Verrocchio's scrupulous and eminently dilatory character also passed over to his brilliant pupil. Verrocchio remained a bachelor and wholly devoted to his art, yet he took eighteen years to give to his famous bronze group of Christ and St. Thomas its dignity and sensitive feeling. Leonardo remained some ten years or more with Verrocchio, painting many works that are lost to us, and a few, I believe, that we may identify. In this most contested matter I follow in the main the views of Dr. Sirén.

For many years Leonardo ventured little on his own account, following with docility the directions of his master. The single painting which we may with certainty ascribe to Verrocchio, the Baptism of Christ, Figure 146a, in the Uffizi, already bears traces of Leonardo's hand. The general composition is borrowed from an insignificant panel of Baldovinetti's. The

Fɪɢ. 146.   Leonardo da Vinci, Head at Left; Verrocchio, Head at Right.
Details from Verrocchio's Baptism. — *Uffizi.*

stalwart ugly forms derive from Pollaiuolo. Delightful features added in oils by Leonardo are the exquisite angel at the left, Figure 146, and the vaporous distance and mountain skyline. We may surmise that these improvements were added about 1470 to a picture started several years earlier. One other picture was designed by Verrocchio and finished after his death in 1488 by his assistant, Lorenzo di Credi. This Madonna, in the cathedral of Pistoia, affords an excellent contrast between the puffy forms of Lorenzo and the firm and living contours of Leonardo. The famous Annunciation in the Uffizi, Figure 147, seems a kind of joint product, the actual painting being by Leonardo, the badly balanced composition

and intrusive heavy lectern, as well as the rather cheap attitude of surprise of the Virgin, representing a perfunctory
mood of Verrocchio. The vista of remote mountains hanging
pale in the blue sky is such as only
Leonardo could have created.
The delightful Gabriel also seems
wholly his invention. The composition again rests on one of
Baldovinetti's, at S. Miniato,
and the date of the picture may
be about 1475. Of about the
same date is a Madonna with an
Angel in the National Gallery,
which may well be a composition of Verrocchio interpreted by
Leonardo. The note of sweetness is a little forced, as in most

Fig. 146a. Verrocchio and Leonardo. Baptism of Christ.—*Uffizi*.

work of this kind. We meet Leonardo in his own right a little
earlier, in a pen sketch of a broad landscape dated in mid-

Fig. 147. Leonardo da Vinci under Verrocchio's Direction. Annunciation.
— *Uffizi*.

summer of 1473, Figure 148. Its spaciousness and schematic
handling of horizontals ally it to the landscape backgrounds
we have been considering. The last work of this Verrocchian

character is the Portrait of a Girl, in the Liechtenstein Gallery, Vienna. Here we are in a field where Leonardo and his master are almost indistinguishable, but the picturesquely

FIG. 148. Leonardo da Vinci. Landscape. Pen Drawing. — *Uffizi.*

broken background, the bit of landscape, and the ease of the contours, speak for the younger man. As late as 1476, his twenty-fifth year, Leonardo was still with Verrocchio. He probably set up his own *bottega* a year or so afterwards.

FIG. 149. Leonardo da Vinci. Annunciation. — *Louvre.*

There followed four or five years of eager experiment, much being planned and rather little carried to completion. Relieved from the pressure of a master, actual painting seems to have become irksome. He loves to sketch, to turn his designs over until they reach perfection, leaving them in the condition of the swiftest and most accurate notations. Lack of system and paralysis of will are already apparent. For about two years of this joyous and irresponsible creation he remained a primitive. Such he is in the idyllic little Annunciation of the Louvre,[6] Figure 149, which should be for its fluent technic no earlier than 1476. He takes the motive which he had previously done under restrictions, reduces it to a symmetrical order, rejects distracting details, floods it with warm light breaking through ragged apertures of the trees, and invests it with a penetrating humility and grace. The little picture, which many critics set too early, is really Leonardo's declaration of independence. It shows features which anticipate his mature style — a combination of a severe geometrical symmetry in figure composition with a romantically strange setting and lighting.

Of less import is the unpretentious little Madonna of the Flower, recently discovered, and in the Hermitage, at Petrograd. It is authenticated by numerous composition sketches. Its vivacity and youthful lightness of effect are entirely in Verrocchio's manner, nothing is new but heavier shadows and more emphatic modelling.

On a sheet of drawings in the Uffizi, which characteristically combines with sketches of men's heads studies of machinery, we read "This day I began the two Virgin Marys." The day is effaced, but it is a month in 1478, ending in -bre — September, October or November. One of these Madonnas is, no doubt, the Madonna of the Flower.[7] As to the other we have no certainty, but the sketches of this time show at least five madonnas in process of invention. A Madonna holding a mischievous Child who hugs a writhing cat, a Madonna with a Dish of Fruit, a Madonna kneeling before the Child, a theme later developed into the Madonna of the Rocks; a Madonna seated on the Ground, and a Madonna seated in the

open with the Christchild and St. John.   Dr. Jens Thys thinks
the last composition may be the one actually begun as a
picture, since such early Raphaels as the Belle Jardinière
seem to imply such a picture as their model.   We do well to

FIG. 150.   Leonardo da Vinci.   Pen Sketches for the Madonna of the Cat.
— *British Museum.*

turn from such speculations to the marvelous sketches for
these Madonnas, Figure 150.   Nothing firmer, lighter or
more charming can be imagined.   Of the line, thinned to a
hair or widened to a blot, there is the completest control.
These little figures, a couple of inches high at the most and
often of thumb-nail minuteness, may be enlarged to life size
without losing in structure or character.   Nothing shows better

the sheer fecund genius of Leonardo than these sheets, crowded with figures, scribbled with his right-to-left hand-writing, and slantingly shaded from upper left downwards, after the fashion of a lefthanded draughtsman. They show how Leonardo worked in spurts of inspiration, creating a dozen lovely compositions and contented with none. They represent so many tensely joyous halfhours, with doubtless long intervals of other activities and withal of sheer brooding and unrecorded observation. They help one grasp the spas-modic and discontinuous quality of Leonardo's genius — why the actual execution of pictures was ever a matter of pain and drudgery to him. Up to his twenty-ninth year he apparently made no prolonged effort of any sort, but spent himself furiously in separate investigations. Then he pulled himself together for a great picture, and though it too never got beyond the underpainting, it broke the new path to the Golden Age.

For several years Leonardo had turned over the theme of an Adoration of the Child in his sketch books. These desul-tory inventions were brought abruptly to a focus in March 1481, when he agreed to do an altar-piece for the monks of S. Donato at Scopeto. We have the best circumstantial evi-dence for identifying this piece with the unfinished Adoration of the Kings, now in the Uffizi. When we live ourselves into this dusky and mysterious sketch we step out of the early Renaissance into a new, ardent, rich and ordered region of invention such as the world had not witnessed since the glory of Greece faded. The composition went through at least three main stages. At first, as we see from a pen study in the Bonnat Museum, at Bayonne, an Adoration of the Shepherds was considered, the Madonna kneeling over the Christ between flanking groups of worshippers. The scheme was rejected as too thin and obvious. A picture of Lorenzi di Credi's shows us its limited possibilities. Then the picture became an Adoration of the Kings, with the thatched shed, much action in the foreground group and a ruined amphitheatre in the background. This sketch in the Louvre, Figure 151, contains all the elements of the picture, but an extra-

ordinary work of clarification and refinement remained to be done. The figures were studied and restudied till they reached both highest expressiveness and individuality,[8] and an exact relation to the dense and intricate articulation of the foreground group. Often there are half a dozen separate studies for each motive. The central group was more closely massed till it became a rose of eager faces and flickering hands and kneeling forms pressing inward towards

Fig. 151. Leonardo. Sketch for Adoration.— *Louvre.*

the Child. To increase this concentration, a mound is erected behind the group shutting it off from the wide background. To steady the group, the Madonna is no longer swung athwart the motion, but her nearly straight position becomes a sort of axis carried up by the trees above. In the richness, variety and animation of the compact group of adorers, Leonardo has met the Early Renaissance on its own ground and outdone it. In the wider setting he still observes the old precepts, but in a profounder and more significant sense. He has swept the traditional shed aside and opened up a world, a world furtive and active and combatant in its own wilfulness — playing, hiding, and fighting amid the crumbling ruins of old civilizations, and before distant towering crags which were there before civilization or man himself was; a world oblivious of the sublime mystery accomplishing itself in the kings who pay homage to a Babe. What an ironic substitute for the joyous pastoralism with which contemporary artists invested their pictures of the Epiphany!

The Adoration of the Kings, Figure 152, is the richest, most complicated, most beautifully ordered picture of its century;

Fig. 152. Leonardo da Vinci. Adoration of the Magi. Underpainting.
—*Uffizi.*

even Leonardo was not to surpass it simply as a composition. Like all rich things it will bear many analyses. You may consider it as a triangle, with the reciprocal forms enriched, or, with Dr. Thys, as the combination of two radiating motives, one centred on the Madonna's face, the other on the soft alert body of the Child. Such analyses are only important as temporary aids to understanding of the main fact that in the making of such a masterpiece a clear and subtile geometry is involved. Later Leonardo was to declare that there is no science which cannot undergo mathematical demonstration, and he probably would have added — no art. Of his own art at least the saying is true. It may have been not so much his native indolence that arrested a work which had claimed months of passionate preparation at the moment when creation was at its height, as the conviction that it would lose something if fully realized. One can see how he loved the summary touches of dark and light, the swift, sufficient evocation of body and soul which he had learned from Masaccio. He may have hated to cover up such work, and a critic today may well be in doubt whether the gain in finishing it would have atoned for the loss. Or Leonardo da Vinci may already have been called to Milan and a new artistic life. However that be, the monks of Scopeto, after a long wait, turned to Filippino Lippi, who had already undertaken one lapsed commission for Leonardo, and he promptly achieved an Adoration of the Kings which only shows how inimitable Leonardo was, and how little mere richness counts in any picture.

For two years between 1481 and 1483, there is silence. It seems to me that in this time we may set the crowning of his early work in the Madonna of the Rocks at the Louvre and the Cartoon of St. Ann at London. The Madonna of the Rocks, Figure 153, is the logical outcome of a half dozen Adorations which we may trace through the drawings of 1478. A sheet of sketches in the Metropolitan Museum shows him turning the theme over, rejecting the established profile arrangement of Fra Filippo, and hitting on the formal pyramidal pattern which appears in the picture itself. There the pyramid is felt not merely in plane, but also in depth. The forms and faces are superbly tense without either rigidity or the fluency of Leonardo's later work. The setting is primitive, with minutely studied textures of rock and crisp shapes of wall flowers.

Everything derives from Fra Filippo and Botticelli, but with new meaning. The romantic strangeness of the setting, the glimpses of sky and opening in the rock, the sifting in of light from the heart of the picture itself, the broad contrast of the formality of the figure arrangement with the picturesque wildness of the setting — all this is purest Leonardo and represents the culmination of many experiments. One can trace this idea of irregularly broken light and an informal screen as foil for a geometrical pattern, from the little Annunciation of the Louvre, through the unfinished St. Jerome of the Vatican. The Early Renaissance steps into the background, where it belongs. Leonardo never rejects it; he fulfils it with an exquisite sense of proportion.

Fig. 153. Leonardo. Madonna of the Rocks. — *Louvre*.

If the first Madonna of the Rocks was painted before 1482, in Florence, so probably was the cartoon of the Madonna with St. Ann, Figure 127, perhaps the most precious single work that Leonardo has left us. The inwardness of the relation between the two women is in the mood of the Adoration of the Kings, single motives suggest the drawings for the Madonna of the Cat. Later Leonardo was to lend to the motive greater complication and formal elegance, somewhat at the cost of emotional insight. Pictures of intense and natural feeling Leonardo does not produce after his thirtieth year. Instead we have dramatic objectivity in one phase, and in another, exquisite subtilities, a calculated graciousness sweet to morbidity.

What drew Leonardo from Florence to Milan we do not surely know. Probably he was called directly by the Duke Lodovico Sforza to undertake the colossal equestrian statue of his father Francesco. Moreover, Leonardo seems to have achieved notoriety at Florence without gaining much confidence or achieving much success. After all, he had rather little to show for his genius — just his sketch-books and his good intentions in unfinished masterpieces. He seems, too, never to have mastered the practice which ever brought the best commissions, fresco painting. Thus he had every reason to seek new fortunes.

He heralded his coming to Milan with the most truthfully boastful of letters in which he arrogated to himself all ability as an inventor, civil and military engineer, painter, sculptor, and architect; and he entered the presence of Lodovico bearing a silver lute wrought in the form of a horse's skull. This dramatic entrance was the forecast of arduous duties as an entertainer. He sang, told anecdotes and fables, arranged pageants and masques, conducted debates on his art — in short, accepted the thousand and one duties and distractions of a courtier.

He painted the portraits of the Duke's mistresses, and it is possible that we have the girlish figure of Cecilia Gallierani in the lady with an Ermine[9] at Cracow. The forms and feeling are entirely like Leonardo's work in the early eighties. He agreed to do an altar-piece for the Church of San Francesco, and delivered it only after a delay of twenty-three years. This most postponed of pictures is the version of the Madonna of the Rocks now at London. Meanwhile Leonardo's constant concern was "the horse," as he calls it. For seven years he worked at a rearing horse with a fallen foe trodden beneath. It is shown in many drawings. It was too sensational a theme to please him in the long run. So in 1490, spurred by the risk of losing the job, he restudied the horse, using the walking motive, which had come down from classical antiquity. Eventually the clay model was set up before the Sforza castle, just in time for the invading French archers to make a target of it. The rider was never even definitely planned. The whole project remained a chagrin to Leonardo even after the horse itself had disappeared. One day in Florence he civilly accosted Michelangelo who turned on him with the taunt — "Thou who did'st model a horse and could'st not cast it in bronze."

Amidst the distractions of the court, the irksomeness of the rashly undertaken Sforza monument, and the increasing passion for scientific research, Leonardo managed to carry through his single monumental work, the Last Supper, in the refectory of Santa Maria delle Grazie.

For three years Leonardo worked spasmodically on the Last Supper, and it was finished in 1498. The design had been most carefully elaborated. He started with the customary arrangement of the apostles in pairs, John in Jesus' bosom — a refractory motive, and Judas in sinister isolation on the near side of the table. Almost by accident he fell upon the effective grouping of the apostles by threes. Then he set himself to giving in expression and gesture the maximum emotion that could be contained within a monumental design. He eliminated the old casual accessories and made all the lines of perspective converge on the face of Christ. He gave to all the figures a classical gravity, though admitting many varieties of age and character.

Thus even in its ruined estate The Last Supper, Figure 154, is perhaps the most impressive picture in the world. The moment is that when Christ says "One of you shall betray me." The arrangement is in five great balancing waves. From the Christ there is an outgoing gesture of resignation and love, from the apostles converging, incoming waves of horror, amazement, curiosity and indignation. Each undulation is double.

Extended arms or pointed hands check the motion where it is excessive or connect the separate groups. Only Judas is out of the converging rhythm. He swings back defiantly pondering his part. Highly agitated in details, the whole is held

Fig. 154. Leonardo da Vinci. Last supper.—*S. Maria delle Grazie, Milan.*

within a noble and pathetic decorum. It is the very ideal of a Renaissance composition — dense, rich, energetic, varied, yet unified by a severe and calculated pattern which subordinates to its purpose the most diverse components. Raphael can only imitate it in the lower part of the Disputa, and monumental design ever since has gone to school with it.

It was unhappily painted in tempera, not in oils as older accounts say,[10] on the dry wall, and it soon began to deteriorate. What we see today is merely the wraith of it, yet a wraith that imposes itself and moves us as few better preserved masterpieces do.

In the year 1500 the French overran Lombardy, and, Leonardo, after wandering in Northern Italy and a martial episode as engineer for conquering Caesar Borgia, returned, in 1503, to his native Florence. He is fifty and already in spirit an old man. His always limited will power has given out, he broods incessantly over mathematical and physical lore, wastes himself over fantastic inventions. His exhibit is only a cartoon, now lost, for a St. Ann. He makes portraits by proxy, but

Fig. 155. Leonardo da Vinci. Sketches for the Battle of Anghiari.
—*Windsor Castle.*

paints, himself, only under peculiar incentives. Such he found in the commission for a great battle piece for the Priors' Palace and in the personality of Mona Lisa.

Early in the year 1504 he began to work on the cartoon for the Battle of Anghiari. He chose the incident of a cavalry fight for the standard. He composed a whirl of horses and infuriated riders, hacking and slashing about a flag — a literal picture of bloodlust at its height. The ability he expended on this atrocious theme may be sensed in a dozen preparatory sketches, Figure 155. The portion which he actually painted on the wall is represented only by inferior copies. The original soon faded from deficient technical methods. The old copies tell us that this great piece, while the marvel of its day, was sensational and highly exhibitionistic. We need not too much mourn its loss. The admiration it evoked was that of an age eager for novelty and responsive to display.

Fig. 156.   Leonardo.   Mona Lisa.
—*Louvre*.

While working on the battle-piece, Leonardo met the young Neapolitan wife of Francesco del Giocondo and began her portrait, Figure 156. She had lost children and was habitually sad. He employed musicians to charm the inscrutable fascinating smile to her face. He set her demure and watchful before a romantic expanse of river plain rimmed by blue alps. Against this wild charm of nature, he made Mona Lisa a symbol for all that is cultured, self-contained, sophisticated, civilized. Simple people instinctively dislike her, and are right. Subtle people adore her, and are also right. Such as wish poetic commentary on her mysterious beauty may find it for themselves in Walter Pater's admirable essay. They will do well to temper his eloquence with Kenyon Cox's [11] just if prosaic observation that this portrait is simply the finest, most accurate, and subtle bit of modelling in the world. Its mystery is perhaps merely one of amazing vision and impeccable workmanship. The truth may well lie between two interpretations, each of which is valid in its own field. Had there not been some extraordinary spell in the woman herself, Leonardo, now well weary of painting, would hardly have studied either her soul or her modelling with such tenacity.

During his brief sojourn in Florence, Leonardo did cartoons for two designs of Leda and the Swan, his only mythological picture. One represents her standing, the other crouching. If we may trust the inferior imitations, in which alone we know these subjects, their calculated sensuousness was almost cloying. Their mood is that of his least agreeable imitator, Sodoma.

Fig. 157. Leonardo. Madonna with St. Ann.—*Louvre*.

In May 1506 Florence lent Leonardo to Charles d'Amboise, the French viceroy at Milan, and there he spent the most of the next five years. The Franciscans had been biding their time, and under legal duress made him finish the Madonna which he had promised twenty-three years earlier. Thus the second Madonna of the Rocks, at London, was painted somewhat against the grain. It has more simplicity and breadth than the earlier version and shows improvements in the position of the angel. It also lacks the minute and painstaking delicacy of its original, reveals a tired hand and mind. Otherwise Leonardo achieved in painting only the third version of the Madonna and St. Ann, Figure 157, now in the Louvre. The interweaving of the figures is compact and masterly, the solution of the difficult problems of the two heads consummately clever. It has passages of the utmost loveliness, like the foot of the Madonna, but there is some suspicion of oversophistication, and Leonardo never summoned the energy to finish it. Painting little himself, — for he was busy with

canals, architecture, and the never finished equestrian monument of Trivulzio, — Leonardo gave his stamp to the entire
Milanese school. Such pupils as Boltraffio, Cesare da Sesto,
Andrea Solario, his old partner, Ambrogio de Predis, and his
intimate, Francesco Melzi, readily grasped his mannerisms,
and filled Italy with Leonardesque pictures of inferior inspiration. More robust and independent spirits, like Bernardino
Luini, adapted his manner intelligently to the needs of mural
painting. Lombardy under his influence for a moment seemed
to vie with Florence and Rome.

In 1513 Leonardo was called to Rome by the new Pope
Leo X, Lorenzo de' Medici's son, Giovanni. It was the moment for artistic ambition to flame in one who felt himself a
great painter. Michelangelo had recently unveiled the Sistine
ceiling, and Raphael had completed the Camera della Segnatura. Leonardo was sixty-one, when a painter should be at
his best. Yet he plunged himself into scientific experiments,
perpetrated strange practical jokes on his patrons, produced
nothing but disorderly notes, and after two wasted years left
the repute of one rather an amateur magician than an artist.

Having lived a wanderer, it was appropriate that Leonardo
should die an exile. Francis I, an enthusiastic patron of
Italian art, called him to France and settled him honorably
in the Château of Cloux, near Amboise. We hear of him as
immensely learned and venerable, but palsied, and dependent
on the affectionate care of his pupil Melzi. He died on the
morrow of Mayday 1519 at peace with the church, leaving
money to sixty poor persons who should follow his body with
candles to the tomb. Doubtless you could have marked in that
pitiful procession many of those gnarled, toothless and haggard
faces which Leonardo formerly loved to sketch in the intervals
of his endless quest of beauty. As we study the marvelous
drawing of himself in old age, Figure 158, we may surmise that
he was glad to go. It is hard to see in it the courtier who bore

the fantastic silver lute to Lodovico, the artist who charmed
a smile from the weary and cautious face of Mona Lisa. One
sees a man immensely old, though at an age generally robust
and cheery — one who has tried
to crowd many lives into one and
has paid the inevitable penalty.

Broken and intermittent as it
had been, Leonardo's painting
had sufficed to show the way. He
had substituted mystery of light
and shade for allurement of frank
color, study of the subtler and
finer shades of emotion for obvious characterization, had founded
modern portraiture. He had
shown how to express power and
passion with delicacy, had combined the richest animation and
variety with monumental severity of design. After him the art

Fig. 158. Leonardo da Vinci.
His own portrait. — *Turin.*

of painting was never to be the same again. Its standards
became ampler and more classic. Stolid men like Fra Bartolommeo immediately accepted his principles of composition
and so did miraculously alert intelligences like Raphael's.
His mere passing contact and tradition inspired that admirable
language of light and dark that became poetry in Giorgione
and Correggio. The good and the harm he did is active today
in thousands of academies and art schools. His is assuredly
the finest intelligence that ever applied itself to the painter's
art, and if he failed in will and in fecundity, he has impressed
himself upon posterity as no other Italian painter save Titian.
His art had its limitations, but its capacity for influence, to
which he added the thoughtful eloquence of his written word,
seems limitless; and his glory is imperishable.

Nowhere does the superiority of Florence show more clearly than in the attitude of her artists to Leonardo. Where his Milanese followers aped his superficial mannerisms, his Florentine admirers studied and assimilated his construction in light and shade and his principles of geometrical composition. Unhappily the early years of the sixteenth century were a slack time in Florence. Such transitional painters as Piero di Cosimo, Granacci, Franciabigio, Il Bacchiacca, and Ridolfo Ghirlandaio were not men to carry forward Leonardo's discoveries, but they and others, at least paid him an intelligent homage and sensibly clarified their practice under his influence. Greater intelligences like Fra Bartolommeo and Andrea del Sarto not merely adopted Leonardo's canons, but even at certain points criticized them. Both saw the drawback of Leonardo's passionate concern with chiaroscuro — that it flooded the canvas with colorless shadow, tending to reduce the palette to black and white. Both men then therefore kept their rich shadows colorful. Both worked for a more compact and intricate composition as well as for graceful, abstract poses. In these latter endeavors they simplified and sharpened principles which Leonardo himself only rarely carried to their logical extreme.

Leonardo retained certain primitive qualities. He seldom reduced his compositions to dense arrangements of the figures, loving to allow elbow room and delighting to open up landscape backgrounds. And while in the "Treatise on Painting" he advocated elaborately balanced and counterpoised poses, in practice he usually sought an excuse for them in action. A consummate stylist, he achieved style on a basis of function. The pose, in his own words, must express "the emotions of the soul." Right here his ablest followers took issue with him. Posture with them no longer expressed specific or individual emotion, but abstract beauties of grace, dignity or grandeur. The figures no longer do or feel anything, they are arranged as the general composition and mood of the picture require. Such gradual advance towards pure style heralds the advent of the High Renaissance.

Of the somewhat stolid and occasionally sentimental sublimity of Fra Bartolommeo[12] nothing much need be said except that it was a formative influence on young Raphael. The Dominican monk is an impressive and amiable figure personally. Working solely for the glory of God and the profit of the Convent of San Marco, perturbed by the tragic fate of his cloister mate, Savonarola, he strove incessantly for a fuller color and a greater dignity. In his numerous Holy Families he is stately in a conventional way, nowhere more so than in the unfinished design for a Madonna with St. Ann, in the Uffizi. Occasionally, in such pic-

Fig. 159. Fra Bartolommeo. God appearing to two Saints. — *Lucca.*

tures as the Deposition of the Uffizi, and the Madonna of Pity at Lucca he achieves poignant, one is tempted to say operatic effects, forecasting the mood of the Baroque. Lucca also affords in the great picture God Adored by Two Saints, Figure 159, a fine example of this painter's simple and massive compositions. In the fresco of The Last Judgment, which, being ruined, is better represented by Copies, Figure 160, we find an elaboration, in Leonardo's sense, of the simple symmetries of Perugino. It is the precedent for Raphael's monumental frescoes at Rome. His short career, from about 1495 to 1517, fell on evil times for Florence. In happier days he might have harmonized more perfectly the stylist and the lyrical dramatist that, as it was, never quite came to terms in his grave and noble personality. Yet to have mediated between Leonardo and Raphael would seem glory enough for

Fig. 160. Fra Bartolommeo. Copy of Lost Fresco of Last Judgment. — *S. Marco.*

any painter, and it was also no slight service to borrow for Florentine painting, rapidly becoming starved of color, something of the colorful richness of Giovanni Bellini and Giorgione.

"The Perfect Painter" was what the Florentines called Andrea del Sarto,[13] and he merited the title. He produced no masterpiece of the first order, but his work is singularly uniform on a high level. Its chief qualities are dignity and grace with a great richness of color. The deep shadows are warm and full of dusky light, the stylistic poses of the figures always easy, and the weaving of the complicated groupings ever tasteful and harmonious. To the refractory art of fresco painting Andrea brought a richness, depth and variety of color that others hardly attained in oil painting. Only Luini in the north came near him in this regard. In short he is a consummate technician, carrying his art as far as skill and taste unillumined by sheer genius will reach.

Fig. 161. Andrea del Sarto. Birth. — *Annunziata.*

Little of his excellence can be laid to his early training. Before 1500 he was working with Piero di Cosimo, and Andrea's youthful frescoes of the miracles of S. Filippo Benizzi, in the fore-court of the Annunziata, show the loose and animated arrangements and the exaggeration of picturesque landscape features characteristic of his master. But Andrea learned

Fig. 162. Andrea del Sarto. Madonna of the Sack. — *Annunziata.*

rather of the time-spirit than of any other master. By 1514 his art is complete and one may see its flowering in the frescoes of the Birth of the Virgin, Figure 161, and the Madonna of the Sack, Figure 162, respectively in the fore-court and in the cloister of the Annunziata. It is a sumptuous and grave kind of design redeemed from heaviness by its exquisite balance of color masses, and from conventionality by the hint of portraiture in the artfully disposed figures.

Scores of times Andrea repeats these perfections in the great altar-backs required for the new Renaissance chapels. The Four Saints in the Pitti, the Madonna of the Harpies in the Uffizi, Figure 162a, the Enthroned Madonna at Berlin may serve among many to illustrate his accomplishment in this new vein. Somewhat reminiscent of the heavier monumentality of Fra Bartolommeo, these great pictures add a personal and disquieting note from the presence of the moody, handsome wife, Lucrezia whose caprices and infidelities are the tragic element in an otherwise even life.

Fig. 162a.   Andrea del Sarto.   Madonna of the Harpies. — *Uffizi.*

Andrea in his later years won new glories but added no new note to his art. The monochrome frescoes in the Cloister of the Scalzo representing the Life of St. John Baptist merely show the old gravity somewhat exaggerated. The series which extended over many years (1515–1526) is uneven, and many of these perhaps overestimated compositions are plainly

of student execution. Without his color, Andrea seems somewhat coldly academic. It was precisely this quality of stylistic
grandeur, however, that appealed paradoxically to the romantic monarch, Francis I. He called Andrea to France in 1518
and kept him there in honor for a year. Had Andrea possessed
any of the capacities of a teacher and theorist, he might have
inaugurated the Renaissance in France. As it was he remained
merely a harbinger of such inferior but more influential spirits
as Il Rosso and Primaticcio who a few years later were to
found the School of Fontainebleau.

Often the portfolios of a great technician are more thrilling than his major works. This is the case with Andrea del
Sarto. His numerous sketches in red chalk, have an athletic
charm which his painting lacks. Others have drawn differently
in this medium, but no one has drawn better.

When Andrea died in 1531, "full of glory and domestic
trials," as Vasari recounts, the normal development of Florentine painting ended, and Florence had already seen her artistic
star dimmed by the rising splendors of Venice and Rome.
Artistically she became a city of wit and ingenuity, chroni-
cling and criticizing art rather than producing it. Moreover the
obsession of Michelangelo's sublimity worked havoc with his
dilettante imitators. Some of these have the grace of lucidity,
like Agnolo Bronzino, who (1502-1572)[14] practiced a reactionary
sort of portraiture based on the old tradition of tempera painting. In sheer beauty of surface, enamel one is tempted to call it,
he is little inferior to his great German contemporary, Hans
Holbein, and his sense of character is only less keen because less
individual. In the haughty patricians surrounding the person
of Cosimo, the first granduke, he found congenial sitters,
Figure 163. In the narrow field of portraiture he is nearly in
the first rank, while in his rare mythologies and religious
pictures his limitations appear painfully. He was a vicious
person, a cold æsthete, with few of the generous virtues that

nourish the soul.   Yet in his flinty way he was quite perfect, and as one of the first professionally unmoral artists he cannot be neglected by the psychological critic.

FIG. 164. Pontormo. The Deposition.—*S. Felicità*.

A more appealing figure is his master, Jacopo Carrucci, called from his birthplace Il Pontormo.[15] His was a tender and deeply religious spirit with the poet's capacity for elation and melancholy.   In his altar-pieces, such as the Deposition, Figure 164, at S. Felicità he seeks and achieves a positive pathos.   Influenced by Michelangelo's sublimity, he converts it to more specific and psychological ends.   Often he is restless and over-emphatic as in the frescoes of the Passion in the cloister of the Florentine Certosa, or in the strangely complicated and contorted little picture of the Martyrdom of St. Mauritius and his Legionaries, in the Uffizi.   In such work he moves towards the absolute expressionism of an El Greco, preluding also the more conventional emotionalism of the Baroque.   As a portraitist he had no equal at Florence except his pupil Bronzino.   Often the sensitiveness and moodiness of his characterizations recall his Venetic contemporary, Lorenzo Lotto.   Even when he is robust he is sensitively psychological, as in the superb portrait of a Halberdier, Figure 165.   Above all he was a powerful and subtle draughtsman whether with pen or chalk.   His line writhes in a fashion at times sinister, at times singularly blithe, and his figure sketches have something of the imaginative thrill of the figure studies of Blake.   For the grandducal palace of

Poggio a Cajano, Figure 166, he did in a huge lunette pierced by a great round window a most original decoration for the odd triangles at the base. The unconventional fields are filled each by a rather small figure energetically posed and

Fig. 163. Bronzino. Eleonora of Toledo and her son.— *Uffizi.*

Fig. 165. Pontormo. The Halberdier.— *C. C. Stillman, N.Y.*

surrounded by greenery. The thing is at once monumental and pastoral and its freedom and tonality almost as modern as a Besnard. I would willingly dwell longer on so sympathetic an artist, but can only refer the interested reader to Dr. F. M. Clapp's two authoritative volumes.

For a century and more after Pontormo's death in 1556 there are still occasional artists of talent at Florence, but there is no longer a Florentine school. The masterpieces of Michelangelo were at Rome, those of Raphael widely scattered. Conscious of her decline, Florence begins to import artists — the Flemish portraitist, Sustermans; the Venetian decorator, Luca Giordano. One of her own abler painters, Francesco Salviati, attaches himself to the Venetian manner. Being an academic city, Florence eschews the rugged naturalism of

Caravaggio, but has no longer vitality enough to find a substitute of her own.   In the late sixteenth century her fresco
painting sinks to the pompous emptiness represented by Giorgio
Vasari, or by the hardly better mythologies of the brothers

Fig. 166.   Pontormo.   Frescoed Lunette. — *Poggio a Cajano*.

Federigo and Taddeo Zuccaro.   In the seventeenth century
she still can produce an idyllist of great romantic and sensuous
charm in a Francesco Furini and a genial illustrator in a Giovanni di San Giovanni.   But such names only suggest the
incoherence of the times.   Florence is no longer a main current
but an eddy, and what small flood-tide still runs courses in the
more resolute academism of Bologna, which is to be capable
of inspiring a Poussin; and in the raw naturalism of Naples,
which is about to give lessons to a Velasquez.

ILLUSTRATIONS FOR CHAPTER V

POETRY AND PAINTING IN THE RENAISSANCE

Reversing the maxim *ut pictura poesis*, the Renaissance believed that painting should be poetical. Indeed the term *poesia* is commonly applied to all painting of a mythological or idyllic sort. Angelo Poliziano's unfinished but very popular poem on the joust of 1468 is lavish in descriptions, of which the painters made use. Botticelli surely got more than a hint for the Birth of Venus from stanzas xcix-ci of *La Giostra*, though the mood of the picture is wholly Sandro's own and unlike the pagan joyousness of Poliziano.

"One saw

Born in the sea, free and joyous in her acts,
A damsel with divine visage
Driven ashore by the ardent zephyrs
Balancing on a shell; and it seemed the heavens rejoiced thereat."

"True the foam and true the sea you would have said
True the shell, and the blowing of the winds true.
You would have seen the gleam of the Goddess' eye
And the heavens laugh about her, and the elements.
And the Hours in white garments on the strand,
And the winds toss their spreading soft locks."

. . . .

"You could swear that you could see the goddess coming from the waves
Wringing out her hair with her right hand
And with the left covering the sweet mount of desire,
And the sand, once trodden by her feet,
Clothing itself with grass and flowers.
Then with joyous and expectant glance
You would have seen her clasped by the three nymphs
And wrapped in a starry robe."

Botticelli's charming and even slyly humorous picture of Venus with sleeping Mars, at London, follows afar and discreetly *La Giostra*, I. stanzas cxxii-iii, but Botticelli has taken the motive out of doors and otherwise considerably subtilized it. Venus is

> "Seated in bed outside the covers
> Just released from the arms of Mars
> Who, lies backward on her lap
>
> . . . .
>
> "Above them and around the tiny loves
> Played naked, flying now here now there
>
> . . . .
>
> "One fills the quiver with fresh flowers
> Then comes and empties it on the bed."

Poliziano also supplied to Raphael the theme of the Galatea, in the Farnesina, *Giostra* I, cxviii (Fig. 192a)

> "Two shapely dolphins draw a car;
>   On it is Galatea who holds the reins,
>   And they swimming breathe with equal breath.
>   Around circle the more amorous throng.
>   One spits out the salt wave, the others circle round;
>   One seems to play at love and dallies.
>   The fair nymph with her trusted sisters
>   Laughs charmingly at their hoarse singing."

Titian, too, may have had in mind the *Giostra*, I. cxi, when he composed his Bacchus and Ariadne.   (Fig. 260)

> "Comes upon a car covered with ivy and rushes
> Drawn by two tigers — Bacchus
> And with him it seems that fauns and mænads
> Tread the deep sand and shout with raised voices.
> One we see staggering; others seem to stumble,
> One clashes the cymbal; others seem to laugh.
> One drinks from a horn, one from his hand.
> One has grabbed a nymph, and one turns handsprings."

LEONARDO AND THE ACADEMIC IDEA OF PAINTING

The extraordinary mixture of liberality and dogmatism, of naturalism and taste in Leonardo is best illustrated from his own *Trattato della Pittura*. I quote from the standard edition of H. Ludwig, Vienna, 1882, using his paragraph numbers:

Modelling in Chiaroscuro as the Painter's First Object

¶ 412. "The first object of the painter is to make a flat plane appear as a body in relief and projecting from that plane, and he who in such art excels the others, deserves the greater praise, and such research, or rather crown of such science, is born from light and shade, or I mean chiaroscuro. Then he who flees from shadows, flees also from the glory of our art among noble spirits and gains it with the ignorant herd, which desires nothing in painting but beauty of colors, forgetting entirely the beauty and wonder of showing a flat thing as if it were in relief."

On Judging a Painter's Work

¶ 483. "The first thing is that you consider the figures, if they have the relief which the place and light demand . . .

"The second is that the scattering, or rather distribution of the figures be made according to the way in which you wish the story to be.

"The third is that the figures be alert and intent on their particular purpose."

On the Movements that Mark the Emotions

¶ 122. "The most important thing which can be found in the theory of painting are the movements appropriate to the mental state of each being,— as desire, scorn, wrath, pity and the like."

The Steps in a Painter's Education

¶ 82. "Draw first designs of a good master made in the fashion of nature and not mannered; then from a relief, in the presence of a drawing made from that relief; then from a good natural object."

Judgment versus Dexterity

¶ 62. "That painter who does not doubt learns little. When the work surpasses the judgment of the worker, that worker acquires little, and when the judgment surpasses the work, that work never ceases to grow better, unless avarice prevents it."

On Use of Memory in the Night Watches

¶ 67. "Also I have proved it to be of no little use to me, when you find yourself in bed in the dark, to repeat in the imagination the things studied earlier, or other things of notable sort comprised in subtle thought, and this is truly a laudable act and useful in fixing things in memory."

On Selective Imitation

¶ 58a. "The painter should be solitary and think over what he sees and discuss with himself, selecting the most excellent parts of the species of whatever he sees, acting after the fashion of a mirror which transmutes into as many colors as there are things what is set before it. And so doing he will seem to be himself a second nature."

¶ 98. "Winter evenings should be used by young painters in the study of things prepared in summer, that is bring together all the nudes which you have made in the summer, and make a choice of the better limbs and bodies and practice from them and fix them in mind."

On High Standards

¶ 59. "If you painter will seek to please the first painters, you will make your pictures well, because they alone can guide you truthfully, but if you wish to please those who are not masters, your pictures will have few foreshortenings and little relief or alert movement, and thereby you will fail in that part in which painting is held to be an excellent art, that is in giving an effect of relief where there is nothing in relief."

On Avoiding Harsh Shadows and Sunlight Effects

¶ 87. "The light cut off from the shade too clearly is greatly blamed by painters. Hence to avoid such a fault, if you paint bodies in the open country, you will not make the figures as lighted by the sun, but imagine some sort of mist or transparent clouds to be interposed between the object and the sun, whence, since the figure is not emphasized by the sunlight, the demarcations of light and shade will not be emphasized."

On the Most Pleasing Light

¶ 138. "If you have a court yard that can be covered as you wish with a linen awning, that will be a good light; or when you wish to draw anyone, draw him in bad weather, towards nightfall, and make the sitter stand with his back to one of the walls of this court. In the streets set your mind towards nightfall on the faces of the men and women, in bad weather, how much grace and sweetness appears in them."

On Counterpoise of the Figure

¶ 88. "Do not have the head turned the way the breast is, nor the arm the way the leg is; and if the head is turned over the right shoulder make the parts lower on the left than on the right" [and vice versa].

At first blush this stylistic counsel flatly contradicts Leonardo's principle that poses and emotions should express state of mind, but as a matter of fact many expressive movements obey this law of counterpoise or active equilibrium. Leonardo himself generally finds motives for such poses. Such successors as Raphael and Andrea del Sarto habitually used such poses without other excuse than that of their own inherent gracefulness.

On Freedom in Making a Composition

¶ 189. "Have you never considered the poets composing their verses? They take no trouble to make fine letters, nor do they mind cancelling some of the verses and making them better. Do you, then, painter, make the limbs of your figures roughly and attend first to the movements appropriate to the mental state of the beings composing your story, rather than to the beauty and rightness of their members, because you must understand that if such a composition in the rough will meet the needs of the invention, it will please all the more after it has been adorned with the perfection appropriate to all its parts. I have seen in the clouds and spots on the wall what has aroused me to fine inventions of various things, since these spots though entirely without perfection in any part, did not lack perfection in their movements and other actions."

Painting the Grandchild of Nature

¶ 12. "If you shall despise painting, which is the only imitator of all the apparent works of nature, assuredly you will despise also that careful investigation which with philosophical and careful speculation considers all the qualities of forms: the sea, place, plants, animals, herbage, flowers, which are enveloped in light and shade. And truly this speculation is science and the legitimate child of Nature, since painting is born of this nature. But, to speak more correctly, we will say grandchild of nature, since all apparent things are born of Nature, of which things painting is born. Hence rightly we shall call it the grandchild of this nature and the kinsman of God."

That the Painter Should be Solitary

¶ 50. "The painter, or rather designer, should be solitary, and especially when he is intent on speculations and considerations which continually appearing before the eyes give matter to be well kept in memory. And if you are alone, you will be entirely yours. And

if you shall be accompanied by a single companion you will
be half yours, and so much the less as the indiscretion of your com-
panionship shall be the greater . . . And if you would say 'I will do
in my fashion, I will hold myself apart' . . . one cannot serve two
masters. You will fullfil badly the duty of a companion, and worse
the aim of reasoning on the art . . . And if you say 'I will withdraw
myself entirely,' . . . I tell you you will be held a madman, but, lo,
thus doing you will at least be alone."

Here Leonardo takes sharpest issue with the easy-going sociable
methods which for generations had held in the painter's *bottega*, and
shows himself an individualist of modern type.

Rubens' Praise of Leonardo

Peter Paul Rubens, who had copied Leonardo's battle-piece, has left
the following perceptive tribute to the genius of his predecessor:

"Nothing escaped him that related to the expression of his subject:
and by the heat of his fancy, as well as by the solidity of his judgment,
he raised divine things by human, and understood how to give men
those different degrees, that elevate them to the character of heroes.

"The best of the examples which he has left us is our Lord's Supper,
which he painted at Milan, wherein he has represented the apostles in
places that suit with them, and our Saviour in the most honourable,
the midst of all, having nobody near enough to press or incommode him.
His attitude is grand, his arms are in a loose and free posture, to show
the greater grandeur, while the apostles appear agitated one side to the
other by the vehemence of their inquietude, and in which there is,
however, no meanness, nor any indecent action to be seen. In short
by his profound speculations he arrived to such a degree of perfection,
that it seems to me impossible to speak so well of him as he deserves,
and much more to imitate him."

*The Art of Painting . . . Translated from the French of Monsieur
De Piles*, London about 1725. p. 107 f.

THE GOLDEN AGE

Fig. 167. Raphael. Count Baldassare Castiglione, author of "the Courtier." — *Louvre*.

CHAPTER VI

THE GOLDEN AGE

RAPHAEL AND MICHELANGELO

On pride and humility in Art — The new Grand Style defined — Umbrian
humility in the Early Painters — Gentile da Fabriano — The Fifteenth
Century — Luca Signorelli — Perugino — Raphael; Early development —
Roman triumph — Michelangelesque aberrations — Michelangelo.

Whether the greatest art is grounded in pride or in humility has divided the critics. To most it will seem evident that
the artist's assertion of his own powers is an act of pride —
a pride of person which is often reinforced by that of nation
and race. As fine a critic as John Ruskin, on the contrary,
has insisted that the greatest art springs from humility —
reverence for God, admiration of His works in nature, homage
also to one's earthly master in art and withal to the great tradition of one's craft. The difference is world-wide. According to one interpretation or the other, the work of art becomes
an act of display or of worship. Such opposites in the realm
of analysis often meet comfortably enough in the realm of
practice. A haughty individualist like Leonardo da Vinci
insists that his investigations of appearance and reality lead
to that knowledge of God without which love is impossible.
And the Golden Age of painting itself, though mostly based
on corporate and individual pride, has also its infusion of
humility. If Michelangelo represents the flowering of three
generations of research, of that pride of intellect which ever
ruled Florence, so equally does Raphael represent many generations of humility and teachableness in his native Umbria.

For about ten years pride and humility worked side by side, and that was the Golden Age. Pride prevailed over humility, and the classical style of Central Italy sunk to a pretentious exhibitionism.

Our theme is that brief moment of accomplishment which witnessed the rise of Rome as centre of art, and the greatest painting of Raphael and Michelangelo. We need not hesitate to apply to it the oldfashioned term, the Golden Age. But we shall not use it with quite the oldfashioned unction, knowing as we do the heavy sacrifice involved in attaining the so-called Grand Style, and the still heavier penalty it imposed upon the art that succeeded it.

The Florentines believed that painting had reached its height in the years 1504 and 1505, when Leonardo da Vinci and Michelangelo were designing the great competitive battle-pieces for the Priors' Palace at Florence, and Raphael was painting his loveliest Madonnas. Modern critics might rather be inclined to date the grand climacteric from a pathetic incident of a few years later. In 1508, when Pope Julius II wished to decorate the new anterooms of the Vatican, the famous *stanze* he called the best of the older painters — Sodoma, Perugino, Signorelli, among others. No sooner had they begun to decorate the vaults than their work seemed inadequate. They were turned off incontinently and the young man Raphael called down from Florence to take their place. The incident shows how suddenly the new beauty dawned upon the world of art patronage. Vividly conscious of its advent, the Italians were less conscious of the equally sudden waning of the great style. With the wisdom of hindsight we can now see that the whole development was a marvelous spurt, lasting a bare dozen years, from the battle cartoons of 1505 to Raphael's tapestry cartoons of 1516. Raphael and Michelangelo, who created the lasting glory of the Renaissance, also dug its grave. Before considering the creative and destructive energies of these two giants, we may profitably note the characteristics of what whether for praise or mockery has ever since been called the Grand Style. And here I have little to do beyond condensing Professor Wöfflin's excellent book.

In the Grand Style the accent was on maturity, decorum, and measured power. Vivacious and picturesque incidents are eschewed. The new art demands simplicity and centrality. The human figure dominates the compositions. The frame is filled densely with a complicated group. The figures themselves are ample and mature. The Madonna is no longer a girl, but a gracious woman of thirty years. The Christ Child is no longer an infant, but a well-grown lad, whose supple curves harmonize with those of grown folks. As to pose, the figures no longer are casually arranged or in some posture required by a specific action. They are cast in conventional poses which bring out the active beauty of the body. Heads swing across shoulders, the upper body turns against the thrust of the lower, the arms counter the action of the legs. Such counterpoise is always active, implying motion. Straight lines give way to weavings of S curves — so many springs whose tension is kept equal. Violent motion or torsion of the body is frequent, but one motion or torsion must be immediately taken up and balanced by some equivalent. Following the general principle of centrality, colors are fewer and more studied. In portraiture, for example, we no longer have landscape or elaborate interiors, but plain dark backgrounds. At all points we have left spontaneity and happy accident behind and have entered a world of exquisite calculation. Society had moved with art towards ideals of simplicity and decorum. You no longer find the braided, beribboned and jewelled coiffures of Botticelli's women, but serene brows with the hair drawn back evenly from its part and disposed as a mass in a net. Young gallants wear their abundant locks much the same way and sport seignorial spade beards. Old men are even more magnificently provided with beards of monumental scale. Such men are clothed no longer in particolored raiment, but in richly sober black. The ideal is dignity, composure, and magnanimity. You may trace it through all its intricacies of casuistry in what is still one of the best pictures of what a gentleman and lady should be, the *Cortegiano* of Baldassare Castiglione. It was finished in 1516 while his friend Raphael was designing the tapestry cartoons. And you may read much of this high teaching in Count Castiglione's own sensitive and comprehending face, Figure 167, as Raphael then painted it. It breathes that fine interplay of pride and humility which was the mainspring of the Renaissance, and it brings us back to the double origin of the Grand Style in the pride of Florence and the humility of Umbria.

Umbria in the narrow sense includes only the lovely stretches of the upper Tiber, and the rolling banks of Lakes Trasimene and Bolsena. But all the way over the mountains to the Adriatic the civilization was of a similar type, and so the art. Thus we may reckon the Adriatic Marches from Ancona to Ravenna as Umbrian from the point of view of the historian of painting. There were no great cities and little commerce. It is a region of small hill-top communes within the walls of which the peasants huddled for protection at night, going down to the fields in the day. It was a country of hot passions and violent feuds, and equally of religious enthusiasm and mystical piety. Great heresies had swept the land and so had the joyous and practical Christianity of St. Francis, greatest of Umbria's sons. We have much of the volatility that we noted in Siena, without, however, a capital city to centralize it, and we also have what Siena lacked — an abiding and beautiful humility. Umbria knew her provincial estate and accepted its limitations.

Nowhere is this more plainly shown than in her art. For

two centuries she was in the position of inducing foreign artists to come in, ever in an attitude of admiration and docility. Thus Giunta of Pisa, Cimabue and his Roman contemporaries; Giotto and his Florentine pupils; Simone Martini and other Sienese painters decorated the chief monument of Umbria, the Basilica of St. Francis at Assisi. Their work extended over a century to say 1330. Later still Sienese artists were employed at Perugia, among others, Taddeo Bartoli, and the region promised to become an artistic dependency of Siena. But with the dawning of the Renaissance and the extension of Florentine power beyond Arezzo, Florentine artists are preferred. We find Domenico Veneziano at Perugia, in 1438, in the pay of the ruling Baglioni. A little earlier Fra Angelico had painted for several years at Cortona. In the early fifties Benozzo Gozzoli painted his Franciscan frescoes at Montefalco, and was otherwise active in the Tiber valley. In 1468 Fra Filippo Lippi was called to Spoleto. Soon after, Umbria learned to depend on her own artists. In the Adriatic Marches there had been a limited penetration of Giotto's style, chiefly by way of Padua and Rimini. By the end of the century the Lorenzettian manner dominated. It was succeeded by the influence of the Venetian Renaissance as exemplified by such rather backward artists as the Vivarini and Carlo Crivelli. Still later the diffused influence of Giovanni Bellini meets harmoniously that of Perugino.

Thus in humility and teachableness Umbria very slowly, and through most various stages of discipleship, worked out her own originality. And when it came one felt deeply in it the teaching of her spacious intervales and blue mountains.

It is so with the first notable painter that Umbria produced, Gentile da Fabriano.[1] He felt landscape as no artist before him. Born about 1360, he was trained by his fellow townsman, Alegretto Nuzi. Alegretto had made sound studies at Florence and had also observed with admiration the pictures of the Lorenzetti. His own altar-pieces have the Sienese splendor with a touch of sweetness that is wholly Umbrian. His pupil Gentile prefers more ornate and florid compositions such as we

FIG. 168. Gentile da Fabriano. Adoration of the Magi.— *Uffizi.*

see in his early Coronation of the Virgin at Milan. Soon Gentile gave himself to the panoramic narrative style, outdoing the Lorenzetti in elaboration, vivacity, and gracefulness. Superficially he resembles such Florentine contemporaries as Lorenzo Monaco and Masolino, but his mood is broader and more genial, and his decorative accent more splendid. Before 1410 he was called to Venice to paint in the new Ducal Palace. His animated historical frescoes were soon destroyed by fire, but his sojourn was long enough to impress his manner, through his pupil Jacopo, Bellini, and numerous imitators, on the Venetian narrative school.

Passing to Florence, he left there the fullest expression of his gracious talent in the resplendent Adoration of the Kings, Figure 168, now in the Uffizi, which was painted for Palla Strozzi's chapel in the Trinità. It was signed in May 1423,

FIG. 169.   Gentile da Fabriano.   The Nativity.   Predella piece from Adoration of Magi. — *Uffizi.*

and perhaps because it was the season of flowers, Gentile painted in the rich pilasters growing sprays of morning glory, iris, anemone, and cornflower.   Within its fantastic Gothic frame we witness a pageant such as Italy often saw on holy days — the procession of the Wise men moving through her streets.   Around the Mother and her Child devotion reigns, but soon the scene passes off into the tumult of waiting men-at-arms, of chafing steeds, and snarling animals of the chase. The color is a radiance of scarlet, crimson, azure and gold, after the Gothic fashion.   But the picture is more than Gothic in the tender and almost atmospheric shading of the rolling hills in the background.   Skilfully blending Sienese idealism with narrative breadth and vivacity, the picture is the last and most magnificent memorial to a chivalry now merely an afterglow, but dying with all the iridescence of the sunset hour.

As is usually the case, the modern contribution of the picture is modestly made in the *predella* panels.   The Nativity, Figure 169, with the light radiating tenderly from the Christ

Child and golden stars glimmering above the hill-top pastures is perhaps the first nocturne in art, and still one of the loveliest. The Flight into Egypt, shows a joyous sunrise creeping over the glad hills. The means are conventional, the highlights are touched in with gold, but the mood and effect are there. Young Masaccio surely considered these little panels before he undertook his more naturalistic adventure in structural light and shade.

Fig. 170.   Andrea da Bologna. Madonna of Humility.— *Cleveland.*

Soon Pope Martin V, returning from exile at Avignon and planning to restore the splendors of Christian Rome, called Gentile and set him to decorating the nave of St. John Lateran. Again fire has deprived us of the monumental works which constituted Gentile's contemporary fame. We know that they won the praise of the greatest Flemish painter who visited Renaissance Italy, Rogier de la Pasture of Tournai. And two generations later crabbed Michelangelo declared almost sentimentally that Gentile was gentle both by name and by nature. For us it is important to note that Gentile forecast precisely the future triumphs of Raphael, carrying the glory of Umbrian painting widely through Italy before asserting it at Rome.

Of course such work as Gentile's was highly exceptional in the Umbrian Marches. The average state of things is represented by the shy and humble Madonnas which Francescuccio Ghisi repeated indefinitely. This type of Madonna of

Humility is nowhere more delightfully represented than in the
lovely panel at the Cleveland Museum, Figure 170, for which
I have elsewhere suggested the attribution of Andrea da
Bologna.[2] She is most unlike the majestic Madonnas of Florence and Siena. To assure us that this gentle Mother is after
all Queen of Heaven and the Second Eve come for our salvation, the artist has given her a resplendent aureole with tiny
miniatures of her champions, the apostles, and has stretched
at her feet that First Eve in whom we all sinned. The picture
will have been painted before 1380, and, with its Byzantine
reminiscences, it well exemplifies the mediævalism that held
its own in the Adriatic Marches long after Tuscany had set
her face towards the Renaissance.

It would add little to our survey of Umbria to dwell on
Ottaviano Nelli at Urbino, a gently vivacious story teller;
nor yet on those early painters at Camerino and San Severino
who tinged the softer native style with the splendid severity
of the early Venetian manner. I pass their works with regret,
for they are often lovely in their frank dependence on greater
spirits. In a general survey the middle years of the fifteenth
century in Umbria show rather little to attract us until the
rise of Pietro Perugino. He emerges in an artistic world dominated in the Tiber Valley by the Florentine, Gozzoli, and beyond the mountains by Carlo Crivelli and the Vivarini. Such
predecessor of Perugino as Benedetto Bonfigli of Perugia need
not detain us. He had learned a little, a very little, from the
Florentine, Domenico Veneziano, paints Madonnas with a
modest ideality; and narratives, the life of St. Ercolano in
the Communal Palace of Perugia, with abundant and muddled
detail, after the fashion of Gozzoli and Domenico di Bartolo.
His *bottega* was a factory of those quaint and often terrible
religious banners, Figure 171, which the devout Umbrians
carried processionaly to avert the recurrent plague. We need
not dwell upon Perugino's alleged master, Fiorenzo di Lorenzo,

whose ugly and emphatic draughtsmanship derives from Verrocchio and the Pollaiuoli. We may best appreciate Perugino's extraordinary originality by considering contemporaries who

FIG. 171. Bonfigli Plague Banner. The Virgin protecting her Devotees from plague Shafts hurled by Christ. — *Chiesa del Gonfalone, Perugia.*

FIG. 172. Lorenzo di San Severino. Madonna and Saints. — *Cleveland, O.*

came up with equal advantages. Lorenzo di San Severino exemplifies the usual Umbrian blend of Gozzoli and Venetian influences. And in such a picture as the Enthroned Madonna, Figure 172, in the Holden Collection, at Cleveland, he attains an ideality of feeling and a beauty of workmanship of the most refreshing sort. This picture must have been painted about 1490. It may represent the high mark reached in the Marches towards the end of the century — may thus dispense us from considering such inherently charming painters as Girolamo da Camerino and his fellow townsman Giovanni Boccatis.

A very similar training produces more ambitious but hardly

more pleasing results in Niccolò Liberatore of Foligno, (1430 to 1502). Early influenced by Gozzoli, he later aped the intensity of the Venetian, Carlo Crivelli. Niccolò thus chafes within the modest bounds proper to art in Umbria. He essays tragedy and too often achieves burlesque.

He paints, like most of the Um-brians, processional banners, and also the most complicated altar-pieces, in which cusps, carving and pinnacles almost efface the Madonna and saints, who show a peasantlike uneasiness amid so much splendor. Such is the char-acter of the triptych in the Vati-can, which is dated 1466. It rep-resents rather favorably Niccolò's at once slender and ambitious talent.

Such obscure artists as we have been considering[3] could maintain the idealism out of which a Perugino should grow, could provide his spiritual background. They could do little to nurture him on the positive side. That task fell to men of greater power, who had saturated themselves with Florentine realism — Melozzo da Forlì[4] and Luca Signorelli. Both were pupils of that giant among Umbro-Florentines, Piero della Francesca. Melozzo was born in 1438 and early employed by the Dukes of Urbino. He practices an energetic draughtsman-ship both in decoration and portraiture, indulges the boldest foreshortening, adds a positive athleticism to that pride of life which we have noted in more static form in his master. Thus his frescoes for the domes of the sacristy of the Santa Casa at Loreto, and the justly famous fragments of playing

FIG. 173. Melozzo da Forlì. Pope Sixtus IV and his Court. Fresco. — *Vatican.*

angels now exhibited in the sacristy of St. Peter's, at Rome reveal a strength and measured audacity which at once rival the contemporary effort of Mantegna at Mantua and forecast the more pagan exuberance of Mantegna's greatest

FIG. 174.   Luca Signorelli.   Pan, God of Music. — *Berlin.*

pupil, Correggio. This robust and masculine manner appears in a more restrained and traditional form in the superb fresco portraits of Pope Sixtus IV and his Court, Figure 173, in the Vatican. Such work transcends Umbrian standards.

Even more does the intense and rugged art of Melozzo's fellow disciple, Luca Signorelli.[5] Born at Cortona in 1441, we know little of his early career except that he studied with Piero della Francesca, passed to Florence and was permanently swayed by the anatomical and passionate realism of Antonio Pollaiuolo. Signorelli's early work is obscure to us. We may well study him first in the pastoral mythology, Pan, God of Harmony, Figure 174, now at Berlin. It was painted about 1490 for the Medici, for the villa for which Botticelli designed the Primavera and Birth of Venus. It is inferior to its companion pieces in imagination and delicacy, and particularly in color, but in its own measured way it echoes delightfully the poetic wistfulness of early Florentine humanism. Similar qualities of imagination are in the great fresco The Last Days of Moses, in the Sistine Chapel, painted in 1482 after his design. But the vein is exceptional in Signorelli. Soon he gave himself

to a rugged realism, unpleasing in his religious themes. Meeting little favor in the great cities, he painted many altar-pieces for the Umbrian towns. These pictures are stern in spirit and leaden in color. There is no attempt to please. Relentlessly Signorelli pursued his personal quest of expressive anatomy. Legend tells us that, dry-eyed, he sketched the fair body of his own murdered son for the picture of the Entombment at Cortona. We see him introducing nude figures into the background of the round Madonna at the Uffizi, Figure

FIG. 175. Signorelli. Madonna.
— Uffizi.

175. The experimentalist dominates the artist.

In the year 1500, being nearly sixty, he found the real use for his truculent art. He was called to paint in the Chapel of S. Brixio, in the Cathedral of Orvieto. The subject was the Last Judgment. More than fifty years earlier Fra Angelico had begun the work with angel choirs in the vaults. With a far different temper Signorelli continued the task. At the entrance and back of the Chapel he showed mankind scourged by the final plagues. In the four arched spaces at the sides he set The Preaching of Antichrist, a sinister scene detailed with all the circumstantiality of the Early Renaissance. For the three remaining scenes, the Resurrection of the Dead, Figure 176, the Condemnation of the Sinful, Figure 177, and the Reward of the Just, he invented new modes both of interpretation and of composition. How far we are from the solemn assizes of Giotto or the garden and labyrinth motives of Fra Angelico! In every case we have in the lunette celestial figures, or at least supernal, while below we have swarming masses of nude folk, bewildered at the forgotten light, aspiring heavenwards or shrinking from the clutches of the fiends.

What distinguishes these frescoes is a magnificently just matter-of-factness. Only one question is raised by the artist. Given the literal truth of the Book of Revelations, how would the last judgment look, and how would one feel if he were indeed there? So he reasons it out — the struggle of the skeletons to push up to the light, their reinvestiture successively with sinews, muscles and skin, the embarrassment as a half assembled body vainly seeks recognition. And all this he contrasts with the confident, strong bearing of the archangels above. Again in the Ascent of the Just to Heaven, the aspiration is chiefly physical, magnificently so. These clean strong bodies chiefly wish to escape the corruption from which the last trump has summoned them. And even the guardian angels are less tender than jubilant at the thought of fit recruits to replenish St. Michael's celestial militia. Equally the damned wince, not from conscience, but from physical dread of the chains and claws and the imminence of the eternal fires.

This sturdy, upright art seems hardly Italian. The spirit of it is ruthless and Northern. It mitigates nothing, tells pretty much everything, presents the body in its ugliness, disregards obvious considerations of style. Yet as a successful blend of a vast technical experiment in anatomy with an honest and powerful effort of imagination, this is one of the most re-

FIG. 176. Luca Signorelli. The General Resurrection.
— *Cathedral, Orvieto.*

FIG. 177. Luca Signorelli. The Souls of the Damned. — *Cathedral, Orvieto.*

markable achievements of the Italian Renaissance. It has little of the Italian nobility, but it powerfully influenced those who had. Perugino and Raphael imitated Signorelli's orderly arrangement of his scenes in a double, vertical order, and Michelangelo fed his dream of a heroic world of splendid nudity from the drastic visions of Signorelli. Over-rich and over-emphatic as Signorelli is, he is also an elemental, tonic power. No one is quite the same after a visit to the Chapel of S. Brixio.

If Signorelli was the greatest character in Umbria before Raphael, Pietro Perugino was the finest intelligence and taste. He was born in 1446 at Città della Pieve and at nine years old was put with a poor Perugian painter. His early activity is matter only of ingenious conjecture.[6] There is an ambiguous range of pictures variously ascribed to him and to Fiorenzo di Lorenzo, a difficult and rather unimportant problem which I willingly let alone. What is certain is that in his early twenties Perugino was studying with Verrocchio at Florence alongside of Leonardo da Vinci. By 1481 and 1482 Perugino emerges artistically full-grown in the Sistine Chapel.

His superiority, as shown in the fresco of the Giving of the Keys to Peter, Figure 118, and in numerous works of his forty-two remaining years, is so uniform and almost monotonous that its greatness has until recently passed unnoticed. Only such critics as Mr. Berenson and Professor Wölfflin have done him full justice. He worked upon perfectly clear and conscious ideals of simplicity, symmetry, and spaciousness; in all of which he took issue with his times. Rejecting the picturesque richness and confusion of the Early Renaissance, he took counsel of the Byzantine painters and of Fra Angelico at San Marco. They taught him the worth of simple geometrical forms of figure composition, and how to sacrifice details to broad effects. That his groups disposed in simple pyramids, oblongs, or ovals should not seem too bare, he cunningly varied the positions of the figures, thus relieving the severity of the underlying symmetry. Every tilted head, pointed foot and swaying thigh has its precise compositional value. As for the figures, there is no strenuousness of draughtsmanship, they are

Fig. 178. Perugino. Mystical Crucifixion. Fresco. —
Santa Maria Maddalena de' Pazzi. Florence.

simply good enough. A principle of artistic economy, alien to the spirit of the moment, rules here as elsewhere.

So far he appears as a critic and amender of the Early Renaissance style. His positive contribution was a particularly spacious and lovely sort of landscape, an immensity of light and air to set behind the restricted patterns of his figures. This landscape is a beautiful generalization of the scenery of the upper Tiber valley. The forms are few. Feathery trees mark the middle distance; a river valley opens gently with interlocking banks toward distant blue mountains. Above a silvery horizon, the heavens gradually deepen to an intense blue, accentuated by sparse floating clouds. There are few colors, a warm brown, a fresh green, a paler and a deeper blue, a variety of grays. With these simple means is attained a sense of infinite space and of encompassing peace.

All these perfections are in the great frescoed Crucifixion Figure 178, in the convent of Santa Maria Maddelena dei

Pazzi, at Florence. The date is 1495, Perugino's fifty-second year. The lyrical quietism of the effect rests on delicate evasions of the very formal symmetry. Such features as the

FIG. 179. Perugino. Enthroned Madonna. — *Vatican*.

tilted head of the Saint John and the three trees at the left balancing the Magdalen at the right of the cross are essential. Indeed any slight change either in the position of the figures or the lines of the landscape would produce a discord.

We have a very similar effect with the addition of a stately and simple architecture in the enthroned Madonna of the Vatican. Figure 179. Again the formality of the pyramidal pattern is relieved by varied dispositions of the figures which individually considered may seem affected, but which are essential to the composition. More overtly emotional but still restrained is the Deposition, Figure 180a, of the Uffizi Gallery. It is arranged as an oval with catenary internal curves, anticipating much more complicated patterns of Raphael. At this moment, 1494, no living artist but Leonardo could have woven this group together with such certainty of taste, and he could have hardly equalled its broad and serene landscape.

In the first years of the new century Perugino decorated the merchants' exchange of Perugia, the Cambio, with frescoes partly religious, partly moral and symbolical. The most famous represent the Virtues, Figure 180, in pairs, hovering in the heavens with their representatives below. For example, Prudence and Justice with the great law-givers. So Fortitude and Temperance are represented respectively by the venerable forms of brave Horatius, and Leonidas; of Cato and

Cincinnatus. It seems that Perugino executed most of this
latter decoration through assistants, and it has been suggested
that Raphael is responsible both for the design and painting
of the beautiful Sibyls.[7]

Fig. 180. Perugino.   Prudence and Justice with their Representatives.   Fresco. — *Cambio, Perugia.*

Like most of his contemporaries Perugino outlived his
fame. He was insulted by Michelangelo, criticized for repeating his figures, thrust out of the Vatican in 1508 and superseded
by his former helper, Raphael. And his exquisite art in his
later years shows a certain relaxation. He died of the plague
in 1524 and was denied Christian burial, although in his day
he had painted plague banners to protect the faithful.

The known atheism of Perugino affords a curious problem.
How reconcile it with the mild and gentle religiosity of his
art? Were he a modern artist, one might hold that he entered
by æsthetic sympathy into experiences of religion which his
rational self denied. For an atheist of the Renaissance the

explanation seems too subtle. They were of tough fibre and kept their sympathy logically in hand. Mr. Berenson has offered the ingenious explanation that in his noble composition

in space Perugino appealed to emotions which are so nearly akin to religion as to be readily substituted therefor. In the great spaces of Perugino the spirit finds liberation and a sense of the infinite. Such intuition of infinity one finds also in personal religion, and the two experiences are in a degree interchangeable. Æsthetically satisfactory, this explanation may fail to convince a devout person. He will want to know how the art of an avowed

FIG. 180a.   Perugino.   The Deposition. — *Pitti*.

atheist enthralled the pious folk inhabiting the valley sanctified by the memory of St. Francis. Whatever be the explanation, the space composition of Perugino later sufficed to express Raphael's vision of the central mystery of Christianity, of the nobility of pagan intellect and of the serene splendor of the Grecian Olympians.

Raphael Sanzio [8] is the finest example of the Umbrian virtue of teachableness. His course is a series of exquisitely felt admirations. His readiness to assimilate any sort of excellence was his strength, and at times his weakness, for he was not always self-critical enough to reject merits alien to his own personality. His admitted primacy rests on perfection of composition, and that perfection represented a beautiful synthesis of the methods of Perugino, Fra Bartolommeo, and Leonardo da Vinci. In dramatic power, force of draughtsmanship, and charm of color many of his contemporaries surpassed him. His, indeed, is a triumph of tact and judgment, and not of any single achievement. He seems one of the young men of the Platonic dialogues come back to earth — graciously prudent, gently effective, superior yet companionable. He approached art as his fellow Umbrian, St. Francis, approached life, with friendly confidence. He was equally at home with noble and artisan, with austere prelate and libertine humanist. Men readily gave him their loyalty and women their love.

Raphael Sanzio was born at Urbino in 1483. His father, Giovanni, a mediocre poet and painter, left him an orphan at eleven. Raphael's first steps in painting were probably guided by Timoteo Viti, who practiced, partly under Perugino's influence, the timidly idyllic style of the Northern Marches — Bologna and Ferrara. Such boyish efforts of Raphael as the Orleans Madonna, the Three Graces, and the Dream of a Knight, in the National Gallery show Raphael's complete assimilation of this idyllic manner. The little picture at London in which a stripling Hercules slumbers between an attractive girlish Wisdom and a most innocent effigy of Vice — holding the flower that signifies the primrose path — shows us Raphael at seventeen and by no means precocious.

In the year 1500 he was called from Urbino to work in Perugino's home shop at Perugia, soon rising to the position of foreman. In four years he made the most devout and complete assimilation of his master's style. Such pictures as the Coronation of Mary, in the Vatican, and the Marriage of the Virgin, Figure 181, at Milan, would surely be reckoned as consummate Perugino's were it not for signatures and old tradition. The Marriage of the Virgin in particular is merely a rearrangement of Perugino's composition for the Giving of the Keys to Peter. But Raphael has eliminated unnecessary incidents and has outdone Perugino himself in sweetness and calm. The picture was finished in 1504, and that year Raphael took letters of recommendation from his first patroness, the Duchess of Urbino, to the Magistracy of Florence.

Imagine a youngster of twenty-one who has diligently mastered a pictorial style only to learn that it is already obsolete. That is Raphael taking the manner of Perugino to a Florence agog over the battle cartoons of Leonardo and Michel-

FIG. 181. Raphael. Marriage of the Virgin. — *Milan.*

FIG. 182. Raphael. Maddalena Doni. — *Pitti.*

angelo. The coolness with which young Raphael faced this emergency is characteristic. In four years he made himself over into a realistic draughtsman. Abandoning the ready-made faces and figures of Perugino, he wisely held to Perugino's sweetness and spacious compositional patterns. Young Raphael achieves an extraordinary act of criticism. He takes from the reformers just what he needs and no more — from Leonardo his incisiveness and psychology as a draughtsman and his dense and rich compositional patterns, from Fra Bartolommeo his dignity and monumentality, from Michelangelo very little as yet; and, withal, he retains whatever still seemed valuable from his Umbrian experience. Thus with resolute and unperturbed intelligence within four years he completely reconstructed his style, and put himself on a parity with older contemporaries who had been experimenting for a score of years.

The steps of this re-education are most interesting. In 1505 he did the portraits of Agnolo Doni and his wife Maddalena, Figure 182. The posture of the woman is that of Leonardo's Mona Lisa. The draughtsmanship and characterization are severe, the hint of Umbrian landscape is a survival. In later portraits we shall see the elimination of accessories, the line yielding to the most refined modelling in light and dark, the effect concentrated without insistency. A comparison of the Doni portraits with those of ten years later, the Julius II and the Fornarina, will tell better than words of the tendency of Raphael's portraiture towards its ultimate mastery.

In 1505 Raphael returned for a time to Perugino to paint the fresco of the Trinity at the Convent of San Severo. In the splendid geometrical pattern he has already improved on the flat groupings of Perugino. The consistory of Saints bends back in depth after the fashion of a semi-dome. Raphael borrows the new motive from Fra Bartolommeo's fresco of the Last Judgment painted in 1499 for the Florentine Hospital of Santa Maria Nuova. Sixteen years later Perugino added the languid saints at the base of the Trinity, a touching reversal of the natural relations of master and pupil. As for Raphael, in a single experiment he has mastered the sort of symmetrical composition in depth which should suffice within five years for his masterpiece, the Disputa.

The matronly sweetness of Raphael's early madonnas has won them affection from the first. With increasing dignity, they retain a hint of the girlish refinement of their predecessors of the Early Renaissance. But they are less assertively fastidious, more normal and natural. All these obvious reasons for liking them are sound, and these pictures afford as well an insight into Raphael's consciously directed studies. The effect is ever towards richer and more complicated composition, and towards more interesting and stylistic dispositions of the figures. The naturalness is that of taste

FIG. 183. Raphael. Madonna del Granduca. — *Pitti.*

FIG. 184. Raphael. La Belle Jardinière. — *Louvre.*

and calculation. Near the beginning of the series we have the lovely Madonna of the Grand Duke, 1505, Figure 183. The upright, frontal position and form and serene oval of the face recall Perugino. But reality has supervened, — Perugino never painted such a Bambino, — and for the sake of concentration the background is kept plain. We see in the Madonna of the Tempi Family, at Munich, the Madonna turned in three-quarters position, the pose energized, the body swaying in a slight counterpoise. Then he tries seated poses which offer the triangular pattern of Leonardo. Perhaps the earliest of this series is the lovely Cowper Madonna, now in the Widener Collection. Soon he adds figures, constructs the pyramids more ornately and restores the background of landscape. At the head of this line is the Madonna of the Finch in the Pitti. It illustrates that gracious formality which Leonardo established in the Madonna of the Rocks. Finding the balance of the two standing nude children a little too obvious, Raphael carries the motive to its perfection in the Belle Jardinière of the Louvre. Figure 184. Here, to break the rigid symmetry, the St. John kneels, and superfluous trees have been cleared away from the background. He seeks' further to enrich the pyramid, and in the Madonna of the Canigiani family, at Munich, Figure 185, finished in 1507, we have at once the densest of symmetries and the stylistic handling of all the figures in active and counterpoised attitudes. In two years the process is complete. Later, in the Madonna of the Fish and of the Pearl, executed by students, Raphael will adopt diagonal arrangements, he will take up the old Circular form in the Madonna of the Chair, and will amplify the simple patterns of Perugino in the Sistine Madonna and the Madonna of Foligno. The forms and faces will become graver, nobler, more mature, but the whole course is fully anticipated in the joyous and lucid years of experiment from 1505 to 1507.

Fig. 185. Raphael. Canigiani Holy Family. — *Munich*.

In that year Raphael pulled himself together to produce a masterpiece and signally failed. So far he must have seemed only a charming painter, a more gracious Fra Bartolommeo or a more learned Albertinelli, he will now surpass Leonardo and equal Michelangelo — a perilous competition for a man of twenty-five. In 1507 Atalanta Baglioni of Perugia ordered a

Deposition to be set over the tomb of her murdered son, the tyrant Astorre. Raphael, in a theme properly lyrical and pathetic, tries to add tumult and drama — tries too hard. At first he adopted a scheme very similar to that of Perugino's

FIG. 186. Raphael. The Entombment.
— *Borghese, Rome.*

masterpiece, with the dead Christ on the ground, a quietly mourning group and a spacious landscape. The design is shown in a pen sketch at Oxford. He rejects this motive as too quiet and familiar. By successive efforts and exaggerations he arrives at the picture which we now see in the Borghese Gallery. Figure 186. It has become a disagreeable tangle of legs, a display of over-muscular arms which support nothing — a welter of histrionic gestures. The clew to the trouble is in the effective but meaningless pose of the woman at the right, which is borrowed directly from Michelangelo's Madonna of the Doni Family. Figure 195. The landscape no longer liberates the spirit, but almost crowds the figures out of the frame. Doubtless so self-critical an artist as Raphael learned much from this failure. It must have shown him that the rich density and measured dramatic effect of Leonardo were not as accessible as he had thought, and he accordingly restudied the whole problem of energetic monumental design. Moreover it showed him, at least for some years, that Michelangelo was the worst of models for him and threw him back upon his proper exemplars, Perugino and Fra

Bartolommeo — in short, upon that native humility which was at once his charm as a man and his strength as an artist.

In 1508 Raphael was called to Rome through the influence of a former Urbino friend, Bramante, now the architect of new St. Peter's. The task set by Pope Julius II was the decoration of the four new antechambers called the *Stanze*. About the same time Michelangelo began on the ceiling of the Sistine Chapel. Thus the two artists worked within two hundred feet of each other, but held apart partly by a natural rivalry, and even more by the irascible and suspicious nature of Michelangelo. And two masterpieces were produced as from two different worlds — Michelangelo's all tragic and perturbed, Raphael's all hopeful and serene. Between 1509 and 1511 Raphael frescoes the Camera della Segnatura, mostly with his own hand. The scheme comprised the finest leading ideals of contemporary humanism, and the little room is the most important of documents for the student of the Renaissance. Religious authority, legal justice, secular philosophy and science, the arts — such are the four great themes impersonated on the side walls, and echoed in symbol and human illustration on the beautiful ceiling; these are the props of a perfect society.

Religious authority and theology are represented by the famous fresco called erroneously the Dispute concerning the Sacrament, Figure 187. Christ, as the fully revealed member of the Trinity, sits in a heaven rayed and studded with gold; beside him sit the prophets and apostles — the actual witnesses of his passion. The seated group sweeps grandly back describing a sort of semi-dome in space. Below and precisely in the centre, on an altar, glitters the wafer which in the recurrent miracle of the Mass becomes Christ's body. To right and left of the altar are closely compacted and agitated groups insisting on the truth of the miracle of transubstantiation. These are the martyrs and church doctors, those who after the apostolic age either in experience or divine intuition certified to

the central mystery of the Church. The upper group is composed after the fashion of Fra Bartolommeo and Perugino,
is a mere expansion of Raphael's fresco at San Severo; the
lower group is held together after the fashion of Leonardo da

Fig. 187.   Raphael.   La Disputa — The Truth of the Eucharist.   Fresco.
— *Vatican.*

Vinci's Last Supper, the vehemence of the particular gestures
being assimilated in a running balance of thrust against thrust,
so that the whole effect is of a rich and energetic harmony. The
figures themselves are established adequately, but in draughtsmanship are inferior either to Leonardo's or Michelangelo's.
With the thriftiness of a born decorator, Raphael makes the
figure count in its place and beyond that takes no unnecessary
pains. It might indeed be argued that the decoration would be
worse as a whole if the parts were more perfect. Finally, note
how essentially classical, Roman, juridical the motive is; how
concrete and material. Raphael seeks to express nothing more
mystical than the obvious equation of Christ and the host, and

he merely cites a multitude of witnesses to prove that the equation is true. This very simplicity of motive has thoroughly humanized what might have been a tenuous theme. The pic-

Fig. 188. Raphael. The School of Athens. Fresco. — *Vatican*.

ture is a magnificent conclave out of many ages, a symbol of the cumulative splendor of the Catholic tradition.

On the opposite wall, in the School of Athens, Figure 188, Raphael pictures a similar continuity of human thought on the secular plane. The arched space opens into a vast basilica whose gods, represented as colossal statues at the sides, are Apollo and Minerva. Raphael has studied the Basilica of Constantine and has modestly scanned Bramante's plans for new St. Peter's. He invents a vaulted interior more impressive than any that man has ever built. Within finite bounds he suggests the infinity of Umbrian space. Without the figures, or with quite other figures, we should still have a great picture. But the group is as nobly disposed as the architecture.

You may imagine a foreshortened ring of which the reverend forms of Plato and Aristotle are the twin jewels. Aristotle at the right is in the vigor of middle age as a scientist should be. His disciples crowd towards him or gather in secondary groups about some leader. Science is social and co-operative. Raphael puts himself in this group. Plato at the left is immensely old and feeble. Speculative philosophy requires only strength of spirit. His disciples are generally isolated in personal meditation. Philosophical truth is arrived at not in society but in solitude. Certain ardent young faces recall Leonardo da Vinci, and the construction of the group is his. We have linking motives, like that of sprawling Diogenes on the steps, curves that repeat or counter the vault above, turns and thrusts of bodies in active balance, an energetic variety within a serene harmony. The mood is less agitated than that of the Disputa, while the composition is freer. Human science and philosophy are at once less bound than is theology, and move more equably because they strive for more readily attainable ends. Like its companion piece, the School of Athens is both a citation of witnesses and a profession of faith, of faith in the capacity of the human mind.

The fresco of Parnassus repeats approximately the grouping of the School of Athens, but changes the mood to one of lyrism, and shifts the scene to a hill top. About Apollo and the Muses wander the forms of the elder and recent poets. Often the faces are a bit insipid, but no one thinks of that, so easy are the postures, so gracious the whole effect, so instinct with the quiet good breeding of an academic pastoral. All the Umbrian reticence and discretion and humility of Raphael are in this beautifully calculated work. It betrays, too, certain ominous symptoms of display, in the way, for example, in which the figures at the window protrude beyond the wall. Primarily this is only a way of softening two ugly angles of the window opening, but it is also a concession to Michelangelo's

dangerous habit of painting away the architecture. All the forms
have an amplitude and dignity akin to that of classical sculpture. Hellas is for Raphael no longer a far-away, inaccessible
world, as it was, for example, to Botticelli. Raphael has effec-

FIG. 189. Raphael. Prudence, Temperance, Force — generally called
Jurisprudence. Fresco. — *Vatican.*

tively reconstructed it, in part by a gracious act of intuition,
in part by study of the wall paintings and statues of old Rome.

The decoration of the Camera della Segnatura was completed
triumphantly with the fresco symbolizing Jurisprudence, Figure 189, in which Raphael invents a new and beautiful compositional formula. Having to deal with a lunette awkwardly
shortened by the window, he used three seated figures signifying the judging, restraining and rewarding aspects of justice.
There is no strict centrality and no exact symmetry. The
large curves of the figures play off from each other in a continuous rhythm melting into the bounding curve. One may conceive it in terms of the growth of plants, as so many sprays
meeting, diverging, opposing each other, and all managing to
conform to the line of an arch. It is a type of composition that
Raphael will develop with still greater subtlety in the Sibyls
of the Madonna della Pace.

When Raphael finished the Camera della Segnatura he was

about twenty-eight years old. His remaining nine years added certain remarkable portraits, the Castiglione, the Leo X, Figure 190, the Fornarina and the young Cardinal at Madrid, one

FIG. 190.   Raphael.   Pope Leo
X. — *Pitti*.

sublime altar-piece, in the Sistine Madonna; a dramatic master-piece in the Transfiguration, and a few frescoes. But in the main these are years of retrogression. His popularity had got beyond his power to utilize it. Michel-angelo in 1512 had unveiled the ceiling of the Sistine Chapel. Raphael, with all Rome, felt qualities of energy and grandeur which he himself lacked, and, with less than his usual intel-ligence, began a fruitless emula-tion. The last three *Stanze* show in their very look that Raphael is no longer his unperturbed self. The figures no longer hold up their place on the wall, they crowd out toward the spectator appallingly. The compositions no longer show restful patterns which conform to the flatness of the wall. There are disturbing flashes of light and obscure gaps. The figures themselves are contorted and vehement; straining sinews and knotted muscles are advertised for their own sake. Emulating the sublimity of Michelangelo, Raphael only achieves sensationalism. Then he is no longer a painter but a director of painting. Nothing but the designs are now his own. The working sketches and cartoons are by his pupils, who work under the sway of a young Mantuan of facile and brutal talent, Giulio Romano. One passes through the last three Stanze with mixed feelings. The high pleasures of art are left behind; remains the spell of great power and intelli-gence now almost untouched by taste.

The Stanza of Heliodorus finished in 1514 contains a superbly dramatic fresco of Heliodorus, Figure 191, thrust by a celestial horseman from the temple he would profane. The execution is mostly by Giulio Romano. Raphael himself appears

Fig. 191. Raphael. Heliodorus driven from the Temple by a Celestial Horseman. Fresco. — *Vatican.*

in one of his most massive designs, the Mass of Bolsena. The theme is a sceptical priest persuaded of the truth of the sacramental miracle through the bleeding of the wafer. The miracle takes place in the presence of Pope Julius II. There is a weight of character in the picture which is unique in Raphael's mural painting. The adjustment of masses is in an impeccable symmetry all the more difficult that the space is irregular and refractory. The fine figures that carry the theme down into the narrow rectangles alongside the window are in part repainted by a young rival of Raphael, Michelangelo's protegé, Sebastiano del Piombo.

The Chamber of the *Incendio*, finished in 1517, shows even more plainly the devastating influence of Michelangelo. The subject is a fire arrested miraculously by Pope Leo IV, Figure 192. It is a magnificent display of poses and anatomy, an

artistic show window rather than a decoration. The eye
wanders in bewilderment to find the picture and finds
nothing but isolated, splendid forms posing superbly or simu-
lating unfelt emotions. From the point of view of decora-

FIG. 192.   Raphael's Design executed by Giulio Romano. Il Borgo.
The Fire at Rome. — *Vatican.*

tion, the space has been systematically violated. Again the re-
morseless hand of Giulio Romano is everywhere felt. This is
the last anteroom of the Vatican which Raphael saw finished,
though he left to his helpers many sketches for the two remaining *Stanze*.

In 1516 and 1517 Raphael is superintending half a dozen
great tasks at once. From the early months of 1515 he had

been Bramante's successor as architect of new St. Peter's, the same year he became superintendent of all archæological excavations at Rome. To these heavy administrative charges he adds the decoration of the Farnesina, the continuation of the *Stanze*, designs for mosaics in Santa Maria del Popolo, plans for two private palaces, sixteen cartoons for the Vatican tapestries, and the preliminary studies for the Loggia of the Vatican. He designs half a dozen great altar-pieces and paints with his own hand the Portrait of Leo X, the marvelous St. Cecilia at Bologna, the Sibyls of the Pace, and the Sistine Madonna. He was rich and beloved, great nobles pressed him with social attentions, and a cardinal vainly sought to ally him with his family by marriage.

We can consider these multiform activities of the later years only in general terms. The tapestry cartoons at South Kensington representing the miracles of St. Peter and St. Paul complete that magnificent line of narrative painting that begins with Giotto. Raphael works for simplicity and concentration and dignity in an eminently classic spirit. One feels the influence of Masaccio. Though rudely executed to guide the Flemish weavers and executed by the assistant, Penni, the mind of Raphael controls the form throughout. Such designs as the Miraculous Draught of Fishes, Paul Preaching at Athens, the Death of Ananias, the Blinding of the Sorcerer Elymas are among the marvels of our art. Yet many of these designs are over-studied, and few I feel fully bear the comparison with the best of Giotto and Masaccio. A little over-emphasis of style recalls the bitter word of Michelangelo concerning Raphael—that he succeeded not by grace of nature but by study.

The frescoes of the Life of Psyche, in the Farnesina, are beautiful in arrangement and full of a robust paganism. But the wall is overcharged with the weight of figures which too often show Giulio Romano's heavy and insolent hand. All

the same, the whole effect is gracious and the garlanded
borders of the coves and spandrels by Giovanni da Udine are
delightful. To realize how much these frescoes lost from
student execution one has only to consider the Galatea, Figure

FIG. 192a.   Raphael.   Galatea.
Fresco. — *Farnesina, Rome.*

FIG. 193.   Raphael.   The Sistine
Madonna. — *Dresden.*

192a, in the same Palace, which Raphael painted himself in
1514. It is on the verge of over-ripeness, but keeps its saving
element of restraint. In answer to an inquiry from that great
diplomat and gentleman, Count Baldassare Castiglione, Raphael wrote that though beautiful models were not rare, for the
Galatea as for other figures, he had followed only an idea;
and indeed the mind's eye is what ever counts with Raphael.

Raphael's final work for the Vatican was the decoration of
an open, vaulted Loggia. He invented fifty-two little Bible
stories, leaving most of the painting to his assistant, Penni,
and he drew about the arches, pilasters and window frames the
most delicious arabesques. From study of similar decoration
in the Baths of Titus he worked out a style, crisp, formal and
sophisticated, and as various as Gothic ornament itself. Geometrical, animal, and plant forms meet and blend audaciously.

There is interplay of spiral and angular motives, the whole effect is highly playful and ingenious. The style has had vogue to our own day and still speaks to us charmingly of the unserious side of Raphael.

Perhaps in the harassed, competitive years we have been describing, Raphael turned occasionally upon his own ingenuity, and refreshed himself by renewing these simple and gracious modes in which he had been bred. Such a theory would account for the Sistine Madonna, Figure 193, and in part for his last picture, the Transfiguration. The most memorable of Raphael's Madonnas is based on the lucid symmetry of Perugino. Although, for greater concentration, the background is merely a sky, the hovering figures are

FIG. 194. Raphael. The Transfiguration. — *Vatican.*

easily spaced in the usual triangle. The effect is ineffably grand and gentle. A quiet silvery cloudland is created and filled by the devotion of the attendant saints and the inspired glance of the Virgin and her Son. With all the resources of the Renaissance, Raphael has expressed an emotion as intense and reverent as that of Fra Angelico. It is an amazing act of the sympathetic intelligence, for there is no reason to suppose that the painter was ever a deeply religious spirit.

Almost as traditional was the unfinished picture before which in springtime of 1520 Raphael's body lay in state. The Transfiguration, Figure 194, repeats the method of the Disputa. The celestial group of Christ and Moses and Elijah is disposed as Perugino would have counselled, in a swaying triangular group set before the gulf of the firmament. Raphael painted this part with his own hand. The lower part, which was left to Giulio Romano to finish, rests on the maxims and practice of Leonardo. An energetic variety compelled into a close balance is the ideal, a formal order which contains and softens otherwise extravagant expressions and gestures. There is perhaps intended not merely an illustration of the Gospel text, but also the contrast between that life of contemplation towards which the soul aspires, and that world of suffering of mind and body which presses closely upon our rare moments of spiritual escape.

Even that world of facts had been very kind to Raphael. It was fitting then that in his last days he should forget the haunting spectre of Michelangelo's sublimity, and should use his last forces in an imitation which was a sort of gratitude to those two great masters who had set him on the right way. One would like to believe that the Sistine Madonna and the Transfiguration are the sign that Raphael when overtaken by an untimely death was purging himself of an unfruitful rivalry, and becoming once more master of his own soul. Yet since even Michelangelo shipwrecked on the Michelangelesque, it is an open question whether Raphael could ever have permanently recovered his natural equipoise. However that be, Raphael in the glorious years from 1500 to 1512 resumes and perfects every gentle, orderly, and reasonable strain in Italian painting. Whether in portraiture or narrative, in mythology or symbolism, in pictures of the Madonna or in pure decoration, he gave to Italian painting its final stamp. He achieved a grandeur of space composition akin to the movement of a symphony, a hidden structure more appealing than any separate hue or form. His best work rests on a great humility, and his later pride went far towards undoing him as an artist. Such pride was the breath of life and the source of strength to his rival Michelangelo, the fulfiller and perfector of everything that had been insurgent, unbounded and not quite reasonable in the art of Florence.

By a peculiar irony all that was valuable in such truculent and self-sufficing predecessors as Donatello and Bertoldo, Andrea del Castagno, Antonio Pollaiuolo and Luca Signorelli was finally concentrated in the small and ill-favored body of a neurasthenic. There is the tragedy of Michelangelo[9] in its simplest terms. A Titan in capacity to feel and work, he lived in an atmosphere of suspicion and fear. Thrice he ran away from physical danger, once was virtually a military deserter. To unworthy dependent relatives he gave lavishly, scolding and fretting as he gave. He deliberately affronted two of the most courteous and accomplished colleagues, Leonardo da Vinci and Perugino. He suspected the worst of his gracious and generous rival, Raphael. From a Roman studio as unkempt and filthy as its owner, he snarled at the world and himself like a dog from a kennel.

Yet, note the paradox, this snarling is embodied in fine poetry, and this haggard and more than untidy artist is the friend of such elect spirits as Tommaso Cavalieri and Vittoria Colonna. Transient solaces. Near the end of his long life he writes: —

> "Alas! Alas! again and once again
> I see my past and there I find not one —
> In all, not one whole day that has been mine."

These were the words of a man who was admired like a god and had achieved a lifework of unexampled copiousness and athleticism.

The great enigma, how Michelangelo converted what are usually weaknesses into sources of artistic strength, may best be faced in his life and works. He was born at Caprese in 1475, soon taken back to Florence and put to nurse with a stonecutter's wife, with whose milk he later used to say he sucked in the mallets and chisels he wielded so powerfully. At thirteen he was articled to Ghirlandaio as a paid assistant and doubtless did some minor work on those prettiest of frescoes in the

choir of Santa Maria Novella. Extricating himself from an uncongenial task, he became one of the protegés of Lorenzo de' Medici, studying the antique marbles of the Medici Gardens under the kindly guidance of old Bertoldo. There he mingled freely for three years in the most learned and gentle society of the time. He mastered anatomy and modelling, searched the compositional secrets of Masaccio.

Fig. 195. Michelangelo. Holy Family of the Doni. — *Uffizi.*

Soon Savonarola's revolution dismantled that artistic paradise which had been the Medici Gardens, and Michelangelo became what he frequently was afterwards, a fugitive and a solitary man, without either fixed friendships or abiding place.

How he made himself great in sculpture is not our theme. He was thirty and already the master of the David and the Pietà before he began to be a painter. His first commission, in 1505, was for a Holy Family, Figure 195, in medallion form for Agnolo Doni, who at the same time was having his portrait painted by Raphael. The picture as we see it in the Uffizi shows a master who thinks in fresco. The brown flesh, the dull yellows and blues of the draperies could have come from the Brancacci chapel. Remarkable is the complete waiver of charm and sweetness. The superb figures are skilfully contorted into interesting poses, the circle is densely filled and the few interstices left by the main figures are filled with athletic nudes. The aim, which is successfully attained, is an austere grandeur.

There is to be no ordinary human appeal in our youthful Lord and his parents.

At this moment Leonardo was already well advanced on the cartoon for the Battle of the Standard, treating it in terms of literal narrative. In 1505 Michelangelo received a signal honor in the commission for the companion fresco, the Battle of Pisa. Both were for the Hall of the Great Council. We can imagine Michelangelo casting about for a reason to abandon a narrative treatment and to find one that could be expressed by the nude. He found it in an incident in Leonardo Aretino's Chronicle. It seemed that the trumpet found the Florentine men-at-arms bathing in the Arno. Here was the theme of

FIG. 196. Michelangelo. Detail from Cartoon of the Bathers, by the contemporary engraver, Marcantonio.

what was properly called The Bathers. Great muscular forms are drawing themselves up the bank, and are hurrying into clothes and armor. We have not a fight, but its alarm and imminence, a fine imaginative substitute for the obvious event. The picture was never executed, and the cartoon, which was the marvel of its day, was soon destroyed, but Michelangelo's sketches tells us something of the composition, and the contemporary engraver, Marcantonio, Figure 196, has left us a masterly print of the central group. It is plain that Michelangelo made a display of minute anatomy that put his contemporaries to shame, plain also that he subordinated this feature to monumental effect. The failure to execute the fresco and the destruction of the cartoon must count among the capital losses in the history of art.

Burdened already with the impossible task of the tomb of

Julius II, Michelangelo was called to Rome to fresco the vault
of the Sistine Chapel. Contemporary gossip believed that he
was proposed by the jealous and shifty Bramante, architect of

FIG. 197. Michelangelo. The two Western Compartments of the
Ceiling of the Sistine Chapel: God parting Light from Darkness; God
creating the Sea and Plants. Example of the Decorative Scheme.

St. Peter's, in the hope of discrediting him. If so, Bramante
reckoned ill. At first Michelangelo planned a very modest
scheme of colossal figures of Apostles in the twelve spandrels.
Soon, dismissing his incompetent helpers, he attacked single-
handed the present great scheme. He worked at it four bitter
years, and came out of it temporarily crippled and with eyes
distorted from the constant strain of looking upwards. The
ceiling was unveiled on All Saint's Day of 1512 and has been a
portent ever since.

Enter the Sistine Chapel, turn your back to the overwhelming apparition of the Last Judgment, and your eye will naturally seek the lightest part of the rich decoration. In a long

strip, down the centre of the ceiling, made up of nine oblongs
alternately large and small, colossal figures stand out against
the sky. We see the drama of the Creation and Fall of man.
Nude titans play the minor parts in so many simultaneous

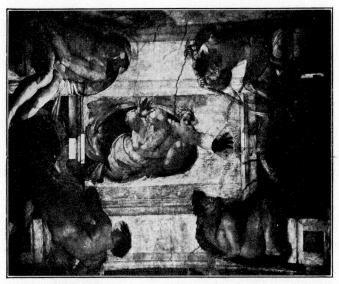

FIG. 198. Michelangelo. God hovering over the Waters. Shows the
decorative use of the so-called "Slaves." — *Vatican.*

scenes. The gigantic, draped form of the Eternal dominates
the first five. We see him an aged athlete, an expression of utmost physical force, rending chaos asunder into light and darkness; by his touch illumining the sun and moon; Figure 197,
drawing out the plants from the earth. I know no more sublime conception in painting than the figure of God assigning
the oceans their place, Figure 198. Here is a form that would
weigh tons hovering with the lightness of an eagle in space,
with extended beneficent arms as solid as reality but coaxed
out of the wet plaster with touch and hues as delicate as those
of a Whistler symphony. A miracle of conception and of workmanship.

The eye will dwell longest on the great fresco of the Creation of Adam, Figure 199. It is all noble energy in the figure of God giving life by His touch, all noble languor in the relaxed form of Adam only dimly conscious of himself and wistful.

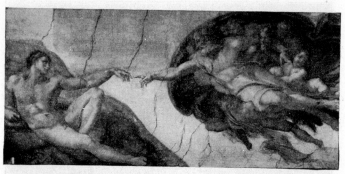

Fig. 199.   Michelangelo.   Creation of Adam.

There could be no truer or more striking illustration of the pessimistic view that life was imposed upon the earth and brought sadness with it. The titan form of Adam has a singular and enigmatic relaxation. He undergoes a gift he has never besought and faces it with something between confusion, mistrust and resignation. Perhaps the splendid body would have been more at ease, had the soul not been added. So in a spirit of Christian pessimism Michelangelo represents Deity sharing its divine powers with the first man.

At the centre of the ceiling is the creation of Eve, again an extraordinary study in lassitude, but with a significant difference in the figure of Eve. The woman, the chosen receptacle and transmitter of life, accepts the gift eagerly. She presses up to God in thankful adoration. No doubts or ambiguities here. And what a figure — fit to be the mother of a race, exulting already in a fecundity that is to be most grievous. Compare her action with the languid and almost disdainful gesture of Adam in the last fresco, and learn that if the world is still peopled it is due to the unreflective and un-shaken fealty to life of all Eve's true daughters.

Perhaps the most decorative subject, if one may use the word of themes so morally impressive, is that which repre-

FIG. 200. Michelangelo. The Temptation and Expulsion from Eden.

sents the sin of the forbidden fruit and the expulsion from Eden, Figure 200. The elements of pathos which are strong in the story of Genesis are absent. Michelangelo has not deigned to show us a habitable or desirable Eden. We see instead the swiftly changing episodes of a great doom, which culminates in this scene. Marvelous are the paired groups, superb the con-trast between careless appetite under the tree of knowledge and utter shame in the exiled pair. One feels that Eve, who shrinks most, will soonest recover. Her mission is still valid in the world of sin and shame. The composition is the first one made up entirely of nudes.

We may pass quickly over the three compartments devoted to the story of Noah. The scale of the figures, especially in the Deluge, is too small to count at the distance from the eye. These three frescoes were the beginning of the work, the proper scale being arrived at through trial and error. In-herently the two small oblongs are among the most beautiful

in the ceiling, having a stylistic grace that is less marked in
the earlier more august themes. With the charm of Greek
intaglios these stories of Noah combine monumentality.

I have tried to put myself in the position of a visitor to the

FIG. 201.   Michelangelo.   The Prophet Ezechiel.

Sistine Chapel following the instincts of his eye. At this point,
having glanced over the ceiling, his mind might well come in
and ask the meaning of a whole of which he is becoming dimly
aware. The nine scenes above are simply the historic axioms
upon which the Christian scheme of redemption is based. The
abstract sparseness of the nine episodes from Genesis is justifed
by the fact that they are less human events than terms in a
great argument, which runs as follows: We were created innocent, sinned in our first parents, were spared in the world-
flood and promised eventual redemption.

This prolonged drama of redemption is witnessed by a
solemn chorus of draped male and female figures enthroned

impressively in the spandrels. Here, representing respectively the pagan and Hebrew world, are seven sibyls and five prophets who had the dim but certain vision of a coming Redeemer. These figures as Hawthorne has well said are "neces-

FIG. 202. Michelangelo. The Delphic Sibyl.

FIG. 203. Michelangelo. The Libyan Sibyl.

sarily so gigantic because the weight of thought within them is so massive." They brood quietly or sway with the burden of yearning. They are magnificently draped and contrast most decoratively with the many nudes of the ceiling. They vary in age and disposition. Contrast the actively inspired and youthful Daniel, or the fiery Ezechiel, Figure 201, with the ponderous gravity of Jeremiah. What shades of delicate characterization are in the athletic loveliness of the Delphic Sibyl, Figure 202, the powerfully concentrated senility of The Cumean Sibyl, she who predicted to Virgil the new era of salvation, and the aristocratic aloofness of the Libyan seeress, Figure 203, most daintily preparing her day's work in divination.

Magnificent is the indignant sprawling form of the unwilling prophet Jonah, remanded by the sea to an ungrateful mission.

He is the active counterpart of the passive Adam on the ceiling. He obeys under protest. The form itself, foreshortened against the curve of the spandrel, is a masterpiece of draughtsmanship. Decoratively it is the link between the nudes of the ceiling and the draped prophets and sibyls.

Below the prophetic figures, in the older frescoes of the side walls, are set the foreshadowing of the work of salvation in the life of Moses and its accomplishment in the life of Christ, and the drama closes with Michelangelo's Last Judgment on the altar wall. There Christ separates eternally the saved from the damned, echoing the definitive gesture with which God in the adjoining ceiling separates light from darkness. So the scheme closes with the inexorable logic with which it began.

The decorative task of Michelangelo was to mediate between the prophets and sibyls and the ceiling frescoes above, and likewise to link the great figures with the side walls below. Above, he set a multitude of nude forms. On the massive sides of the twelve thrones are four caryatids in two pairs. At the top of these piers are seated the lithe forms of nude youths, Figure 198, forty in all, supporting medallions and bent into every conceivable attitude that might set off the flexibility and power of these superb young bodies. But however extravagant any single pose may be, it is immediately balanced by an opposing thrust from some other body, so that the whole composition is locked together into an active and thrilling equilibrium. Even the triangles over the coves are filled with huddled nudes most adroitly disposed in the narrow and refractory spaces.

Below the prophets and sibyls, the linking motives are made up of draped figures. Weakest are the carytid genuises below each throne. The triangular splays at the corners contain those four bloody and sensational acts which assured the perpetuity of God's Chosen People — the Raising of the Brazen Serpent,

the Slaying of Goliath and of Holophernes, the Hanging of
Haaman.

In the triangles roofing the coves and in the lunettes about
the arched window heads are family groups of the ancestors

Fig. 204.   Michelangelo.   Decoration of Cove over Window.

and precursors of Christ. Figure 204. The mood of anticipa-
tion which has been calm and official in the prophets becomes
agitated, passionate, personal in these half hidden groups.
So many pilgrims of eternity yearn for the fulfillment that
shall give meaning to their wanderings — a promised goal
and rest. Very subtle and beautiful is the contrast between the groups sundered by the window heads, individually
meditative, and those which blend their longing in the
close relations forced by the triangular coves. What has
begun as noble abstraction finishes in terms of almost inex-
pressible tenderness. In color the whole gigantic composition
is unified by a sonorous chord of yellow and violet which is
moderately asserted in the ceiling and pushed to the utmost in

the spandrels. Of the color John La Farge has written: "The unity is so great, the balance of effects so harmonious, that it is only by study that we see expressed in the methods of the painting the ancient rules, handed down by practice,

FIG. 205. Michelangelo. The Last Judgment.

which unite with the latest teaching of modern scientific coloring." What a mind it took to hold the tumultuous and pathetic details of this great work within an enveloping order and calm!

In framing his great work out of nudes relieved by draped figures, Michelangelo renewed the Grecian practice. Precisely the difference between the Sistine ceiling and the metopes of the Parthenon, or the frieze of Pergamon, raises the question —

What does the nude of Michelangelo express? I do not find in it, at least in the Sistine ceiling, much of that terribleness, *terribiltà*, which has been remarked by critics from Vasari to Henri Beyle. It seems to me rather an art of lassitude and relaxation, the reluctantly awaking Adam being the clue to the mood. Except for the gestures of God and Eve, the gestures and poses are unspecific. The lithe bodies of the slaves are twisted only that they may attain consciousness of powers which have no use. The relaxation which marks nearly all the nudes, whether in the stories or in the incidental ornament, is not that of fatigue after action, nor yet that of preparation for an ordeal. In barren lassitude we have expressed powers which do not imply action or use, but breathe a great melancholy. We are far from the splendors of passion and achievement, we see humanity confused at a fate that calls itself God, a passive factor in an arbitrary process that makes

the glory of the flesh a vain thing. As a humanist, Michelangelo asserts that failing glory, as a Christian he accepts the
nothingness of mankind and the rightness of God's inscrutable
and apparently cruel designs. Perhaps the spell of Michelangelo, his æsthetic, to put it pedantically, is simply the noble
resignation with which the humanist accepts the Christian
pessimism as regards this world. And here I may note that
Rodin has significantly shown that even the forms of Michelangelo are not uprising and resilient like the antique, but com-
pressed and yielding like those of the Christian Gothic sculptors.

Twenty-one years after the Sistine ceiling was unveiled,
Michelangelo began reluctantly the great fresco of the Last
Judgment, Figure 205. He worked on it for seven years,
and it was unveiled on Christmas Day of 1541. How the choristers had the heart to chant the angelic message of peace and
good will before it, I cannot imagine. Michelangelo was sixty-
six years old, a disillusioned and embittered man, an alien in
the corrupt and pleasure loving Rome of Paul III. He has
put into the Christ all his contempt for mankind. The Christ
who earlier wrathfully hurled the darts in the Umbrian plague
banners has become a far darting Apollo, Figure 206, rejoicing in his dire task. Behind him the murky air is full of
hurtling contorted angels, in aspect quite indistinguishable
from fiends, who bear the implements of the Passion. Below,
the just and unjust rise or fall in knots and festoons of writhing
nude bodies all equally sinister. The conception is violently
corporeal, and never elsewhere in painting has the human body
been used with such ingenuity and power. But it is a power
that defeats itself. I believe the spectator is not so much
appalled as confused before the Last Judgment. Its vehemence
seems so unrelieved and insensate. If this be indeed the goal
of mankind, no wonder moody Adam in the ceiling above
faces his Creator with doubt and a hint of distrust.

Its sheer display of force won all contemporaries, and the

French critic and superman, Stendhal, has highly praised the work for its burning energy. While not sharing his enthusiasm, I gladly refer the reader to his admirable pages. In my own opinion the creative ardor of Michelangelo had waned by

FIG. 206. Michelangelo. Christ with the Virgin and the Apostles.
From the Last Judgment.

this time. He offers, instead, his spleen, which is more valuable than most men's genius, and his amazing technical skill. Michelangelo has become Michelangelesque. That is deplorably true in the frescoes for the Pauline Chapel which were finished in 1547, his seventy-second year. Nothing is left but sensationalism, and the Pope does well not to exhibit these works. As regards humanity, Michelangelo's vein is completely exhausted. He still is capable of exquisite calculation, as in the design for the dome of St. Peter's, still retains a dæmonic capacity for work and emotion, but the sculptor in him is nearly dead and the painter completely so. The poet of

the rugged sonnets has superseded them both. When he died
at 89, in 1564, the little illfavored body was honored like that
of a king. His sheer power had swept the whole rising generation of artists under his sway. To their own hurt and to the
bankruptcy of the Golden Age.

Such forms as Michelangelo's are tolerable only when possessed by that melancholy poetry of his which gives them
meaning. If the serene intelligence of a Raphael had not
found emotions to fill such forms, if Michelangelo himself
in his later years falls back on a monotonous formula of terribleness, what hope was there for such uninspired imitators as
the Venustis, Volterras, and Vasaris? One and all, they en-
tertained monstrous delusions of effortless attainment —
cleverly contorted their nudes, shrewdly calculated their terrors.
And the Roman art of the Golden Age, forgetting both the wise
humility of Umbria and the reasonable pride of Florence,
suddenly collapsed in the ugliest and most irrational ostentation. Michelangelo had passed — to fulfill and to destroy.

ILLUSTRATIONS FOR CHAPTER VI

A CONTEMPORARY LIST OF GREAT ARTISTS, BEFORE 1510

In an offhand mention in *The Courtier* Baldasarre Castiglione tells
us who seemed to be great artists to a cultured and well-informed
gentleman about the year 1508. Titian had not yet emerged and of the
older men only Leonardo da Vinci and Mantegna are remembered.
As seniors, they are the first mentioned.

"Again various things give equal pleasure to the eyes, so that we can
with difficulty decide what are more pleasing to them. You know that
in painting Leonardo da Vinci, Mantegna, Raphael, Michelangelo,
Giorgio da Castelfranco are very excellent, yet they are all unlike in
their work; so that no one of them seems to lack anything in his own
manner, since each is known as the most perfect in his style."

The Book of the Courtier by Count Baldesar Castiglione, translated by
Leonard Ekstein Opdycke, New York, 1903, p. 50.

MICHELANGELO ON RENAISSANCE COUNTERPOISE

It is said then that Michelangelo once gave his advice to Marcoda Siena, his pupil, that "one should make the figure pyramidal, spiral, (*serpentinata*) and multiplied by one, two, and three." Lomazzo *Trattato*, Milan, 1484, p. 23. The pose, that is, should be contained geometrically, should display opposing thrusts, and should be mathematically proportioned within the inclosing geometrical form.

VASARI ON THE "MODERN STYLE"

Vasari's account of the Grand Style or "Third Manner," in the Preface to Part III (De Vere's translation, Vol. IV, pp. 79-85) is still authoritative. He praises the artists before Leonardo, but finds in them a certain hardness, lack of finish and uncertainty of proportions. The change to the perfect manner was caused by the discovery of ancient marbles.

"After them [the predecessors of Leonardo], their successors were able to attain to it through seeing excavated out of the earth certain antiquities cited by Pliny as amongst the most famous, such as the Laocoon, the Hercules, the Great Torso of the Belvedere, and likewise the Venus, the Cleopatra, the Apollo, and an endless number of others, which, both with their sweetness and their severity, with their fleshy roundness copied from the greatest beauties of nature, and with certain attitudes which involve no distortion of the whole figure but only a movement of certain parts, which are revealed with a most perfect grace, brought about the disappearance of a certain dryness, hardness, and sharpness of manner . . .

[He mentions the contemporary admiration of such precursors as Francia and Perugino.]

"But their error was afterwards clearly proved by the works of Leonardo da Vinci, who, giving a beginning to that third manner which we propose to call the modern — besides the force and boldness of his drawing, and the extreme subtlety wherewith he counterfeited all the minutenesses of nature exactly as they are — with good rule, better order, right proportion, perfect drawing, and divine grace, abounding in resources and having a most profound knowledge of art, may be truly said to have endowed his figures with motion and breath.

"There followed after him, although at some distance, Giorgione da Castelfranco, who obtained a beautiful gradation of colour in his pictures . . .; and not inferior to him in giving force, relief, sweetness, and grace to his pictures, with his colouring, was Fra Bartolommeo di San Marco. But more than all did the most gracious Rafaello da Urbino, who, studying the labours of the old masters and those of the Moderns, took the best from them, and, having gathered it together, enriched the art of painting with that complete perfection which was shown in ancient times by the figures of Apelles and Zeuxis, nay, even more, if we may make bold to say it, as might be proved if we could compare their works with his. Wherefore nature was left vanquished by his colours . . . .

"In the same manner, but sweeter in colouring and not so bold, there followed Andrea del Sarto, who may be called a rare painter, for his works are free from errours.

. . . .

"But he who bears the palm from both the living and the dead, transcending and eclipsing all others, is the divine Michelangelo Buonarotti, who holds the sovereignty not merely of one of these arts, but of all three together. This master surpasses and excels not only all those moderns who have almost vanquished nature, but even those most famous ancients who without a doubt did so gloriously surpass her; and in his own self he triumphs over moderns, ancients, and nature, who could scarcely conceive anything so strange and so difficult that he would not be able, by the force of his most divine intellect and by means of his industry, draughtsmanship, art, judgment and grace, to excel it by a great measure; and that not only in painting and in the use of colours under which title are comprised all forms, and all bodies upright or not upright, palpable or impalpable, visible or invisible, but also in the highest perfection of bodies in the round, with the point of his chisel."

UNITY OF DESIGN IN THE RENAISSANCE

The humanist Benedetto Varchi, renewing the debate which Leonardo da Vinci had started concerning the relative rank of sculpture and painting, sent the text of his lecture to Michelangelo and asked for his opinion. The sculptor writes in 1549:

"In my opinion painting should be considered excellent in proportion as it approaches the effect of relief, while relief should be considered bad as it approaches the effect of painting. I used to consider that sculpture was the lantern of painting and that between the two things there was the same difference as that between the sun and the moon.

But now that I have read your book, in which, speaking as a philosopher, you say that things which have the same end are themselves the same, I have changed my opinion; and I now consider that painting and sculpture are one and the same thing, unless greater nobility be imparted by the necessity for a keener judgment, greater difficulties of execution, stricter limitations and harder work. And if this be the case, no painter ought to think less of sculpture than of painting and no sculptor less of painting than of sculpture. By sculpture I mean the sort that is executed by cutting away from the block: the sort that is executed by building up resembles painting. That is enough, for as one and the other, that is to say, both painting and sculpture proceed from the same faculty, it would be an easy matter to establish harmony between them and to let such disputes alone, for they occupy more time than the execution of the figures themselves. As to that man [Leonardo da Vinci] who wrote saying that painting was more noble than sculpture, as though he knew as much about it as he did of the other subjects on which he has written, why my serving-maid would have written better!"

From Robert W. Carden, *Michelangelo, a Record of his Life*, Boston and New York, 1913, a book which from Michelangelo's letters gives a very intimate view of the sculptor's character.

SIR JOSHUA REYNOLDS ON THE GRAND STYLE

No critic of art has better expressed the ideal of the Grand Style than Sir Joshua Reynolds. I quote from the third of his *Discourses*, in the admirable edition of Roger E. Fry, New York, 1906. pp. 51 ff.

"Every language has adopted terms expressive of this excellence. The *gusto grande* of the Italians, the *beau idéal* of the French and the *great style*, *genius* and *taste* among the English, are but different appellations of the same thing. It is this intellectual dignity, they say, that ennobles the Painter's Art; that lays the line between him and the mere mechanic: and produces those great effects in an instant, which eloquence and poetry, by slow and repeated efforts, are scarcely able to retain." . . . [The grand style is seen to rest upon a sort of generalizing tendency.] "The whole beauty and grandeur of the Art consists, in my opinion, in being able to get above all singular forms, local customs, particularities and details of every kind." [The artist] "being enabled to distinguish the accidental deficiencies, excrescences, and deformities of things, from their general figures, he makes out an abstract idea of their forms more perfect than any one original; and, what may seem a paradox, he learns to design naturally by drawing his figures unlike to any one object." [Sir Joshua advocates the study of the antique, not to imitate any single work, but to master the principle that underlies them all.] "Beauty and simplicity have so great a share in the composition of the great style, that he who has acquired them has little else to learn. It must not, indeed, be forgotten that there is a nobleness of conception, which goes beyond any thing in the mere exhibition of perfect form; there is an art of animating and dignifying the figures with intellectual grandeur, of impressing the appearance of philosophic wisdom, or heroic virtue. This can only be acquired by him that enlarges the sphere of his understanding by a variety of knowledge, and warms his imagination with the best productions of ancient and modern poetry."

KENYON COX ON THE CLASSIC SPIRIT

The ideals of the High Renaissance are eloquently, if incidentally, defined by the late Kenyon Cox in *The Classic Point of View*, New York, 1911. pp. 3–5.

"The Classic spirit is the disinterested search for perfection; it is the love of clearness and reasonableness and self-control; it is, above all, the love of permanence and of continuity. It asks of a work of art, not that it shall be novel or effective, but that it shall be fine and noble. It seeks not merely to express individuality or emotion, but to express disciplined emotion and individuality restrained by law. It strives for the essential rather than the accidental, the eternal rather than the momentary — loves impersonality more than personality, and feels more power in the orderly succession of the hours and the seasons than in the violence of earthquake or of storm. And it loves to steep itself in tradition. It would have each new work connect itself in the mind of him who sees it with all the noble and lively works of the past, bringing them to his memory and making their beauty and charm a part of the beauty and charm of the work before him. It does not deny originality and individuality — they are as welcome as inevitable. It does not consider tradition as immutable or set rigid bounds to invention. But it desires that each new presentation of truth and beauty shall show us the old truth and the old beauty, seen only from a different angle and colored by a different medium. It wishes to add link by link to the chain of tradition, but it does not wish to break the chain."

THE END OF THE RENAISSANCE AND THE COMING OF FEAR

An artistic collapse whether in an artist or a nation is usually due to a prior collapse in morale. Florence suffered such loss of face when the Imperialists stormed the city and crushed the Republic. We may study the disaster in Michelangelo's personal case and in its effect on the citizenry at large. Michelangelo was military engineer. Writing from Venice, Sept. 25, 1529, he describes his desertion with singular objectivity:

"I had intended to remain in Florence to the end of the war, having no fears for my own safety. But on Tuesday morning, the 21st of September, a certain person came out by the Porta a San Nicolò while I was engaged in inspecting the bastions, and whispered in my ear that I must remain there no longer if I valued my life. He accompanied me to my house, dined there, brought me horses, and never left my side until he had carried me out of Florence, declaring that it was for my good that he so acted. Whether it were God or the devil I cannot say."

From Robert W. Carden, *Michelangelo, a Record of his Life*, Boston and New York, 1913, p. 168.

Florence suffered not from hallucinations, as this seems to have been, but from the humiliation and confusion incident upon defeat and foreign occupation. I translate from Benedetto Varchi's *Storia*, the extract in Ancona and Bacci's *Manuele della Letteratura Italiana*, Vol. II, p. 506.

"The city of Florence when her liberty was lost was full of such sorrow, of such terror, of such confusion, that it can hardly be described or even imagined. . . . The nobles were indignant among themselves and inwardly resented being scorned and vilified by the lowest classes; the plebeians in extreme need, would not refrain at least from relieving their minds about the nobility; the rich, how they could manage not to lose their property; the poor, day and night, what they should do not to die utterly and of famine; the citizens were dismayed and desperate, because they had spent and lost a lot: the peasants, much more, because there remained for them nothing at all; the priests were ashamed of having deceived the laity; the laity grieved at having believed the priests; men had become extraordinarily suspicious and covetous; women immeasurably incredulous and distrustful: finally, every one with lowered face and staring eyes, seemed beside himself, and all without exception pallid and bewildered feared at all times every sort of ill."

From such a shell-shocked community as this, no serene or noble art was to be expected. It was much that Florence in bondage still could nurture the exquisitely morbid art of a Pontormo and the aristocratic detachment and *finesse* of a Bronzino.

VENETIAN PAINTING BEFORE TITIAN

FIG. 207. Giovanni Bellini. St. Francis receiving the Stigmata.
— *H. C. Frick Coll., New York.*

CHAPTER VII

VENETIAN PAINTING BEFORE TITIAN

On the splendor of Venice — Italo-Byzantine painters of the 14th Century —
    Paduan, Veronese, and Umbrian Painters at Venice — Jacopo Bellini —
    Squarcione's school at Padua, Carlo Crivelli — Andrea Mantegna, mentor
    for Northern Italy — Antonello da Messina's Realism — The flowering
    of the old Narrative School in Gentile Bellino — Giovanni Bellini — The
    backward Vivarini — Carpaccio and the end of the old Narrative Style —
    Literary background of Giorgione's Art — Giorgione of Castelfranco.

When, about the middle of the fifth century, a pitiful throng
of refugees sought safety from Attila and his Huns in the fens
at the head of the Adriatic, they took with them what was
left of the constructive genius of the Roman Empire. They
raised amid the lagoons a healthful and convenient city, which
in the course of centuries became the most beautiful in Europe.
They developed a strong and wise oligarchy, under forms sufficiently democratic to satisfy the people. They attained an
extraordinary capacity for diplomacy and overseas trade —
a brilliant commercialized civilization. Secure in their isolation and wealth, the Venetians mediated the long strife between the popes and the Teutonic emperors, making favorable
terms with both. Venice enjoyed a wholly exceptional political
stability. No other commune of Europe could have fittingly
assumed the title, Serenissima. Her galleys and sailing craft
plied to Candia, Rhodes, Smyrna, Alexandretta, Constantinople. Down the Adriatic to Malta, her trading stations shone
white under the yellow cliffs. Her incoming ships brought back
the splendid rugs and silks and embroideries from the Levant,
the beautiful potteries of Asia Minor, Persia and distant China,
the veined marbles and porphyries of Egypt and of Istria to

build into her churches and palaces. She was astute and powerful enough to divert a crusade into a plundering expedition against her rival, Constantinople. And thus she got the four antique bronze horses still chafing above the portico of St. Mark's and many a relic of the later Byzantine splendor. Her doors ever opened to the Orient. Her quays swarmed with turbaned traders. The Greeks had their churches and confraternities at Venice, and so had the Slavonians. For articles of luxury the northern caravans came to Venice over the Brenner to load from the German warehouses on the Grand Canal.

So stable, rich and proud a city was singularly slow in producing its own art. Venice was never primarily a manufacturing community, and from the first she expected to import most articles of luxury and display. Thus when the many-domed Basilica rose over the body of her patron, St. Mark, Venice called masters from Constantinople to enrich the surfaces with mosaics, and when, towards the end of the fourteenth century, she wished to picture the new Palace of the Doges, she called not her own artists to the task, but those of Padua, Verona and distant Fabriano. Her originality and greatness in painting do not clearly assert themselves until about 1475 in the work of the brothers Bellini, and by 1577, the year of Titian's death, the period of her artistic supremacy has passed. The whole development is comprised within a century; its acceleration is even more remarkable than the tardiness of its appearance. In three generations Venetian painting made the progress that had required six in Tuscany, and the whole preparatory period, which in Florence stretched over a century and three quarters, is included in the single life of such a master as Giovanni Bellini.

This means that Venetian painting followed simpler and more unperturbed ideals than that of Florence. The composure, complacency, and self-centered quality of the Venetians was a source of strength to their artists and as well a limitation. The city stuck closely to its chief business of gaining greatly in order to live magnificently. And unlike Florence, Venice interprets magnificence in the most material terms, in terms of velvet and veined marbles, fair skins and lustrous hair, in feasting and measured revelry, grave and gentle manners, colorful pageantry in honor of God, his saints and the Serenissima Republica. You will not find poets, scholars, scientists a-plenty at Venice. Her painters have no tendency to be also architects, sculptors, mathematicians, theorists in æsthetics; they stick placidly to the main business of painting. And perhaps just because the Venetian painter refused to be diverted from the problems proper to his craft, his progress was so rapid and assured, and the Venetian school, simply as painting, the most beautiful school of painting the world has ever seen.

It was written in the lagoon itself that Venetian painting should be a school of color. Long before the marble and porphyry palaces and the shining bridges of Renaissance Venice spanned the canals, the brown water gave its satiny reflections of rude hut, coppered galley, tawny sail, and, in days of complete calm, of the serrated ivory of the Julian Alps or the velvety azure of the Euganean Hills. As the city grew palatially, the marble and gold of the palace fronts, and spires and domes, with the buff and red of soaring bell towers, further enriched the shimmering of the lagoon. Its waters were ruffled not merely by winds blending and effacing the weaving of borrowed colors, but also by the passing of gilded processional barges with rhythmical oars celebrating the Assumption of the Virgin or the marriage of Venice to the Adriatic.

Ashore the splendor was hardly less. Along the balustrades of innumerable little bridges, the rose or yellow marble got an ineffable finish from the touch of countless hands. Dusky archways gave upon courts encrusted with variegated marbles, porphyry and mosaics. In the gloomy streets, gay pictorial frescoes enlivened the fronts of the less pretentious houses. In the great Piazza of St. Mark and other open spaces, often passed in solemn procession the religious confraternities called Schools, the members garbed with a splendor rare even in the

Renaissance. There were clubs of young fops, not yet broken to the paternal commerce, who gave themselves to the invention and display of the finest tailoring and haberdashery. And the unorganized kindred activities of the women of all ages were as effective from the point of view of social display. Such was the spectacle that Venice offered the painter for record and even more for inspiration. And the great-

FIG. 208. Presentation; Flight to Egypt; Miracle at Cana; Temptation. From an Italo-Byzantine Altar-front of about 1350. — *Trieste.*

ness of the Venetian painters lay in their capacity to lend to this chiefly material splendor their own kind of ideality.

When Venetian painting about the year 1350 made its first timid assertions of originality, the leading influence was that of the late Byzantine artists of the Slavonian coast and the Ionian Islands. We see their narrative painting assuming a very slightly Italian guise in the composite altar-front preserved in the museum of Trieste. Figure 208. Its date cannot be very late in the fourteenth century, and the stereotyped religious compositions represent models vividly before the Venetian painter up to the Renaissance. Such Venetian masters as Paolo, active from 1332 to 1358, and Lorenzo, whose work falls a generation later, make slight and external improvements on the Byzantine manner.[1] They reject its more rigid formulas — the gold web over drapery, the multiplied small folds, the painfully schematized muscles. They add on their own account radiant blond coloring, splendid brocades, more gorgeous fashions of gilding, and a new type of architectural arrangement. The elaborate altar-backs with perforated pilasters, and flamboyant arches and cresting; with full-length figures below and half-length of like scale above, become the standard form of Venetic *ancona* about 1350 and remains so for nearly a century and a half. We may see the form, with the upper central panel modernized, in Lorenzo's Annunciation of 1357, in the Venetian Academy. The effect depends largely on the frame-maker. Such altar-pieces are made more thoughtfully by Caterino and Donato and indeed persist in all Northern Italy until after 1450. Figure 211. We may study a similar type of *ancona* with narratives instead of single figures in the very accomplished and colorful work doubtfully ascribed to Nicolo Semitecolo, towards the beginning of the new century. Though the narratives follow pretty closely the old Byzantine requirements, the whole surface shows the flower-bed variety and harmony of color which is proper to Venice. Such work, as a blend of Byzantine and Gothic features, repeats what Siena had effected with far greater originality and *finesse* about seventy years earlier under Duccio and Simone Martini. Modena and Bologna and Padua through the latter half of the fourteenth century share this development, but again on a basis of rather marked inferiority to Siena.

The Venetian authorities were fully conscious of the backwardness of their own artists. When the Ducal Palace was finished in 1365, they called to fresco its great hall not any of the various local followers of Paolo and Lorenzo, but Guariento from neighboring Padua. He executed the great Coronation of the Virgin which was later damaged by fire and covered by Tintoretto's Paradise. The temporary removal of Tintoretto's canvas showed for a time the crumbling remains of Guariento's fresco. It is in an elaborate Gothic-Byzantine style and abounds in incidental architectural ornament. Below the ceremony of the Coronation there is a screen of pierced marble niches occupied by graceful angels. It is a motive that will often recur in the new century. On the whole Guariento brings little new to Venice, but he does demonstrate the decorative possibilities of the local style. His influence was restricted because the Venetians soon ceased to work in fresco.

The impetus necessary to lift Venetian painting out of its routine condition was supplied in the fifteenth century by Gentile da Fabriano and Pisanello. Gentile, who worked in the Ducal Palace about 1410, commanded both the exquisiteness of the Sienese style and its narrative breadth. Unhappily his Venetian frescoes which are lauded in contemporary accounts have perished. His sweetness and ideality are attested by various Madonnas. We may infer his raciness and vivacity as a narrative painter from the predella of his master work, the Adoration of the Kings (1423). The little panel of the Presentation in the Temple is admirable for its architectural inscenation and for the actuality of its incidental figures. We have a man whose eye takes in the look of things. This is even more the case with Pisanello (1397–1455), who worked a little later in the same hall. He has severe notions of draughtsmanship, as befitted the greatest of all medallists. He brought from Verona, where his artistic ideas were formed, the ideal of elaborate and credible setting, especially as regards the relations of figures to architecture. In his ruined fresco of St. George of Verona, Figure 209, we may catch his quality. But the Veronese style is really better represented by such immediate predecessors as Avanzo and Altichiero. Jointly about 1385 they frescoed the great Oratorio of St. George at Padua. Especially remarkable are the legends of the titular saint, Figure 210. Through repainting one may still discern the dignity and discretion of the arrangement, and in particular

FIG. 210. Altichiero of Verona. St. George baptizes the Family of the Princess. Fresco. — *Oratory of St. George, Padua.*

FIG. 209. Pisanello. St. George meets the Princess. Fresco. — *Sant' Anastasia. Verona.*

the just and tasteful elaboration of contemporary architectural features. Florentine and Sienese frescoes of the time are hardly as accomplished. The festal value of the architecture persists as a leading ideal of the school of Verona down to her greatest master, Paolo Veronese, and the ideal was taken up with conviction at Venice — became indeed the distinctive feature of her narrative school.

Jacopo Bellini,[2] the first great painter whom Venice herself developed, was the pupil of Gentile da Fabriano and also profoundly influenced by the Veronese. Thus he combines in himself the two main strains of early Venetian painting — its desire for sweetness and its desire for vivacity and elaborate truthfulness in narrative. Alongside of Jacopo Bellini worked the faithful imitators of Paolo, Lorenzo, and Guariento. Such artists as Jacobello del Fiore and Michele Giambono, while often inherently attractive, are of small importance. Their contemporary, Antonio Vivarini, though in most ways less sensitively the artist, prepared the way for the conservative school of Murano. Antonio's quality is somewhat obscured by his habit of working with a German partner, Giovanni. Yet the part of Antonio, as represented by his altar-piece in the Vatican, dated 1464, Figure 211, seems to have been merely to build cautiously on the work of Guariento and Lorenzo. His nephew, Alvise, and his younger brother, Bartolommeo, become influential figures towards the end of the century.

The hope of the future rested with that far more searching spirit, Jacopo Bellini. He gave to art not merely his own indefatigable curiosity but two sons of genius, Gentile and Giovanni. All the leading tendencies of the Early Renaissance in Venice originate with this remarkable family. We first meet Jacopo Bellini in 1424 as an assistant of Gentile da Fabriano and he worked on till 1470. The great decorative canvases which he made for the Ducal Palace, and for the Schools of St. Mark and St. John the Evangelist have perished, while the few pictures remaining from his brush are mostly of late date and inadequately express his ambitions. His Madonnas

Fig. 211. Antonio Vivarini. St. Antony (polychromed wood statue)
and Saints. 1464. — *Vatican Gallery, Rome.*

at the Uffizi, Venice, Paris, and Milan retain the exquisite sweetness of his master's vein. Their modest grace may be felt in the little Madonna, Figure 212, at Venice. Of admirable gentleness and spirit is the ornate Annunciation painted in 1444, in Sant' Alessandro at Brescia. Its predella panels, although probably of student execution, show how definitely his narrative compositions derive from Altichiero and the Veronese.

FIG. 212. Jacopo Bellini. Madonna. — *Venice.*

But we get the full stature of the man, not from the minor paintings which chance has spared, but from the two extraordinary sketch books respectively in the Louvre and the National Gallery. Here we trace his day by day exercises. Perspective is his constant concern. He piles up elaborate architecture with an extravagance which even his Veronese exemplars never ventured. The subject matter gets lost in the setting. The Annunciation becomes a mere episode in an architectural extravaganza. So does the Feast of Herod, Figure 213. The buildings generally are of ornate Early Renaissance type. He loves to adorn them with swags and statues and low reliefs. Sometimes he sketches actual Roman sculptures and coins, medallions, and inscriptions. He makes strange, stern backgrounds for his outdoor scenes, with twisted stratified mountains and stately distant cities. He loves wild beasts; draws capital horses for St. George or for Perseus. He is a bit of a humanist, doing bacchanals, with mischievous satyrs. There are a few fine portraits and designs for Madonnas. Thus these sketches with the silver point and quill pen anticipate every mode of the next generation — the narrative style, the altar-piece, the pastoral mythology. One feels in the sketch books a nature rather alert and curious than thorough — a certain lack of concentration and real seriousness. But the sketches evince an inexhaustible fancy, and if they are ever published cheaply, they should rival in popularity the most loved picture-books of fairyland. Jacopo was not only a versatile but a travelled artist. Active for a time at the brilliant court of Lionello

FIG. 213. Jacopo Bellini. The Feast of Herod (in upper right loggia).
— *From the Paris Sketch Book.*

d'Este at Ferrara, he had also visited Florence and probably Rome. But his most important move as regards the history of art, was to Padua, about 1453. There the whole course of Venetian painting was shaped by the apparently casual fact that an austere young painter named Andrea Mantegna fell in love with Jacopo's daughter, Niccolosia, and married her. Through that alliance, the most formidable of brothers-in-law became the artistic mentor of Gentile and Giovanni Bellini.

For a moment, indeed, Padua and Mantegna quite efface Venice in interest. For ten years before this lucky marriage, Padua had been the scene of intense artistic activity. Donatello, the most powerful realist sculptor of Florence, was at work on the bronze reliefs for the altar of Sant' Antonio, and on the Gattamelata statue. He gave young Mantegna a

strong impulse in the direction of constructive realism. Such
Florentine realists as Paolo Uccello and Fra Filippo Lippi
were also transient visitors at this time. And Padua, ever an
academic city, saw the first systematic art school started by
a shrewd and able master, Francesco Squarcione. Squarcione
collected Roman marbles and bronzes, concerned himself with
the new mysteries of perspective, foreshortening and precise
anatomy. He made his students acquire a line with the re-
siliency of bronze. He made them copy minutely veined
marbles and sculptured reliefs. He insisted that every picture
should have garlands of laurel mixed with vegetables and fruits.
The whole surface had to be brought to the lustrous surface of
an enamel. Severe teaching usually attracts good pupils.
So it was in Squarcione's case; he had scores of pupils from all
of the Venetic region and even from Dalmatia beyond the
Adriatic. He was too sensible to paint much himself; it
didn't pay so successful a teacher. So the few pictures ascribed
to him are either of small importance or of dubious authen-
ticity. But his stamp is on all his pupils. What his teaching
meant may be grasped in early Mantegna and even better in a
painter who never emancipated himself — Carlo Crivelli, of
Venice, "Eques Aureatus."

Crivelli's[3] fame was great but provincial. Originally most
of his altar-pieces adorned churches of the Adriatic Marches.
Dozens have passed thence to the museums of Europe and
America. One and all they seem less painted things than the
most splendid of mineral productions. It is incredible that
mere brush and paint can achieve so tense a line and such
jewellike surfaces. Entirely typical is an early Madonna, at
Verona, Figure 214. The great ancona of 1476 in the
National Gallery shows him faithful to the arrangements of
the early Venetians. The Annunciation, in the same gallery,
painted ten years later, reveals him affected by the narrative
tradition of Jacopo Bellini. In America fine Pietàs at Boston,

Figure 215, New York, and in the Johnson Collection, Philadelphia, exemplify his rectitude and energy.   While Mrs.
Gardner's St. George and the Dragon, as the most fastidious

FIG. 214. Carlo Crivelli. Madonna.
Angels bearing Symbols of the
Passion. — *Verona.*

FIG. 215. Carlo Crivelli. Pietà.
— *Boston.*

of fairy tales, consoles us for the absence of this subject among
the few pictures of Jacopo Bellini. From his beginnings about
1460 to his death in 1493, Carlo Crivelli remained true to his
early teaching.   Whoever understands his works has little
need to consult further the entirely similar achievement of
such great Ferrarese painters as Marco Zoppo (1440 ca.-1498)
and Cosimo Tura (1430 ca.-1495). The influence of Squarcione
passed to the conservative painters at Venice, and influenced the
entire Murano school. We have a resplendent masterpiece of
this sort in the single known work of Antonio da Negroponte,
Figure 216, in San Francesco della Vigna, at Venice. It combines with its evident Squarcionesque features, the mag-

FIG. 216.   Fra Antonio da Negroponte.   Madonna. — *S. Francesco della Vigna.*

nificence of the old Gothic-Byzantine style, and much of
the sweetness of Jacopo Bellini. Its date is about 1450, and the
picture is an excellent point of departure for our understanding
of the radical reform that came
into Venice and all Lombardy
with the activity of Andrea
Mantegna.

Born in 1431 at Vicenza, we
find Mantegna[4] enrolled at the
tender age of thirteen in the
painters' guild at Padua. He is
described as an adoptive son
of Squarcione. Mantegna was
scarcely twenty-four when he
engaged with other fellow pupils
to decorate a chapel in the
Church of the Eremitani, the
subject being the legends of St.

FIG. 217. Mantegna. St. James
led to Execution. Fresco. —
Ermitani, Padua.

James and St. Christopher. In the six panels assigned to
Mantegna, his quality and superiority are already manifest.
His style is severely archæological and Roman. He endeavors
honestly to reconstruct the times of the apostles. But his
method is more severe than that of the Romans themselves.
The line moves with the slow authority of an engraved contour. The relief is dry and harsh. There is little sense of
difference between living forms and sculptured figures. The
landscape is built in spiral strata as if worked out of metal.
Here transpires clearly the influence of Jacopo Bellini, which
is as evident also in the ornate architectural settings. The
colors are at once dull and garish, the textures scrupulously
studied after Squarcione's precepts. A most strenuous art
this, and with all its pedantry full of power and dignity.

Certain innovations in perspective should be noted. In the
fresco, St. James led to Execution, Figure 217, Mantegna

avoids the usual conventional perspective, which tilts the picture towards the spectator; and treats the group as if it were on an actual stage set at the height of the fresco. Thus no ground is seen; the projecting floor cuts off the feet of the fig-

Fig. 218. Andrea Mantegna. Madonna with Saints. — *San Zeno, Verona.*

ures; and all vanishing points are precisely set at the level of the spectator's eye below. The aim is to create illusion.

Before the completion of the Eremitani frescoes, Mantegna had married Niccolosia Bellini, had profited largely by her father's advice, and had influenced strongly her two brothers, Gentile and Giovanni. They seem to have been the first eager pupils of the man who was soon to be the artistic schoolmaster for all Northern Italy. Two years after his marriage, in 1455, Mantegna liberated himself from legal bondage to Squarcione, and soon after began the masterpiece of his developed Renaissance style, the altar-back for San Zeno Maggiore at Verona, Figure 218. It was finished in 1459, the artist being twenty-eight years old. It is a little over-rich, finished throughout like a miniature, and very stately. In arrangement it obeys the artist's new law of illusion. The base of the picture is precisely at the level of the eye, so no floor is seen. The carved classical frame is regarded as the front of an actual pavillion which is continued in paint. Without the frame, the architectural perspective of the picture would not explain itself, and if the picture were set higher or lower all the perspective relations would be wrong. At Siena, a century and more earlier, the Lorenzetti had devised this motive of an open box of which the frame is the plastic front. Mantegna made this sort of illusionism standard for Venice and all Northern Italy. Its value is open to question, but I believe that the monumental altar-pieces of Mantegna and Giovanni Bellini gain something in gravity and stability from this careful adjustment of the perspective to the actual position of the spectator. At any rate it was the rigid logic and probity of Mantegna that gave to Venetian art precisely the tonic stimulus it needed.

By thirty he was famous, and yielding to repeated persuasion, he left Padua for Mantua and the court of the most generous art patrons of the moment, the Gonzagas. His most notable work for them was the decoration of the Camera degli Sposi, 1474, in their great palace, and the canvases of the triumphs of Cæsar, 1481 to 1494, which, sadly damaged and repainted, are now seen at Hampton Court. The two series represent strikingly the dual and never completely harmonized strains in Mantegna's genius — realism and archaism. He was never more the realist than in the room decorated in honor of the marriage of Lodovico Gonzaga and Barbara of Brandenburg, the Camera degli Sposi. The motives are wholly novel — no religious subjects, nothing mythological, just the Gonzaga family and their courtiers, sitting in conversation, meeting ceremoniously, or preparing for the hunt. Nowhere before had such a consistent use of the principle of illusionism been made, not even in Roman mural painting of the Antonine age. Mantegna has completely painted away the real walls of the room, and has replaced the real architecture by a simulated classical pavillion, with arcades looking out to the country side and a round opening above. All the figures are out of doors. To see the scheme properly you must stand precisely in the centre of the room and turn on your heel. The arrangement in short

FIG. 219.   Mantegna.   Detail of Ceiling. — *Camera degli Sposi, Mantua.*

is periscopic. As you look up you will see a balcony with cupids, Figure 219, standing on the outside ledge and maids of honor and peacocks looking down over the balustrade. You see everything feet foremost as if it were actually there. Then you look out through the arcades where the view of outside doings is sometimes interrupted by a curtain. Generally it is drawn aside that you may see these great folk at ease outside their pleasure house, Figure 220. The portraits are of utmost dignity and authority. In dealing with real people Mantegna's style is less pinched than in his classical decorations. If I have insisted on the point of illusionism, it is only because the audacious logic of Correggio and a host of baroque followers for a century and more really grows out of this scheme at Mantua. You will see the open well with figures outside the parapet in Correggio's dome at Parma, and the figures outside the painted roof in the Convent of San Paolo. In-

FIG. 220. Mantegna. Portraits of the Gonzaga Family. Fresco. — *Camera degli Sposi, Mantua.*

deed, you have only to let the clouds come down through such open roofs and seat decorative figures on the clouds to arrive at the fully developed baroque style. And it is odd enough that its most romantic extravagances are clearly deducible from this rather sober and pedantic illusionism of Andrea Mantegna.

Of the painted cloths representing the Triumphs of Cæsar, Figure 221, (1484-1492), nine remain in debased condition at Hampton Court, England. Here the classicism of Mantegna finds its most legitimate expression. The designs are better seen in the engravings of his school and in the later woodcut copies by Andreini.

Despite such great commissions, Mantegna lived in something near poverty. He could never resist a beautiful antique, and he was proud and difficult in his relations to exacting patrons. His style after his Roman visit of 1488 to 1490 loses

Fig. 221. Mantegna. Triumph of Caesar. — *Hampton Court, England.*

something of its tension and develops breadth. Perhaps the most impressive picture of this time is the Madonna of Victory, Figure 222, in the Louvre, which was painted in 1495 to celebrate Gianfrancesco Gonzaga's drawn battle with the French at Fornovo. Its severity is mollified by the graciousness of the evergreen bower in which the group is set and by the contrasting seriousness of St. Elizabeth and the kneeling donor. These figures forecast a mystical and tender quality in certain of the later Madonnas.

In his last years Mantegna undertook an attractive but difficult task in decorating the study of the famous blue-stocking, Isabella d'Este, wife of Gianfrancesco. With the pertinacity of a suffragette born out of due time, this great lady framed the most elaborate written programmes, upon the literal accomplishment of which she insisted. Her correspondence with such unfortunate protegés as Perugino and Lorenzo Costa is among the delightful eccentricities of Renaissance annals. The resultant decorations reflect the sophisticated and somewhat brittle grace of Isabella's own personality. None are better than those of Mantegna which were done about the year 1500. His Parnassus, Figure 223, with its romantically picturesque gods and godesses, and its admirable round of dancing muses, is the

FIG. 222. Mantegna. Madonna of Victory. — *Louvre.*

best that Northern Italy can show in comparison with Botticelli's mythologies, unless it be the companion-piece, Minerva expelling the Vices, Figure 224, which is wonderful alike in energy, inventiveness and grotesque humor, anticipating in its mood similar refinements in Spenser's " Faerie Queene" and Milton's "Comus." Mantegna in these works becomes the true precursor of that poetic pastoralism which in Giorgione soon dominates the Venetian scene.

Mantegna lived on, none too well treated by the younger Gonzagas, until 1506. To relieve his poverty he offered for sale his most treasured marble, an Agrippina. He left in his

FIG. 223. Mantegna. Parnassus. — *Louvre*.

FIG. 224. Mantegna. Minerva Expelling the Vices. — *Louvre*.

studio his most rigid and painful piece,— the Foreshortened
Christ he called it. All his probity is in the picture. For
Giovanni Bellini and others it served as the highest model of
the tragic style, and it refutes the shallow views of such as
find Mantegna merely academic and cold. He left many
engravings and marvellous drawings in which perhaps better
than in the paintings we may feel the exquisiteness of his
austerely fastidious taste. Such a drawing as the Judith in
the Uffizi, Figure 225, is an epitome of all that Mantegna had
to bequeath to the Renaissance.

Well his contemporaries knew the value of his example.
It rebuked the slackness of their own practice. Alongside
the exquisitely modelled foot of his St. Sebastian in the Louvre,
stands the severed marble foot from a Greek statue. As
he ever measured his work against the antique, so the
painters of Milan, Vicenza, Ferrara, Verona and Venice had
to measure their work against his. And that simple act of
honest comparison in a single generation furthered the art of
Northern Italy to a degree that in Tuscany it had taken a
century to attain.

At the moment when Mantegna's influence was at its height,
it was happily modified in a realistic direction by the advent
of Antonello da Messina.[5] Despite recent discoveries, the
career of this great Sicilian realist remains obscure. Vasari
imagined him a traveler in Flanders and a direct pupil of
Jan van Eyck, whose invention of oil painting he was believed
to have adopted. The legend is thoroughly discredited by newly
discovered documents. Antonello came up in Sicily under the
influence of visiting Spanish masters. From them he caught at
second hand the point of view of Northern realism, from them
he learned the advantages of the more fluid and lustrous oil
vehicle. But he must also have seen and carefully studied
fine paintings of the Flemish school. There were such in Sicily
and at Naples. Antonello emerges about 1470 as the most

FIG. 225. Andrea Mantegna. Judith. Wash Drawing. — *Uffizi*.

energetic and truthful draughtsman of his time, and a portraitist of powerful character equipped with a new and better
technique. In 1475 he was in Venice and Lombardy.   Such

Fig. 226. — Antonello da Messina.   The   Condottiere. —
Louvre.

Fig. 227.   Antonello da Messina.   St. Jerome in his Study.
— *London.*

portraits as the captain of mercenaries, Il Condottiere, Figure
226, at the Louvre, immediately set the standard for the entire
region. We no longer find flat profiles, but heads perfectly
drawn in three-quarters aspect, modelled minutely, but with
no loss of character and effect. No such eye as Antonello's,
unless it were that of Piero della Francesca, had as yet applied
itself to the problems of painting. Whether in the nude, in
his St. Sebastians and Crucifixions, or in his rare interiors,
such as the St. Jerome in his Study, Figure 227, in the National
Gallery, he announced new perfections in lighting, modelling
and perspective. He painted for the Church of San Cassiano
at Venice a stately and massive Madonna which led the local
painters in the direction of mass and monumentality. Recent
criticism has recognised the mutilated central panel in the
Vienna gallery. Antonello's work imposes itself primarily
by its mere intensity of existence. It has no charm, and no

especial emotion. Precisely this impersonality makes it an admirable and safe model. Before his coming the Venetians had experimented with oil mediums, but they gladly adopted his lustrous enamels, and strong shadows. He returned soon to his native Sicily, where he died in 1479, but his brief sojourn in the North had left its stamp. Montagna of Vicenza, Cima of Conegliano, Buonsignori of Verona, Alvise Vivarini of Venice are among his conscious emulators, and all the figure painting of Venice assumes new gravity and authority. And we may mark his influence even in the leading masters of the new school, Gentile and Giovanni Bellini.

The tardy emergence of these two brothers of genius is one of the puzzles of the Venetian school. Neither makes any impression till he is in his forties, and their work has no directive influence till after 1480. The simplest explanation is that of Mr. Berenson. He suggests that the brothers loyally contented themselves with the position of partners in their father's *bottega* until his death in 1470. From that moment their progress is swift. Giovanni enlarges the style of the altar-piece in a Renaissance and monumental sense, and later moves gradually in a pastoral direction. Gentile brings to its perfection the complicated narrative style of his father. Both paint admirable portraits. Since Gentile is less an innovator than a perfector of an established mode, we may well begin with him.

Such early works as the organ shutters of St. Mark's and the processional banner with the portrait of the Blessed Lorenzo Giustiniani, 1465, show that he based himself on Mantegna. His career, however, is associated with narrative mural paintings for the schools, in which work he develops a real originality. Whatever he painted in 1466 for the Great School of St. Mark was soon destroyed in a fire. It was presumably the fame of these canvases that got him in 1469 the titles of knight and count palatine. In 1479, being fifty years old, he was called to Constantinople to serve that cruel voluptuary, Sultan Mahomet II. Gentile's portrait of him, now in the National Gallery, Figure 228, is an appalling piece of

FIG. 228. Gentile Bellini. Sultan Mahomet II. — *London.*

FIG. 229. Gentile Bellini. A Turkish Youth. Miniature — *Mrs. John L. Gardner, Boston.*

exact characterization. One feels the malignity of a character softened by vices, but retaining all mental lucidity and capacities for both cruelty and calculated self-indulgence. A more amiable souvenir of this trip is the exquisite miniature portrait of a young Moslem prince, Figure 229, which is at Fenway Court. Gentile brought back to Venice the new title of Pasha. We do not find him about his proper work until 1492, when he agrees to do "not for money but by superhuman inspiration" the new canvases necessitated by the fire in the Great School of St. Mark.

The greatest of these is the view of the Piazza of St. Mark's with the procession made by the School itself on Corpus Christi day, Figure 230. In the centre is their venerated relic of the True Cross. About it attention is fixed and almost military, relaxing gradually at the sides. There are hundreds

of figures and scores of portraits in the picture, yet there is no
smallness of presentation. Such eighteenth century town
painters as Canale and his followers could hardly improve
upon the truthfulness of the scene as regards light and air

FIG. 230. Gentile Bellini. Corpus Christi Procession in Piazza of
S. Marco. — *Venice.*

even. Its value as record is immense. And, barring a certain
stiffness, its value as art is hardly less.

Another panel from this series shows Gentile's really great
capacity as an out-of-doors painter. It represents the miraculous recovery of the reliquary of the cross which had fallen
into the canal. How perfectly the play of light over the
encrusted and plastered palaces is felt, its shimmer upon
the smooth water and through the moving crowds! In the
essentials of *plein-airisme* we moderns have not so much
surpassed this work. And if Gentile seems after all not quite
a great artist, it is due to that impassivity which is proper to
a luminist. With equal realism, Gentile's imitator, Carpaccio,
added sentiment, hence he is beloved and Gentile ignored. Yet
early Venetian narrative painting is complete with Gentile,
and from every consideration of naturalism it is immensely
superior to anything produced at Florence in this period. It
gains all the smaller points of representation with the most

amazing ease, perhaps because it waives the greater issue of monumentality. It is well put together, but shows little selection, is even at its best rather casually full of persons and things.

Fig. 231. Giovanni Bellini. Pietà. — *Milan.*

This produces, as compared with Florence, an odd reversal of conditions. The altar-piece, which in Florence is rather intimate, is in Venice far the most monumental type of painting. We study the development of monumental design better in Giovanni Bellini's altar-backs than in his brother's narratives. To Gentile, at once a searching spirit in details and a conservative on the whole, it must have been a great satisfaction to have perfected the narrative mode that his father had so brilliantly inaugurated.

After 1500, being in the seventies and ailing, old Gentile acquired the ominous habit of frequently making and unmaking wills. His last one, which became effective in 1507, left

to his vigorous brother, Giovanni, the precious paternal sketch-
books and the heavy duty of finishing for St. Mark's School
the vast Canvas of St. Mark Preaching at Alexandria, which

FIG. 232.   Giovanni Bellini.   Christ at Gethsemane. — *London.*

is now at Milan.   Giovanni was nearly eighty himself, but he
put the great work through handsomely.

Giovanni Bellini[6] was a natural son, but as was the humane
Italian custom, taken into his father's family.   He was born
about 1430, and his early efforts were completely dominated
by Mantegna.   Indeed he hardly finds himself artistically
until he is fifty, and then he develops a most gracious capacity
for growth which ceases only with his death at eighty-five.
Of the score of pictures which are Mantegnesque in quality
the earliest and most remarkable is the Pietà at Milan, Figure
231.   In the tragic power it outdoes Mantegna himself, and
with all its hardness, it is more painter-like.   The distribution
of light and dark is broader, the expression more homely and
genuine.   Only a little later, perhaps towards 1470, is the
Christ on the Mount of Olives, at London, Figure 232.   With

a very similar picture by Mantegna in the same gallery, it is based on a sketch of Jacopo Bellini's. Although Giovanni frankly imitates the rigid folds of drapery and landscape from Mantegna, it is with a distinct difference. The mood is gentler, details are less obtrusive, there is an exquisite sense of evening sky, and of hills in gloom, and of the coming of twilight over a river plain. It is the first greatly felt landscape in Venetian painting, and though Giovanni was far to surpass it in fineness and accuracy, even he never excelled it in depth and truthfulness of feeling. The serenity of the eventide is the fitting foil to Our Lord's single moment of human weakness and despair.

Fig. 233. Giovanni Bellini. Madonna.— *Estate, Theodore Davis.*

Giovanni's early Madonnas are singularly various. We have one very stately and tender in the estate of Theodore M. Davis, Figure 233. The Madonna in the John G. Johnson collection, Philadelphia, is wistful and emaciated. One belonging to Mr. Philip Lehman, New York, is of sensuous, peasant type, while the painting, unlike the soberness of the two earlier ones, shows the utmost resplendence of Mantegnesque enamels. Its date may be about 1470. So we see Giovanni wholly flexible and experimental at forty, and developing chiefly under Mantegna's influence.

Giovanni's emancipation from Mantegna takes place very gradually. It is virtually complete in the Transfiguration, Figure 234, at Naples which may be dated towards 1480. Bellini asserts himself fully in the gracious monumentality of the chief group, while his Arcadian mood is forecast in the ample landscape softly invested with a colorful light and shade. There is a more specific emotion and a more romantic richness of setting in St. Francis receiving the Stigmata, Figure 207,

FIG. 234.   Giovanni Bellini.   The Transfiguration. — *Naples.*

Frick Collection, which may be a year or two later. These are both Wordsworthian pictures, imbued with a mystical tenderness for natural appearances. Such are the sources from which Giorgione will soon draw his pagan pastoralism.

Towards 1480 Giovanni Bellini's work assumes monumental breadth, and withal a new sweetness. His Madonnas settle into what was to be the Venetian type — superb, mature forms at once queenly and maternal. Earlier there had been no Madonna type in his work but a singular variety of forms and faces. In generalizing the stately charm of Venetian motherhood, Giovanni moves towards the grand style, and does so nearly twenty years sooner than the Florentines. His charac-

teristic works are now great altar-pieces, with monumental distribution of the figures within fine architectural spaces.   Generally the frame is a part of the pictorial organism, the plastic front of a pavilion.   It is about the only survival of Man-

FIG. 235. Giovanni Bellini. Madonna with Saints. — *Frari, Venice.*

tegna's practice in these solemn and gracious pictures.   Unluckily the first of the series perished in 1867 in the disastrous
fire which robbed us also of Titian's Death of St. Peter Martyr.
But surviving copies of this altar-back for the Church of S.
Giovanni e Paolo confirm the tradition that it was painted
well before 1480.   In its arrangement and details, especially
in the tendency to crowd the many figures forward, it reveals
to me the influence of Antonello da Messina's great altar-
piece for San Cassiano.   It had apparently a somewhat rigid

formality like that of the slightly earlier piece at Pesaro.
Bellini is not yet quite at ease in his new and broader style,
but he has at least glimpsed the ideal of monumentality and

acquired a new technique, that
of oil painting, in which to express it.

We find him full-grown in the
noble Madonna of St. Job, Figure 235a, made for the church of
that name about 1480 and now
in the Venice Academy. In this
picture the new Venetian ideals
of ardor and gravity unite harmoniously with the old ideal of
material splendor. What play-
ings of light and half-lights there
are over mosaics, polished marbles and carvings! How admirably the strict symmetry of the

FIG. 235a. Giovanni Bellini. Madonna of St. Job. — *Venice*.

group is relieved by varying the postures of the six saints
and by contrasting the sober garb of the monkish saints with
the superb nudity of Saints Job and Sebastian and the shimmering silks of the playing angels below. And the great
picture, with all its monumentality, retains much of that old
lyrical fire, which is gradually yielding to more sedate and
reflective aims.

We shall find the two great Madonnas of 1488, for the
Frari, Figure 235, and for St. Peter's at Murano, conceived
more impassively. For the city church, Bellini insisted on
hieratic effect and incidental splendors, reverting to the form
of the triptych and arranging it after Mantegna's fashion with
the frame and picture in one perspective. It is perhaps the
grandest as it is the most formal of his altar-backs, consciously
regal in the attitude of the Virgin, with saints as magisterial

as so many Venetian senators. For the suburban church at
Murano he set the Madonna low amid her paladins and opened
up delicious landscape vistas at the sides. The thing, with

Fig. 236. — Giovanni Bellini. Madonna with St. Paul and St. George.
— *Venice.*

all its dignity, is lyrical, and almost intimate. It anticipates
the mood of the later open-air Sacred Conversations.

In the nineties and the early years of the new century,
masterpiece follows masterpiece, and we must proceed by
selection. Giovanni invents a charming form of altar-piece
for private chapels. These Madonnas and saints at half
length have already the mood of the later conversation pieces,
and need only the less symmetrical scheme which Bellini's
pupil, Titian, will soon give them. For harmony one might
prefer the Madonna with two female saints, or for robust
contrast and vitality the Madonna with two burly military
champions, Figure 236. Both are in the Venetian Academy.

The single, half-length Madonnas, Figure 237, of this period are counted by scores, and are in many public and private collections in Europe and America. They are singularly uni-

FIG. 237. Giovanni Bellini. Madonna of the Trees. — *Venice.*

form in inspiration, and yet the mood is so rich and noble that an apparent monotony is never cloying. Bellini's gift in these pictures is to combine a kind of serene obviousness with great delicacy. There are hints of wistfulness and sadness through the series, but such sentiments are never much insisted on. The real mysticism of these pictures is nothing but the notation of the most natural and mysterious thing in the world — the bond between mother and babe, the pride of it, the exclusiveness of it, the joyous burden of it. Art could hardly be less theolog-ical or more genuinely religious than in these Madonnas. I think no human being could miss either their naturalness or their sacredness.

As Giovanni Bellini approached the scriptural term of years, and the century drew to its close, he cultivates by way of recreation certain old leads which become new and powerful influences on his successors. The element of tact in the man is miraculous. He does nothing till the time has come when the doing will be most useful. Thus such pastoral recreations as the Religious Allegory in the Uffizi, Figure 238, and the little symbolical panels in the Venice Academy lead directly to the fantastic Arcadianism of Giorgione. The Religious Allegory is vaguely an illustration for the old French poem "Man's Pilgrimage." We have a Paradise, with the new souls in in-

fant form. The apostles Peter and Paul stand guard outside
the celestial barrier, while the Madonna presides within.
Beyond a dark stream is the hazardous world, a place of caverns
and crags, and hermits and centaurs; of mystery and uncer-

FIG. 238. Giovanni Bellini. Religious Allegory, Souls in Paradise.
— *Uffizi.*

tainty. Perhaps Giovanni Bellini cared rather more for the
darkling shadows over water and river bank, for the broken
light under a veiled sky than for the formal allegory. Certainly the element of strangeness and glamour is evident
enough in the five little panels depicting virtues and vices.
Again the faery quality, our earth grown strange to us, is the
basis of the charm. We have noted similar fantastic inventions at Florence, notably in the work of Piero di Cosimo.
Bellini evokes a more normal poetry which is based on a more
intimate study of nature. Such landscapes as his, even when
unpeopled, suggest nymphs and shepherds.

At seventy, at the opening of the new century, Giovanni
Bellini's mind was still flexible, so much so that we hardly
know whether he leads or follows such pupils of genius as
Titian and Giorgione. His color acquires a deeper glow, his

warm shadows are heavier and more carefully graduated; he drops his few remaining Mantegnesque habits.   In the

Madonna for San Zaccaria, Figure 239, dated 1505, we have no longer the illusionistic perspective of the altar-pieces of the '80s. The group is set well back, the suffusion of the niche with air is more dense, the saintly figures have exchanged the old resolute, hieratic attitudes for a gentle dreaminess; the mood is that of Giorgione's contemporary altar-piece at Castelfranco.   In

FIG. 240. Giovanni Bellini. Doge
Loredano. — *London*.

the portrait of Doge Loredano, Figure 240, of the same year resolution and wistfulness blend fascinatingly.   The delineation has the force and certainty of Antonello da Messina with a refinement Antonello never even glimpsed.

In these later years Giovanni Bellini multiplied, largely through student aid, conversation pieces with gracious gatherings of saints in the open air. The mood is that of courtly revery. Titian and Palma will later repeat the theme indefinitely. One of the best is at S. Francesco della Vigna, and bears the date 1507. It is an idyl borrowing religious forms.   In the altar-piece painted in 1513, Figure 241, for the church of

FIG. 239. Giovanni Bellini. Madonna with Saints. — *S. Zaccaria.*

S. Giovanni Crisostomo, Giambellino anticipates the new and compositional forms of the rising generation. The rich architecture opens upon a contemplative old man reading on a crag, with majestic mountain lines behind him athwart a serene sky. Everything above is off-centre and diagonal, stability being preserved by the great vertical figures of the saints in the foreground, and by the formality of the parapet behind them. We have almost a picture within a picture, the maximum of formality and informality, of nature and artifice — all those elaborate and calculated beauties which we associate with Titian's maturity. There is withal a mystical earnestness of which Titian himself lacked the secret.

FIG. 241. Giovanni Bellini. St. Jerome Crisostom. — *S. Giov. Crisostomo.*

In his remaining two years Bellini designed the lovely and modest nude Lady at her Toilet, at Vienna. and the Feast of the Gods, Figure 242, now in Mr. Joseph Widener's collection at Philadelphia. His career ends in a rather skeptical acceptance of the sensuous graces of the new humanism, for the gods are merely Venetian picnickers on an excursion. The penetrating poetry of the picture is of a homely sort without pretensions to grandeur. The landscape is partly by Titian.

Giovanni died in 1516, being more than eighty-five years old. As late as 1506, Albrecht Dürer found him the greatest artist at Venice. He had begun with the faint dawn of the Renaissance and ended in its midday glow. He had raised

Venetian painting to monumental estate, had mastered the secrets of landscape and its illumination, had initiated a delightful pastoralism, had conveyed religious emotion in forms humanly sweet and grave, had made the best of every world.

FIG. 242. Giovanni Bellini. Feast of the Gods. — *Widener Coll. Elkins Park, Pa.*

Scores of his pupils extended his manner to Brescia, Bergamo, Vicenza, and Treviso. His genius knew neither haste nor hesitation, he was almost never below his best. The Renaissance produced a few painters of greater scope and powers, but none more consistently great as an artist or more venerable as a personality.

To appreciate his value a glance at less progressive contemporaries will suffice. We find Bartolommeo Vivarini normally continuing the routine of the Murano School. In the polytych at Bologna, done with his elder brother Antonio in 1450, we have with slight Squarcionesque improvements the old attenuated Venetian forms. In the highly decorated

FIG. 243. Bartolommeo Vivarini. Madonna with Saints. — *Naples.*

Madonna at Naples, dated 1465, we have an intelligent use of both the Squarcionesque realisms, and the refinements of Jacopo Bellini. Figure 243. Later pieces such as the triptych of 1487 at the Frari reveal a heavy-handed imitation of Mantegna, and any little originality of the master soon gets lost in the voluminous output of the shop. Bartolommeo died in the last year of his century, whose fair average he had well represented. His nephew Alvise Vivarini deserves notice as the transmitter of the realism of Antonello da Messina to such artists as Montagna, Cima, and Lorenzo Lotto. As a portraitist he has real power. His great altar-pieces have their bleak and unattractive nobility. Venice greatly honored him in confiding several of the new panels for the Ducal Palace to his care. But since these works of the eighties were soon burned, our view of Alvise remains imperfect. I suspect modern criticism has somewhat exaggerated his importance. He was active from about 1460 to 1503, and his altar-pieces afford the best foils for Giovanni Bellini, as revealing a lesser capacity for growth.

We have now to trace the old narrative style to its climax and end in Vittore Carpaccio.[7] He inherited all the panoramic and luministic accomplishments of Gentile Bellini, but applied them with far greater imagination. He deals with legend, giving it contemporary color, and in his sensitive hands it becomes the most veridical and charming of fairy lands. Carpaccio's training is obscure to us. It may be that the very mediocre narrative painter, Lazzaro Bastiani, first taught him. In any case he drew more from Gentile Bellini's resolute handling of light, textures and costume. We first meet Carpaccio as an artist in the decoration of the Great School of St. Ursula from 1492 to 1495. He was probably all of fifty years old. The child-like legend, with its numerous embassies, meetings and partings, settings out and arrivings, gave him spectacular opportunities of which he made the most winning use. In the nine canvases now in the Academy we find an epitome of the courtesy, circumstance and adventure that accompanied travel in those days, and the mere spectacle is underlaid with a pensive ideality; for these are no ordinary journeys, but the quest of martyrdom by a princely youth and maiden. Nothing is insisted on, however, but the gayety of the events, and the picturesqueness of their settings. As in all good story telling, the persuasiveness depends on veracious minor episodes.

There are the most attentive scribes and secretaries, as if to carry off the unlikely matter they are inditing. The heavy ease of men-at-arms and self-conscious elegance of young Venetian fops make them credible witnesses to else incredible

Fig. 244.   Carpaccio.   Prince Hero Taking Leave of his Father (L) and Greeting Ursula (R). — *Venice.*

legend. To adorn his tales Carpaccio borrowed from the wood-cut illustrations to Breydenbach's "Itinerary to Jerusalem." It is remarkable how he invests these mere skeletons of cities with color, sunlight, the glamour of the orient. About all he draws a veil of air saturated with sunlight, concentrated into rising clouds whose shadows darken the lustrous blue of the tranquil lagoon. There never was a more ravishing racon-teur in the art of making incidentals count for essentials. Such a picture as Prince Hero taking leave of his father and greeting St. Ursula, Figure 244, is the fulfilment of all that old Jacopo Bellini and his Veronese precursors had dreamed of. It is typical of a series which has its more intimate phases only by way of exception. The virginal beauty of the legend gets a real expression only in the Vision of St. Ursula. Figure 245. The character of the earnest, slumbering face and the sweet slight body carries through the exquisitely indicated space, and we hardly need to be told that the wistful boyish angel is offering a martyr's palm. Possibly it takes a mundane person like Carpaccio to realize the beauty of the more fantastic religious ardors. A completely devout person takes them as in the day's work.

Before the end of the century, Carpaccio painted for the

Fig. 245.   Carpaccio.   Dream of St. Ursula. — *Venice.*

School of S. Giovanni Evangelista the Miracle of the healing of a Demoniac. The picture is now in the Academy. It is a marvellous panorama of contemporary Venice, with the bustle of eager crowds, the slipping of gondolas over the canal, and light flickering over and caressing the manifold colors of the gay scene. It has the fidelity of Gentile Bellini without his dryness.

The most delightful if not the most important monument of
Renaissance Venice is unquestionably the School of St. George
of the Slavonians. It is the only school that retains its primitive paintings still set in the original carved and golded wain-

FIG. 246. Carpaccio. St. George and the Dragon. — *School of St.
George of the Slavonians.*

scoting. There one sees in the ground floor the legends of
St. Jerome, an odd mixture of gravity, richness, and humor.
Nothing more sumptuous than the Saint in his exquisitely
appointed study, or more archly comic than the scene of con-
sternation when the Saint brings home his lion from the desert.
The series was painted about 1502. Opposite we have the
chivalric legend of St. George of Cappadocia, painted some
eight years later. Nothing could be more romantically entrancing than the boyish champion charging intrepidly over
the sun-dried shreds and tatters of his predecessors into the
very jaws of the most confidently virulent of dragons, Figure
246, unless it be the scene where he leads his tame dragon into
the astounded court, or that in which he proudly baptizes his
future bride and her parents while a Turkish band plays a fanfare. About the blowing of these horns of elfland there is no
faintness whatever. We are in the realm of most palpable
adventure and romance, and the emphasis depends on splendid
color and on drawing of a magical alertness.

Carpaccio's merit as the liveliest and most persuasive of *raconteurs* seems so definite that it is almost a shock to meet him in other capacities. Also a disappointment to find in the

New Testament subjects from the School of the Albanians, 1504, that in such stereotyped subjects he can be almost mediocre. Certainly in the great altar-piece of the Presentation in the Temple, Figure 247, at the Academy, he shows that he fully understands the new monumentality of Giovanni Bellini. The date is 1510. The picture is of the most reverent composure, and as tender as it is grand. In the portrait of Two Courtesans on a Balcony, in the Correr, Carpaccio shows a

FIG. 247. Carpaccio. The Presentation. — *Venice*.

force of character wholly modern. With a kind of irony he has taken the moral emptiness of his sitters out of doors, flooded it with sunlight and air, given it harshness and ugliness, lavishing upon the rich costumes and fair skins the most delicate pains. John Ruskin will tell you that these are honest women. Such faith is more worthy of reverence than of imitation. The greatness of Carpaccio lies in the impartiality with which he renders a certain kind of life on its own terms. The romancer is capable of appalling truthfulness.

That he was also a mystic of the most intense sort is hard to believe. Yet if the marvellous Meditation on the Passion, Figure 248, in the Metropolitan Museum, be really by him, such is the case. In a desert the Dead Christ sits in a crumbling throne, while two grim sages, St. Job and St. Onophrius, sit in rapt contemplation. Their mood has evoked the bodily

vision of their Lord. Art has produced few such symbols for
the hallucinative intensity of the life contemplative. These
weather-beaten forms seem an emanation from the sands and
blistering sunlight. They have few relations to our world.

Fig. 248. — Ascribed to Carpaccio, perhaps Giovanni Bellini's Design.
Desert Hermits Meditating the Passion. — *New York*.

Their souls move in vast uninhabited spaces. That Carpaccio
can have produced this masterpiece as late as 1520, and cast
it deliberately in a style learned forty years earlier seems to
me a fantastic hypothesis, even if it has enlisted grave authority. The abundant similarities of the landscape with
that of the St. Francis of the Frick Collection make me feel
that the invention of this picture is Giovanni Bellini's, at his
moment of highest emotional power, about 1480. Since the
actual painting is evidently in large part Carpaccio's, I am
driven to the by no means satisfactory hypothesis that Car-

paccio may have executed this masterpiece, and the group to which it belongs, while serving as studio assistant to Giovanni Bellini. Such a view at least expresses my conviction that the picture transcends Carpaccio's powers.

As for his later years, his work goes off, he loses most of his Venetian patronage, and paints for the obscure Istrian and Dalmatian seaports, the critics mock him, he dies some time after 1523, leaving no deep impression. Vasari dispatches him with a few condescending lines, and nobody cares for him till young Burne-Jones came to Venice some sixty years ago. He plainly stands out of the main line of progress. He was too romantically traditional in his themes, and too minutely naturalistic in his vision to fit into the monumental development of the Renaissance. In a sense he merely brings the old narrative tradition to a splendid close. But in so doing he preserves the look of an exquisite moment — of Venice still in her mediæval gayety and splendor, not yet reduced to her ultimate magnificent decorum. In him we glimpse the eager comeliness of patrician youth, self-sufficient in love of living. And this we see between the glistening waters of the lagoon and the lambent blue heavens, with pearly domes and bell towers rising as lightly as the drifting summer clouds above. All this may or may not be a-part from what the wise esteem artistic greatness. In any case it is charm of the most persuasive and durable kind.

Whether Giorgione of Castelfranco is to be regarded as the last of the Venetian primitives or as the first of the men of the Renaissance is no simple problem. It is further complicated by the fact that we do not surely know what pictures he painted. According to the austerity or geniality of the critics, the lists vary from eight, Lionello Venturi's, to over seventy, Herbert Cook's. Naturally I also have my own list, which, with old copies, runs to twenty-four, but I am unwilling to claim demonstrative weight for what are merely strong subjective convictions. Walter Pater daintily evaded the issue by writing the most subtle of essays not on the person, but on the School of Giorgione. I shall in part imitate him in defining first the Giorgionesque mood before considering the canon of his works.

On the side of minor technique Giorgione marks a great advance. He early abandons the old frank coloring of Giovanni Bellini for a mysterious method which abolishes line, builds in mass, invests the picture with deep shadows that are marvellously warm and colorful. What contemporaries loved to call the Venetian fire originates with him about 1505. Vasari may well be right in say-

Fig. 249. Giorgione. Portrait of a Youth. — *Berlin*.

ing that he learned the method directly from Leonardo da Vinci, who was a fugitive in Venice in the year 1500. Only Leonardo never taught him that shadow is color. That was Giorgione's own beautiful discovery, one immensely important for all decorative painting ever since.

In his early phase, if I am right in thinking that Sir Martin Conway's two stories of Paris, Figure 250, and the Ordeal of the Infant Moses and Judgment of Solomon in the Uffizi, are his, Giorgione was merely a graceful continuer of the slighter narrative mood of Giovanni Bellini and Carpaccio, — that is, distinctly a primitive artist. In his fully developed Arcadian vein he is neither a primitive nor fully of the Renaissance, but midway between, and his work constitutes not so much a pioneer effort as a delectable episode quite complete in itself. Unhappily we are almost without biographical details. Giorgione was born in 1478, in Castelfranco, a long day's ride towards the Friulian Alps. The country abounds in streams, meadows, and immemorial trees — is a subalpine Arcadia. He came pretty young to Venice and worked with Giovanni Bellini. Legend tells us that he was big and handsome, amor-

Fig. 250. Giorgione. The Infant Paris found by Shepherds. — Sir Martin Conway. *Maidstone, England.*

ous, and a musician. We know that he died of the plague of 1510, in his thirty-third year. The rest is conjecture from pictures some of which are his, and all of which are inspired by him.

These breathe a single mood, that of Arcadian revery. It is a world of desire indulged for its own sweetness, of day dreaming apart from will, action, and results. More blithely it had pre-existed in the Idyls of Theocritus; more pensively, in the Eclogues of Virgil. This world revives a faraway pastoral golden age, of lovers and their lasses, of nymphs and fauns, of vague ardors at once tempered and reinforced by a sympathetic nature. We are dealing with one of the oldest resources of poetry, and we can only understand this most beautiful visualization of the old theme by associating it with the tradition of literary pastoralism.

Of course the Eclogues of Virgil were read generation by generation, if not very understandingly, through the Middle Ages. Still the more sensitive felt the appeal of mountain shadows lengthening over the evening meadows and the pathos of love-lorn shepherds sighing musically for hard-hearted shepherdesses. By the middle of the fourteenth century, the pastoral mode becomes once more contemporary, incidentally in the interludes of Bocaccio's *Decameron*, explicitly in his idyl of alternate prose and verse, the *Ameto*. These are pale lights before the dawn. Pastoralism becomes widely current in the *Arcadia* of Jacopo Sannazaro, the bulk of which was ready by 1489. It is the parent of those slow-moving, sentimental, and ever lengthy romances in verse and prose of which Sir Philip Sidney's *Arcadia* is the most familiar to the modern reader. Dante had once longed for a magic boat in which congenial souls should drift forever and do nothing but discourse of love. Transfer these discourses to a leafy nook beside a running stream, with the herds in view below the branches, and nymphs and satyrs overhearing the debate — and you have Sannazaro's *Arcadia*. We have the eternal poetry and perhaps eternal fallacy of a bygone golden age where duty and effort are absent, where love and poesy reign.

In his most famous song, *Alma beata*, Sannazaro, celebrating a dead beauty, makes heaven itself merely an Arcadia —

"Other mountains, other plains,
  Other groves and streamlets
  In heaven I see, and withal new blossoms.
  Other fauns and sylvans, through sweet summer places,
  Pursue their nymphs in happier loves than ours."

You find the mood clear cut in the Venetian nobleman and prelate, Pietro Bembo, both in his *Asolani* and in the separate poems. These were being handed about in Giorgione's time, from 1500 on. Thus Bembo sings of the shepherd's life:

> "Tryphon, who in place of ministrants and lackeys,
>   Loggias and marbles, woven gold and purple,
>   Lovest about thee willows leafy, cloister
>   Of joyous hillocks, plants and rivulets —
>   Well may the world admire thee."

Naturally the denizens of such paradises live and dress in a state of nature. The nymphs are lightly clothed and readily discard their slight draperies for the joys of the bath, which they considerately take within the range of their shepherd swains. Bembo warmly praises those "courteous garments" which do not too much hide the fair throat and bosom, and roundly curses more churlish concealing fashions.

Sannazaro describes with a confusing mixture of metaphors what may be called a fortunate bath fall.

> "Leading one day my herds beside a stream,
>   I saw a light amid those waters fair,
>   Which bound me fast straightway with two blond tresses,
>   And stamped a face all milk and roses
>   Forever on my heart."

Earlier painters than Giorgione [8] had essayed these pastoral themes. Botticelli, Signorelli; in a sardonic way, Piero di Cosimo; Giovanni Bellini and even Andrea Mantegna had variously attempted this sort of painted poesy. But the flavor of the Giorgionesque poesy is fuller and richer. His beauty is that of languor, revery, dream. Whatever the ostensible theme may be, his painting is Arcadian. His people have not merely no relation to our world, but slight and ambiguous relations to each other within the picture. They are isolated in their own musings, rarely look at each other, never suggest an action, but only a mood. Even the portraits sug-

gest rather temperament than character or will. The proud
youth, at Berlin, Figure 249, withdraws himself from purpose
and deed. It is an early Giorgione. The Shepherd with a
Flute, at Hampton Court, is bemused with his own fancy.

FIG. 251. Giorgione. Fire Ordeal of Infant Moses. — *Pitti.*

FIG. 252. Giorgione. "Soldier and
Gipsy." — *Giovanelli Palace.*

It is of the later years. The fastidious patrician, at New York,
reveals an almost worried and sickly detachment. If indeed
a Giorgione, which I cannot doubt, it is of his latest manner.

Take the little Carpaccian idyls at Florence which cannot
be much later than 1500. How far we are from real narrative!
In the Ordeal of Moses, Figure 251, a child is thrusting his
tender fingers among live coals. Ladies and gentlemen stand
languidly about and bask in the pleasantness of their own
thoughts. There is a similar nonchaiance in the Judgment
of Solomon where a newborn babe is threatened with the
sword. The horror is treated as a negligible incident of an
al fresco party.

Again what is the meaning of the mysterious idyl in Prince
Giovanelli's gallery? Figure 252. In view of the picturesque
walls and moat of Castelfranco, a half nude mother, oblivious

of a coming thunder shower, nurses her child. Equally oblivious of her and the weather, a fashionably dressed youth
turns away. Ruins reflect the ominous lightning flashes.
Old records call this (one of the few certain Giorgiones) The

Fig. 253.   Giorgione.   The Three Philosophers. — *Vienna*.

Soldier and the Gipsy — evidently a bad guess. A learned
Viennese professor chooses to think that this is Prince Adrastus
finding the forsaken Princess Hypsiphile. Nobody can pre-
vent such conjectures or disprove them. It is safer to imagine
that coming rain and thunder at Venice recalls some old memory of similar weather and state of mind at Castelfranco,
evokes some old desire of which this richly fanciful masterpiece is the enigmatic symbol. Some story of loving and parting surely underlies the poesy, it would be foolish to be more
specific than Giorgione himself has chosen to be. The Three
Philosophers, at Vienna, Figure 253, again has been explained

as Aeneas surveying the future site of Rome. What we actually have is a glowing nook at eventide in which three grave

FIG. 254. Giorgione. Madonna with St. George and St. Francis. —
Castelfranco.

men of different ages go separately about some task requiring
thought and mathematical calculation. And even this duty

is yielding to the spell and mystery of the evening hour. These pictures are probably a little earlier than the altar-piece of 1504 at Castelfranco.

That lovely work, Figure 254, has much of the intimacy of

Fig. 255. Giorgione. Landscape by Titian. Sleeping Venus. — *Dresden.*

Bellini's altar-piece at S. Zaccaria, in formal arrangement iv is rather monumental. The mood, however, is one of revery. St. Francis of Assisi makes his gesture only for himself, and St. George, exponent of the active life, broods moodily beneath his slackly held pennon. The Arcadian landscape quietly reinforces the idyllic feeling. Externally the thing is splendid in color, and as saturated with atmosphere as it is with mood.

From now on the question of chronology becomes at once difficult, and, since we are dealing only with five years or so, relatively unimportant. The sleeping Venus at Dresden, Figure 255, may have been designed about 1505. A Cupid slumbering at the Goddess's feet has been painted out, and the landscape was finished by Titian. The noble sleeping body, to use a word of Lucretius which Montaigne commends, seems "poured out" on the receptive earth — so grandly and easily it lies. The gestures are unconscious caresses. The Goddess dreams of old joys. What faun or sylvan even would not respect that dream? Not with passion, then, though himself knowing all its sting, does Giorgione deal, but with ardors sublimated in memory. The marvellous lines of this Venus, as sweeping as the curves of hills or river currents, were imitated again and again, but neither Titian, Palma Vecchio, nor the rest ever recaptured the evasive poetry of their model.

FIG. 256. Giorgione. Judith.—
Petrograd.

In 1508, working with Titian, Giorgione finished certain frescoes for the outside of the German Warehouse. The remaining red blurs, and Zanetti's fragmentary copies, tell us that the postures begin to have the breadth and conscious counterpoise of the advancing Renaissance, but that the mood is still that of languor. Very like one of these figures is the fascinating Judith, at Petrograd, Figure 256. After the horrors of the night, she stands dreamily. Her lovely left leg escapes from the courteous draperies, and the foot touches lightly the brow of the peaceful, severed head of Holophernes. The touch of the foot is almost careless, as if merely to assure herself that the portent is really true. Her head bends gently, her nerveless beautiful fingers barely feel her girdle or support her great sword. Behind her, morning forests and fields stretch towards a tranquil sea and sky. The gestures are those of one between sleeping and waking, irresolutely feeling for some basis in reality. We are in a realm where the most awful deeds and experiences count only as raw material for delicate imaginings.

Fig. 257. Giorgione. Pastoral Symphony. — *Louvre.*

In the later works problems multiply, and a critic is pretty well reduced to personal intuitions. No doubt, however, should attach to the pathetic and nearly effaced Christ of St. Roch. The Christ is nobler than the earlier example at Fenway Court, the feeling more expansive. Still nobody, not even the executioner, seems to will the atrocity of the deed. The thing is not an act but a vision, pervaded by a dreamy tenderness.

The completely repainted Pastoral Concert, Figure 257, at the Louvre is never the less fraught with Giorgione's peculiar poetry. A courtly lover has struck a chord on the lute, and gazes intently, perhaps sadly, at a shepherd sitting close to him. A rustic, nude nymph whose back only is seen takes the pipe from her lips to listen. A proud beauty turns toward a fountain, light draperies slip away from her superb form, and with a graceful gesture of idleness she pours back into the fountain a tinkling jet from a crystal pitcher, while she bends to note the ripple and catch the pleasant, idle sound. This strange scene takes place on the edge of a vale that winds down to a glittering sea, affording a path to a shepherd and his flocks. The meaning? Modern criticism is loath to look beyond contrasts of nude and clothed forms, swing of treetops and of sky, subtle interplay of light and shade. My own reading is merely based on the contrast between the rustic and urban lovers, and an intuition that the courtier in peering so wistfully at the shepherd is merely seeing himself in a former guise. In lassitude, perhaps in satiety, beside a courtly mistress who is absent from him in spirit, there rises the vision of earlier simpler love and of a devoted shepherdess who once piped for him in the shade. The vision rises as his listless hand sweeps the lute strings in a chord unmarked by the far lovelier mistress at the fountain. The golden age of love, like Arcady itself, is ever in the past. Such may be the reading of this poesy. Indeed all Giorgione's pictures are less facts than apparitions born of roving thought in idleness, — such stuff as dreams are made of.

The famous Concert, Figure 258, of the Pitti since Morelli's time has been generally classed as an early Titian, I think erroneously. The precise and powerful execution of the Monk's head is certainly his, but I question if the motive itself lay within the scope of his lucid and uncomplicated imagination. An Augustinian monk holds the initial harmony on the clavicord and turns towards the 'cellist while the singer waits impassively. And this simple theme becomes a universal symbol for thwarted desire. The player asks a kind of sympathy which this world rarely affords, which certainly these companions cannot give. As in the Pastoral Symphony, the music awakens impossible longings, is the accompaniment of inadequacy. Titian was too robust ever to have imagined such a thing, and I feel we need only modify the old tradition to the extent of giving Titian a hand in an unfinished Giorgione to account for this poignant and most characteristic master-piece.

There remains old and good tradition for crediting Gior-

FIG. 258. Giorgione *cum* Titian. The Concert. — *Pitti*.

gione with the design of the altar-piece in San Giovanni Crisos-tomo. The execution is unquestionably by Sebastiano del Piombo. If this view be correct, Giorgione attained the ex-ternal features of the coming Renaissance style, missing its athleticism. Certainly the abstraction of the saint and the unmotivated appearance of the three virtues, and their unre-lated gracefulness, is entirely in Giorgione's manner, while the whole invention is alien to Sebastiano's heavy and forthright talent.

For the view I have tried to give of this poet picture-maker I may claim at least the merit of consistency. There is only one theme — languor of love and of remembered happiness; and there is only one setting — the Arcadia of the pastoral poets. Giorgione is the first painter who realized Leonardo's definition of painting as "mute poetry," yet not quite mute for there is generally a suggestion of music. And the music is less heard than contemplated, as is the case in one of his latest pictures, the Shepherd Boy, Figure 259, who hesitates to set the flute to his lips lest the melody fall short of that which the imagination has already heard.

FIG. 259. Giorgione. Shepherd with a Flute. — *Hampton Court.*

For ten years after Giorgione's death his mood dominated Titian with most of the rising artists. It seemed likely to replace the sturdy and objective art of Venice with a quite alien subjectivism. Meanwhile the normal effort of old Giovanni dele Bellini and of young Titian continued. The Renaissance offered to the outer eye new dignities and splendors. The inner eye went bankrupt in the numerous imitators of Giorgione, in trivial symbolism and merely playful mythology. After her brief pause in Arcadia, Venice once more took account of her own proud charms. The nymphs paled before the comparison, Arcadia vanished. But it never was wholly forgotten, and, ever since, those who have craved actually to see the golden age of poesy have had to consult Giorgione of Castelfranco.

ILLUSTRATIONS TO CHAPTER VII

Praise of Mantegna in the Renaissance

The immense authority of Mantegna kept his name on all honor lists of painters long after his death.

Lorenzo of Pavia, writing in 1504 to Isabella d'Este, says of a Madonna by Giovanni Bellini:

"The Painter has made a great effort to do himself honour, chiefly out of respect to M. Andrea Mantegna, and although it is true that in point of invention it cannot compare with the work of Messer Andrea, that most excellent master, I pray Your Excellency to take the picture, both for your own honour and also because of the merit of the work."

Julia Cartwright, *Isabella d'Este*, New York, 1903, Vol. I, p. 351.

A little later Lorenzo writes:

"And, as I have said before, in point of invention no one can rival Andrea Mantegna, who is indeed a most excellent painter, the foremost of our age. But Zuan Bellini excels in colouring." l. c. 352.

On Oct. 16, 1506, Lorenzo writes, on learning of Mantegna's death:

"I am much grieved to hear of the death of our Messer Andrea Mantegna. For indeed we have lost a most excellent man and a second Apelles, but I believe that the Lord God will employ him to make some beautiful work. As for me, I can never hope to see again a finer draughtsman and more original artist."

Isabella replied:

"Lorenzo, — We were sure that you would grieve over the death of M. Andrea Mantegna, for, as you say, a great light has gone out." l. c. I. 369.

Titian's View of Mantegna

As late as 1519, Titian admired the Mantegnas at Mantua. Girolamo da Sestola, Isabella's music master, writes to her:

"M. Dosso and M. Tiziano, another good master who is making a fine picture here [The Bacchanal, at Madrid] for the Lord Duke, went to Mantua. He saw all Mantegna's works, and praised them greatly to our signor, and he also praised your studies. But above all, he admired your *Tondo* [the frescoed ceiling of the Camera degli Sposi, Fig. 219] exceedingly, and calls it the finest thing he has ever seen. Our Signor has one here, but Titian says yours is incomparably the finest." l. c. II. 171, 2.

Ariosto's Honor List of Painters

Ariosto as late as 1515 still includes Mantegna and Giovanni Bellini among the best artists. The list is instructive as to the fallibility of contemporary judgments. The two Dossi and Sebastiano del Piombo today have lost their place in the roll.

> "And those who were and still are in our days —
> Leonardo, Andrea Mantegna, Giambellino,
> The Dossis, he who chiselled and colored equally
> Michel, more than mortal, Angel divine,
> Sebastian, Raphael, Titian who honors
> No more Cadore, than they Venice and Urbino."
>
> *Orlando Furioso*, Canto XXXIII, 2.

Lomazzo's List of Great Painters and Their Kindred Poets

"Each painter has naturally had a genus more conformable to one poet rather than another, and has followed that poet in his work, as it is easy to see in the modern painters. For one sees that Leonardo has expressed the movement and decorum of Homer, Polidoro the grandeur and sweep of Virgil, Michelangelo the profound obscurity of Dante, Raphael the pure majesty of Petrarch, Andrea Mantegna the keen judgment of Sannazaro, Titian the variety of Ariosto, and Gaudenzio Ferrari the devotion which one finds expressed in the books of the saints."

Paolo Lomazzo, *Trattato dell'Arte delle Pittura*, Milan, 1584, p. 283.
See also Castiglione's list in Illustrations to Chapter VI, p. 313.

Giorgione — Leonardo on Rural and Pastoral Delights

"What moves thee, O man, to quit thy city habitations and leave thy friends and kin, and go in places wild by reason of mountains and valleys, if not the natural beauty of the world, the which, if thou well considerest, thou enjoyest only through the sense of sight? And if the poet wishes to call himself also a painter in such matters, why do you not take such sites as described by the poet and stay at home without feeling the excessive heat of the sun? And would not this be more useful and less wearisome since it is done in coolness and without moving about and risk of illness?

But the mind cannot enjoy the benefit of the eyes, windows of its habitation, and cannot receive the varieties of delightful spots, cannot see the shady valleys furrowed by the play of winding streams, cannot see the various flowers which with their colors make a harmony for the eye — and so with all the things which can be represented to that eye."

"But if the painter in the cold and harsh winter time sets before thee those same places painted, and others, in which thou mayest have experienced thy pleasures beside some fountain, thou canst see again thyself as a lover, with thy loved one in blossoming meadows, under the sweet shadow of verdurous trees — wilt thou not receive quite an other pleasure than from hearing such an effect described by the poet?"

Leonardo, *Trattato*, Wien, 1882, p. 44.

This is so fully in the mood of Giorgione's idyllism that one likes to think that he may have talked over such themes with Leonardo when they met in Venice in 1500.

VENETIAN PAINTING OF THE RENAISSANCE

FIG. 260. Titian. Bacchus and Ariadne. — *London.*

Chapter VIII

VENETIAN PAINTING OF THE RENAISSANCE

Titian before 1545 — Some contemporaries, Sebastiano del Piombo, Palma
Vecchio — The advent of Modern Sensitiveness in Lorenzo Lotto —
Moretto of Brescia — Correggio — Titian's last Manner, its subjectivism
and impressionism — The Portraitist Moroni — Tintoretto and the new
dramatic emotionalism — Paolo Veronese, his spectacular mastery and
impressionism, his characteristic works — Eighteenth Century Venetians:
Tiepolo, Canaletto and Guardi — Longhi.

The glory of Venetian painting is to an unusual degree that
of a single individual, Titian[1] of Cadore. He lived nearly
a hundred years, from 1477 to 1576, and we can trace his painting for more than seventy years of serene and unbroken progress. He had great contemporaries — Sebastiano del Piombo,
Palma Vecchio, Tintoretto, Paolo Veronese, Lorenzo Lotto,
Moroni, Moretto of Brescia — but so various and comprehensive is his achievement that their work seems merely so many
extensions of the paths first explored by him. In his noble
and measured sensuousness, he seems nearer the Greeks than
any other Italian painter.

If he is something less than admirable as a character, it is
because of an unpleasantly calculating side. He schemed
ruthlessly for preferment and lucrative sinecures, had the
repute of envying young artists of talent, flattered to the limit
his Hapsburg patrons, bargained and begged concerning prices,
let himself be puffed egregiously by his blackguard friend,
Pietro Aretino, first and most formidable of yellow journalists.

Yet this element of craft in the man was eminently Venetian. They schemed for splendor and pleasure, and measured even their indulgences. Thus we should not expect lyrical raptures or extremes of any sort in Titian. His art is one of judgment and moderation. Indeed that calculating spirit which makes him unamiable as a man was a source of strength to him as an artist. One of his pupils, Palma Giovine, has described his manner of working. First he laid in his pictures heavily in neutral tones. Then he turned them to the wall for months to dry. Then he would pass from one to the other, scrutinizing each "as if it were his worst enemy." He would add color, amend drawing and composition, thus systematically carrying many pictures forward at a time, and subjecting each to repeated criticism and correction. He never painted a figure at one go, saying that "he who improvises his song never achieves learned verses or well turned." Precisely the greatness of Titian lay in his capacity to put ardor into these prolonged critical processes. Thus if certain raptures are denied him, he is never below himself, but always as noble in sentiment as he is resplendent in color.

Tiziano Vecellio was born at Cadore, in the Dolomites, in 1477.[2] Its shadowy oaks and blue alps live in his backgrounds. At eleven he was put with a mosaic worker, Zuccati, at Venice. He may have worked for a time with Gentile Bellini, but attained his real development in the studio of Giovanni Bellini, under the stimulus of his fellow pupil, Giorgione. This intimate and poetical phase of Titian's genius lasts from before 1505 to 1516 and the Assumption.

His second period is that of fullest color and vitality. It runs from 1517 to say 1536, Titian's fortieth to fifty-ninth year, and the characteristic works are the monumental altarpieces at Venice and the Mythologies painted for the Este family at Ferrara.

The third period extends from about 1537 to 1548. It is

marked by deeper resonances of color that is tending towards tone, and by a more objective and static ideal. Energy is no longer squandered, and intimate poetry is not sought. Typical

Fig. 261. Titian. Portrait so-called "Ariosto." — *London.*

Fig. 262. Titian. Portrait of a Youth. — *Temple Newsham, England.*

works are those mythologies and portraits done for the Duke of Urbino, and the early Hapsburg portraits.

The fourth period begins with 1548 or a little earlier, Titian's seventieth year, and lasts nearly thirty years till his death. A looser and more synthetic construction, the substitution of broken shades and tone for frank color, a more tragic and ardent mood, a more energetic grandeur of composition, with lesser formality, are the marks of this amazing last phase, in which Titian becomes a precursor of Rembrandt and Velasquez. Since he now works chiefly for the Hapsburgs, the great examples are at Madrid and Vienna.

The earliest Titians show the sultry shadows of Giorgione, and are distinguishable from his work only by a more linear quality, and by a greater explicitness of mood. Titian's poetry is direct and rarely ambiguous. What ardors of flesh and spirit are suggested in his early portraits of men! The portrait of a bearded man in London, Figure 261, is conceived entirely in Giorgione's fashion, as a short bust showing the hands, and the mysterious envelopment in warm shadow is Giorgione's

FIG. 263. Titian. The Tribute Money. — *Dresden.*

as is the sensitiveness of touch and characterization. But with all his gentle beauty, the man is formidable. His aloofness is no revery, but some preparation of will for action. Again Giorgione would hardly have labored to suggest the material splendor of the silvery satin sleeve. Even more perfect is the half-length of a young patrician at Temple Newsham, Figure 262, England. It is full of a reserved poetry, yet the effect is as well almost shrewd and diplomatic. This youth has the Venetian capacity for both passion and affairs. Both these portraits should be a little earlier than 1510. Such masterpieces of smouldering ardor as the Knight of Malta, erroneously ascribed to Giorgione and the Man with a Glove, at Paris, must be a little later. In concentration these are as fine as Giorgione's portraits, but quite a different spirit transpires from the investing shadows. These men of Titian are no day-dreamers, but resolute and purposeful. They live little in memory and much in prospect. Their imagination implies action and possession. Even the drawing is more resolute. Study the eye sockets, temples, and cheek bones of these early Titians. Nowhere in Giorgione do you get such a sense of inner bony structure, of thicker and thinner cushions of flesh, of tenser or slacker skin. The method finds its most admirable expression in the two marvellous heads of the Tribute Money (1514–5), at Dresden, Figure 263. Yet how little mystery or pathos is invoked. With a gesture and an expression of exquisite consideration and breeding, the Saviour baffles the most eager and fanatical of inquisitors. Nothing could be more unlike

FIG. 264. Titian. The Three Ages. — *Bridgewater House, London.*

the abstracted and almost morose Christs of Giorgione. As usual, Titian stands on the ground of the finest worldliness, as the Greeks had done. With the supernal, whether in heaven or Arcadia, he has little concern.

In the early poesies Titian at once manifests his adoration of Giorgione and his own independence. In the Three Ages, Figure 264, at Bridgewater House we may grasp at its highest beauty his robust Arcadianism. In a meadow landscape an ardent nymph woos her bronzed swain. Complacently he accepts her unreserved advances. Nothing could be more explicit than the relation between the lovers, and with equal plainness an old man and sleeping child serve to teach us that youth and its sweetest ardors are but a brief pause between childhood and old age. Let us then seize the moments when nature and love are kind to us. Such is the forthright poetry of Titian. It is the poetry of every boy and every girl — simple, classic, unchangeable. Think of the overtones and personal interpretations with which Giorgione would have overlaid such a theme. Such twilight

FIG. 265.   Titian.   "Sacred and Profane Love." — *Borghese, Rome.*

mysteries are alien to Titian's fervent and lucid spirit. He loves the morning hour with work and love ahead, as Giorgione loves the veiling glamour and brooding memories of eventide.

The Three Ages was probably painted about 1512, the far more famous poesy, misnamed Sacred and Profane Love, Figure 265, is two or three years later. The sumptuous variety and richness of Titian are here at their height. Luminous marbles, pearly nude forms, lustrous stuffs, dark shimmer of foliage and sun-swept slopes of grass seem created merely to set off their respective beauties of hue and texture. Purples, azure, rose, saturated greens form a sonorous chord of colors which is so satisfying that one scarcely asks why a Cupid stirs the waters of a magic fountain, and why a splendidly clothed figure sits tranquilly at the side while a superb nude figure turns impulsively and holds aloft a burning lamp.

Explanations of the fable abound. It is Venus persuading Helen to harken to Paris, or Medea to aid Jason. So the Germans. I am sure only that if we knew the meaning it would be quite as simple as these explanations. My friend, the late William P. Andrews, suggested that we have a lovely symbolism for the inquietude of maidenhood and the composure of matronhood — love in prospect and retrospect. The universality of the interpretation is in its favor. Titian's mind worked socially and con-

FIG. 266. Titian. Flora. —*Pitti.*

cretely. Plainly the nude figure is reminiscent of Giorgione's listless beauty by the fountain in the Pastoral Concert, Figure 257. Titian's maiden lacks something of the momentary grace and spontaneity of her model, but has in compensation a fuller grandeur.

Perhaps the ideal portrait of Flora (1515–16), in the Pitti, Figure 266, should be reckoned with the poesies rather than with portraits. In material beauty few Titians excel it. The curded whites of the drapery vie with the flushed ivory of face and bosom. The sweetness of the impression is almost awe-inspiring. What a world it is that thrusts forth carelessly such beauty as this! Think of Giorgione's quite similar Shepherd with the Pipe, Figure 259, and imagine again the twilight mystery with which he would have invested this apparition. Titian on the contrary thinks and feels like every man, but with an intensity and clearness quite his own. The lyrical and subjective note is incidental and superficial in him even when he most seems to resemble his lost comrade.

Titian's progress in composition is best noted in the religious pieces. From the first he seeks to break up the old inert symmetries. He invents active balances, brings the main thrusts to the sides of the pictures rather than to the centre. Thus even his Conversation Pieces gain implications of action and energy. In the altar-piece of St. Peter with Donors, at Antwerp, perhaps as early as 1502, and still somewhat in Bellini's style, we find the enthroned figure moved to the side and the accessory figures arranged in a processional approach.

FIG. 267. Titian. St. Mark with Plague Saints. — *Salute.*

The somewhat later altar-piece of St. Mark at the Salute, painted probably in 1504, Figure 267, again evades the old central symmetries. The Saint is enthroned off centre and his position gains great energy and novelty from its elevation and consequent fore-shortening. The four plague saints keep the old symmetry, their types are partly from Bellini (the St. Sebastian), partly from nature. The structure in glowing shadow is that of Giorgione. We trace the same evasion of old symmetries and the same Giorgionesque fire in the Baptism of Christ, in the Capitoline at Rome, and Christ and Mary Magdalen, at London. Such pictures with their slightly conscious emphasis prepare the way for the more assured and sonorous harmonies of the great altar-backs of the '20s.

The Madonnas and Conversation pieces again show us most vividly how his taste is working. The Gipsy Madonna, Figure 268, at Vienna, painted about 1505, is highly Giorgionesque, but Giorgione never painted such sculptural forms, nor ever conceived so resolute a Christchild. Even the throwing of the outlet to one side reveals Titian. At Madrid and Vienna are superb half-length Madonnas arranged symmetrically after Bellini's fashion, but with greater freedom of pose. Titian soon saw that the old compositional forms could not express the new energy. He makes repeated experiments, shifts the Madonna to one side, as in the unfinished Madonna with St. Anthony at Florence. He adds figures and rearranges them

Fig. 268. Titian. Gipsy Madonna. — *Vienna.*

until the Conversation piece becomes an audience, with the saints and donors approaching the Madonna, as in an Adoration of the Magi. We find the completed form in the admirable Conversation piece, of about 1510 with its two versions in the Louvre and at Vienna, Figure 269; and considerably later, a further development in those numerous full-length Holy Families in landscapes of which the Madonna of the Hare (1530), Figure 270, and The Marriage of St. Catherine, at Paris, are consummate types. And with all the conscious experimentalism of this work, the sense of character and of beauty is unperturbed. As compared with the con-

temporary Holy Families of Raphael, the accent is more individual and local. These superb Madonnas and gracious
female saints with attendant martyrs and church doctors,
are merely the lads and lasses of Carpaccio's legends, grown

FIG. 269. Titian. Madonna with Saints. — *Vienna.*

up to manhood and womanhood, increased in dignity and
sweetness.

Until the death of Giovanni Bellini, in 1516, Titian seems a
little hampered by his example as by that of Giorgione. Then,
as if relieved of a restraint, Titian pursues his own aims. His
design, in such great altar-backs as the Assumption and the
Madonna of the Pesaro family, doubles its breadth and energy.
His mythologies, in the bacchanals for the Alabaster Chamber
of Alphonso d'Este, at Ferrara, are no longer pensive lyrics,
but dithyrambs; primordial lyrics, for animation and power.
The religious pictures, such as the noble Entombment in the

Louvre, are no longer insistently pathetic. Subjective poetry is everywhere giving way to masculine assertion of the splendor of love, motherhood, comradeship. And these great objective commonplaces, which were the very staple in their

FIG. 270. Titian. Holy Family with Rabbit.—*Paris.*

day of Greek Epic and Sculpture, receive in Titian their finest modern embodiment. His new energy requires a changed color. All the hues are brighter and more resonant. Their harmonies no longer require the bond of deep shadow, but are positive and established at the middle of the color scale, where color is most itself. If the music of Giorgione was that of vibrating lute strings, that of Titian has the clarity and clangor of exquisitely harmonized woodwind and brass.

Before sounding this new music, Titian prudently secured the sinecure, a Commissionership of the Salt Taxes, which old Giovanni Bellini had enjoyed. While scheming for it, he was designing also the most famous of his great altar-pieces, the Assumption, Figure 271. It was finished in 1518, set on the high altar of the Friar's Church, whither it has lately returned. Titian adopts a form of composition which Fra Bartolommeo and Raphael had employed. The upper celestial tier is symmetrically arranged, almost in a domical way, the lower tier abounds in swinging turns and gestures, one carefully balancing the others. The forms are large and athletic, such as the Re-

FIG. 271. Titian. The Assumption. — *S. M. dei Frari.*

FIG. 272. Titian. Pesaro Madonna. — *Frari.*

naissance preferred, for greater gravity. Their weight is compensated by the ease with which they hold themselves and by the numerous floating and falling cherubs, playfully at home in their clouds, like so many celestial rose leaves for the crispness and lightness with which Titian's brush has touched them in.

An over-spiritual observer might ask, Why are the Apostles so jubilant at losing their beloved Mistress? Only a little earlier, Giovanni Bellini, who painted the theme for San Pietro Martire at Murano, invested his witnesses with pathos, silence, wonder and awe. In comparison Titian is obvious, and barely reverent. He thinks of nothing but that this is Mary's moment of highest glory, so of course her friends cheer boisterously as they wave her off heavenwards. Titian's mind does not work in half tones of sensibility, yet he is honestly religious in his own way. The Lord's people are good enough for him, and he likes them not in the hush of devotion but in the expansive moments of action. The attitude is operatic. Choruses have no business with overtones, all voices shall be *robusto*. What infallible taste he shows along these simple lines! There is no smallness, no mere floridness of utterance, no hint of over-emphasis. Such art is the despair of the modern artist. He cannot feel so simply. The great enduring commonplaces are denied to his more complicated genius.

Perhaps Titian is even more himself in the Madonna of the Pesaro Family, Figure 272, which was in hand from 1519 to 1526. For animation he sets the throne of Mary to the right, and carries splendid columns back in depth. He gives to every gesture of saint or donor a balancing relation to the gracious curve of the body of the Queen of Heaven. He renews the Giorgionesque mystery in the portraits of children, adds picturesque accessories of armor, velvet, and silken banner. The picture is as rich as it is logical and monumental, as varied in character as it is unified in mood. It is only by chance that it stands almost over Titian's tomb, and yet it would have been hard to find a picture that better represents both his more intimate and his more objective perfections. Even such masterpieces as the Madonna with six Saints in the Vatican (1523), and the lost Slaying of Saint Peter Martyr (before 1530), which enjoyed three centuries of praise, seem a little set and over-reasonable in comparison.

Alphonso d'Este's Alabaster Chamber at Ferrara represented the high point of mythological poesy for the Full Renaissance, as Castello with its Signorelli and Botticellis marked a similar culmination for the Early Renaissance. It is lamentable that we see these essential expressions of two great moments torn from their context and relegated to the promiscuity of museums. Yet the scattered poesies from the Alabaster Chamber remain a delight, at London, Madrid, and Philadelphia, and give us the truest impression of the pagan greatness of Titian in his maturity. For this series old Giovanni Bellini, in 1514, painted a sylvan Feast of the Gods, Figure 242. Titian, succeeding to the work, freely repainted the landscape, to harmonize it with his own poesies. Two years later Titian set up The Worship of Venus, now in the Prado. Before the white image of the goddess the shadowy lawn swarms with winged loves. They frolic, dally, pluck apples shaken down by their mates from the trees above. The strong little bodies glow delicately like the inside of a great shell. A rhythm of joyous life runs through the picture. In due course Rubens, Boucher and Fragonard will fill earth and air with tumbling Cupids like these, but will hardly recapture the spontaneous ecstasy of this scene. It is baffling to learn that its origins are academic — from the imaginary gallery of the Alexandrian philosopher, Philostratus. Again a two year interval, for Titian ever declined to be hurried, and, in 1520, the Bacchanal, or Bacchus among the Andrians, was ready. About the lolling figures of two clothed nymphs, the sleek brown bodies of nude sylvans bend in grand gestures as they pour the wine. At the left Bacchus in professional aloofness goes about the serious business of emptying a flagon. At the right is flung the relaxed body of a nymph overcome by sleep and wine. Her splendid nudity shines forth in competition with a soaring afternoon cloud, while behind her a lightly draped shepherd dances with his lass. The orgy is swept by the clean breeze and dappled with sunlight — purifying elements. We have not intoxication in the gross sense, but the Greek notion of an elemental Bacchic inspiration.

The decoration was triumphantly completed in 1523 with the Bacchus and Ariadne, Figure 260, now in the National Gallery. The noisy train of the god of wine sweeps into the picture oblivious of the heroine. As the leopards swing the car along

FIG. 273. Titian. The Entombment. — *Louvre.*

the strand, the God flings himself rapturously towards the form of startled Ariadne, who with a grand, hesitating gesture turns her head and body away while her legs and feet still bear her towards her wooer. The thing sparkles with wine-red and azure, tingles electrically with passion, gives forth a clamor which is also a harmony. Its exuberance is well contained in noble compositional forms. The passionate yet disciplined soul of Titian approaching fifty is fully expressed in this marvellous work.

Passing to the religious pictures once more, the Entombment, Figure 273, now in the Louvre, which was painted for the Gonzagas about 1525, is again a masterpiece of unaffected feeling and of finest disposition of masses. The central group looms against the sky with the grandeur of a great dome. Whoever has seen strong men caring for the dead or stricken will realize the reserve and nobility of acts which are expressions of sympathies too deep for words. I saw things like that at the Messina earthquake. Equally fine and restrained is the protective attitude of the Magdalen towards a Mary stark and mute with grief. Magnificent is the contrast of the grand nude forms of the dead Christ, with the rich stuffs in which the attendants are clothed. I imagine when Titian conceived this simple elegy with such power and pathos he may have had scornful reference to Raphael's distorted and sensational version of the same theme, Figure 186. And perhaps the æsthetic lesson of the picture is that choice feeling is far more difficult of attainment than fine painting.

In 1533, Titian, by command, met the Emperor Charles V at Augsburg, was promptly made a knight and later a count palatine. From now on he was much employed by the Emperor and his son Philip. With that relationship a change begins to come over his art. He becomes less exuberant, more official and objective. Titian at sixty has said almost every possible thing on his own account, and is content for a space to be observer and recorder of the stately world about him. We have descriptions of him at this time, maintaining a princely hospitality in his palace, and declining to share the dissipations which he willingly provided for such loose-living friends as Francesco Sansovino and Pietro Aretino.

He strangely depoetizes himself. The change comes somewhere about 1536, and a notable evidence of it is in the portrait of a lady in peacock blue velvet, in the Pitti. Posterity has agreed to call her simply La Bella, and so impersonal a style well befits her impassive beauty. Materially Titian has never painted more exquisitely, but it has become a painting of surfaces. The appeal is vague, general, social, there are no personal intimations, merely a magnificent statement of entirely obvious perfections.

Again Titian is content to be the mere painter in the so-called Venus of Urbino, Figure 274. It was painted about 1538, and is in the Pitti. Evidently the sleeping Venus of Giorgione is in Titian's mind, but what a loss in awaking her!

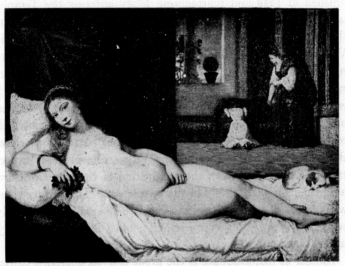

Fig. 274. Titian. Venus of Urbino. — *Pitti*.

Titian sees the gracious forms for what they are of nacreous light and rosy shadow, he sees the room for what it is in distribution of curtained interior and alcove space irradiated by morning light. He studies curiously the delicate nuances of bluer sheet and creamier skin, he models out the slender body with faintest investment of almost imperceptible shadow. In short, he is just a painter, but what a painter he is!

About the same time he did the official portraits of Eleonora and Federigo Gonzaga. He treats them as grandees. They are imposing, almost pompous, every inch the prince and princess. He sees with a courtier's eye, and gives to official portraiture that impersonal cast which it has since only too faithfully retained. He revives the great traditions of Venetian narrative painting. The great wall painting, in the Ducal Palace, of the Imperial Victory at Cadore has perished. Old copies and engravings tell us of its energy, picturesqueness and panoramic breadth. Fortunately the great mural canvas, finished in 1538 and representing Mary entering the Temple, is still in its place; for the old School of the Carità has become the Academy. In this picture Titian realizes all that the Veronese and Venetian painters from Altichiero down had sought for. Like his predecessors, he is chiefly spectacular, subordinating character, but he attains a monumental breadth which they never remotely glimpsed. The scheme is worked out in magnificent oblongs varied by triangular forms which repeat the motive of the steps. The chief narrative motives, the childish determination of the Virgin, the gracious expectancy of the high priest, the admiration of the women below, hold their own amazingly in the vast space. The surface sings with color. The painting was affixed to the wall in 1538, fully ten years before Paolo Veronese had made this sort of pageantry his special domain.

Almost as dispassionate is the great canvas, depicting Christ before the People (1543), at Vienna. It becomes less an expression of the submission of Christ than an exaltation of the Imperial power that has him in charge and of the mob spirit that cries for his blood. The architectural surroundings are magnificent. There are wonderful details, as in the howling boy at the left and the white form of a girl caught in the throng. Her sudden apparition as an element of relief and mystery anticipates by nearly a century a similar device in Rembrandt's Night Watch.

Very characteristic in its patrician decorum is The Disciples at Emmaus, in the Louvre, Figure 275, which was painted about 1545. Here there is no intensity in the moment of surprise and revelation. Benignly the Christ breaks bread; reverently and without excitement the disciples give him his due worship. All the homeliness and surprise that are in St. Luke's narrative, and that Rembrandt later emphasized, have been leveled out in the interest of discretion and nobility.

FIG. 275. Titian. The Supper at Emmaus. — *Louvre.*

The disciples show no more enthusiasm than a Venetian dignitary and prelate should.

Two portraits which were both painted within the year 1545 show Titian at the parting of the ways. The Aretino, in the Pitti Palace, the even finer sketch being in the Frick Collection, New York, Figure 276, reveals the truculent and sensual man of letters in all his formidable massiveness. The satin and velvets in which he is clad are painted lightly but with fullest regard for their textures and material beauty. Titian liked Aretino and had profited by his bitter and venal pen. So without emphasizing Aretino's effrontery and brutality Titian brings out his resolute intelligence.

In the portraits of Paul III, Figure 277, especially in that scene where the decrepit Pope muses craftily between two smooth flatterers and traitors, his own kinsmen, the sinister

air seems filled with contesting wills. A veil of atmosphere
interposes itself before the figures. The touch is light, contrasts are evaded, materials count for very little, there is no

FIG. 276. Titian. Pietro Aretino. — *Frick Coll., N. Y.*

FIG. 277. Titian. Paul III and
his Nephews. — *Naples.*

copying of rich surfaces. Even the color is reduced to tones
of gray merely warmed with reds or cooled with blues.

In its tremulous psychology, in its reticence, in its substitute of richly broken monochrome for a gamut of real color, this
picture is a kind of negation of everything Titian had attained.
His remaining thirty years were given to ideals which are no
longer bounded by the Venetian lagoon, but are as broad
perhaps and indeterminate as the modern imagination itself.
Before exploring this mystery of Titian's renovation of his
art at seventy, and since his Venetian style has closed, we may
do well to consider some of his contemporaries at Venice and in
Lombardy.

Sebastiano del Piombo ³ was born at Venice in 1487, and like
most of his generation emulated the smouldering harmonies of
Giorgione. He paints such admirable portraits as the so-called
Fornarina, at Florence, which long passed for a Raphael. He
soon passes from the lyrism of Giorgione to a dramatic mode

quite his own. He was called to Rome, made keeper of the Papal Seal, became an executant of Michelangelo's designs, and thus indulged a losing rivalry with Raphael. He commands a heavy dignity in his male portraits, and in his various

FIG. 278. Palma Vecchio. Adoration of the Shepherds. — *Louvre.*

pictures of the Dead Christ and Mary, attains a robust and telling pathos. Down to his death, in 1547, he maintained a tradition of Giorgionesque color in the alien air of Rome, and represented something of the gravity of the Venetian Renaissance in a city rapidly giving itself to sensationalism.

Palma Vecchio [4] is a more considerable figure. Born at Serinalta amid the Bergamesque hills, in 1480, we find him at Venice, by 1505 among the pupils of Giovanni Bellini. Like the rest, he is touched by Giogione's poetry, but on the whole he merely intensifies and refines upon simpler methods. He follows Titian in the conversation piece, and does many Arcadian Holy Families which are beautifully lighted, radiantly colored and felt with a warmth and simplicity that just misses sentimentality. Among the best is the Adoration of the Shepherds, Figure 278, in the Louvre.

With Titian, he loves women of generous build and he sets off their impressive charms by careful posing, employing all the new devices of counterpoise. One may see him at his grandest in the altar-piece of St. Barbara, Figure 279, painted aftei 1561. The saint is worthy to be the patroness of artillerymen. She holds her martyr's palm like a field marshal's baton, she is imperiously confident and yet gentle — a lovely Amazon of the Christian pantheon.

FIG. 279. Palma Vecchio.—*S.M. Formosa.*

In the Arcadian nude Palma has delicacy and refinement of workmanship, but the mood is obvious. For him beauty is literally skin deep, and he gives himself to the impossible competition of paint with nature's nacreous shades and ineffable carnations. But he so nearly succeeds that just as a painter of lovely surfaces no Venetian painter quite equalled him, not even Titian, and with this single talent Palma almost made himself a great portraitist. Indeed if painting surfaces were all of portraiture, he would be the greatest portraitist of the Renaissance. But his big, blond models lose condition in his hands. Charming as is such a group as the Three Graces at Dresden, or the dozen or more single portraits of men and women, they lack the last quality of distinction. He tries to gain it by adopting rather overtly the pathos and wistfulness of Giorgione, but it doesn't suit his exquisitely groomed cavaliers nor yet their even more exquisitely groomed and most ample light o'loves. Indeed, despite a handful of superb portraits, Palma has ever the air rather of a consummate beauty doctor than that of a great artist. However that be, his influence was widespread throughout Northern Italy, and especially around his native Bergamo. He died in 1528, leaving a Veronese pupil, Bonifazio, to complete his unfinished canvases and to carry on to the middle of the century his brilliant and gentle style. Within his narrow range Palma is admirable, never uneasy, never below himself. In his unperturbed Arcadianism and even in his harmless sentimentalism, in his delicacy and robustness, he seems more Venetian than the Venetians themselves.

Composure is the very soul of the grand style whether in fifth century Athens or in sixteenth century Florence, Rome, or Venice. It accepts the human spectacle as worthy and thrilling, admires without misgivings the best things that come before its eye. That is why radicals hate the grand style — and rightly, for it is always aristocratic, caring rather little for the average man and much for that privileged remnant which lives in highest bodily efficiency and mental ease. The grand style is on the side of what Matthew Arnold called the barbaric virtues of wealth, health, and generous living. The moment the artist begins to question the social order, to be curious about the foibles and fates of individuals as such, the grand style is in peril. This delicate and inquisitive sensibility makes its appearance in Italy not long after the death of Raphael. You will find it in Pontormo, at Florence, in Lorenzo Lotto, in the Venetic region, in Moretto of Brescia, above all in Correggio, more assertively in Tintoretto, and latent in Titian's last phase. It is a tremor on the sea of history that heralds a new dawn.

Lorenzo Lotto,[5] born at Treviso in 1480, first and most characteristically embodies the new intimacy. He worked widely through Lombardy and the Marches, enjoying a transitory vogue at Venice. Trained in the austere methods of Alvise Vivarini, he soon gave himself to his own native melancholy. One may see his qualities and defects in the great Enthroned Madonna, in San Bartolommeo at Bergamo. Mr. Berenson has well remarked that the saints are no longer demigods and objects of worship, but "pious souls in whose faces

and gestures we discern the zeal, the fervor, the yearning, the
reverie, or even the sentimental ecstacy peculiar to the several
temperaments most frequently occurring among the children
of Holy Mother Church." Note too how the stately architec-

Fig. 280. Lorenzo Lotto. Adoration of the Shepherds. — *Brescia.*

ture derived from Giovanni Bellini and the crowded figure
group mutually dwarf one another. Intimacy and monumentality do not live well together. This picture was finished
in 1516, the year that Titian began the Assumption. Does not
the contrast show Lotto an alien in his time and a harbinger
of ours? In later pictures of less monumental pretensions,
— as in a Nativity, Figure 280, at Brescia, which may profitably
be contrasted with Palma's more assured version, — he attains
a penetrating beauty of a morbid kind, and his sensitiveness
makes him a most appealing portraitist. He has left an extra-

ordinary gallery of shy, inadequate, sometimes morose and invalid men, and women, Figure 281. They have not the confidence of the Renaissance, but hesitations like our own. Which shows perhaps that the Renaissance mood was ever

FIG. 281. Lorenzo Lotto. The Marriage Yoke. — *Madrid.*

urban and the affair of a minority of statesmen, merchants and humanists. In the little cities where there was no enlightened court the human spirit retained and betrayed its immemorial frailties and misgivings. Lotto died in 1556, having widely diffused his sensitive art through the Marca and Lombardy.

It is significantly the provincial painters and not the born Venetians who indulge these quite feminine refinements of sensibility. Such a one is Moretto of Brescia, born in 1498 and active until 1555. Although closely in touch with Palma and Titian, he avoids their positive color and dreams his pictures in delicate harmonies of silver and blue. There is a morning coolness about them which anticipates certain perfections of

FIG. 282. Moretto of Brescia. Madonna with St. Nicholas.— *Brescia.*

early Velasquez and even of the figure painting of Corot. He is a distinguished spirit but an anomaly in the age of Aretino. Milton would have understood him. In portraiture, as in the richly clad nobleman of the National Gallery, he forces the note of picturesqueness to restlessness. In such religious pictures as the Madonna in Glory, (1540), in San Giorgio Maggiore, at Verona, or in the Madonna with St. Nicholas, at Brescia, (1539), Figure 282, he

shows an ecstatic lyrical feeling, and finds the free and florid compositional forms to express it. It has an informality

FIG. 283.   Correggio.   Detail of Ceiling. — *Convent of S. Paolo, Parma.*

which Titian would never have permitted himself at this moment.

Of course the greatest of those who in the name of sentiment undermined the grand style was Antonio Correggio,[6] a provincial painter, a disappointed and unsuccessful man, who lived out his less than fifty short years (1489 ?–1534) in or near Parma. His ideas he took from Mantegna, master of all Northern Italy, whose illusionism he carried a point further. He made in 1518 for the ceiling of the reception room of the Convent of San Paolo, Figure 283, a trellis through the verdurous ovals of which one sees pairs of nude boy geniuses at play. He

FIG. 284. Correggio. St. Augustine. Fresco. Toschi's Copy. — *Cathedral, Parma.*

paints away the domes of the Church of San Giovanni (1524) and of the Cathedral (1530), shows us Christ or His Mother soaring into the clouds with hosts of accompanying angels. He brings the clouds down through the painted wall and sets them before the pendentives. Church Doctors, Figure 284, or Evangelists ride their cloud-thrones easily in the company of the fairest nude angels of either sex. The painting fairly annuls the architecture. These decorative frescoes are so vital and so richly various that they demand admiration and disarm criticism. To walk among the demi-gods and goddesses that loll on the parapet painted about the Cathedral dome, Figure 285, is to have known the company of Homer's immortals. The impression is over-powering and unforgettable. Cautious people have always resented such profusion and such unrestrained assertion of life and joy. At the time they called the dome, with its confusion of wriggling rosy legs of ascending angels, the "frog pond." They cavilled at Correggio's price and appealed to Titian, who knowing a miracle of fine workman-

Fig. 285.   Correggio.   Detail of fresco decoration of Dome of the Cathedral.   After Toschi's Copy. — *Parma.*

ship, told them that if they turned the dome over and filled it with ducats, it would not be too much.

It was Correggio's distinction to fill an immense decoration with lyrical ecstacy. Michelangelo in the ceiling of the Sistine Chapel had done as much in elegiac vein. Both set a destructive example to smaller men who followed. For two centuries after Correggio's death in 1534 the clouds blew into churches, and rosy angelic apparitions cooled their nude charms in these clouds and dangled their delicate legs therefrom, and painters worked their will upon mere architecture, and the baroque style took possession of all Catholic Europe. At its best it is captivating even to an unwilling Protestant imagination, but it never regained the height of its beginnings in Correggio.

In his religious pieces and mythologies, Correggio is respectful to the grand style. He had in one way or another taken account of his Titian, Raphael, and Michelangelo, and he builds his groups in their active symmetries. But such an allegiance to the decorous style is merely superficial, his affinities are with the following centuries and the devotees of sensibility. Even in a grandly composed picture like the Holy Family called The Day, Figure 286, the women are disquieting in their personal loveliness. There is no relation to the Parthenon marbles, as there always seems to be in Titian, no suggestion of a larger air. These Maries know love, and raptures and tears. In the somewhat earlier Marriage of St. Catherine, Figure 287, at Paris, the mood is simply one of great tender-

FIG. 286. Correggio. "The Day." — Parma.

FIG. 287. Correggio. Marriage of St. Catherine. — Louvre.

ness. In later pictures like the Madonna with St George and the Holy Night, at Dresden, the excitement of all the figures becomes almost unpleasant. So, in the mythologies, Leda, or Danae, or Antiope, Figure 288, is not goddesslike but perturbingly feminine and desirable. A most delicate erotic appeal is in all this work. It is like Alexandrian sculpture. It is still noble, but less so than Titian or

Raphael, less abstract and stylistic. The exquisite ambiguity of the mood is not quite compatible with the compositional formulas. One feels it is but a step and a legitimate one from Correggio to the rare, sentimental nudes of Gainsborough and Sir Joshua and Romney.

FIG. 288. Correggio. Jupiter and Antiope. — *Louvre.*

In every phase Correggio's work is distinguishable by the most beautiful handling of color and light and dark. Like Moretto and Lotto he prefers a blonder scale than the Venetian, and makes his surfaces so many miracles of ivory, silvery grays and straw yellows, invested with shadow tenuously modulated, yet of strongest modelling power. He cares nothing about textures or individually rich passages; it is the whole picture that counts. The brush sweeps lightly and swiftly, there is no loading of color, everywhere an exquisite economy and a subtlety that conceals itself. At all points, technically as well as psychologically, Correggio deals in overtones. And by that token he is not of the Renaissance, but is greater or smaller than it, as you may choose to decide. He is more our contemporary than he is Titian's.

Meanwhile Titian himself is passing into a subjective phase. In 1545 he was at Rome. Michelangelo, who offered him unusual courtesies, doubtless showed him the Sistine ceiling and the recently finished Last Judgment. Titian, as he writes himself, studied with humble amazement the "marvellous old stones" that the Roman soil was yielding up to the newly founded museums.

Even before the Roman trip, his style begins to show an old man's restless vehemence. The titanic ceiling decorations for the Salute, of 1543 and 1544, Abraham and Isaac, Cain and Abel, David and Goliath, display at once an almost sensational energy and a lesser regard for the superficial attractions of color. The rugged designs are hacked out in bold splotches of light and dark. The method begins to be luministic. The partial foreshortening of the figures to adjust them to being seen from below is the decorative compromise which prevails at Venice from Tintoretto to Tiepolo. The new point of

FIG. 289. Titian. Charles V. at Mühlberg. — *Madrid*.

view is easiest studied in Christ crowned with Thorns, in the Louvre. Titian passes swiftly through this overtly dramatic stage. The same year, 1548, that saw the Crowning with Thorns, saw also the equestrian portrait of Charles V, Conqueror, Figure 289, after the battle of Mühlberg. What is odd about the picture is the elimination of all military conventions — no battle reek, no stricken foes, no busy staff. Instead just the pale, inflexible, thoughtful face of a slight old man, physically frail but firmly seated on a cantering horse. There is no frank color except the purple scarf and the gold of armor and horse trappings. Everything is expressed in marvellous grays and browns which contain hints of all the colors. There is no linear drawing; edge melts into edge without abrupt contrasts. A twilight mystery, a veiled quality, adds immensely to the expression of melancholy and might. The mere spectacle of life has become relatively uninteresting to Titian. He rather meditates on those creative throes of the mind which underlie action. His conqueror is a thinker.

In Titian's own portrait, of 1550, at Berlin, the new method

FIG. 290. Titian. The Rape of Europa. — *Mrs. John L. Gardner, Boston.*

is more strongly announced. The form grows out of a silvery gloom by reason of hesitating flickers of light which yet have extraordinary modelling power. In character the work is remarkable. One senses smouldering under the weathered surfaces of this man of seventy-three the most formidable capacities for wrath and for passion.

The nudes and mythologies of these final years, the various Danae's and the Nymph and Faun at Vienna, the Calisto and Actæon at Bridgewater House, the Venus and Adonis at Madrid, all show a very different temper from the early poesies. There is no suggestion of meditative dalliance, no shy Arcadianism. These are mortals stung and lashed by desire. Love is not sweet on their lips but bitter and fateful. Even Europa, Figure 290, at Fenway Court, the finest of these later poesies, seems to fill the sunlight sky and sea with a spasm of erotic expectancy. Passion becomes cosmic. Strange capacities for tenderness also appear. Compare the Deposition

FIG. 291. Titian. The Entombment. — *Madrid.*

in the Prado, Figure 291, of 1559, with the masterpiece of forty years earlier, Figure 273, at the Louvre. The noble dome-like arrangement persists, but within the compositional dome what a change! The body of the Christ is no longer grandly disposed. It crumples as it is turned into the tomb. The thing has the unexpectedness of fact. The canvas is soberly incandescent with half-lit faces which gleam through the deep grays and browns. Each light is a focus of compassion.

Titian himself, impersonating St. Joseph of Arimathea, supports the Christ.

In one of the latest poesies, the Education of Cupid, Figure 292, at the Borghese, Rome, the new method may be studied.

FIG. 292.   Titian.   Education of Cupid. — *Borghese, Rome.*

The forms are built up of little and apparently indeterminate touches of russets and grays that glow from within. The form builds itself out vibratingly. It is no longer as palpable to the hand as that of the early Titians, but it is more palpable to the eye and to the mind. Tone has driven out color; atmospheric envelopment has replaced minute description; the artist merely creates gradations of light which afford the illusion of bulk. It is what we call today, rather loosely, impressionism, or, more accurately, luminism. In the character of these goddesses we have no longer wistfulness, that ineffable adolescent quality of Titian's early poesies, but women fully conscious of their power to give or take away.

His later pictures, The Crowning with Thorns at Munich (1570) and the Pietà (1576) in the Venice Academy, are nobly tragic in mood. Titian faces the last great event not as a humanist, but as a humble believer sorrowing in the suffering of his Lord. Carried off by the plague in 1576, Titian had lived nearly a century, for over seventy years had been a famous painter. In that long course there is no sign of failure of power. His dominant mood changes according to his age from the ardent pastoralism of his early maturity, through the dramatic energy of his middle age, and the impersonal splendor of his first old age. And when he had passed the scriptural term, he developed new depths of feeling, and created to contain them a pulsating realm of light and dark in twilight. He had begun with the cool preciseness of Giovanni Bellini and closed with a passionate mystery of expression which foretells Rembrandt. So far as Venice was concerned, he not merely led its Renaissance, but was its Renaissance, both in rise and decay. And it is noteworthy that while Raphael and Michelangelo end in ostentation of power and decline of feeling, Titian ends in deeper capacities whether for passion or sympathy, works away from the daylight realities of humanism towards new depths in natural appearance and new depths in his own soul.

Around such a man a throng of able painters naturally grew up. The poorest imitated him, the better took hints from his marvellous practice and went their own way. Among these was Giambattista Moroni of Bergamo, born in 1520 and trained under Moretto of Brescia. Mediocre as a religious painter, he was a portraitist of acutest vision for character. A provincial, he cared little for the idealizations of the time. In such a portrait as the Tailor, at London, or the amazing old Abbess in the Metropolitan Museum, or the Husband and Wife, at Cleveland, or The Widower, at Dublin, Figure 293, he gives us the very look of people, even to their uneasiness as they submit to the ordeal of being portrayed, and withal their intelligence, diligence, and patience. Titian, when over-driven with portrait commissions, habitually referred his clients to Moroni, as an abler artist in the specialty. And indeed

FIG. 293. G-B. Moroni. The Widower. — *Dublin.*

Moroni, while lacking Titian's style, looked harder at his sitters than Titian ever did. He died in 1572, four years before his generous friend.

The Bassanos, the father Jacopo and his sons Leandro and Francesco, were too popular to be omitted. Their style is pretty eclectic with something of late Titian and Tintoretto in it. They treat the old religious themes, are good portraitists, and carry out on their own initiative a bucolic sort of painting, with abundant horses, cattle and dogs. So homely a tradition has its place in breaking down the decorum of the grand style. The excellent average of the family in their craft may be judged from Leandro's Pietà, at Cleveland.

Sometimes over the velvety calm of Venice and the lagoon will roll up a thunder storm. The radiant color becomes more sombrely rich under the tossing clouds. Their steely edges break into the lightning flash; domes and towers for a moment stagger under the lashing of the rain squall. The storm passes, the leaden clouds show saffron backs against the blue, the evening is here with double serenity and purity. Such is Jacopo Tintoretto amid the reflective tranquility, and confident splendors of Venetian painting — a wind of the spirit, a shattering, yet consoling, apparition. Tenderness, tragedy, romance, are his realm. Where his contemporaries dealt in superb averages, he deals in transcendent exceptions. Thus he has ever been a baffling figure to the critics. For the febrile Ruskin, he is among the greatest of painters; for the coolly

Fig. 294. Tintoretto. Tithonus and Aurora. Tempera color sketch.
— *British Museum.*

analytical Kenyon Cox, he is little better than a reckless sensationalist. Every one, friend or foe of his art, must admit its Shakespearean richness and variety. He lacks Titian's Olympian poise, but is more universal.

Jacopo Robusti,[7] the dyer's son, was born in Venice in 1518. At seventeen he was put with Titian. Once passing through the studio Titian saw on the floor a number of Tintoretto's sketches. Not trusting himself to speak, he sent word that the new comer should never again enter his studio. An act which contemporary gossip ascribed to jealousy, is rather to be referred to disgust at Tintoretto's unbridled vehemence. Whoever has studied Tintoretto's tempera sketches, Figure 294, in the British Museum may realize how Titian felt. The sketches are superb, but Titian in 1535 was in no way to realize their value. Twenty years later he may have appreciated them.

Driven out by the best master in Venice, Tintoretto was reduced to the process of self-education, in which he was

Fig. 295.   Tintoretto.   Presentation of Virgin in the Temple. — S. M. dell' Orto.

aided by that brilliant decorative colorist and ever luckless artist, Andrea Schiavone.   Tintoretto's earliest work of note is the decoration of his own parish church of the Orto, which he undertook about the year 1546 for the costs.   The gigantic canvases of the Deluge and Worship of the Golden Calf in the Choir made his fame, but we see his peculiar quality better in the Presentation in the Temple, Figure 295.   It was finished only a few years after Titian's masterpiece in the Scuola della Carità, hence the contrast between the two works on the same theme is enlightening. Titian's picture is fundamentally a spectacle and a ceremony. Everything goes as arranged and expected. Tintoretto's picture is a sudden and thrilling event full of unexpected graces. The little Virgin is well within the picture, but keeps her prominence through her position against the sky and even more by reason of the focusing of intense interest on her by all the persons in the composition. It is a charming invention that three mothers and their infant daughters on the steps should share in the glory of her consecration. At the left a prophetic figure suddenly grasps the import of the moment and sways with wide stretched arms towards the hope. From him to the head of the steps rises a pathetic line of cripples and beggars mercifully veiled in half light. These are witnesses to the human misery that the Virgin through her Son is to assuage. The unifying principle, apart from the fine linear design, is the light which floods out of the picture over the beautifully carved steps. Everything is conceived in depth, while Titian's Presentation is relatively on one plane. Golden browns and yellows of great luminosity are prevailing colors, the crimsons and blues serving merely as relief and accent. With all its richness of illustrative content, the thing is a noble decoration.

A little later, perhaps in 1548, Tintoretto did the first of three canvases for the Scuola Grande di San Marco. It represents the moment when a Christian slave is about to be brained. The liberating figure of St. Mark, Figure 296, swoops down, the maul snaps in the executioner's hand. With a singular delicacy the entire interest of the bystanders is concentrated on the helpless white body of the martyr. The suspense is breathless. Only the old magistrate high at the right has seen the miraculous breaking of the executioner's sledge. His gesture carries the eye to the figure of the downward swooping saint, thus the most sensational feature is last seen and comes as a climax. Such dramatic modulations are of the very essence of Tintoretto's genius. Again, though the sweeping curves of the linear design are splendidly balanced, the light is the ultimate harmonizer. It ripples out in an increasing wave towards the spectator, kindling as it goes the colors of

Fig. 296. Tintoretto. Miracle of the Slave. — *Venice.*

rich stuffs and the bronzed or pearly roundings of brows, shoulders, throats and limbs. The carrying of a uniform rhythm of motion through earth and sky is again Tintoretto's invention. He uses it here as elsewhere not as a sprightly device — which was later the baroque attitude — but as a necessary factor in emotional expression.

In 1561 Tintoretto finished the great Marriage at Cana for the Salute. The picture is tremendously developed in depth, and the Christ is set in the distance. The foreground figures alone are concerned with the miracle. Very effective is the contrast of the quiet feasters with those who are stirred by the marvel. The lighting is consummately fine. There are passages of extreme loveliness, such as the swaying row of women's faces on the right of the table, but the whole thing is far from clear; illustrative and decorative features are imperfectly harmonized. In this great scale Tintoretto's richness and insatiate inventiveness tend to work against him.

Before considering his colossal labor in the School of St. Roch, we should note his avowed ideal. It might be read on the walls of his studio: "The Drawing of Michelangelo and the Coloring of Titian." In the studio were casts of Michelangelo's sculptures brought up at great expense from Florence and Rome. And to Michelangelo we owe the slender and alert proportions of Tintoretto's figures, quite different as they are from the gravity, almost ponderosity of Titian, Palma, and Paolo Veronese. The color is based on late Titian, but is more sonorous, simple, and uncomplicated by minor tones. The brush stroke is unlike anything earlier — sketchy, impetuous, definitive, working by first intention. Accordingly the surfaces are much broken, and, to a near view, lack preciousness. We have neither the fluent enamel of Giorgione and early Titian, nor yet the muffled richness of Titian's later manner. But in the best Tintorettos the touch is infallibly crisp, right and expressive. To exaggerate these generously avowed influences of the master who repudiated him and the master he never saw would be easy. As a matter of fact, Tintoretto is always more the illustrator than either of his models. If he adopts the grand poses of Michelangelo, he does so not for abstract beauty, but ever seeks a motive for them. If he chooses Michelangelo's slender, athletic proportions, he invests them with tenderness and enthusiasm. Unlike Titian, he avoids both classical draperies and rich contemporary costumes, choosing compromise forms of dress which, without ceasing to be classical, should seem familiar, and fit for a real world. If he adopts Titian's coruscating light, he gives it a special poetry. It does not glow evenly through the picture, but flashes intermittently, as an accent or accompaniment to emotion.

In 1560 the famous charitable confraternity of St. Roch

determined to decorate their beautiful School. They called Federico Zuccaro, and Francesco Salviati, who had Roman honors, Tintoretto, and his friends, Schiavone and Paolo Veronese. The subject in competition was to be a cartoon of St. Roch in glory for the ceiling of the refectory. When the day came, Tintoretto unveiled not a cartoon but the finished oval. That was his drawing, he said; he hoped they would not be offended, but he knew no other way. The misunderstandings due to this summary procedure were soon cleared up. Tintoretto became titular painter to the School, later a member, and worked at the two great halls and ante-rooms for twenty-eight years.

St. Roch was the Physician Saint who cared for the plague stricken. Thus the upper hall was pictured with examples of miraculous mercy and deliverance chosen from the Old Testament. The lower hall was devoted to the more familiar stories of the life of Christ and of His Mother. Sadly darkened and neglected, often in impossible light, these pictures baffle all but the enthusiast. One needs all the vicarious enthusiasm that may be drawn from a Ruskin to do San Rocco with any thoroughness. Whoever persists will be rewarded, for while Tintoretto is by no means at his greatest as a painter in this work, it reveals his inexhaustible inventiveness, his warmth and tenderness, and power, as no other series does, whereas it has in the little moonlit landscapes with St. Mary Magdalen and St. Mary of Egypt faery refinements elsewhere lacking in the master.

Everybody knows at least the great Calvary, with its sense of cosmic disaster. Marvellous is the storm which sweeps towards the cross from behind, superb alike the cluster of faithful friends at the foot of the cross and the proud riders at the flanks. Hate, love and indifference mingle in the scene. It gets its profound tragedy on terms of fact, is free from all mystical sentimentality. What was it like on that awful evening? is the only question the artist asks himself, and his answer, a sheer gift of the imagination, transcends all the lyrical sweetness and measured solemnity of the ritual crucifixions. Humanism and religion unite for once in this masterpiece.

Among the scores of narratives in the two halls the eye will rest upon Moses Smiting the Rock, for its majesty; upon the meeting of Mary and Elizabeth which has the intensity of Giotto's fresco at neighboring Padua, with an abandon all its own; upon the Flight into Egypt, with its idyllic landscape; upon the awful tumult and despair of the Massacre of the Innocents; upon the pathos of the white-robed Christ, awaiting his doom from an indifferent proconsul. These occur among many that are equally memorable. Perhaps the subtle humanism of Tintoretto is best shown in the Temptation

Fig. 297. Tintoretto. Christ Tempted by Satan. — *Scuola di S. Rocco.*

of Christ, Figure 297. Instead of the ignoble bat-like Satan of the mediæval painters, we have a magnificent starry-eyed youth, a veritable genius of the pride of life. With outstretched, generous arms he offers unstinted power and pleasure. The Christ regards him with tranquil kindness, as one might a splendid animal fawning too eagerly. For so Christian a man as Tintoretto, it implies extraordinary sympathy to imagine a Satan in his own way gloriously sure of his case. In these compositions the method is most various. But where there are many figures Tintoretto generally avoids the convention of placing the chief personages on the picture plane. You look over heads or between bodies to glimpse the Saints or the Blessed Virgin or Christ. And curiously this procedure does not confuse the eye. On the contrary these apparently casual but really most thoughtful arrangements heighten the sense of reality; one feels like a witness, like one himself on the edges of the throng.

Along with the decoration of San Rocco, Tintoretto undertook frequent commissions for the Ducal Palace. But the fire of 1577 consumed his picture of the naval victory at Lepanto, with much else. In the mythologies of the Anticollegio painted in 1578 we have the loveliest poesies of the Venetian school. These are the Marriage of Bacchus and Ariadne, Mercury and the Graces, Minerva expelling Mars and the Forge of Vulcan. From the point of view both of decoration and sentiment these are perhaps the finest nudes in painting. They glow with outdoor health, the firm wholesome bodies sway from sheer joy in motion, or hover lightly in the limpid air. The noble forms are fixed for us in transparent shadows, and broad dapplings of light. There is little of the sheer dreaminess of Giorgione, who yet counts for something in the work, nor yet of the explicit sensuousness of Titian. These noble creatures go about our business, — marrying, seeking grace in life, composing strife, providing munitions should strife arise. Miss Phillipps is probably right in divining here an allegory of the greatness of Venice, bride of the Adriatic, protected by her diplomacy, admired for her arts, yet ever ready in her arsenals. What is better worth noting is the combination of breadth and delicacy in the finest of these poesies, The Marriage of Bacchus and Ariadne, Figure 298. The interlocking of the superb forms in a flowing rhythm or pattern, the technical miracle of Venus's easy turn in the air as she offers the ring and the starry crown, the exquisite alternations of light and half light others might conceivably have invented. What is proper to Tintoretto and to him alone is the hesitating hand of Ariadne and her almost resigned and reluctant acceptance of

FIG. 298. Tintoretto. Bacchus and Ariadne. — *Ducal Palace.*

a new love, being mindful of love once betrayed. Also the delicacy of Bacchus's ardent gesture, as knowing himself to be not only wooer but consoler, is purest Tintoretto. The picture with its companion pieces is the effulgent after-glow of the Arcadianism that began with Giorgione. It breathes a charm that has never since been fully recoverable.

While these poesies were in progress, about 1575, Tintoretto painted for the Church of San Cassiano the most original of his Crucifixions, Figure 299. One looks over the narrow top of Golgotha to a peaceful expanse of marbled evening sky. The heads and serried pikes of the Roman legionaries suggest a throng behind the hill. The sharpest note of color is a banner, and the purple robe just stripped from the Christ.

Between John and Mary and the executioners on the ladder and against the sky the strangest episode passes. It is the moment when a Pharisee hands up to the executioner the mocking placard "Jesus of Nazareth King of the Jews."

FIG. 299. Tintoretto. Calvary. — *S. Cassiano.*

With a sudden impulse John points out the act to Mary, to console her. Christ's enemies affirm the truth of him. Even in the hour of defeat and death he is eternally his people's king. The level light which ripples softly over the nude forms of Christ and the thieves takes away all harshness. At San Rocco Tintoretto presented an epic and cosmic terror. Here he suggests all the intimate and lyrical hopes that have grown out of the sacrifice on Calvary.

Like all the Venetians Tintoretto was an admirable portraitist. His sober and powerful vein is well shown in the Madonna with Three Magistrates, Figure 300.

Among the later altar-pieces none is finer than the Miracle of St. Agnes in the Orto. It has all of Tintoretto's sweetness,

FIG. 300. Tintoretto. Madonna with Three Magistrates. — *Venice.*

power and suddenness, and is nearly in its original condition of color. In 1587, being nearly seventy years old, he got the commission for his greatest and perhaps his last picture, the Paradise, in the Hall of the Great Council in the Ducal Palace. Darkened and dried, it is still to the perceptive observer a billowing sea of rapturous faces of the blest, obeying in its widening circles of cloud-borne angels an oceanic rhythm. During the three years that Tintoretto was painting it, his young daughter and comrade, Marietta, dressed like a Shakespearean page for greater convenience, worked and chattered beside him on the scaffolding. She hardly lived to see the great canvas set on its wall. Tintoretto lived on till 1594, and then his aged and withered body was carried across the canal from his palace to his vault in the Orto. Such friends as Schiavone and Paolo Veronese had gone before him, the old merrymakings and impromptu concerts in his home had ceased. It was a very tired old man who bid his sons continue the honorable trade of painting. He had shared nobly the greatest range of human emotions, and his last artistic vision was of an ecstatic peace in Paradise.

After Tintoretto, Paolo Veronese[8] seems an anti-climax. His imagination is very limited. His greatest pictures treat the sole theme of stately feasts. His soul is that of a very high class society editor. But no well-advised person looks to Paolo Veronese for soul. One rather seeks in him judgment and fine painting. Both are at their maximum.

Paolo Caliari was born at Verona in 1528, trained by a half primitive master, Antonio Badile, and influenced by the energetic compositions of Brusasorci. Paolo inherited the long Veronese tradition for spectacular narrative painting with splendid architectural accessories, and he carries the local tradition to its close and height. He came to Venice at twenty-seven, a finished and famous artist, bringing with him a novel sort of color. He avoids the contrasts and keen resonances of the true Venetians, painting rather in luminous half tones based on gray and blue. His forms are rich and solid without heavy shadow, and his canvases have the generally blond and uniform color quality of the modern out-of-door school.

His preference is for feasts and pageants. We have the spectacle of a rich and gentle society, dignified in its pleasures and resplendent in its costume. Gold brocade sets off the pearly skins of the portly and gracious ladies in his pictures, and their cavaliers are as magnificently clad in satins, velvets and furs. The feasts are generally half out of doors in great colonnades, with the light glinting impartially upon fair throats and faces and upon channeled columns and sculptured balustrades. Behind, pale cornices and spires swim against a blue sky.

It was the habit of the wealthy chapters of monks who maintained the great Venetian churches to paint in their refectories some Scriptural feast, as a warrant perhaps for their own daily convivialities. Earlier, the most solemn of all meals, The Last Supper, would have been chosen. Not so with Veronese and his contemporaries. They chose instead the Marriage at Cana or the Feast in the House of Simon or of Levi, Figure 301, — splendid events of small or only incidental religious significance, and treated merely as contemporary banquets.

Of the four great feasts painted by Paolo Veronese the

Fig. 301. Paolo Veronese. Feast in Levi's House. — *Venice.*

Marriage at Cana, in the Louvre, painted in 1563, is earliest, and most imposing. It builds up indefinitely from the marble pavement, with tier upon tier of people, clinging to columns and peering from balconies. One may count no less than two hundred and fifty heads. It has all the stir of a public banquet and everywhere the greatest richness of table accessories and constumes. The theme called for little religious emotion. The miracle itself is a convivial one. Yet Veronese has made this different from other feasts by a most complicated system of guiding lines which always lead the eye to the gentle face of the Christ in the centre. He fairly dominates all this animation and splendor. In the trio of musicians in the foreground Veronese has given us a precious hint of the part music played in the life of all Venetian artists. Paolo himself plays the viola, Tintoretto the 'cello, and Titian the bass. What is remarkable about the great canvas is its unity. Bathed in equable cool light, the eye takes it in at a glance; there is no confusing or distracting emphasis; the whole thing is nobly tranquillizing.

In 1569 Veronese was in Rome. We may possibly see some

slight influence of Michelangelo in the frescoes of the Villa Barbaro, at Maser. These contain the only nudes of Veronese that have a real athleticism, and the whole decoration has a more positive and sprightly spirit than is usual in Veronese's placid style. Working in a country house for liberal and congenial patrons, Daniele Barbaro was himself an architect of merit, Veronese sheds something of that professional dignity which is sometimes excessive in his official work.

FIG. 302. Paolo Veronese. Marriage of St. Catherine. — *Santa Caterina.*

Among his numerous altarpieces, the Marriage of St. Catherine, Figure 302, in the Venetian Church of that name is perhaps the most gracious. The women are adorable — hothouse flowers, incredible for poise, hue and delicate surface bloom. They are not very personal, their charm is a social one. But they are very gentle, reasonably unconscious of their own beauty, and quite unforgettably lovely. It took a wonderful eye to see them at once so simple and so regal.

In the last twelve years of his life, Veronese was constantly employed in the Ducal Palace and the adjoining public buildings. He employed assistants freely, and the work affords difficult critical problems. The work is uneven. In mythology he belies the hopes based on the frescoes at Maser, where it seemed as if he too might attain the Olympian mood. It is sadly lacking in the hoydenish group that enacts Europa and the Bull, Figure 303, in the Ducal Palace. Why are these

Fig. 303. Paolo Veronese. Rape of Europa. — *Ducal Palace.*

heavy Venetian lasses risking their skins and skirts and shins near the seaside and a bull? The flat prose of the feeling, or rather the absence of any real feeling, makes one forget the splendor of the painting. Such also is the effect of the superbly painted Venus and Mars, at New York, and of most of the mythologies. We have to do with sheer prose and not very sincere prose at that.

When, however, the theme can be drawn from everyday Venice, Veronese is overpoweringly fine. Again and again in looking at the ceilings of the Ducal Palace one catches his breath before such visions of magnificence as Venice as Justice, Figure 304, Venice as Queen of the World. For all its

contemporary quality, it attains a strange other-worldliness.
It is as if some one had looked at superb Venice through a
magnifying glass that ennobled the forms and greatly enhanced the colors. You feel how
Veronese loved it all and how
little he cared for anything beyond the splendor, dignity and
prosperity of his adoptive city.
He gives us the look of Venice
at her climax of Renaissance
glory, as Carpaccio had given the
dying radiance of her mediæval
estate. From the point of view
of judgment, style and fine
craftsmanship, it is impossible to
overpraise Veronese. He should
be regarded rather as a great
painter in the narrower sense
than a supreme artist. When

Fig. 304. Paolo Veronese. Venice attended by Force and Justice. Ceiling Panel. — *Ducal
Palace*.

he died in 1588, only fifty years old, he left a very enduring
inheritance.

It was on the whole his moderate and judicious sumptuousness that inspired the painters of the next century. It was well
that they sought his imitable merits and not the passion of
Titian and Tintoretto. It was largely thanks to Veronese
that Venetian art suffered no such sharp decline as befell that
of Florence and Rome. The decorative tradition of Veronese
sufficed to nourish a Piazetta and a Tiepolo a century and a
half after his death.

For Giovanni Battista Tiepolo [9] (1695-1770) in sheer force
and fertility yields to none of his Renaissance predecessors.
There never was a more valiant draughtsman or a more splen-

did colorist. Such decorations as those of the Scuola del Carmine, and the Labia Palace fall little behind Veronese's pag-

Fig. 305. G–B. Tiepolo. Time revealing Truth. — *Villa Biron, Vicenza.*

eantry in grandeur while representing an audacity of stroke and coloration which Veronese lacked. So the tragic scenes of Christ's Passion at San Luigi have the intensity of Tintoretto if lacking something of his nobility. In the ceiling decorations of Tiepolo, Figure 305, we see the freest fancies of the Baroque, its customary tumult of shimmering clouds and hovering pearly figures, repeated with a lightness and audacity and withal measure which the Baroque itself never attained

FIG. 306.   Antonio Canale.   Island of San Michele. — *Royal Collections, Windsor.*

save in its great initiator Correggio.   Such powers as Tiepolo's soon won him international patronage.   He painted in Austria and died at Madrid.   With him perishes the grandeur of the Venetian school.   Only a tinge of masquerade and exhibitionism puts him lower than his constant exemplar, Paolo Veronese.

Indeed the simplicity which is the most enduring charm of any art is more felt in the minor Venetians of Tiepolo's time, as in Antonio Canale, called Canaletto, Figure 306, who painted the irradiated panorama of the Venetian lagoon and canals with the ardent precision of a reborn Gentile Bellini. Francesco Guardi[10] (1712-1765), Canaletto's pupil, with a freer brush and fancy paints the spectacle of Venice, Figure 307, its balls

FIG. 307. Francesco Guardi. Scuola di San Marco. Pen and Wash Drawing. — *Lamperti Coll., Milan.*

and promenades and water pageants, with the sensitiveness of a Carpaccio. But Carpaccio's youthful world is no longer there to paint. Romance has given way to casual amorous intrigue, sentiment to show. But out of the welter of sophisticated gayety still rise clean against the heavens the pale domes and bell towers of an older and finer Venice. Guardi is perhaps at his best in the numerous tiny oil sketches which deal with the remote and solitary groves and ruins of the lagoon. Here we have felicities of broken color and niceties of observation, accurate notations of evanescent effects of light, which can still give lessons to the most modern landscapists.

In Pietro Longhi (1702-1762) Venice developed a sympathetic chronicler of her social pleasures, Figure 308. The world of his delicate and witty little canvases is that of the

card party, the formal call, the vanity and ceremony of philandering, the shop, the musicale, the masked ball. Only Holland has given so true and sympathetic a record of her smaller affairs, and at the moment, only Hogarth in England and Chardin in France were doing the thing with equal ability.

Nothing better shows the slightly anachronistic quality of Tiepolo's grandeur than a fine Longhi. The Venetian imagination had moved indoors, so to speak, had foregone in favor of

FIG. 308. Pietro Longhi. Maskers at the Zoo. — *London.*

individual gratifications the old vision of the collective splendor. Venice no longer dines grandly in the open with Veronese, she coquettishly sips coffee with Longhi. If she had declined in nobility, she had at least kept her sincerity and taste. Her affair had ever been rather with appearances than with ideals or interpretations. But since the Greeks no other nation had considered appearances with such noble candor. She kept to the end the good pictorial habit of letting appearances explain themselves. Thus if a Titian will stand beside a Pheidian marble, so will a Tiepolo beside an Alexandrian masterpiece, while a trim belle of Pietro Longhi need feel no confusion before a Tanagra figurine. Time passes gently over a city whose artistic aims are as limited as her taste is sure. Venice had ever been gracious in her grandeur, and gracious she remained even after she had ceased to be grand.

ILLUSTRATIONS FOR CHAPTER VIII

Titian's Assumption the Beginning of the Venetian Grand Style

Titian's contemporaries were fully aware that the Assumption (1518) marked the beginning of the Grand Style at Venice and that the change was revolutionary. The critic Lodovico Dolce writes in his *Dialogo della Pittura*, Florence, 1735, p. 286 f. putting the words into the mouth of Aretino:

"After not much time [after the Fondaco frescoes, 1508] he was given to paint a great panel for the high-altar of the Friars Minor; where Titian, still young, painted in oils the Virgin, who rises to heaven among many angels who accompany her, and above her he figured a God Father flanked by two angels. It seems really as if she rises with a face full of humility, and her robes fly lightly. At the bottom are the disciples who with various attitudes manifest joy and amazement, and are mostly larger than life, and assuredly in that picture is contained the grandeur and terribleness of Michelangelo, the pleasingness and grace of Raphael, with the coloring proper to nature, and, moreover, this was the first public work which he made in oils; and he made it in very little time, and young."

"Thereupon the stupid painters and the vulgar herd who up to then had seen nothing but the cold and dead things of Giovanni Bellini, of Gentile, and of [Alvise] Vivarini (since Giorgione, working in oils, had not yet had any public work; and for the most part made no other works than half figures and portraits) which were without movement and without relief, spake great ill of that picture. Afterwards, as envy cooled, and opening their eyes a little to the truth, the people began to be amazed at the new manner discovered in Venice by Titian: and all the painters from then on strove to imitate it; but being off their own path, became confused. And surely it must seem a miracle that Titian, without having at that time seen the antiquities of Rome, which were the light of all the good painters, solely with that little spark, which he had discovered in the works of Giorgione, saw and perceived the idea of perfect painting."

The general critical justness of this statement must condone its abundant overstatements and errors of fact.

AURELIO LUINI ON TITIAN'S IMPRESSIONISM

"Aurelio Luini has excellently understood this art [of landscape]. To whom it once happened that visiting Titian, and asking him his opinion about the background of trees, besides many reasons which he heard from him about making the foliage sparkle against the background, he saw one of his [Titian's] wonderful landscapes which he had at home, which, having seen quietly, Aurelio thought a daubed up thing, but afterwards, having withdrawn to a distance, it seemed to him that the sun shone resplendently in it, making the paths retreat on this side and that; so that Aurelio had to say that he had never seen a rarer thing in the world in the way of landscapes."

Lomazzo, *Trattato*, Milan, 1584, p. 474, 5.

ON BELLE NATURE AND THE ANTIQUE

The Renaissance idea that Nature must be ennobled and corrected by the Antique is plainly formulated by Dolce, again under the name of Aretino, *Dialogo*, p. 190.

"One should then choose the most perfect form, imitating nature in part. . . . And partly one should imitate the beautiful marble and bronze figures of the ancient masters. Whereof who so shall taste and possess fully the marvellous perfection, will be able with certainty to correct many defects of nature, and make his pictures noteworthy and grateful to all. Inasmuch as the ancient things contain the entire perfection of art, and can be the exemplars of all beauty."

This is one of the earliest full statements of the notion of *belle nature*, and of the antique as normative. The dogma persists with unabated rigor down to Sir Joshua Reynolds (see Illustration to Chapter VI, p. 316) and Jacques Louis David.

GEORGE FREDERICK WATTS ON THE GREEK AFFINITIES OF VENETIAN PAINTING

"The revival of the Greek Language and Greek Literature raised the long ebb into a wave that swept over civilized Europe. On its glittering crest the Venetian painters especially were lifted into the society of gods, goddesses, nymphs, and satyrs. They might see sky, sea and earth peopled with radiant beings; perhaps with a sort of semi-belief such as we accord to the Lorelei and fairies, creations that somehow easily worked in with creeds and experience. Anyhow, they might see

Pan come dallying down the sparkling brook-side, now shouting to the laughing brown nymphs rustling through the reeds, and pretending to be afraid, now scattering a shower of notes from his pipes that would fall upon the ears as the brightness of the iris over a fountain falls upon the eye." . . .

"It may seem strange if I place the Venetian school and Titian, with his liberal line — which, however, is by no means wanting in reticence — in closer relationship with Greek art of the great period than the more classical schools of Tuscany and Rome. Supposing one were to endeavor to paint a restoration of the pediments of the Parthenon, it would be possible to interpolate with figures by Titian, never with any by Poussin, or, I think, even by Raphael or Michael Angelo." . . .

"In spite of extravagant and even absurd defects (for the great artist's eyes no longer served him faithfully), when Titian, towards the end of his life painted the 'Europa' . . . the muse who inspired Pheidias laid her hand on the old man's shoulder, and she inspired the wealth of volume, ease of line, and glowing sense of nature's exuberance."

George Frederick Watts, his Life and Writings, London and New York, Vol. III., pp. 251, 253, 254.

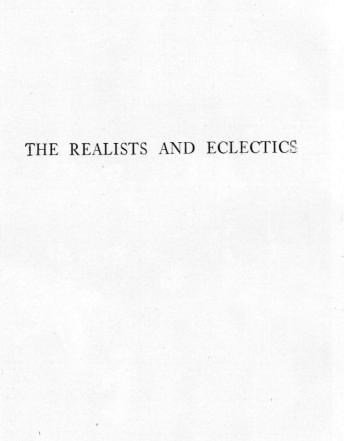

THE REALISTS AND ECLECTICS

Fig. 309. Caravaggio. Death of the Virgin. — *Louvre.*

CHAPTER IX

THE REALISTS AND ECLECTICS

The Confusion following Raphael and Michelangelo — Giulio Romano — Caravaggio and realistic Revolt — Salvator Rosa, romantic Individualism
and the Picturesque — The Carracci and the Eclectic Ideal — Later
Eclectics; Guido Reni — Domenichino — The Waning of Italian Greatness — Influence of Italy on the Schools of France, Flanders, and Spain.

Italian painting suddenly declined for lack of taste. The
followers of Raphael and Michelangelo possessed astonishing
power and knowledge, but, save their own cleverness, no
longer had anything to express. Thus painting became merely
an art of self-exploitation and display, a matter of difficult
foreshortenings, complicated groupings, and novel construc-
tions in light and shade. Such at least was the case at Rome,
and partly at Florence. At Venice, Milan, Cremona, Ferrara,
and generally in the North the decline was gradual and be-
nign. Sincere art of a minor character was still produced.
But in the artistic centre the collapse was complete, and all
the more disastrous that nobody realized that a collapse had
come.

It is staggering to find that Vasari, in the face of merited
ridicule, had no doubt that he was a great painter. How he
boasts of his own powers! "But what matters most for this
art, is that they have made it so perfect today, and so easy
for him who possesses design, that where formerly a picture was
made by one of our masters in six years, today our masters
make six in one. And I am the credible witness of this both
by my observation and by my work. And many more perfect

and finished pictures are now seen, than formerly were made
by the important masters." (Vol. IV, p. 13.) Nothing is more
appalling than to find Vasari at Florence and Lomazzo at Milan
regularly naming Giulio Romano, Polidoro and Maturino along

FIG. 310. Giulio Romano. Battle for Troy. Fresco. — *Palazzo del
Tè. Mantua.*

with Raphael and Michelangelo. Evidently the old sure
taste of the Renaissance has yielded to confusion.

Indeed patronage had changed. It is no longer spontaneous
but organized. We now have academies, art schools, art
criticism, exhibitions, archæologists, picture dealers. Art no
longer rests on generally accepted ideas and broad approba-
tions, but is a game between experts.

To enumerate the followers of Michelangelo and Raphael
and allot to each his due dispraise would be in no way profitable.
Giulio Romano may represent them all. With extraordinary
powers as a draughtsman of the figure, and with paradoxical
taste in minor decoration, we know him already as the vul-
garizer of Raphael's designs in the Stanza of Heliodorus and
of the Burning City. Later (1524-46) removed from Raphael's

influence, at Mantua, he develops a coarse titanism. The old
Castello of the Gonzagas and the Palazzo del Tè, Figure 310,
are tediously full of sensational and occasionally obscene mythologies which are done with amazing energy and facility, but are
as restless and undecorative in design as they are hot and foxy
in color. And the immoderations and indecencies have not
even the excuse of naturalness, they are coldly calculated and
studied. Such talented Florentine imitators of Michelangelo
as Pontormo and Bronzino we have already considered. At
Rome, he left at least one disciple of talent, Daniele da Volterra,
in the composition of whose masterpiece the Deposition in the
Convent of the Trinità, at Rome, the master himself may have
had a hand. Rather than delay over these complacent epi-
gones we do well to pass to those few more intelligent artists
who saw that something was amiss.

Michelangelo Amerighi, (1569–1608), called from his Lombard birthplace Caravaggio, and Annibale Carracci of Bologna
are here the outstanding names. The former bitterly fought
the grand style in the name of naturalism, the latter attempted to reintegrate it through a critical eclecticism. Their influence is dominant from the last decade of the sixteenth
century.

Caravaggio[1] had carefully studied the impressionistic manner
of late Titian but finally adopts a harsh and resolute chiaroscuro with the light restricted and the canvas mostly black.
Thus his modelling is both brutal and academic. His real
fight was with the nobility of Raphael. His saints are taken
from the streets and often from the gutters. He loves character above all, and wants it proletarian. Within his chosen
limitations he is a powerful and sincere artist. His masterpieces are the Entombment in the Vatican, and the Death of
the Virgin in the Louvre, Figure 309, which created so much
disapproval that it had to be removed from its altar. Both
pictures take the theme out of the realm of legend, making it

drastic and contemporary.   Both, while rejecting all grandeur
in the figures, preserve the tradition thereof in the composition.
One gets Caravaggio in epitome in The Peter denying his
Lord of the Vatican.   Figure 311.   It is a powerful character
study from low life.   Indeed character is his watchword.
One finds it extravagantly over-emphasized in his famous
pothouse and gambling scenes, a revolutionary innovation.
The most famous and one of the best is The Card Players, at
Dresden, Figure 312.   It is the symbol of the painter's love
of low life.   He killed his man in a duel, and died himself
when turned out of prison into the August sun.

Before that fitting end he had fled to Naples where amid
the corruption of the Spanish overlordship his proletarian ideals
became generally contagious.   They were taken up eagerly
by the Valencian, José Ribera, who with an equal sense for
character and a more genuine religious feeling transmitted
the manner to Seville and eventually to Velasquez.   So Caravaggio became the founder of the modern realistic and impressionistic schools, a precursor of Courbet and Manet.
Except for a surplusage of too emphatic character studies,
smiling and weeping philosophers, Ribera was a true and most
skilful artist.   Having no quarrel with an earlier grand style,
he had the grace of simplicity.

Both at Rome and Naples swaggering Caravaggio had enor-
mous success.   His heads, we read, brought more than other
men's compositions.   He boasted himself the greatest painter
of all time, and was often believed.   From his swarthy tones
his entire school took the name, the Tenebrists.   His experiments in interior and artificial lighting were widely imitated,
and again ultimately passed into recent Impressionism.   His
rejection of noble form in favor of what one sees, and of decorative color in favor of natural, was the sharpest possible chal-
lenge of the Renaissance style, and outside of Italy where the
noble tradition was only incipient did much to arrest its dif-

FIG. 311. Caravaggio. St. Peter denying his Lord. — *Vatican.*

FIG. 312. Caravaggio. The Card Players. — *Dresden.*

fusion. From the point of view of modern art there are few more important figures. From the point of view of art broadly he has his serious limitations. Most damaging is his waiver of civilization, he looks at low life not with the eyes of a detached artist but with those of a ruffian. He did not have the intelligence to live up to his own formula. Annibale Carracci was once looking at Caravaggio's Judith, and, being pressed for an opinion, remarked that it was "too natural." He spoke as an admirer of the grand style. A modern realist would make the far more radical criticism that Caravaggio is never natural enough. He really makes no close study of the subtleties of natural appearance or of the actual refinements of illumination, but rather substitutes for the old stately formulas a new, more ugly, and less studied formula of his own. Logically he should have gone forward with Ribera and Velasquez to a real investigation of appearances. But his logic was only that of scorn, and it would doubtless have somewhat compensated him for a sordid and premature end, could he have forseen that his biographers would credit him with the ruin of Italian painting.

Through Ribera, Caravaggio's influence passes to the Neapolitan, Salvator[2] Rosa (1615-1673). With greater vivacity and better color Salvator repeats the character studies and tavern scenes, also bringing the proletarian mood into mythology. He painted battle pieces of real ferocity. He was an irascible, vain and capricious person, proud of being so; a scorner of his own patrons and of the bourgeois generally; a maker of epigrams, and a writer of satires. His specialty is the sinister and picturesque, and he practices it with gusto and ability, Figure 313. Salvator is the real discoverer of the picturesque, the first enthusiast for the savage aspects of nature. Likewise he was one of the first artists to study effects — sunsets, storms, mists, and whirling clouds. He excursioned in the Abruzzo, equally savoring its crags, torrents, and forests, and its ferocious banditti. His letters on these wanderings are among the first and most important documents of the modern cult of nature. He writes: "You have saddened me by giving me the news of your having been in Garfagna, and having rejoiced in the savagery of that country so congenial to my nature. . . . To be merely reminded of it brings the tears to my eyes." Again he writes from the Adriatic Apennines: "I have been two weeks in continual travel and the trip is much more strange and picturesque than that of Florence, beyond comparison so, since there is such an extrava-

Fig. 313.   Salvator Rosa. Landscape with figures — *Pitti*.

gant mixture of the rough and cultivated, of the level and precipitous that nothing more could be desired for the satisfaction of the eye." . . . "At Terni, four miles off the road I saw the famous falls of the Velino, a thing to haunt and possess the most insatiable mind because of its horrid beauty. To see a river that plunges straight down a mountain for half a mile, and sends up its foam as high!" Much of the stormy and energetic character of such scenes is transcribed in the best landscapes of Salvator, Figure 314. In their age they evoked little following. But these forests, cascades, evening seaports, and ruined sites were freely bought by the English, greatly admired and had their part in producing the literary enthusiasm for wild nature in the eighteenth century.

Salvator avows his "extravagant genius," is driven by the lust for novelty, is a modern and romantic spirit. Withal he was a man of capacity and taste with an open-minded understanding of quite alien merit. "Here, we esteem M. Poussin," he writes in October, 1665, "more than any one else in the world."

Poussin could never have returned the compliment. His approbation was for Raphael, the Carracci and Domenichino.

FIG. 314.   Salvator Rosa.   Landscape. — *Pitti.*

Indeed a chief glory of the Bolognese Eclectics was that their critical method sufficed to nurture so classic a spirit as Poussin's and so to establish the academic tradition for Northern Europe.

Though the Eclectic movement is properly associated with the cousins Lodovico and Annibale Carracci,[3] it somewhat antecedes them. The impetus comes from Flanders with the painter of Antwerp, Denis Calvert, who came to Bologna late in the sixteenth century and founded an art school. Like all the better educated Flemings, he represented a profound nostalgia for Renaissance grandeur, and also a certain detachment from the particular Italian artists who had embodied the ideal of *grandezza*. Such a man is, perforce, an eclectic, studying widely the methods of his great predecessors and seeking to assimilate in his own art their various perfections. Besides, methods of comparative study which had formerly been extremely difficult if not impossible were now easy. Casts were available of the antique marbles, fairly faithful engravings were at hand for all the great painters. It is significant that both the Carracci were reproductive engravers. Denis Calvert was no genius, but a prudent and sagacious artist who made the most of a slender endowment. His critical and assimilative spirit passed over to his best pupils. Their reform, unlike Caravaggio's, was not revolutionary, but based on a careful restudy of the grand style, which they had never wavered in venerating.

Annibale Carracci was reared in devotion to Raphael, whose fine St. Cecilia was at Bologna. Venice lured him, but he was rebuffed by Tintoretto. Annibale made profound studies of Correggio at Parma, whence he writes that Raphael now seems wooden to him in comparison. He is now launched on the impossible quest of combining with the austere grandeur of the Roman School, the charm of Venetian coloring and the emotional instability of Correggio. Thus it was an attempt to restore the grand style largely in the name of one of its chief disintegrators, and as such it was from the first headed for failure. Yet it was an attempt dictated by the times, and the inevitable choice of any superior spirit who wished to reknit the Renaissance tradition.

It was the moment of the Catholic Reaction and of the endeavor of the new Jesuit Order to rebuild a shaken Church on the basis of persuasion. Largely shorn of authority, the Church must now be popular or perish. It wisely chose to be popular, adopting the thrilling novelties of Baroque architecture, borrowing from the opera its swelling choral cadences,

everywhere stressing the note of charm, surprise and emotion.
So the moderation and austerity which underlay the Renaissance style were forbidden to the Eclectics, and they chiefly
differed from the rival Naturalists in choosing to make their

FIG. 316. Annibale Carracci.
Madonna in Glory. — *Bologna.*

FIG. 315. Lodovico Carracci.
Assumption. — *Bologna.*

sensationalism as decorous as the circumstances permitted.
Such is the social background of the Carracci's reform, and they
deserve utmost credit for achieving so much under such limitations.

Agostino (1568-1602) was the brains of the family, courtier,
scholar, man of the world. Annibale (1560-1609) was the
nerves, — moody, shy, solitary, with titan ambitions in a small
and unprepossessing frame. His cousin, Lodovico (1555-
1619), was possibly the best artist of the three if only because
he attempted less and followed sentimentalism frankly without too much bothering about grandeur.

Lodovico, Figure 315, and Annibale, Figure 316, enriched

the churches of Bologna with great animated altar-pieces which enthralled their contemporaries, and today seem more than a little affected. But that is merely because we no longer share what was an entirely sincere way of religious feeling. They started an Academy in which the antique, the nude, and competitive composition were the staple of instruction quite as in French and British State art schools today. In the Bolognese palaces the Carracci did in fresco great mythological series, consulting Homer, Virgil and Ovid and Apollonius of Rhodes. In the main they had friezes to do, and they drew heavily from Correggio, tempering his alacrity with something of the heavier energy of the Roman style.

In 1585 the Carracci set up their Academy. It was soon thronged. Agostino, a courtly, learned and accomplished person, was the leading influence, being lecturer as well as drawing master. Even, Annibale, habitually an offish and difficult man, is said to have been affable and helpful to his disciples.

In studying his pictures, one feels that he was thwarted of his true development. Not only was he much of a realist, painting tavern scenes, Figure 317, after Caravaggio's lead, but also a studious and charming landscape painter, Figure 318. His soberly colored and gracefully composed landscapes were an important influence on Poussin. Annibale's adventures in the grand style, though audacious and loudly applauded, really did some violence to his modest and sensitive spirit. His was the least academic temperament imaginable, and the final disastrous quarrel with his eminently academic brother, Agostino, was inevitable.

Annibale and Agostino were called to Rome in 1595 to fresco Cardinal Odoardo Farnese's palace. Annibale was thirty-five years old, Agostino a few years younger. Both had reaped all honors possible at Bologna, and they came to the Eternal City at a fortunate moment. The favorite decorators were men of routine talent, Taddeo Zuccaro and the Cavaliere

FIG. 317. Annibale Carracci. The Bean Eater. — *Prince Colonna, Rome.*

FIG. 318. Annibale Carracci. Flight to Egypt. — *Doria, Rome.*

d' Arpino. Caravaggio's amazing and perturbing genius had already asserted itself, but he was not a mural painter. After a preliminary series of mythologies in the riverside casino of

Fig. 319. Annibale Carracci. Ceiling Detail. — *Farnese Palace, Rome.*

the Palazzo Farnese, Annibale turned, in 1597, to the decoration of the great hall. It was a lofty tunnel-like room of refractory proportions. The theme was to be the loves of the gods. But the great spaces in which are represented Bacchus and Ariadne, the Judgment of Paris, Polyphemus and Galatea, Cephalus and Aurora, Hero and Leander, amongst other subjects, yield in effect to the general plan and the incidental decoration. Annibale, who despite contemporary accounts to the contrary, controlled everything, has taken as his motive the architectural framework which Michelangelo designed for the Sistine, with its burden of decorative nudes. One looks past heavy painted cornices, Figure 319, to painted statuary in profusion, thickly set, and, behind, more nudes in natural hues, the whole echoed by nudes in stucco relief on the walls.

We have instead of the relative flatness of Michelangelo and his predecessors a consistent lumpiness, which, while theoretically tasteless, is actually rich, satisfying, and even light

Fig. 320.   Annibale Carracci and Helpers.   Grand Hall, Farnese Palace.
— *Rome.*

Only an extraordinary ability could have kept any kind of unity in this wilful and extravagant complexity, Figure 320. But unity there is and coherent expression of a mood at once pompous and festal.

The pictures, as we have noted, seem to count for less than their borders.   When we examine the love scenes, we find them at once coarse and mannered.   They are superficially like Giulio Romano at Mantua but without his self-satisfied brutality.   To this extent they are inferior, and indeed the strain to be at once grand, graceful, and passionate is only too apparent throughout the pictorial part. Yet as a whole the decoration seems hardly inferior in power, ingenuity, and rhythmical fulness to such ancient masterpieces of kindred inspiration as the Pergamon frieze. For the moment the decoration was enthusiastically acclaimed, after three-quarters of a century it taught Charles Le Brun the way to decorate the Louvre and the Palace at Versailles, and even today the admirer of the fountains of Rome and of her Baroque churches must admit that Annibale caught the very spirit of his day, in its superfluity of learned vaingloriousness and shortage of the simpler and more noble passions.

FIG. 321. Guido Reni. Madonna with two Saints. — *Vatican Gallery*.

For the artist the work brought only chagrin. The Cardinal treated him with stinginess and personal despite. His irritation with his brother reached the explosive point. Agostino left him staggering under the weight of an ungrateful task, he fell into a dangerous melancholy, and in 1609 died miserably, leaving his helpers Albani and Domenichino to finish the gallery.

Of the followers of the Carracci, Guido Reni (1575–1642) and Domenichino (1581–1641), are the most important. At his worst Guido Reni is the most repellant of sentimentalists, at his best a realist of the calibre of Ribera himself. In his time there are no grander old men than his, better painted or more fully realized as characters. You find them at their best in the Madonna of St. Paul, at Berlin, or the Immaculate Conception at Petrograd, or the Madonna with St. Jerome, in the Vatican, Figure 321. It is hard to reconcile them with his sleek and cheaply seductive Magdalens, Cleopatras and Venuses. What steadies him in his inconsistency is a fine

FIG. 322. Guido Reni. Aurora. Ceiling Fresco. — *Casino Rospigliosi, Rome.*

and simple sense of composition. He is lucid where his masters, the Carracci, tend to be confused. His taste is more coherent than his character. Under other conditions than those of academic Bologna and Papal Rome he might easily have become a realist of Zurbaran's type. As it was, he undertook the usual synthesis of the grand style with the new sentimentality. Generally speaking he is neither grand nor sentimental enough, but superficial in both regards. Yet his discretion saves him in such works as the ceiling of the Villa Rospigliosi (1615) and the supremely elegant St. Michael, Figure 323, of the Cappucini. I like the Aurora, Figure 322, nay love it well this side of idolatry, for the same reason that I like Kipling's lines

> "An' the dawn comes up like thunder
> Outer China 'crost the bay."

Both the fresco and the verses have the same pounding and obvious, yet thrilling cadences, both bring lyricism to the brink of bombast without letting it go over.

Domenico Zampieri, called Domenichino, (1581–1641) is a far more serious figure. We see him best not in the sentimental sibyls which he multiplied nor even in the studied emotionalism of his most famous altar-piece, the Last Communion of St.

FIG. 323. Guido Reni. Saint Michael. — *Cappucini, Rome.*

FIG. 324. Domenichino. Last Communion of St. Jerome. — *Vatican.*

Jerome, in the Vatican, Figure 324, but, rather in such decorations as those in S. Andrea della Valle, and in the monastic church of Grotta Ferrata. Here we find a heavy and simple emphasis, a great clarity both of figure construction and of composition. For his personal awkwardness, patience and quietism his comrades mockingly called him the Ox. It took character to play the ox amid the febrile sprightliness of the Catholic Reaction. His gravity is marked also in his color. He forsakes the old decorative conventions of the Renaissance and works in olive and silvery tones which suggest in a generalizing way the coolness and freshness of nature. Above all he is not facile like most of his contemporaries, but studious,

dilatory, and considerate. At times he yields to the prevailing
sentimentality, but usually he is both spontaneous and reticent.
He seldom insists, but candidly lets the picture be seen. All
these qualities appear in the modestly hoydenish masterpiece,

Fig. 325.   Domenichino.   Diana and her Nymphs. — *Borghese, Rome.*

Diana and her Nymphs, in the Borghese Gallery, Figure 325.
It is completely captivating for its element of surprise, its
manly wholesomeness, its winsome setting of lithe girlish
bodies amid verdure under a gray sky. This unaffected mood
in mythology has rarely been recaptured. We have it in
Vermeer's little Diana at the Hague and, only yesterday, in
the Nausicaa of Lucien Simon. Such qualities of lucidity,
reserve, and simple nobility made Domenichino the natural
model for Nicholas Poussin. We can trace the influence through
Poussin's masterpieces, and had France been wise enough to
understand her greatest painter, her academic tradition, which
was promoted in Poussin's name, might have taken a much
more fruitful course than it actually did.

An ill fate finally took Domenichino to Naples. There he found the ruffianly local painters banded against every foreigner, and in particular he met the systematic animosity of the truculent Spaniard, Ribera. Outright terrorism alternated with petty persecution. They defaced his work and tampered with his materials. Soon they broke his delicate and timid spirit, even turned him against the wife with whom he had lived on terms of ideal affection. Today it remains uncertain whether he died of shattered nerves or was actually poisoned. Presumably the barbarous Neapolitans would have done about the same to any visiting artist, but doubtless they turned the screw a shade harder upon a gentle idealist who brought into their realistic stews some afterglow of the quietistic dignity of a Montagna or a Cima.

When all reservations are made, the Eclectics had fairly done their work of correcting the disorder of the late Renaissance and of restoring something of the old decorum. They made possible the revival of the grand style at Rome, in the eighteenth century, by Carlo Maratta and Raphael Mengs. The Eclectics were the bridge by which the classical manner passed over into Western Europe, an indispensable link in the chain of the great hellenistic tradition. That should be enough to keep them in memory if not in unqualified honor.

Our review of the late sixteenth and early seventeenth century in Italy will have served its purpose if it has convinced the reader that this was no time of stagnation. We have rather to do with activities of exploration and reconstruction which are much too restless and various. The intellectual power of the Italian painters had not greatly diminished in comparison with the Renaissance. Italy still was capable of giving the leads which have guided painting elsewhere ever since. What was lacking was not energy but patience, reflection and taste. The Italian artist tended to regard himself as a swift and resolute executant first of all, and no longer knew how to nourish his spirit as a man. Even as executants, the realists and eclectics had the humiliation of finding themselves outdone by foreigners. Successively in the seventeenth century Ribera, Rubens, Van Dyck, Velasquez, Claude Lorrain and Poussin came to Italy and sojourned there. It was in every case apparent that the foreigner excelled all native artists in his field. The traditional authority of Italian painting still held, but its contemporary glory was evidently waning.

But even in decline Italy was strong enough to hand on her torch to newer hands. From Titian stems the florid classicism and aristocratic portraiture of Rubens and Van Dyck, which dominated the whole eighteenth century in France and England; through Caravaggio and Ribera, Italy made Velasquez the founder of those most characteristic nineteenth century movements, realism and impressionism; through Raphael, the Carracci and Domenichino, she fed the white flame of Poussin's classicism, which in one way or another has determined the academic development of all Western Europe. Thus Italian painting, eternally alive in the timeless region where dwells the fame of Giotto, Masaccio, Leonardo, Giorgione, Raphael, Michelangelo, Titian, is as well most practically and actually alive in the recent and present struggles, failures, and triumphs of our modern schools. Without understanding Italian painting we cannot understand our own painting. And while the modern world will hardly return to the coherence, solidity, and grace of the great Gothic and Renaissance masters, I am confident that there can be no exit from our present confusion and incoherence until our painters learn at least to consult those great Italian predecessors who dwelt on the heights above which is the abode of the human spirit's creative rest.

ILLUSTRATIONS FOR CHAPTER IX

ON THE ECLECTIC IDEAL

The nearly contemporary account of Carlo Cesare Malvasia, *Felsina Pittrice*, Bologna, 1841, Tom. I. p. 263 is instructive.

"Lodovico . . . was the first who supplied a firm prop to tottering painting and was able to save it from imminent harm and ruin. He was the one who courageously opposed that vainglorious time, which succeeded the most perfect age, and liberating it from the common ills of those erroneous mannerisms which dared to tyrranize that fair profession that had been raised so high, not only wished to restore it to its first vigor, but also to a state still more perfect and sublime. . . . Taking the best from all the best artists, one sees him, with a facility no longer used and valued, form from them a brief compendium, rather a precious extract, outside of and beyond which little more remained for the studious to desire. And coupling and uniting with the discretion of Raphael the intelligence of Michelangelo, and adding withal with the color of Titian the angelic purity of Correggio, he succeeded in forming from all these manners a single one, which had nothing to envy in the Roman, Florentine, Venetian and Lombard manners."

A Sonnet supposed, without complete evidence, to have been addressed by Annibale Carracci to the painter Niccolò d'Abate gives an even more complete and correct account of the elements that blended in the style of the Carracci. I quote it from Rouchès, *La Peinture Bolonaise*, Paris, 1913, p. 123, note 1.

> "To make a good painter let him have
> At ready and eager hand the drawing of Rome,
> The movement with the shading of Venice,
> And the dignified coloring of Lombardy.
> The terrible manner of Michelangelo
> And Correggio's pure and sovereign style
> And the true symmetry of Raphael,
> Tibaldi's decorum and substance,
> The inventiveness of learned Primaticcio
> And a little of Parmigianino's grace.
> Not without having strenuously made such studies
> Let him place before himself for imitation
> The works which our Niccolò has left here."

THE END

NOTES

CHAPTER I

1. For the altar as tomb-shrine see Yrjö Hirn's learned and fascinating book, *The Sacred Shrine*, London, 1912.

2. For the Byzantine pictorial style see the excellent summary in *Fogg Art Museum, Collection of Mediaeval and Renaissance Paintings*, Harvard Univ. Press, 1919, pp. 3–10; also a more extended treatment in O. M. Dalton, *Byzantine Art and Archaeology*, Oxford, 1911, chapters V, VI, VII. C. R. Morey, *Christian Art*, New York, 1935.

3. For the influence of St. Dominic, St. Thomas Aquinas, and St. Francis read the respective chapters in Taylor, *The Mediaeval Mind;* and in Ferdinand Schevill, *History of Florence;* for St. Francis, Thomas Okey's translation, *The little Flowers of St. Francis* in "Everyman's Library." E. Gebhart, *Italie Mystique*, Paris, 1908, is also enlightening.

4. *Burlington Magazine*, Vol. XXXII (1918), pp. 45–6. Mr. Berenson in "*Dedalo*," Vol. II (1921) fasc. V, makes this superb Madonna a Constantinople picture of the late 12th century. His confessedly slight argument fails to convince me. The picture is Greco-Italian, and its date about 1300. Where it was painted is uncertain.

Cimabue. Andreas Aubert, *Cimabue Frage*, Leipzig, 1907, is the standard work. *Cimabue, a Critical Study*, by Alfred Nicholson, Princeton, 1932, gives a clear and interestingly written survey. The predecessors and contemporaries of Cimabue are best studied in Raimond van Marle, *The Development of the Italian Schools of Painting*, Vol. I, The Hague, 1923. The various views on the early frescoes of the Upper Church at Assisi are well summarized in Brown and Rankin, *A Short History*, pp. 54 and 57–59.

An unsuccessful attempt to reduce Cimabue to a myth has been made by Langton Douglas in his edition of *C. & C.*, Vol. I, pp. 187–193. The constructive and accepted view is that of Aubert. My list differs slightly from his and is:

Louvre Madonna, about 1275, Louvre.

Trinità Madonna, about 1285, Uffizi.

The frescoes of the Choir and Transepts of S. Francesco at Assisi, saving possibly the big Ascent to the Cross, circa 1296, Assisi.

Madonna with St. Francis (fresco), after 1290, Assisi, Lower Church of S. Francesco.

St. John in mosaic in the Apse of the Cathedral at Pisa, 1301.

Venturi's endeavor to attach to Cimabue some of the later New Testament mosaics in the vault of the Florentine Baptistry, see *Storia*, Vol. V, p. 229, is plausible but not convincing. In *The Isaac Master, a Reconstruction of the Work of Gaddo Gaddi*, Princeton, 1932, I have ascribed these mosaics to Gaddo Gaddi. Venturi's attribution of lost frescoes in the portico of old St.

Peter's, known from sketch copies, *Storia*, Vol. V, p. 195, has no solid basis. Two fresco fragments, heads of Peter and Paul, remain, and are published by Wilpert, *Die Mosaiken &*, bd. I, fig. 144, and by him correctly assigned to Cavallini or some Roman follower.

R. van Marle, in *La Peinture Romaine*, Strasbourg, 1921, has made a most careful study of all the earlier frescoes in the Upper Church. See his fuller treatment of the problem in *The Development* etc., Vol. I. Beda Kleinschmidt, *Die Wandmalereien der Basilika San Francesco in Assisi*, 2 vols. Berlin, 1930, offers superior illustrations of good scale. Generally I concur in his conclusions, but cannot see Cavallini in the far abler work of the Isaac Master, who for me is Gaddo Gaddi, see my *Isaac Master*. A papal bull of 1288 authorized collections for enlarging and embellishing the Basilica. So the frescoes in the Upper Church were probably painted between 1290 and 1300.

In *Toskanische Maler im XIII Jahrhundert*, Berlin, 1922, Dr. O. Sirén makes a comprehensive survey of the earliest painters of Lucca, Pisa, and Florence. He endeavors to reconstruct the works of Coppo di Marcovaldo whom he regards as a formative influence on Cimabue. To the usual list of Cimabue's works Dr. Sirén adds, with Aubert, a great Madonna in the Servi, Bologna; and also a Madonna in the Verzocchi Collection, Milan; and an extraordinarily fine crucifixion formerly in the d'Hendecourt Collection, London and now in the Fogg Art Museum. Dr. Sirén also accepts for Cimabue the triptych of Christ, St. Peter and St. James, which Berenson first published in *Art in America*, for 1920. Of these accretions none is persuasive to me.

5. The latest and fullest discussion of Pietro Cavallini is by Stanley Lothrop in *Memoirs of the American Academy in Rome*, Vol. II, 1918. I think he is in error in seeing Cavallini at Assisi and Perugia. Van Marle, note above, has thrown additional light on the continuity of a Roman school.

6. *C. & C.* (Ed. Hutton), Vol. I, pp. 194–5. Zimmermann (*Giotto* &c., Leipzig, 1899), H. Thode (*Franz von Assisi*, Berlin, 1904), and Fr. Hermanin (*Gallerie nazionali Italiane*, Vol. V (1902), p. 113) ascribe the Stories of Isaac and some other superior frescoes of the upper row to youthful Giotto. This view has gained the weighty adherence of Toesca and Berenson. To me these frescoes seem too mature for any young artist. See my *Isaac Master*.

7. *Giotto*. Oswald Sirén, *Giotto and Some of his Followers*, Cambridge, Harvard Univ. Press, 1917, in 2 vols., gives a reasonable chronology and is valuable for illustrations.

Complete illustrations for the Giotto problem, in Curt Weigelt, *Giotto des Meisters Gemälde*, Berlin and Leipzig, 1925.

Roger E. Fry, *Monthly Review*, Vol. I, pp. 126–151; Vol. II, pp. 139–157; Vol. III, pp. 96–121 is an admirable critical analysis of Giotto's style, but the ascriptions and chronology are often doubtful. Excellent on the frescoes at Sta. Croce. The essay is reprinted in *Vision and Design*, London, 1921.

J. B. Supino's startling views in the chronology of Giotto, expressed in *Giotto*, Florence, 1920, in 3 vols., seem to me fantastic. He virtually follows the unsafe and eccentric leading of Franz Rintelen, *Giotto und die Giotto-Apokryphen*, Basel, 1923.

Supino's general order is the Allegories of the Lower Church and the Baroncelli altar-piece about 1300, the Arena frescoes 1305, the St. Francis

series in the Upper Church about 1310, the Peruzzi Chapel about 1312, etc.
Supino's illustrations are perhaps the best available.

My list would be:

The Early Part of the St. Francis Series (II–XVIII)	before 1298
The Mosaic of the Navicella (completely restored)	about 1300
Crucifix, S. M. Novella	" "
Stigmatization of St. Francis (Louvre)	" "
The Arena Frescoes and Crucifix	" 1305
The Madonna of Ognissanti	" 1308 ca.
The Franciscan Allegories, Lower Church (design only)	" 1312–20
The Stefaneschi Altar-piece (in part)	" 1320
	(perhaps earlier)
The Peruzzi Chapel, Santa Croce	after 1320
The Bardi Chapel, " "	about 1325
The Dormition of the Virgin, at Berlin	" "
Madonna, Ancona, Bologna (design only)	" 1330
The Paradise in the Bargello	after "
Part of the Magdalen Legends there	" "
Part of the Magdalen Legends, Lower Church, Assisi	" "
Baroncelli Altar-piece (design only)	" "
Small panels of the Life of Christ	
at New York, Fenway Court, Boston	" "
Munich and Berenson Collection	" "
Settignano (bottega works)	" "

Perhaps the fine *Stigmatization of St. Francis*, Fogg Art Museum (about
1302–1303) and the stately Madonna (about 1320) in the National Gallery,
Washington (Mellon Foundation) should be added as bottega works, as also
the Crucifixes at Ognissanti, S. Marco and S. Felice, Florence. See my articles
in *Art Studies*, III, p. 25, VIII, 1, p. 47.

8. Padre Angelis, *Collis Paradisi*, 1704, I, p. 33.

9. About the 28 stories of St. Francis there is no agreement except that
Nos. I and XXVI–XXVIII are by the "Cecelia Master." Venturi sees Giotto
only in the later stories. I agree with Berenson that the ruder frescoes, II–
XVIII, which are based on the so-called Roman work above show us Giotto at
his beginnings. For the various views consult Brown and Rankin, *A Short
History*, pp. 48–9, 59, 61.

10. Alex. Romdahl's attempt to set the upper row many years later than the
rest is entirely unconvincing to me. See *Jahrbuch der K. Preussischen Kunst-
sammlungen*, 1911, pp. 3–18.

11. John Ruskin, *Mornings in Florence, passim.*

12. *Giotto's Followers.* Oswald Sirén, *Giotto and Some of his Followers*,
see note 7, may be freely consulted for illustrations and very cautiously for
attributions.

This ground is admirably covered with good illustrations by Raimond
van Marle, in *The Development of the Italian Schools of Painting*, Vol. III, The
Hague, 1924.

Richard Offner, *A critical and historical corpus of Florentine Painting*,
New York, 1930–1934, in 5 vols., in progress, treats exhaustively and with

superior illustrations most of the Florentine painters who were active before Giotto's death.

Pietro Toesca, *Florentine Painting of the Trecento*, Pantheon Series, New York, 1935 *ca.* Superior illustrations.

13. Peleo Bacci's ascription of the recently discovered Passion frescoes in the Badia to Buffalmacco seems reasonable, *Bollettino d'Arte*, V (1911), pp. 1–27. Dr. Sirén ascribes these frescoes to Nardo di Cione and follows Venturi in identifying Buffalmacco with the "Cecelia Master." *Burlington Magazine*, Vol. XXXVI, p. 10. The hypothesis still lacks solid foundation.

14. By Vasari the Spanish Chapel was divided between Taddeo Gaddi and Simone Martini. *C. & C.* discovered that the work was by an Andrea da Firenze who as a document attests painted stories of S. Ranieri at Pisa, in 1377. The contract which proves this Andrea to have been Andrea Bonaiuti, active 1343–1377, was published in *Arte e Storia*, Florence, Feb., 1917, p. 34. It gives the date of the contract for the Spanish Chapel, 1365.

The very elaborate decoration of the Spanish Chapel is fully described in *C. & C.* (Hutton), Vol. I, pp. 309–312. There are useful literary illustrations in Venturi, *Storia dell' arte italiana*, Vol. V, pp. 792–809. Ruskin in *Mornings in Florence* gives a partial analysis which is fascinating from a literary point of view, but badly overestimates the merit of the work.

CHAPTER II. — SIENA

GENERAL WORKS:

Langton Douglas, *A History of Siena*, New York, 1902.

Ferdinand Schevill, *Siena, the Story of a Mediæval Commune*, New York, 1909.

Edmund G. Gardiner, *The Story of Siena and San Gemignano*, London, 1902.

William Heywood and Lucy Olcott, *Guide to Siena, History and Art*, London, 1903.

PAINTING, THE SCHOOL:

Emil Jacobsen, *Sienesische Meister des Trecento in der Gemälde Galerie zu Siena*, Strassburg, 1907; *Das Quattrocento in Siena*, Strassburg, 1908; *Sodoma und das Cinquecento in Siena*, Strassburg, 1910; all very valuable for illustrations.

Venturi, *Storia dell' Arte Italiana*, Vols. V and VII.

Bernard Berenson, *The Italian Painters of the Renaissance* and *Italian Pictures of the Renaissance*, New York and London, 1932.

C. Ricci, *Il Palazzo Pubblico di Siena e la Mostra d'Antica Arte Senese*, Bergamo, 1904, offers a good and inexpensive survey of Sienese handicraft in general.

G. H. Edgell, *A History of Sienese Painting*, New York, 1932, a clear and fully illustrated survey.

R. van Marle, *The Development*, etc., Vols. II, IX, XVI.

Curt Weigelt, *Sienese Painting of the Trecento*, Pantheon Series, New York, 1930, superior illustrations.

SIENESE PICTURES IN THE UNITED STATES. Consult the illustrated catalogues of the Fogg Museum, Harvard, The Isabella Stewart Gardner Museum,

Boston, and the Jarves Collection, Yale. Also many special articles in *Art in America*, especially the series in Vols. VIII–IX, by F. Mason Perkins, *Some Sienese Paintings in American Collections*.

1. The fact that the Madonna of the Palazzo Pubblico had been much repainted in Duccio's time not unnaturally threw Milanesi and other critics off the track. But the date is entirely genuine (see *C. & C.* [Douglas], Vol. I, p. 162, note 1*; and E. Jacobsen, *Das Trecento*, p. 18). The latter writes, "The signature and date are genuine. There is no tenable ground for doubting them." I have satisfied myself by close inspection that such is the case, and the half dozen or so other panels associated with this Madonna stylistically all seem to belong to the first half of the 13th century.

2. Sirén, *Burlington Magazine*, XXXII (1918), p. 45, ascribes this panel to Cavallini. Berenson in *Dedalo*, Vol. II, fasc. v, allots it to Constantinople at the end of the 12th century. Neither view is even plausible to me.

3. *Duccio*. A. Lisini, *Notizie di Duccio* &c., Siena, 1898. Curt Weigelt, *Duccio di Buoninsegna*, Leipzig, 1911, the standard monograph, well illustrated.

4. The whole matter of the Rucellai Madonna is well discussed by Douglas in his edition of *C. & C.*, Vol. I, Appendix to chapter VI. Andreas Aubert, *Cimabue*, pp. 138 ff., and Curt Weigelt, *Duccio*, both agree that the Rucellai Madonna is the picture called for by the contract of 1285, hence is by Duccio Aside from many stylistic similarities to Duccio's early Madonna with Franciscans in the Siena Academy, the exquisitely drawn bare feet of the Angels in the Rucellai Madonna amount almost to a signature for Siena's greatest painter. H. Thode and O. Sirén hold that a picture designed and begun by Duccio was finished by Cimabue, *Toskanische Maler*, pp. 308–9, and note 41 to latter page. The hypothesis that Duccio was strongly influenced by Cimabue in this work seems simpler.

5. The contract is worth quoting in part from G. Fontana, *Due documenti inediti riguardanti Cimabue*, Pisa, 1878; it is reprinted in Strzygowski, *Cimabue und Rom*, Wien, 1888. The papers were recovered from a grocer who was about to use them for wrappers.

"Which picture of the Majesty of Divine and Blessed Virgin Mary and of the Apostles and other saints is to be made in columns and in the predella and [main] spaces of the picture good and pure florin gold shall be used; the other pictures which are to be made in the aforesaid panel above the columns in tabernacles, gables, and frames shall be made . . . of good silver gilt."

The picture apparently was a polyptych of three, five, or seven panels with columns and round arches, with an upper order of gables and tabernacles. It seems to have been the first well-peopled Madonna in Majesty, and it probably served as Duccio's exemplar. Cimabue died before finishing it, but since in Nov. 1302 he received a large installment of 40 Pisan *lire*, he must at least have fully drawn the composition on the panel.

6. *Simone Martini*. See the standard work by Raimond van Marle, *Simone Martini*, Strasbourg, 1920.

There is considerable difference among critics in dating these frescoes, and no objective evidence. The early date, 1322–1325, suggested by Venturi and Van Marle, is confirmed by the stylistic character of the work. It lacks the calligraphic, linear formulas which abound in Simone's works after 1330.

The early date also agrees with the general probabilities of the course of events in the decoration of the Lower Church at Assisi.

7. Frey's ed. Berlin, 1886, p. 42.

8. The contract for this altar-piece is translated in the illustrations to chapter II, p. 106.

9. Venturi, Vol. V, pp. 680–694, offers a sensible compromise view of the authorship of this series, assigning to Pietro himself only the Deposition, Entombment, Stigmatization of St. Francis and a Madonna and Saints, ascribing most of the subjects to an assistant. E. T. Dewald, *Pietro Lorenzetti*, Harvard Univ. Press, 1930. S. L. Faison, *Barna and Bartolo di Fredi*, The Art Bulletin, Vol. XIV, No. 2, pp. 285 ff. Millard Meiss, *The Problem of Francesco Traini*, The Art Bulletin, Vol. XV, No. 2, pp. 97 ff. Proves that the Pisan Traini painted these frescoes about 1350.

10. However the "Cecelia Master," active about 1300, deals ably with such spatial problems. See O. Sirén, *Burlington Magazine*, Vol. XXXIV, p. 234, and XXXVI, p. 4, and *Giotto*, plates 11–13, Vol. II.

11. *Sassetta*. Bernard Berenson, *A Painter of the Franciscan Legend* (Sassetta), London and New York, 1909. John Pope-Hennessey, *Giovanni di Paolo*, New York, 1938.

12. *Matteo di Giovanni*. We have the standard work of G. Hartlaub, *Matteo da Siena*, Strassburg, 1910. Mr. Berenson in *Essays in the Study of Sienese Painting*, New York, 1918, essay on Cozzarelli, has made useful criticisms of the list of pictures usually ascribed to Matteo.

13. *Sodoma*. Hobart Cust, *Giovanni Antonio Bazzi, usually styled "Sodoma,"* New York, 1906.

CHAPTER III.— MASACCIO AND THE NEW REALISM

On the general matter of the realists of the Early Renaissance not much has been added to Crowe and Cavalcaselle, but Mr. Berenson's comment in *The Italian Painters of the Renaissance* is of high critical value. Vasari is, as always, interesting, but never more inaccurate than when dealing with this group. As usual the latest collected information is in Venturi, *Storia*, Vol. VII, part I, and elsewhere and R. van Marle, *The Development*, &c., Vols. XI, XII, XIII, XIV.

1. Matteo Villani, *Istorie*, Florence, 1581, Lib. I, cap. iv, pp. 5–6.

2. *Lorenzo Monaco*. The standard work is by O. Sirén, *Don Lorenzo Monaco*, Strassburg, 1905.

3. *Fra Angelico*. Langton Douglas, *Fra Angelico*, London and New York, 1900.

Vasari's *Life* is admirable and in essentials correct.

4. *Masolino-Masaccio*. The summary in *C. & C.* (Douglas), Vol. IV; (Hutton), Vol. II, reasonably brings the controversy up to date. A good review is by Dr. Richard Offner, *Art in America*, Vol. VIII, pp. 68–76, *A St. Jerome by Masolino*.

The large album of plates accompanying August H. Schmarsow's *Masaccio, der Begründer des Klassischen Stils* &c., Kassel, 1900, is indispensable to the serious student. It is available in the great libraries. More accessible and in illustration a fair substitute for Schmarsow, Enrico Somaré, *Masaccio*, Milano, 1924. Cuts of all the works involved in the controversy are readily attainable in P. Toesca's *Masolino da Panicale*, Bergamo, 1908, in Venturi, *Storia*, Vol. VII, pt. I and in Van Marle, *The Development* etc., Vol. X.

5. The rider with his back turned at the left of the fresco of the Calvary has a rondel protecting the nape of his neck. It is a short-lived and unsuccessful invention which was not used before 1435–1440. This information, which I owe to Dr. Bashford Dean of the Metropolitan Museum, dates the Calvary well after Masaccio's death, and, inferentially, all the other frescoes in the same chapel.

6. *Cassoni* and other Furniture Panels. The standard work is by Paul Schubring, *Cassoni* &c., Leipzig, 1915. *Supplement*, 1923.

Many of the examples in American Collections have been published and discussed by William Rankin and myself in the *Burlington Magazine*, Vol. VIII, IX. See also a popular sketch by me in *Arts and Decoration*, Dec. '05. The furnishing and decoration of a patrician Florentine house in the 15th century is learnedly and delightfully treated by A. Schiaparelli, *La Casa fiorentina* &c., Florence, 1908.

7. See my article in *Art in America*, Vol. VIII, p. 154, and in *Arts and Decoration*, Note 6, above.

8. *Masaccio*, bibliography in Note 4 above.

In essentials the view and chronology of Masaccio's works here given differs from Cavalcaselle's only in relegating the frescoes in S. Clemente to Masolino and their proper date in the late 30s or early 40s. In this I have been partially anticipated by Pietro Toesca, *Masolino da Panicale*, Bergamo, 1908.

The reader may justly wish me to commit myself on this most disputed question to the extent of a list. I give it in a tentative chronological order assuming that Masaccio may have begun to work as early as 1420.

Early Works under Masolino's influence:

Madonna and Saints (fresco). Shrine at Montemarciano near S. Giovanni.
Pietà (fresco). Cathedral, Empoli.
Miracle of healing by Christ (ruined by repainting). John C. Johnson Coll., Philadelphia.
Madonna and St. Ann. Uffizi, Florence.
Adam and Eve Tempted (fresco). Brancacci Chapel.
Resuscitation of Tabitha (fresco). Brancacci Chapel.

Later Works:

St. Peter Preaching (fresco, possibly earlier). Brancacci Chapel.
Birth of St. John (salver), doubtful. Kaiser Friedrich Museum, Berlin.
Madonna of Humility. National Gallery, Washington (Mellon Foundation).
Polyptych for the Carmine, Pisa, 1426.
> The Madonna, some small pilaster pieces, and a small rondel with bust of God Father. National Gallery, London.
> Three predella panels (largely school work) and some small pilaster pieces. Kaiser Friedrich Museum, Berlin.

Crucifixion central pinnacle. Naples Museum.
A Saint (upper order). Civic Museum, Pisa.
A Saint (upper order). Lanckoronski, Vienna.
The Trinity (fresco). S. Maria Novella, Florence.
All the remaining frescoes of the Brancacci Chapel save the parts and panels now universally assigned to Filippino Lippi.

9. Schmarsow, *Masaccio Studien*, bd. 3, p. 27, 8.

10. *Andrea del Castagno*, see the important articles by Herbert P. Horne in the *Burlington Magazine*, Vol. VII, 1905. Richard Offner, in *Art in America*, Vol. VII, pp. 227–35, first published the admirable portrait in Mr. Morgan's Library, New York. Now in the National Gallery, Washington (Mellon Foundation). A magnificent tournament shield with the figure of a David is in the Widener Collection, Elkins Park, Penna., and was first published by Guido Cagnola in *Rassegna d' Arte*, Vol. XIII (1913), p. 49.

Andrea worked at Venice in 1442. See G. Fiocco, *Burlington Magazine*, Vol. XL, p. 11.

11. *Alesso Baldovinetti*. See E. Londi, *Alesso Baldovinetti*, Firenze, 1907.

CHAPTER IV. — FRA FILIPPO LIPPI AND THE NEW NARRATIVE STYLE

1. *Fra Filippo Lippi*. I. B. Supino, *Les deux Lippi*, Firenze, 1904. Vasari's *Life* is capital. Robert Browning's poem, in *Men and Women*, an admirable side-light.

2. *Benozzo Gozzoli*. I accept Col. G. F. Young's date for these frescoes. See *The Medici*, New York, 1909, Vol. I, chapter vii, where there is a good analysis of this decoration.

3. *Antonio Pollaiuolo*. Maud Crutwell's *Antonio Pollaiuolo*, London and New York, 1907. For later information consult Venturi, *Storia*, Vol. VII, pt. 1, pp. 558–578; and R. van Marle, *The Development*, etc., Vol. XI.

4. *Piero della Francesca*. W. G. Waters, *Piero della Francesca*, London, 1901; and Corrado Ricci's superbly illustrated folio, *Piero della Francesca*, Rome, 1910; or H. Graber's, *Piero della Francesca*, Basel, 1920, fine plates.

5. *Early Frescoes of the Sistine Chapel*. Magnificently reproduced in the album accompanying Ernst Steinmann's *Die Sixtinische Cappelle*, Munich, 1901.

6. *Francesco Pesellino*. Consult Dr. W. Weisbach's able and beautifully illustrated work, *Francesco Pesellino und die Romantik der Frührenaissance*, Berlin, 1901. For cuts of *Cassoni*, Paul Schubring, *Cassoni*, Leipzig, 1915, and the books and articles already cited in note 6 to chapter 3.

7. *Domenico Ghirlandaio*. A copious and satisfactory life is that of Gerald S. Davies, *Ghirlandaio*, London and New York, 1909. Briefer but of greater cultural scope is *Ghirlandaio*, by Henri Hauvette, Paris, "Les maîtres de l'art." For a summary criticism my article in *The Nation* (N. Y.), Aug. 20, 1908, p. 167. Ruskin's famous assault on Ghirlandaio in *Mornings in Florence* is joyous reading if whimsically exaggerated.

CHAPTER V. — BOTTICELLI AND LEONARDO DA VINCI

1. *Botticelli.* The standard work is Herbert P. Horne, *Sandro Botticelli*, London, 1908. A little additional information may be found in Crowe and Cavalcaselle, *A History of Painting in Italy*, Hutton ed., Vol. II, and in Venturi, *Storia dell' Arte Italiana*, Vol. VII, pt. 1. Yukio Yashiro, *Sandro Botticelli*, in 3 vols., London, 1925. Superbly illustrated. Cheaper revised edition in one volume, London and Boston, 1929. Admirable illustrations at a very reasonable price in *Botticelli*, New York and Vienna, 1938.

Walter Pater's essay in *The Renaissance* offers beautifully a one-sided view. The essays, the *Soul of a Fact* and *Quattrocentisteria*, in Maurice Hewlett's *Earthwork out of Tuscany* are poetically illuminative. Mr. Berenson's essays in *The Italian Painters of the Renaissance* are important. I have written more fully on Botticelli in *Estimates in Art*, New York, 1912.

Botticelli's Dante illustrations are published both in a cheaper and more sumptuous form by Friedrich P. Lippmann, *Botticelli, Zeichnungen von Sandro Botticelli*, Berlin, 1896.

Lists of Botticelli's works differ considerably. I incline to accept a number of early paintings which are rejected by such exclusive critics as Berenson and Horne. My own list, which for reasons of space cannot be given here, would not differ much from that of A. Venturi, in *Storia*, VII, i, 588–642.

2. *Filippino Lippi.* Katharine Nielson, *Filippino Lippi, a Critical Study*, Harvard University Press, 1938.

3. *Piero di Cosimo.* Fritz Knapp, *Piero di Cosimo*, Halle, 1899. As usual later information in Venturi, *Storia*, Vol. VII, pt. 1.

4. This extraordinary series of which four have been recovered is fully discussed and somewhat differently interpreted by Roger E. Fry, in *Burlington Magazine*, Vol. XXXVIII, pp. 131 f. See also letter on page 257.

5. *Leonardo da Vinci.* The standard life is by W. von Seidlitz, *Leonardo da Vinci*, Berlin, 1909. The early work of Leonardo and his relations with Verrocchio have been thoroughly and lucidly analyzed by Jens Thys, *Leonardo da Vinci*, London, 1913. Amid the confusingly rich bibliography, the student may do well to stick to Vasari's admirable *Life* in any of the translations, to Dr. O. Sirén's scholarly and cautious book *Leonardo da Vinci*, New Haven and London, 1916 and to the late Dr. J. P. Richter's incomparable work "The Literary Works of Leonardo da Vinci," London, 1883, a new edition in preparation. Giovanni Poggi, *Leonardo da Vinci*, Firenze, 1919, has thoroughly edited Vasari's *Life*, and should be consulted for latest views and for illustrations. My own view on the early development of Leonardo, a most disputed matter, is set forth more fully in *Art and Archæology*, Vol. IV, pp. 111–122.

For literary side-lights Walter Pater's essay, in *The Renaissance;* for an iconoclastic view Berenson in *Study and Criticism of Italian Art*, Fourth Series, New York, 1920. Edward McCurdy's selected translations from *The Notebooks of Leonardo da Vinci*, New York, 1938, are valuable for those to whom Richter is inaccessible. Leonardo's drawings, which are no less important than his paintings, may best be approached through Mr. Berenson's monumental work, *The Drawings of the Florentine Painters*, New York and London, 1903 — an enlarged and cheaper edition is about to appear — while the drawings before 1480 are clearly and ably discussed by Dr. Thys.

6. The capital mistake of the more exclusive critics of Leonardo's early work is that they set this delightful little masterpiece at the beginning of the series in an impossibly early date. There is no such manipulation of paint and no such feeling for unity of landscape before 1475 or so. Being a revision of the design of the Uffizi Annunciation, it is necessarily later.

My list of Leonardo's would include, in approximate order:

1. In Verrocchio's Baptism. The landscape at left and distance, the Angel kneeling to right, about 1470, Uffizi.
2. Madonna and Child with an Angel, design by Verrocchio, London.
3. The Annunciation, design mostly by Verrocchio, about 1475, Uffizi.
4. Portrait of a Girl, possibly a Verrocchio, Prince Liechtenstein, Vienna.
5. Annunciation, Louvre.
6. Benois Madonna, about 1478–1479, Petrograd.
7. St. Jerome, unfinished, Vatican, Rome.
8. Adoration of the Magi, left unfinished about 1481, Uffizi.
9. Cartoon of St. Ann, Burlington House, London.
10. Madonna of the Rocks, between 1480–1483, Paris.
11. So-called Belle Ferronnière, perhaps bottega piece, about 1490, Paris.
12. Girl with an Ermine, perhaps a bottega piece, about 1495, Cracow.
13. Clay model of the Sforza horse, destroyed in 1500.
14. Last Supper, 1498, Santa Maria delle Grazie, Milan.
15. Cartoon for a St. Ann, lost but represented by sketches at Venice, 1503.
16. Madonna of the Distaff, represented by old copies.
17. Cartoon for Battle of Anghiari, only central group painted, partly represented by sketches and old copies, 1504.
18. Portrait of Mona Lisa, Paris.
19. Cartoon for a standing Leda, probably only the figure, since numerous old copies have widely varying accessories.
20. Madonna of the Rocks, 1507, London.
21. Cartoon for a Kneeling Leda, the figure only. Sketches and old copies.
22. Madonna and St. Ann, Paris.
23. St. John, half-length, Paris.

All Leonardo's main activity as a painter lies from 1470–1500. He painted a picture about every two years.

Various sculptures have been ascribed to Leonardo. Of these only two, which will have been made in Verrocchio's *bottega* and under his direction, seem to me to deserve consideration. A terra cotta Madonna and Child in the Metropolitan Museum, there ascribed to Verrocchio's school, may represent Leonardo's modelling about 1465. A stucco Madonna at All Souls' College, Oxford, is perhaps ten years later. The first is discussed by me in *Art and Archæology*, Vol. IV, p. 122; the second is reproduced and accepted as a Leonardo by Prof. A. Venturi in *L' Arte*, Vol. XXV, p. 131.

7. The best study of this picture and of its contemporary influence is that of George Gronau in *Zeitschrift für bildende Kunst*, N. F., Vol. XXIII, pp. 253–259. He fails to perceive that so primitive a picture as late as 1478 furnishes the best reason for accepting most of the rejected early Leonardos.

8. In all this matter Jens Thys's admirable studies are indispensable. See note 5 above.

9. The Lady and the Ermine and the Belle Ferronnière are thoroughly discussed by H. Ochenkowski, *Burlington Magazine*, Vol. XXXIV, pp. 186 *f.*, where a full bibliography will be found.

10. This error which has persisted since Vasari was finally corrected by the great restorer Cavenaghi in his report of the last restoration. Malaguzzi Valeri in *Milano*, Bergamo, 1906, pt. 2, p. 14, first advanced the correct view that the painting was done in tempera.

11. Kenyon Cox, *Concerning Painting*, New York, 1917, p. 73.

12. *Fra Bartolommeo*. The standard work is Fritz Knapp's *Fra Bartolommeo della Porta*, Halle, 1903. H. v. d. Gablentz, *Fra Bartolommeo* in 2 vols., Leipzig, 1922.

13. *Andrea del Sarto*. H. Guinness, *Andrea del Sarto*, London and New York, 1901. Andrea's drawings are finely reproduced and analyzed by Bernard Berenson in *The Drawings of the Florentine Painters*.

14. *Bronzino*. Hans Schulze, *Die Werke Angelo Bronzinos*, Strassburg, 1911.

15. *Pontormo*. We have two admirable books by the same writer, Dr. F. M. Clapp: *Les Dessins de Pontormo*, Paris, 1914; *Pontormo, his Life and Work*, New Haven, 1916.

Pontormo's supreme masterpiece of portraiture, The Halberdier, is published by myself in *Art in America*, Vol. X, p. 66.

CHAPTER VI

THE HIGH RENAISSANCE. The indispensable books are, for leading ideas, J. C. Burckhardt, *Civilization of the Renaissance in Italy*, 293 illustrations, New York, 1930; for the stylistic development in Art, H. Wölfflin, *The Art of the Italian Renaissance*, New York, 1913. Very valuable for history and biography are J. Addington Symonds's *The Renaissance in Italy*, 5 vols., London; and H. O. Taylor's *Thought and Expression in the Sixteenth Century*, New York, 1920. For Renaissance ideals of nobility and moderation the capital contemporary work is *Il Cortegiano*, by Baldassare Castiglione, translated as *The Courtier* by L. E. Updycke, New York, 1905. For stylistic analysis Berenson's *The Italian Painters of the Renaissance* is of first importance.

1. *Gentile da Fabriano*. A. Colasanti, *Gentile da Fabriano*, Bergamo, 1909. Also my Essay review. *The Nation*, Vol. 89 (1909) pp. 168–170.

2. *Andrea da Bologna*. *The Nation* (N. Y.) Vol. 95 (1912) p. 392.

3. *Fifteenth Century Umbrians*. Walter Rothes, in *Anfänge . . . der Alt-Umbrischen Malerschulen*, Strassburg, 1908, gives excellent illustrations for the Early Umbrian Artists. R. van Marle, *The Development* etc., Vol. XIV. Also for cuts, U. Gnoli, *La Mostra Umbra*, Bergamo.

4. *Melozzo da Forlì*. A. Schmarsow, *Melozzo da Forlì*, Berlin, 1886, and C. Ricci, *Melozzo da Forlì*, Rome, 1911, are the standard works.

5. *Luca Signorelli*. Maud Crutwell, *Luca Signorelli*, London, 1901. R. van Marle, *The Development* etc., Vol. XVI. *Signorelli, des Meisters Gemälde*, Stuttgart, 1927. Complete works in fair cuts.

6. *Pietro Perugino*. Venturi, *Storia*, Vol. VII, pt. 2, ch. v, makes Perugino the direct pupil of Piero della Francesca, ascribing to Perugino many pictures formerly ascribed to Fiorenzo di Lorenzo. The view while attractive is not wholly convincing to me. All of Perugino's works are published in *Klassiker*

der Kunst, No. XXV, Stuttgart, 1914. The best general estimate of Perugino is that of Wölfflin and of Berenson, in *Italian Painters of the Renaissance*.

7. The *Cambio* frescoes. While it is inherently likely that Raphael worked on these frescoes, Prof. Venturi's plea for Raphael's authorship of God, the Prophets and Sibyls, *Storia*, Vol. VII, pt. 2, pp. 828 *ff*. depends largely on the shaky evidence of drawings attributed arbitrarily to Raphael.

RAPHAEL AND MICHELANGELO. From the point of view of pure style the best treatment of these artists and of the High Renaissance is that of Heinrich Wölfflin in *The Art of the Italian Renaissance*, New York, 1913. It is a book that every student should read and if possible own. Mr. Berenson's treatment of Perugino's and Raphael's space composition, in *Italian Painters of the Renaissance*, is perhaps his finest achievement in criticism. Sir Charles Holmes, *Raphael and the Modern Use of the Critical Tradition*, New York and London, 1933.

8. *Raphael*. Hermann Grimm's two volume *Life of Raphael* is still valuable for background. Among the numerous popular books in English none is outstanding. Henry Strachey's *Raphael*, in "Great Masters of Art," is good, and so are Julia Cartwright's two monographs: *The Early Work of Raphael* and *Raphael in Rome*, in the *Portfolio Series*, London, 1895.

For Raphael's participation in the frescoes of the Cambio it seems to me that Professor Venturi, in *Storia dell' Arte Italiana*, Vol. VII, part 2, makes out only a plausible case.

Reproductions of all of Raphael's works in *Klassiker der Kunst*, No. I, *Raphael*, Stuttgart and Leipzig.

Among the innumerable essays on Raphael none is more understanding than John La Farge's, in *Great Masters*, New York, 1903.

9. *Michelangelo*. The best source for the study of Michelangelo, painter, is the superb plates in Ernst Steinmann's *Die Sixtinische Cappelle*, Munich, 1901. Among recent short biographies that of Charles Holroyd, *Michelangelo*, London and New York, 1911 and Romain Rolland (a longer study, *The Life of Michelangelo*, New York, 1912; a different and shorter work, *Michelangelo, a Study, &c*, New York, 1915) are perhaps the best. The two volume biographies by Hermann Grimm and by J. Addington Symonds are valuable, especially for historical background. But the reader may be wise to content himself with one of the brief biographies and such contemporary lives as Vasari's, Ascanio Condivi's, and Francesco d'Olanda's. The two latter are translated in Holroyd's book. The drawings of Michelangelo are admirably discussed and presented in a perfect selection by Mr. Berenson in *The Drawings of the Florentine Painters*. The drawings are chronologically arranged and beautifully reproduced by Karl Frey, *Die Handzeichnungen Michelangelos*, 2 vols., Berlin, 1911. W. R. Valentiner treats *The Late Years of Michelangelo* (New York, 1914) with insight, devoting himself chiefly to the more finished drawings. For a brief yet comprehensive survey, John La Farge in *Great Masters*, New York, 1903. The works are completely reproduced in *Klassiker der Kunst*, No. VII. *Michelangelo*, Stuttgart and Leipzig.

CHAPTER VII. — EARLY VENETIAN PAINTING

1. Little literature of a general sort is available to the English speaking reader. Crowe and Cavalcaselle, *A History of Painting in Northern Italy*,

admirably edited by Tancred Borenius, in three volumes, London, 1913, is the chief repository of facts. Evelyn March Phillipps, *The Venetian School of Painting*, London, 1912, is an excellent brief survey. Frank Jewett Mather, Jr., *Venetian Painters*, illustrated, New York, 1936, treats the later period more fully than is usual in handbooks. R. van Marle, *The Development* etc., Vol. XV. For readers of Italian Lionello Venturi's *Le Origini della Pittura Veneziana*, Venice, 1911, is the best book. A treasure house of materials in Laudadeo Testi's two volumes, *La Storia della Pittura Veneziana*, Bergamo. John Ruskin's masterpiece, *Stones of Venice*, may be consulted with profit and delight. There are treasures of antiquarian information in Pompeo Molmenti, *La Storia di Venezia nella Vita Privata*, 3 vols., Bergamo, 1905.

2. *Jacopo Bellini.* The extraordinary and fascinating sketch books are published in two forms, by Corrado Ricci, *Jacopo Bellini e i suo libri di designi*, 2 vols., Florence, 1908, and by V. Goloubew, *Les Dessins de Jacopo Bellini*, Bruxelles, 1908.

3. G. McNeill Rushforth, *Carlo Crivelli*, London, 1900.

4. *Andrea Mantegna.* The standard work is by Paul Kristeller, *Andrea Mantegna*, London and New York, 1901. Maud Crutwell's short biography, *Andrea Mantegna*, London, 1901, is excellent. Mr. Berenson's subtle analysis in his *Italian Painters of the Renaissance* perhaps overstresses Andrea's defects. Mantegna's complete works are reproduced in *Klassiker der Kunst*, No. XVI, Stuttgart, 1910.

5. *Antonello da Messina.* See L. Venturi, *Le Origini*, and A. Venturi, *Storia*, VII, pt. 4. Recent attributions, Bernard Berenson, *Study and Criticism of Italian Art*, 3rd Series, London, 1916, p. 79 ff. R. van Marle, *The Development* etc., Vol. XV.

6. *Giovanni Bellini.* Nothing notable in English except casual criticism by Ruskin and Roger E. Fry's admirable little book, *Giovanni Bellini*, London, 1899, which is unfortunately out of print. For such as read German — Georg Gronau, *Die Künstler-familie Bellini*, Leipzig, 1907, with abundant illustrations. Recently discovered pictures and a better chronology, in Bernard Berenson, *Venetian Painting in America*, New York, 1916.

Georg Gronau, *Giovanni Bellini*, New York and Stuttgart. Cuts of all the works and attributions. Far too generous in the latter.

Luitpold Düssler, *Giovanni Bellini*, Frankfort-A-M., 1935, the latest and best critical study.

R. van Marle, *The Development* etc., Vol. XVIII.

7. *Vettor Carpaccio.* Ludwig and Molmenti's *The Life and Works of Victor Carpaccio*, London, 1907, gives, aside from its main topic, a vivid picture of the cultural condition of Venice about 1500. See my essay-review of it in *The Nation*, Vol. 86 (1908), pp. 315 ff. John Ruskin's delightful comments on Carpaccio are mostly in the *Guide to the Academy* at Venice and in *St. Mark's Rest*, chapter *The Shrine of the Slaves*, Library ed., Vol. XXIV.

8. *Giorgione.* For the smallest list L. Venturi, *Giorgione e il Giorgionismo*, Milan, 1913; for the longest list Herbert Cook, *Giorgione;* for a middle view L. Justi, *Giorgione*, 2 vols., Berlin, 1908, 2nd fully rewritten edition, 1926. Most useful plates. George Martin Richter, *Giorgio da Castelfranco called Giorgione*, Chicago, 1937. A very thorough study superseding earlier biographies on the scholarly side. Excellent illustrations.

Duncan Phillips, *The Leadership of Giorgione*, Washington, 1937. An eloquent and enthusiastic monograph, like Richter too generous with attributions.

The general conditions of the problem are clearly stated by the late Richard Norton in *Bernini and other Studies*, New York, 1914. L. Hourticq, in *La Jeunesse de Titien*, Paris, 1919, has lately worked over the pictures which lie between Titian and Giorgione in an interesting but highly subjective fashion. Kenyon Cox, *Art in America*, Vol. I, pp. 115 ff., makes the plausible suggestion that the several portraits, signed V or VV are by Titian, the letters meaning Vecellius Venetus. This would make the Berlin portrait a Titian.

Walter Pater's essay on *The School of Giorgione*, in *The Renaissance* is as masterly for insight as it is for verbal beauty.

Sir Martin Conway's *Giorgione, a New Study of his Art as a Landscape Painter*, London, approaches the problem from a novel and interesting point of view.

I hesitate to add one more to the varying opinions concerning Giorgione's paintings. At least I may introduce a novelty by classing them according to probability, or rather according to the completeness of my own conviction. In the whole matter we are largely in the field of taste and opinion. E means early.

Paintings, m. j. surely by Giorgione

1. The Shepherds finding the Infant Paris (repainted fragment, E) Budapest
2. "The Soldier and the Gipsy" E   Prince Giovanelli
3. Madonna with St. Francis and St. George (1504) Castelfranco
4. The Three Philosophers (finished by Sebastiano del Piombo) Vienna
5. Orpheus and Eurydice (*cassone* panel) Bergamo
6. The Sleeping Venus (landscape by Titian) Dresden
7. Fresco of Nude Woman, nearly effaced (1508), represented by Zanetti's print Fondaco de' Tedeschi
8. Judith (cut down at sides) Petrograd
9. His own Portrait (much cut down and damaged) Brunswick
10. Christ with his Cross   Church of S. Rocco
11. The Concert (finished by Titian? or repainted in his manner?)   Florence

Paintings probably by Giorgione. I accept these, but do not think the evidence demonstrative.

12–13. Stories of the Infant Paris (two *cassone* panels, E) Lady Allington, Allington Castle, Maidstone, England
14. The Fire Ordeal of Moses (door panel, E) Florence
15. The Judgment of Solomon   "   "   "
16. Christ bearing his Cross, E Fenway Court, Boston
17. Infant Paris exposed   My collection
18. Portrait of a Young Man (possibly an early Titian) Berlin
19. Boy With an Arrow (old copy?) Vienna
20. Shepherd with a Flute Hampton Court
21. David with Goliath's Head (copy? or ruined original?) Vienna
22. Altar-piece of St. John Chrysostom (mostly executed by Sebastiano del Piombo) S. Giovanni Crisostomo

23. The Pastoral Symphony (radically repainted in recent times)   Paris
24. Portrait of a Man   New York
25. Daphne (much repainted)   Vienna

This list might still be extended by half a dozen numbers by including pictures which may represent lost originals by Giorgione, but here we are in a field too subjective for profitable discussion in a handbook.

Pictures generally ascribed to Giorgione, I think erroneously.
The Knight of Malta (probably a Titian about 1515)   Florence
Portrait of Broccardo   Budapest
Storm Calmed by St. Mark (probably a Palma)   Venice
Judgment of Solomon (Hourticq plausibly regards as copy of lost fresco by Titian)   Banks Coll., Kingston Lacy
Madonna with St. Antony and St. Roch (probably a Titian)   Madrid
Portrait of a Woman   Casino Borghese, Rome
The Allendale Adoration of the Shepherds (probably an early Titian)
The reason for excluding such works is their over-pathetic or over-dramatic quality.   The argument applies especially to the Adulteress before Christ at Glasgow.   Corroborative technical evidence against this group may be found in L. Venturi's excellent monograph.

CHAPTER VIII. — TITIAN AND THE VENETIAN RENAISSANCE

On the Venetian Renaissance in general we have the works cited at the head of Notes for Chapter VII and for biographies and lists D. V. Hadeln, new ed. Ridolfi, *Le Maraviglie dell' Arte*, Berlin, 1914.   A brief survey by the late Kenyon Cox; in *Concerning Painting*, New York, 1917, pp. 98–132, is valuable. My *Venetian Painters*, note to last chapter.

1. *Titian.* Crowe and Cavalcaselle's *The Life and Times of Titian*, in 2 vols., London, 1881, is still the fullest repository of information.   Georg Gronau's popular but carefully done *Titian*, London and New York, 1904, takes account of later documentary discoveries.   As a painter's analysis of technical aims Charles Rickett's *Titian*, London, 1910, is noteworthy.   Nearly all of Titian's works are published in *Klassiker der Kunst*, No. III, Stuttgart, 1906.   Fuller and better illustrations in *Titian, Paintings and Drawings*, edited by H. Tietze, Phaidon Press, Vienna, 1937.   Several newly discovered pictures are reproduced in the recent volumes, 1918–1922, of the *Burlington Magazine*, *Art in America*, and *Zeitschrift für bildende Kunst*.

2. *Titian's Age.* The problem of Titian's span of life has been exhaustively discussed by me in *The Art Bulletin*, Vol. XX, pp. 13 *ff*.

The whole weight of evidence points to the fact that Titian told the broad truth about his age, perhaps, indulging in a round number.   I am sure he was well over ninety when he described himself as ninety-five in the letter of 1571, and that he died all but a centenarian.

3. Pietro d'Achiardi, *Sebastiano del Piombo*, Roma, 1908.
4. A. Spahn, *Palma Vecchio*, Leipzig, 1932.
Palma Vecchio, des Meisters Gemälde und Zeichnungen, Stuttgart, 1937. Fair cuts of the entire work.

5. Bernard Berenson, *Lorenzo Lotto*, London, 1905. Comprises also careful studies of Alvise Vivarini, Cima, Montagna and other Venetic painters. In *The Study and Criticism of Italian Art*, 3rd series, London, 1916, the superb Saint Justine of the Valsecchi Collection is rightly restored to Giovanni Bellini, l.c. pp. 38 *ff*.

6. *Correggio*. The standard work, C. Ricci, *Antonio Allegri da Correggio*, New York, 1896. A delightful critical study, T. Sturge Moore, *Correggio*, London and New York, 1906. The complete works in *Klassiker der Kunst*, No. XVII, Stuttgart.

A new and convincing view of Correggio's date of birth and early development in Venturi, *Storia*, Vol. VII, pt. iii, pp. 1152 *ff*.

7. Evelyn March Phillipps, *Tintoretto*, London, 1911. F. P. B. Ogmaston, *The Life and Genius of Tintoretto*, London and New York, 1915. Fully illustrated. Many of the extraordinary tempera sketches are reproduced in the *Burlington Magazine* for January and February, 1910. Erich von der Bercken und August L. Mayer, *Jacopo Tintoretto*, in 2 vols., München, 1923. Good stylistic discussion and virtually complete illustrations.

Many eloquent criticisms by Ruskin in *Modern Painters* and *Stones of Venice* (see indices) and in the *Guide to the Academy at Venice*, Library ed. Vol. XXIV.

8. *Paolo Veronese*. See Kenyon Cox's masterly essay in *Old Masters and New*, New York. G. Fiocco, *Paolo Veronese*, Bologna, 1928. The standard work.

9. *G. B. Tiepolo*. The standard work is by Pompeo Molmenti, *G. B. Tiepolo*, Milan, 1909.

10. G. A. Simonson, *Francesco Guardi*, London, 1905. Numerous additions by the same author in the *Burlington Magazine* for succeeding years.

CHAPTER IX. — THE REALISTS AND ECLECTICS

On this period there is little available literature in English, but there are excellent sketches of many of the artists treated in this chapter in C. Ricci, *Art in Northern Italy*, New York, 1911.

A. Pérate in A. Michel, *Histoire de l'Art*, Vol. V^a, gives a fuller summary.

U. Ojetti. *et al*, *La Pittura italiana del Seicento e Settecento alla Mostra di Palazzo Pitti*, Milano and Roma, 1925. Excellent illustrations. Of equal value in this respect, Max Goering, *Italiënische Malerei des 17 und 18 Jahrhunderts*, Berlin, 1936.

1. *Caravaggio*. W. Kallab, Austrian *Jahrbuch*, Vol. XXVI (1906), pp. 272 *ff*., brief illustrated essay. Felix Witting, *Michelangelo da Caravaggio*, Strassburg, 1916.

2. *Salvator Rosa*. Lady Morgan, *The Life and Times of Salvator Rosa*, in two vols., Paris, 1824. Leandro Ozzola, *Vita e opere di Salvator Rosa*, Strassburg, 1908.

The passages translated in the text are from Bottari, *Raccolta di lettere sulla Pittura* &c., Vol. I, pp. 447, 450 *f*., Milan, 1822.

3. *The Carracci*. The fundamental source is Carlo Cesare Malvasia's highly contentious and anecdotal work *Felsina Pittrice;* I have used the two-volume edition, Milan, 1841.

Gabriel Rouchès, *La Peinture Bolonaise à la Fin du XVIᵉ Siècle*, Paris, 1913, is the standard work on the Eclectic School. On the landscape of this school, which is highly important as preparatory to Claude and Poussin, Rouchès has two remarkable essays in *Gazette des Beaux Arts*, 5ᵉ période Tome, III (Jan. and Feb. nos. 1921), pp. 7 *ff.*, and 119 *ff.*

Hans Tietze, in Austrian *Jahrbuch*, Vol. XXVI (1906), pp. 51 *ff.*, *Annibale Carracci's Galerie im Palazzo Farnese und seine Römische Werkstätte* — a very thorough and richly illustrated monograph on the Carracci, including such scholars as Francesco Albani, and Domenichino.

4. *Guido Reni.* Max von Boehn, *Guido Reni*, Leipzig, 1910, fully illustrated.

5. *Domenichino.* Luigi Serra, *Domenico Zampieri detto Domenichino*, Rome, 1909. Also Tietze's article, above, note 3.

HINTS FOR READING

COMPREHENSIVE HISTORIES OF ITALIAN PAINTING. Every well-appointed library must have Raimond van Marle, *The Development of the Italian Schools of Painting*, 18 vols., The Hague, 1923–1936. For its generally complete and judicious treatment, abundant illustrations and bibliographies, it is the best resource for the studious reader. It carries the story to about 1500, at which point the later volumes of A. Venturi's, *Storia dell'Arte Italiana*, Milano, continue up to 1600. The old standby, Crowe and Cavalcaselle, *A New History of Painting in Italy*, editions by Langton Douglas in 6 vols. (New York, 1908), and by Edward Hutton, in 3 (New York, 1908) are still valuable for documentary citation and discussion of disputed points. These volumes cover Central Italian painting, and are supplemented by Tancred Borenius's edition of Crowe and Cavalcaselle, *History of Painting in Northern Italy*, in 3 vols., New York, 1912. The Italian chapters in A. Michel's, *Histoire de l'Art*, Paris, are excellent and more succinct and readable than the encyclopaedic works already cited.

MANUALS. Bernard Berenson's, *The Italian Painters of the Renaissance*, critical essays on the four main schools, and *Italian Pictures of the Renaissance*, a list of the principal artists and their works, with an Index of Places, are indispensable to the student. The Oxford University Press, New York and London, 1932, are the publishers.

Among the numerous brief histories only *A Short History of Italian Painting*, by Alice van Vechten Brown and William Rankin, New York, 1936, seems to retain present value. It is a brilliant and uneven book, with much distinguished criticism and enlightened discussion of the more difficult problems.

TECHNIQUE. Consult the delightful *The Book of Art by Cennino Cennini*, edited by Christiana J. Herringham, London: George Allen, 1922, for methods of painting in tempera and fresco. A later and more scholarly edition of the original text with a new translation, Daniel V. Thompson, *Il Libro dell'Arte* (text), *The Craftsman's Handbook* (translation), New Haven, 1932, 1933.

Sir Charles Holmes, *The National Gallery, the Italian Schools*, London and New York, 1923, critical and technical observations by a painter.

BIOGRAPHY. Giorgio Vasari's picturesque *Lives of the Painters* may most profitably be read in the translation of Gaston DuC. de Vere, in ten volumes, London: Philip Lee Warner; New York: The Macmillan Company. There are many color-prints. The matter is available inexpensively in the handy "Temple Classics." Mrs. Ady, "Julia Cartwright," has epitomized the chief lives agreeably, with necessary corrections, in *The Painters of Florence*, E. P. Dutton and Company, 1916.

PERIODICALS. The reader may most profitably cultivate the habit of paging over the files of *The Burlington Magazine* and *Art in America, Rassegna d'Arte, Pantheon, Belvedere* and *l'Arte*, which contain good reproductions of many fine Italian pictures in private collections.

HISTORICAL BACKGROUND. Excellent are the many Italian Chapters in Henry Osborn Taylor's *The Mediaeval Mind*, in two volumes, 5th Edition, 1938, and *Thought and Expression in the Sixteenth Century*, in two volumes, 2nd Edition, 1930, The Macmillan Company. For Florentine conditions consult Guido Biagi, *Men and Manners of Old Florence*, Chicago, A. C. McClurg and Company, 1909, and *The Builders of Florence*, by J. Wood Brown, London, Methuen and Company, 1907. Ferdinand Schevill, *History of Florence from the Founding of the City through the Renaissance*, illustrated, New York, 1936, is especially recommended.

PHOTOGRAPHS, etc. The ideal way to use a handbook would be to skim it before visiting a great European gallery and to reread it carefully while the impression of the pictures themselves was still vivid. But the student must also depend much on photographic reproductions. For Italy those of Messrs. Alinari and Brogi at Florence and of Dominick Anderson at Rome are comprehensive, finely made, and remarkably cheap. Alinari has most of the Italian paintings of the Louvre and Dresden Gallery; Anderson, those of the Prado, Madrid, and National Gallery, London. The collections of Hanfstaengl and of Bruckmann, Munich, cover most of the galleries of Northern and Central Europe. Photographs of the Italian pictures in the Metropolitan Museum, New York; the Museum of Fine Arts, Boston; the Isabella Stewart Gardner Museum, Boston; the Fogg Museum, Cambridge, Mass., and the Jarves Collection, Yale University, New Haven, Conn., may be purchased from those museums. Considerable collections of photographs are available in many colleges (notably Harvard and Princeton) and public libraries. At New York the extraordinarily rich Frick Art Reference Library is open to students. Besides the five main collections of Italian pictures in America, that of the New York Historical Society, New York, and the Isabella Stewart Gardner Museum, Boston, are noteworthy. The art museums of Baltimore, Md., Worcester, Mass., Providence, R. I., Princeton University, Philadelphia, Cleveland, O., Indianapolis, Detroit, Chicago, St. Louis, Kansas City and Minneapolis have Italian pictures of quality. When the National Gallery (Mellon Foundation) is opened at Washington that city will be very rich in Italian paintings of the first order. The student should not fail to utilize such local resources, however slight they may seem, for one minor original thoroughly enjoyed is worth days of poring over reproductions.

For students who cannot afford a considerable number of photographs, the *University Prints*, Newton, Mass., afford a tolerable substitute. For quick reference the numerous cuts in Venturi's monumental *Storia dell' Arte Italiana*, Milan, Ulrico Hoepli, and in R. van Marle's *The Development of the Italian Schools of Painting* are very useful. The halftones in *Klassiker der Kunst*, Stuttgart and Leipzig, serve a similar purpose. Hanfstaengl publishes albums of most of the important European galleries. The Phaidon Press, Vienna, has begun to publish complete works of Italian artists in superior reproductions at a very reasonable price. Details may be had from any importing bookseller.

INDEX

Where an artist has a family name, that is the indexed word, e.g., Bellini, Giovanni. Where there is no surname, the Christian name is used, e.g., Nardo di Cione, Andrea da Bologna. So is the Christian name the index word when an apparent surname is really only descriptive of birthplace or civil estate, e.g., Domenico Veneziano, Lorenzo Monaco. In the case of well-known artists, the most familiar name is employed, e.g., Angelico, Fra; Giorgione, Titian, Perugino, Raphael, Andrea del Sarto, Pontormo, Botticelli, Michelangelo, etc.